BIBLICAL FOUNDATIONS
FOR LIFE

LARRY KREIDER

Coordinates with a *FREE*
365 Day Devotional Video Series

House To House Publications
Lititz, Pennsylvania USA

How to Use This Resource

Use this manual alongside a **FREE** 365 Day Devotional Video Series with Larry Kreider available at dcfi.org/devos.

Daily devotional

Use as a devotional for a daily study of God's Word. Additional scriptures can be used for further study. Each day includes reflection questions and a place to journals. It coordinates with online video devotions at dcfi.org/devos.

Mentoring relationship

Use for a spiritual mentoring relationship to study, pray and discuss life applications together.

Personal study

Read this book from start to finish as an individual study program to build and a develop spiritual maturity. Each part has seven days of readings. Additional scriptures can be used for further study. Each reading includes questions for personal reflection with room to journal.

Small group study

Study these important biblical foundations in a small group.

Biblcal Foundations for Life
By Larry Kreider
Copyright © 2020 DOVE International

Published by House to House Publications
11 Toll Gate Road, Lititz, PA 17543 USA
Telephone: 800.848.5892
www.h2hp.com

ISBN-13: 978-1-7357388-2-6
ISBN-10: 1-7357388-2-4

Unless otherwise noted, all scripture quotations in this publication are taken from the *Holy Bible, New International Version* (NIV). © 1973, 1978, 1984 by International Bible Society. Used by permission of Zondervan Publishing House. All rights reserved.

All rights reserved. No portion of this book may be reproduced without the permission of the publisher.

CONTENTS

Foundation 1	Knowing Jesus Christ as Lord	5
	1. Building a Solid Foundation	6
	2. Counting the Cost	12
	3. Total Trust	17
	4. Hot, Cold or Lukewarm?	22
Foundation 2.	The New Way of Living	29
	1. Works vs. Faith	30
	2. Faith In God	36
	3. The Potent Mixture: Faith and the Word	41
	4. We Can Live Victoriously	46
Foundation 3.	New Testament Baptisms	51
	1. Baptism in Water	52
	2. More Baptisms	58
	3. Baptism in the Holy Spirit - Part 1	63
	4. Baptism in the Holy Spirit - Part 2	69
Foundation 4.	Building For Eternity	77
	1. Imparting Blessing and Healing	78
	2. Imparting Authority	83
	3. We Will Live Forever	88
	4. God Judges All	93
Foundation 5.	Living in the Grace of God	99
	1. What Is Grace?	100
	2. Responding to God's Grace	106
	3. Speaking Grace to the Mountain	111
	4. Grace for Everyday Living	117
Foundation 6.	Freedom from the Curse	123
	1. What is a Curse?	124
	2. We Can Reclaim What the Enemy Stole	130
	3. Receiving Freedom in Jesus' Name	136
	4. You Can Be Completely Free	142

Foundation 7.	Learning to Fellowship with God	151
	1. Knowing God Through His Word	152
	2. Knowing God Through Prayer and Worship	158
	3. How Can We Hear God's Voice?	164
	4. Hearing His Voice Clearly	170
Foundation 8.	What is the Church?	177
	1. The Importance of the Local Church	178
	2. Spiritual Family Relationships	184
	3. Who Is Watching Out For You?	190
	4. Our Commitment to the Local Church	196
Foundation 9.	Authority and Accountability	203
	1. Understanding the Fear of the Lord and Authority	204
	2. Delegated Authority in Government, Workplace, Family and Church	210
	3. The Blessing of Authority	216
	4. The Blessing of Accountability	221
Foundation 10.	God's Perspective on Finances	227
	1. We Are Managers of God's Money	228
	2. The Tithe	233
	3. Give Both Tithes and Offerings	239
	4. Managing Finances God Has Given	244
Foundation 11.	Called to Minister	251
	1. Everyone Can Minister	252
	2. We Are Called to Serve	257
	3. Ministering With Compassion	262
	4. We Are On Jesus' Team!	267
Foundation 12.	The Great Commission	273
	1. What is the Great Commission?	274
	2. Ready for Action! Spiritual Warfare	280
	3. Reaching the Lost and Making Disciples	286
	4. Be a Spiritual Father or Mother	293

FOUNDATION 1

Knowing Jesus Christ as Lord

1 | Introduction to foundation 1

The foundation of the Christian faith is built on Jesus Christ and His Word. Jesus said, *"Whoever hears these sayings of Mine, and does them, I will liken him to a wise man who built his house on the rock"* (Matthew 7:24). If we want to be wise, we will build our lives on the solid foundation of Jesus Christ and the Word of God.

In the city of Pisa in Italy, workers laid the first stone for a magnificent bell tower. It took 199 years to build. The building materials and workmanship were second to none in the Renaissance era. Yet it soon became clear that something was terribly wrong: a slight "lean" was visible. The building's brilliant design was already becoming less important than its flawed foundation. Unfortunately, the tower was built on marshy soil only three meters above sea level. Today, the "Leaning Tower of Pisa" has a reputation as an oddity in architecture.

As Christians, we sometimes erect faulty towers, using the building blocks of our personal abilities, gifts, and vision. Through more than fifty years of experience in Christian ministry, I have noticed that many believers who have a lot of zeal start to sink when hit with discouragement and problems. Unfortunately, their foundation is as unstable as the marshy soil underneath the Tower of Pisa! Without exception, every person desperately needs a solid, biblical foundation for their lives.

Psalm 11:3 says, *"When the foundations are being destroyed, what can the righteous do?"*

If you are a new believer, the teachings in this series will help you build a solid foundation. If you are already a mature Christian, they can be used as a spiritual refresher or as tools to assist you as you disciple others. The lessons include modern-day stories that bring clarity to and make practical the basic truths of the Christian faith found in the Bible.

I am committed to helping you build a strong spiritual foundation. May His Word become life to you today.

Why is it important to build a solid biblical foundation in our lives?

_____
_____
_____
_____

PART 1

BUILDING A SOLID FOUNDATION

2 | Foundation of Jesus Christ

Years ago, I worked on a construction crew. I learned quickly that the first step to building a house is to *put in a solid foundation*. Likewise, our Christian lives must be built on the sure foundation of Jesus Christ. He is the foundation of the Christian faith. *For no one can lay any foundation other than the one already laid, which is Jesus Christ* (1 Corinthians 3:11). If we build on anything else, our spiritual foundation is faulty and will collapse when tests and storms come our way—and we can be sure they will come. If our foundation is strong, we will be able to stand, no matter how hard the winds blow.

This book helps you continue to build, once you lay the foundation of a personal encounter with Christ who claims, *"...I am the way and the truth and the life. No one comes to the Father except through me"* (John 14:6).

Many people have a false understanding of what it means to be a Christian. Some people think that if you live in a "Christian nation," such as the United States, you are a Christian. Others think they are Christians because their parents are Christians. Being a follower of Jesus is not based on our ethnic or family background. It is based on a relationship. Knowing *about* God does not mean you know Him personally. You may know about the Queen of England, but you probably do not know her personally. You cannot know God without having a relationship with Him. Christianity is all about having a relationship with the living God.

Liz was attracted to Christianity when a neighbor moved in next door. She recalls: "Judy talked about God in intimate terms and I could tell she really knew Him. She acted like God lived in the house with her." Liz longed for that same relationship with God, so she, too, yielded her life to Christ.

The basic foundations for a Christian's life must be built on Jesus Christ who wants to know us personally. In this book, we will come to know that God is revealed to us through Jesus Christ. *Now this is eternal life: that they may know you, the only true God, and Jesus Christ, whom you have sent* (John 17:3).

3 | Our personal relationship with God

Our universe and everything in it has order and design. Its complexity and beauty suggest an intelligent creator behind it. God intended for the beauty of the universe to point to Him (Psalms 19:1). In Romans 1:20, the apostle Paul tells us that God has made Himself known to us through nature and an inner, instinctive recognition of God. *For since the creation of the world God's invisible qualities—his eternal power and divine nature—have been clearly seen, being understood from what has been made, so that men are without excuse.*

In nature, we find evidence that He exists, but He really must be accepted by faith. *And without faith it is impossible to please God, because anyone who*

Jesus—the foundation of Christianity

Isaiah 28:16
Matthew 16:18; 11:27
Acts 4:11-12
Ephesians 2:20; 2:18
1 Peter 2:6-8; John 10:9
1 John 5:20

How is it possible to know all about God but not really know Him?

According to John 14:6, how can you know God?

comes to him must believe that he exists and that he rewards those who earnestly seek him (Hebrews 11:6).

If a person does not want to believe in God, he can find a million reasons not to believe. Yet, when you think about it, it really takes more faith not to believe in God than it does to believe in Him.

Many people think of God as a distant, impersonal being, presiding over His creation disinterestedly and intervening only when humans beg Him to act on their behalf. Such a view is entirely incorrect.

The Bible reveals a God who seeks mankind because He wants to fellowship with them. God, the creator of the universe and ruler over it, who existed before the beginning of time, created humans in His image. God said, "*Let us make man in our image, according to our likeness...*" (Genesis 1:26). He wants mankind to reflect His image. The creator of the universe wants to have a personal friendship and relationship with you! He wants you to know Him and to be your closest friend. *This is how God showed His love among us: He sent his one and only Son into the world that we might live through him* (1 John 4:9).

4 | Jesus—The only way to God

We were created to share in a close, loving relationship with God and one another. Relationship is central to God. He created us to live in unbroken fellowship with Him. But the first human beings, Adam and Eve, created without sin and in perfect fellowship with God, rebelled against God in the Garden of Eden. When Satan tempted them to eat the forbidden fruit from the only tree in the Garden that God commanded them to avoid, their sin of disobedience alienated them from God (Genesis 3:6, 14-19).

Did God leave mankind to perish in their sin? No! He loved them and continued to reach out to them. In the Bible we do not see man seeking after God; we see God reaching after man. *You did not choose me, but I chose you...* (John 15:16).

But what possibility does man have to know the eternal God? God is infinite, all-powerful, and all-wise (Isaiah 40:12-18; 55:8-9). How can we ever relate to such an awesome God? It is possible through Jesus Christ. God took the initiative to reveal Himself in Jesus Christ. He reached out to us through Christ. We can know the Father through knowing Jesus. Jesus Himself said, "*If you really knew me, you would know my Father as well...anyone who has seen me has seen the Father...*" (John 14:7, 9).

When we see Jesus, we see Father God. We must accept and believe Jesus Christ in order to know God.

Some people say there are many ways to God, but the Bible is clear—no one can come to God and go to heaven except through Jesus Christ (John 14:6; Acts 4:12). The Bible tells us that not everyone will be saved (Matthew 25:41-42), and it really does matter what we believe, regardless of how sincere we are (Acts 17:22-31).

You can see God in nature, but how can you truly believe that He exists (Hebrews 11:6)?

Why does God seek mankind?

Why were you created?

What alienates you from God?

How can you know God, according to John 14:9?

Biblical Foundations for Life

The sin problem of mankind

Ecclesiastes 7:20
Galatians 3:22
1John 1:8-10
Romans 5:12
Ephesians 2:13

What evidence have you seen in your experience or observation that convinces you humanity is lost?

_____

_____

_____

_____

Repentance

Luke 13:3, 5; 5:32
1 Timothy 2:4
Romans 2:4
Acts 17:3

We must believe, by faith, that Jesus is "the way, the truth and the life," because we can only come to God through Jesus Christ.

5 | Realize we are lost in our sins

In order to be saved and know Jesus as Lord, we need to first realize that we are lost. *For all have sinned and fall short of the glory of God* (Romans 3:23).

We have all sinned. The word "sin" literally means to miss the mark [of God's perfect will]. It would be highly unlikely for a person practicing target shooting to hit the bull's eye every time. Every now and then he or she will miss. Sin misses the mark of God's perfect will, as revealed in His Word, and separates us from God. All of us have sinned. Jesus came to solve the sin problem of mankind. He first convicts us, or makes us aware, of our sin...*He will convict the world of guilt in regard to sin...* (John 16:8).

Someone once asked D. L. Moody, an evangelist in the nineteenth century, "I only have one or two little sins. How can God reject me?"

Moody responded: "If you are trying to pull yourself up on a roof by holding onto a chain, it only takes one weak link to cause you to fall to the ground. The other links may be in perfect condition. And it only takes one sin to cause us to spend eternity separated from God." Moody was right. Even one sin separates us from God. God loves us, but He hates sin.

Sin is like cancer. If one of my family members had skin cancer on his arm, every time I would see it, I would hate it. That is how God feels about sin. He knows that sin will destroy the people that He has created to be in fellowship with Him. God loves us. He does not want to destroy us. But if we stubbornly cling to our sin, we will be destroyed by it.

Once we realize we have missed the mark, we must believe Jesus can save us from our lost state that condemns us. *Whoever believes in him is not condemned, but whoever does not believe stands condemned already because he has not believed in the name of God's one and only Son* (John 3:18).

6 | Repent and believe

God, in His great mercy and love, could not leave mankind in a state of sinfulness and condemnation. He loved us so much and did not want to see us perish in our sin...*not wanting anyone to perish, but everyone to come to repentance* (2 Peter 3:9).

It is God's will that we do not die in our sins because our sins demand a terrible penalty—the death penalty. Or you could say, our sins pay horrible wages—the wages of death, according to Romans 6:23. *For the wages of sin is death....*

We earn or deserve what we work for. If we work for sin—living in confusion and disorder outside of God—death is the wage that we receive for our sins (spiritual separation from God for all eternity). But the good news is that God provides a way out. Even though "the wages of sin is death," God offers us the free gift of salvation and eternal life through Jesus Christ...*but the gift of God is eternal life in Christ Jesus our Lord* (Romans 6:23b).

God sent Jesus to offer us a new kingdom that He came to set up in our hearts. This happens when we repent of our sins and believe in the truth of His gospel...*Jesus went into Galilee, proclaiming the good news of God. "The time has come," he said. "The kingdom of God is near. Repent and believe the good news!"* (Mark 1:14-15).

God's will is for everyone to turn from their sin to Him. He wants everyone to come to a place of true repentance because it is God Himself who...*commands all people everywhere to repent* (Acts 17:30).

The word *repentance* means *to change, to turn around, a reversal of decision, and to transform*. If you are heading in one direction, "to repent" means you make a decision to turn around and head the other way. If you're driving somewhere and discover you're going the wrong way, you must turn around and go in the other direction. It means you change your mind and change your actions.

A friend of mine was driving in his car one day while listening to a Christian speaker. The speaker began to say: "Someone is driving on the road right now and you need to turn your life over to God." My friend was convicted of his sin. "That's me!" he said. He pulled his car off to the side of the road, weeping as he repented of his sins and gave his life to Jesus. His life was totally changed from that time on. He made a decision that involved an outward action of turning away from sin and turning to the Father.

A good description of repentance is this: "[Repentance is] resolutely turning from everything we know to be displeasing to God. Not that we make ourselves better before we invite Him in. On the contrary, it is because we cannot forgive or improve ourselves that we need Him to come to us. But we must be willing for Him to do whatever rearranging He likes when He comes in. There can be no resistance, and no attempt to negotiate on our own terms, but rather an unconditional surrender to the lordship of Christ."[1]

[1] John R. W. Stott, Basic Christianity (Downers Grove, IL: Inter-Varsity Press, 1971), p. 125.

7 | Confess Jesus as Lord

We come to Christ by confessing and believing that Jesus Christ can save us from a life apart from God. In the same way a couple confesses their commitment to each other on their wedding day to begin their marriage relationship, we confess Jesus Christ as our Lord to begin our relationship with God.

That if you confess with your mouth, "Jesus is Lord," and believe in your heart that God raised him from the dead, you will be saved (Romans 10:9).

A man struggled with knowing if he was a Christian. I took his Bible and showed him Romans 10:9 and told him to read it. He read it over and over, and suddenly faith rose up in his heart. He announced excitedly, "Now I know I am really a Christian!" Why? He was no longer basing his belief on his feelings, but

---

What wages does sin pay according to Romans 6:23?

Describe "repentance" in your own words.

on what God said in His Word. He confessed with his mouth that Jesus is Lord and experienced true salvation.

Jesus as Lord
Acts 2:36; 10:36
John 13:13
1 Corinthians 8:6; 12:3

What does it mean to know Jesus Christ as the Lord of our lives? Lord means: ruler, king, boss, one in complete control of our lives. Yet it is more than that. Confessing Him as Lord is also a confession of Christ's deity. When we confess Jesus as the Lord of our lives, we are not only confessing that He is in total control of our lives, but that He is God.

When Jesus walked on the earth, Caesar, the ruler, was called "lord." When a Roman soldier greeted another person, he would say, "Caesar is lord!"

The other person would respond, "Caesar is lord!" They really were saying that the emperor was god.

What does having Jesus as the Lord of your life mean to you personally?

But when a soldier made that statement to a Christian, the Christian would answer, "Jesus is Lord!" Subsequently, he or she would be punished, most likely thrown to the lions. Many were martyred for the cause of Christ. The early Christians clearly understood Lordship! It required a total commitment on their part.

In the Bible, the word "Savior" is mentioned 37 times. The word "Lord" is mentioned 7,736 times. In the New Testament, "Savior" is found 22 times and "Lord" 433 times. Both are very important, but the emphasis is on Jesus as the *Lord* of our lives.

Today, we have the privilege of confessing Jesus as Lord because we choose to, not because we have to. But on the judgment day, when Jesus returns, everyone will acknowledge His Lordship and kneel before Him, according to Philippians 2:10-11. *That at the name of Jesus every knee should bow, in heaven and on earth and under the earth, and every tongue confess that Jesus Christ is Lord, to the glory of God the Father.*

8 | Receive salvation and become God's child!

Jesus took your place on the cross two thousand years ago so that you can know God. *For Christ died for sins once for all, the righteous for the unrighteous, to bring you to God...*(1 Peter 3:18).

When you receive Him as your Lord, He makes you His child. *Yet to all who received him, to those who believed in his name, he gave the right to become children of God* (John 1:12). One time while speaking to a group of teenagers in Scotland, I took some money out of my pocket and offered it to a young man in the audience. I told him that he could say, "I *believe* in the money," but he needed to *receive* the money for it to be his. I said, "If you receive it, it is a free gift from me. You didn't do anything to earn it, but it is yours." Of course, he took it!

Receiving Christ
Hebrews 9:28
Romans 5:6-8; 8:3
2 Corinthians 5:21
Galatians1:4; 3:13
John 20:31
1 John 5:12

You can believe in Jesus, but you only have salvation if you receive God's gift to you—Jesus Christ. Salvation is a free gift; you cannot earn it. You do not deserve salvation, but God gives it to you anyway because He loves you. You have salvation and eternal life if you accept God's gift to you and invite Jesus to be the Lord of your life.

Biblical Foundations for Life

Have you asked Jesus Christ into your life as your Lord and King? If not, you can do it right now. The scriptures tell us that now is the day of salvation (2 Corinthians 6:2).

Take a moment and pray the prayer of salvation appearing below. Start your new life in Christ today! Find someone to talk to who can encourage you and help you grow spiritually. Expect the Lord to use you in amazing ways as you get to know Him and respond to His voice. God bless you!

What is the difference between believing and receiving Christ?

Prayer for Salvation

I confess Jesus Christ as the Lord and King of my life. I believe in my heart that He is alive from the dead. Lord, I confess to you that many times I have "missed the mark" and gone my own way. But from this moment on, I receive Jesus Christ as the sacrifice for my sins, and I am a new creation in Jesus Christ. Old things have passed away and all things have become new. Christ lives in me!

As I have confessed Jesus Christ as my Lord and I believe in my heart that He is alive from the dead, I know that I am saved! I have received eternal life as a free gift from you! Amen.

Salvation is a free gift—Do you want to receive God's gift of Jesus Christ?

Biblical Foundations for Life

PART 2

COUNTING THE COST

9 | Total commitment required

When I was involved in youth ministry, years ago, I used to tell the young people, "If you want friends, peace of mind, and things to work out in your life, come to Jesus. He will help you." Many of the youth made a commitment to Jesus, but two months later they were back doing their own thing instead of obeying the Lord. In many cases, they were worse off than before they made a commitment to Christ. They did not understand that Jesus must be their Lord. They "came to Jesus" for what they could get, rather than receiving Jesus Christ as Lord—the complete boss of their lives.

The Bible tells us in Romans 10:13 that, *"everyone who calls on the name of the Lord will be saved."* "Calling on the "Lord" means we are willing to make Him the master, boss, and complete ruler of every part of our lives, every minute of the day. It requires a total commitment.

Many times Christians preach a "weak" Jesus. I was guilty. I changed my approach and saw lasting fruit. I told the next group of young people, "Jesus must be Lord over everything in your life. Are you willing to die for Jesus if you have to?" I was amazed at their response. They seriously counted the cost before they made a commitment to Christ, just as Jesus requires, according to Luke 14:33, *"...any of you who does not give up everything he has cannot be my disciple."* As a result, they experienced lasting change.

Someone once asked a Christian statesman from Switzerland: "What if you were talking to a young person interested in God, and you told him he must give up everything to follow Christ, but he was not ready? Then he walks away and is hit by a car and is killed. How would you feel about your 'hard line' then?" The elderly Swiss gentleman said, "I would sit down and cry, then I'd pick myself up and go tell the next person the same thing." He knew that a total commitment would be a lasting commitment. He had to tell the truth and allow individuals to make up their own minds.

Jesus requires total commitment. True Christians have Christ as the Lord of every area of their lives, and it will show. To make this kind of commitment, we need to seriously count the cost.

10 | Consider the cost

Large crowds were following Jesus. They were excited about following this new leader who spoke with such authority. But Jesus knew their attachment to Him was mostly superficial. He wanted them to really think about what it meant to follow Him, so He spoke to them in a parable. *Suppose one of you wants to build a tower. Will he not first sit down and estimate the cost to see if he has enough money to complete it? For if he lays the foundation and is not able to finish it, everyone who sees it will ridicule him...*(Luke 14:28-29).

Commitment to Christ
Luke 18:22-23; 18:28-30
Philippians 3:7-8
1 John 2:15-16

In what ways did you count the cost before you made a commitment to Christ?

Jesus spoke a very clear message concerning the cost of following Him. He stressed that an individual should understand the terms of discipleship and not take it lightly. *If anyone comes to me and does not hate his father and mother, his wife and children, his brothers and sisters—yes, even his own life—he cannot be my disciple* (Luke 14:26). The difference between our love for God and our love for even our dearest family members is as great as the difference between love and hate. We are commanded to love all men and our neighbors as ourselves. Yet when we compare that love to the love we have for God, there is no comparison. If Jesus is the Lord of my life, then He is Lord of my marriage, my money, my family, my possessions, my future; He is Lord of everything!

Years ago, we led a Jewish friend to faith in Christ. As a result, her family and many of her friends rejected her and refused to talk to her. She clearly understood the cost of her commitment in making Jesus the Lord and ruler of her life.

Charles Finney, who lived about 200 years ago, was an evangelist who often preached to students on college campuses. After his death, a survey was taken which revealed that 80% of those who had made a commitment to Jesus at those campus meetings were living for God and victorious in their Christian lives several years later. Finney would preach to students and then tell them to go to lunch and come back later if they really wanted to repent and get right with God. He wanted them to count the cost and make sure they knew what they were doing. When they *did* repent, they were counting the cost of their commitment to Jesus, not just making a flippant, emotional decision.

11 | Bear the cross

What does it mean to be totally committed to Jesus? There is an old story about a chicken and a pig walking down the road and passing some hungry-looking men. The chicken said to the pig, "Why don't we give them a breakfast of eggs and ham?"

"That's easy for you to say," replied the pig. "For you, that's only a sacrifice but for me it's total commitment." The pig would have to die to feed those men.

The same is true of Christians—we must literally die to our own desires when we commit our lives to Jesus because He gave His life for us. Jesus said we must bear a cross or we cannot be His disciples. *And anyone who does not carry his cross and follow me cannot be my disciple...any of you who does not give up everything he has cannot be my disciple* (Luke 14:27,33).

Publicly carrying a cross in biblical days was the brand of a criminal doomed for execution. Everyone knew he was going to die. The cost of becoming a follower of Christ is a complete renunciation of all claims to one's own life. Bearing a cross is symbolic of dying to self. Luke 9:23, 24 says we must "take up our cross" daily and follow Jesus. *Then He said to them all, "If anyone would come after me, he must deny himself and take up his cross daily and follow me. For whoever wants to save his life will lose it, but whoever loses his life for me will save it"* (Luke 9:23-24).

When you die to your sins, you save your life! You are set free from slavery to sin and become engaged in the service of God, according to Romans 6:22.

Counting the cost
Luke 14:33
Matthew 10:22;20:22-23

What does it mean to "hate" family members, including your own life before you can become a disciple of Jesus (Luke 14:26)?

Denying self (taking up the cross)
Titus 2:12
Romans 6:14;6:18;8:2
Matthew 10:38;16:24-26
Mark 8:34-37

Biblical Foundations for Life

In your experience, how has losing your life for Jesus actually saved it?

But now that you have been set free from sin and have become slaves to God, the benefit you reap leads to holiness, and the result is eternal life.

A young lady in Philadelphia was enslaved in prostitution and drug abuse for years. When she surrendered her life to Jesus, she started wearing a cross-shaped earring to remind herself she was now a bondslave to Jesus. She was no longer in slavery to sin, but had chosen to take up the cross and follow Jesus.

Salvation is a free gift from God, but when we receive this free gift, we have a responsibility to serve God and hold nothing back.

12 | Jesus must be Lord of everything

Suppose I offer to sell you my car but mention I want to keep the glove compartment. You say, "That's ridiculous! The glove compartment is part of the car. If you sell me the car, it belongs to me—all of it." That's how some people think they can come to Jesus. They say, "Jesus, I give you my life—all but this one thing. (It may be their finances, their future, their thought life, or some sinful habit.)

A rich, young ruler asked Jesus what he must do to inherit eternal life (Matthew 19:16-22). Jesus knew the one area the man clung to was his riches, so He told him to sell his possessions and give them to the poor. The young man went away sorrowful because his riches meant more to him than the opportunity to walk with Jesus. His riches took first place in his life. Jesus did not give him an installment plan of 25% down and easy monthly payments. He did not give him an easy way out. No, Jesus knew this young man's god was *money* and he would have to let it go and allow Jesus to take the place of riches in his heart. **Either Jesus is Lord of all or not Lord at all!**

How do you try to keep "glove compartments" for yourself?

When you put a puzzle together and one piece is missing, it's so frustrating! Why? It's never complete. There is no fulfillment. Sin frustrates people. Something is missing in their lives; they have no peace. But when Jesus becomes the Lord of their lives, they now have a reason to live. He comes to give abundant life, filled with purpose and meaning (John 10:10). The Bible says, "*And this is the testimony: God has given us eternal life, and this life is in his Son. He who has the Son has life; he who does not have the Son of God does not have life*" (1 John 5:11-12).

When we receive Jesus as our Lord, we begin to experience His life. The Lord wants us to be excited about living!

God has an awesome plan for your life today. But you will never walk in the fullness of what the Lord has in store for you unless you give your entire being to the Lord!

13 | Sell out!

Jesus expects us to sell out completely to His lordship because He gave up everything to seek and save us. We see this amazing concept in a story Jesus told in Matthew 13:45-46, called the Parable of the Pearl. *Again, the kingdom of heaven is like a merchant looking for fine pearls. When he found one of great value, he went away and sold everything he had and bought it.*

The merchant (Christ) came seeking men and women (pearls) who would respond to Him and His message of salvation. Jesus gave His life (gave all that He had) to purchase one pearl of great value. Each Christian is that "one pearl" bought at a great price (1 Corinthians 6:20).

We can also look at the Parable of the Pearl to mean that Jesus gave everything to save us, and He expects us to sell out completely to Him once we find Him. Individuals who seek for God and find Him (the Pearl of great value) should be willing to sacrifice all other things for Him.

The early Christian disciples knew what it meant to give up everything for Jesus. When Jesus said to fisherman, James and John, "Follow Me," they left their boats and nets—their business, their livelihood—and followed Him. As Matthew sat in his tax collecting station, Jesus came by and said, "Follow Me." Matthew left his position and job, and followed Jesus. Zacchaeus, a wealthy tax collector, climbed a tree to catch a glimpse of Jesus as He passed by. Jesus stopped, looked up at him and told him He was coming to his house that day.

Zacchaeus didn't hesitate. He climbed down, took Jesus to his home and declared he would pay back those he had cheated.

Jesus told him, "Today salvation is come to this house" (Luke 19:9). Jesus is calling us today. Jesus wants to live His life through us. Let's respond to Him today like Zacchaeus and give it all to Jesus.

14 | It all belongs to Him

Jesus said that if we are attracted to earthly things, our heart will be enslaved to those things. *For where your treasure is, there your heart will be also* (Luke 12:34).

Selling out to Jesus means our interests change from selfish ones to Jesus Christ. Earthly treasure no longer holds us in its grip because we are no longer enslaved to it. We have to surrender all in this world that prevents us from putting God first. This includes every material, physical and emotional attachment we have to this world. We have to give God our wallets, savings, homes, families, jobs, hopes, pleasures, past, present, future—everything!

What happens then? When we are willing to lay it all down, we discover that God entrusts it back to us. He says, "I'll give you back your home and family and money but whenever I want them, you must give them to me. They are mine. They all belong to me." That is what it means to give everything to Jesus. We then realize that we are managers of these things instead of owners. He is the owner!

My family belongs to Jesus. My bank account belongs to Jesus. My house belongs to Jesus. My car belongs to Jesus. Sometimes I stop to pick up a hitchhiker because my car belongs to Jesus, and I believe He wants me to help those in need.

Juan Carlos Ortiz tells the story of people in Argentina who became Christians and sold their homes, cars and other possessions and gave them to the church. The church gave them back and said, "These all belong to Jesus, use them to serve Him. When someone needs a house to stay in or a ride in a car, we will contact you." That's just how God wants it!

Biblical Foundations for Life

Bought with a price
Mark 10:28-31
Acts 20:28
1 Corinthians 7:23

In the Parable of the Pearl, how much was the pearl worth?

How do you give everything to the Lord?

What are some things that enslave people today?

How do you manage, rather than own, earthly things?

15 | How to be spiritually reborn

When we trust Jesus, we believe in Him and have a personal relationship with Him as Lord. We allow Him to change us from the inside out. We must trust Him to change us.

One day, an influential religious leader, Nicodemus, secretly met with Jesus in the night and told Him he was convinced that He was the Messiah. Nicodemus was a good Pharisee who believed that the Messiah would come to set up a political kingdom to free the Jews from Roman domination, and he believed Jesus would accomplish it. Jesus caught the man by surprise when He answered, *"...I tell you the truth, no one can see the kingdom of God unless he is born again"* (John 3:3).

Nicodemus was not ready to believe that Jesus came to change people's hearts or that they could be reborn spiritually. He could not understand that a second birth is a supernatural, spiritual rebirth of our spirit into the heavenly realm of God's kingdom.

Indeed, understanding the rebirth requires faith on our part because it is a miracle of God. You might wonder, "I'm not sure if I'm reborn yet. How do I know?" Well, a newborn baby never says, "I'm not sure if I'm born yet." You are either born or you're not. In the spiritual sense, either Christ lives in you and you are a new creature or He does not and you fail the test (2 Corinthians 13:5).

If you are born again, start living the new life of Christ who lives in you. *I have been crucified with Christ and I no longer live, but Christ lives in me. The life I live in the body, I live by faith in the Son of God, who loved me and gave himself for me* (Galatians 2:20).

What an amazing statement. Christ actually lives within you when you receive Him into your life! The same Jesus, who walked the face of this earth two thousand years ago, lives within you!

Why is it so important to be spiritually reborn?

How has the Lord changed your heart?

TOTAL TRUST   PART 3

16 | The difference between belief and trust

A Christian must be totally committed to the Lord. You can't straddle the fence in the kingdom of God. God loves us so much that He sent Jesus to die for our sins. God's Word says we must believe in Him to have eternal life. *For God so loved the world that he gave his one and only Son, that whoever believes in him shall not perish but have eternal life* (John 3:16).

What does it mean to "believe in Him?" Many people today profess to believe in God or believe there is a God. But even the demons believe in the existence of God. *You believe that there is one God. Good! Even the demons believe that—and shudder* (James 2:19).

To say that you believe is not enough. There is a big difference between mental belief and trust. To truly believe means to totally trust. When my children were younger, they used to stand at the top of the steps in our house and say, "Daddy, catch me!" They did not simply believe in my existence—they completely trusted me, and were absolutely confident that I would catch them when they leapt into my arms.

There's a story of a tightrope walker who walked a tightrope across Niagara Falls. He asked the audience if they believed he could push a wheelbarrow across the rope and they said, "Yes!" But, when he told them he needed someone to sit in the wheelbarrow, no one volunteered. Their belief did not involve total trust!

You might say, "Well, as long as I am sincere." It's not good enough to be sincere. Some people are sincerely wrong. I have a friend who thought he was traveling on a highway heading west to Harrisburg, Pennsylvania, but he was going in the wrong direction and ended up in Atlantic City, New Jersey, hundreds of miles from his destination. He was very sincere, but he was sincerely wrong.

Others sometimes say, "As long as I have my doctrine right, I'll be okay." Believing in the right doctrine or having a biblical foundation, in itself, will not save us. We must truly trust in Jesus Christ as Lord and enter into a personal love relationship with Him.

17 | We trust God because He is God!

We trust God for one reason, because He is God. When we believe He is who He says He is, we will love Him with all our hearts.

Before Jesus was the Lord of my life, I saw Christianity as a type of spiritual "fire insurance;" that is, I did not want to go to hell! I have met many people who do not want to go to hell but are not willing to truly trust Jesus as the Lord of their lives.

Paul, the apostle, revealed his confident trust in Christ when he declared in 2 Timothy 1:12, "*...I know whom I have believed, and am convinced that he is able to guard what I have entrusted to him for that day.*" Paul did not say, "I know

In your own words, explain the difference between mentally believing in Jesus vs. trusting fully in Him.

Biblical Foundations for Life

what I believe," he said, "I know *whom* I believed." He had a deep and abiding relationship with a Person—Jesus Christ.

God does not expect a blind trust in Him. He reveals who He is in scripture so that as we get to know who He is, we can more fully trust Him based on knowledge (scripture). Trust is based on predictability and character. We learn about God's consistency and character through the scriptures that reveal what God is like and how He has shown His love and commitment to man throughout history.

We do not trust in the Lord for His benefits. Although it is true He will "daily load us with benefits" (Psalms 68:19), we trust Him because we love Him. A young man complained to me once, "God doesn't work for me. I served God faithfully, and was hoping a certain Christian girl would develop a relationship with me, but it didn't work out. I just cannot trust God anymore." Clearly, he was serving God for selfish reasons. He was trying to use God to gain something for himself.

As a young lady, could you imagine finding out the day before your wedding that your future husband only wants to marry you because your dad owns a big company and he wants to get a good job or "marry into money"? The Bible calls this idolatry. Anything that means more to us than Jesus is an idol in our lives. 1 John 5:21 says, *"Dear children, keep yourselves from idols."*

We trust Jesus because He laid down his life for us. If we truly love Him, we will obey Him and trust Him completely to guide our lives. When we trust Him, He will fill us with joy and peace. *May the God of hope fill you with all joy and peace as you trust in him, so that you may overflow with hope by the power of the Holy Spirit* (Romans 15:13).

18 | We cannot trust our feelings

During the first few months after I came to Christ, I sometimes felt like I wasn't a Christian. Sometimes I felt close to God and the next time, He seemed a million miles away. I grew depressed and defeated because I thought my feelings reflected my spiritual condition. Then, a wise counselor encouraged me to turn to 1 John 5:13 where it says, *"I write these things to you who believe in the name of the Son of God so that you may know that you have eternal life."*

Believing and trusting God's Word to be true caused faith to rise up in my heart. I knew that I had chosen to believe in Jesus Christ as my Lord and Savior. His Word settled it for me because I believed it to be true. I knew I could not base my relationship with God on my feelings; in fact, I had to realize that sometimes my emotions do not line up with the truth. I am in relationship with God because He says I am. He gives so many promises in His Word that I can trust. God's Word brought a deepening sense of His love for me and caused me to trust Him regardless of how I felt at the moment.

Our lives are completely changed when we see ourselves and others according to what God says about us and about Himself, not by how we feel. People's misperceptions about themselves are often based on their misperceptions of God. When we know what God's Word says, we will be guided by the Holy Spirit to walk in repentance, faith and discipline in our new lives.

What are some idols you may have in your life?

Why do you serve God?

Why are feelings so unreliable?

How has God's Word caused faith to rise up in your life?

You are a new man (woman) with a new nature who is being renewed and changed, according to Ephesians 4:22-24. *You were taught, with regard to your former way of life, to put off your old self, which is being corrupted by its deceitful desires; to be made new in the attitude of your minds; and to put on the new self, created to be like God in true righteousness and holiness.*

19 | What if I don't change completely after I give my life to Jesus?

Becoming a Christian happens in a moment. When we give our lives to Jesus, we enter into a new life. Because of God's great mercy, He saves us by washing us clean of our sins...*not because we were good enough to be saved but because of his kindness and pity—by washing away our sins and giving us the new joy of the indwelling Holy Spirit* (Titus 3:5 TLB).

Your spirit is washed clean in an instant as the Holy Spirit comes to live within you. This does not mean, however, you will never sin again. Your old nature continues to battle with your new nature, and you have a part to play so you can live victoriously. *So I say, live by the Spirit, and you will not gratify the desires of the sinful nature. For the sinful nature desires what is contrary to the Spirit, and the Spirit what is contrary to the sinful nature. They are in conflict with each other, so that you do not do what you want. But if you are led by the Spirit, you are not under law* (Galatians 5:16-18).

Sinful desires still may tug at you, but now you also have the Holy Spirit pulling you toward holiness. Your very nature has been changed, and it is your new nature to obey God. The power that sin had in your life is now broken and a way of victory is provided: the Holy Spirit helps you to overcome sin. As a Christian, it will be impossible for you to live *habitually* in sin because you are born again into a new life. The Lord will bring to mind any unconfessed sin in your life because He is a merciful God. Suppose I give you a book and three weeks later discover I still have two pages that belong in that book. I make sure you get the pages so you do not miss anything. Similarly, the Lord does not want us to miss anything that would keep us from experiencing a Spirit-led Christian life. He will reveal areas of our lives that need cleansing and help us to become victorious in those areas.

A man grew up hating a group of neighbors who were of a different nationality. Even after he became a believer, he looked at those people with disdain just because of their nationality. Finally, he read in the scriptures that everyone is on the same footing in the family of God regardless of their background (Romans 10:12). He broke down and repented to God for his sin of hatred toward these people. God gave him a new heart toward his neighbors, and he became friends with several of them. If we are open, God will continue to purify us, change us, and give us victory over sin in our lives.

Living victoriously
1 Peter 1:22
Romans 6:6;8:1,4-5,12-14
Galatians 5:25; 6:8
Hebrews 3:13; 12:1
Titus 2:11-12; 3:3-7
2 Corinthians 3:18

How do you live victoriously over sin after you become a Christian, according to Galatians 5:16-17?

Biblical Foundations for Life

Forgiveness of sin

Isaiah 43:25
Jeremiah 33:8
Ezekiel 18:22; Acts 3:19
Hebrews 9:28;10:10-18

According to 1 John 1:7, what purifies you from sin?

Reflect on how you have experienced God's love and forgiveness of sins.

When God forgives you of sin, does He ever remember it again?

Where does your sin go, according to Micah 7:19?

20 | Trust Jesus to forgive us completely

Remember, when Jesus forgives our sins, He forgives them no matter how many we have committed or how bad they were. All our past sin is gone, wiped spotless by His blood shed on the cross. Blood, in both the Old and New Testaments, stands for death. Christ died, providing a divine substitute for us, as sinners. He became the substitute that would pay the penalty for our sin, permanently! 1 John 1:7 says Jesus' shed blood purifies us from sin. *But if we walk in the light, as he is in the light, we have fellowship with one another, and the blood of Jesus, his Son, purifies us from all sin.*

When our dirty clothes are washed with detergent, they come out spotless. The blood of Jesus is the most potent detergent in the universe. It completely cleanses us from all sin. This purification is an ongoing work of continual cleansing in the life of every believer. As believers, we will make every effort by His grace to walk in the light so that we can have intimate fellowship with God and each other.

A woman once washed Jesus' feet with her tears because she was so grateful for the forgiveness of her sins. Jesus said, "*...her many sins have been forgiven for she loved much*" (Luke 7:47).

Real love for Jesus comes from a deep awareness of our past sinfulness and that He has forgiven us completely. Some say that they have made such terrible mistakes and sinned so horribly that God could never forgive them. No matter what the sin, *everyone* is forgiven for much, because God loves to forgive sin when we repent!

21 | Sins are not remembered

When we repent of our sins, God forgives them and will never remember or mention them again. Psalm 103:12 tells us that, *"as far as the east is from the west, so far has he removed our transgressions from us."*

You can't get any farther than that! It is as far as you can imagine. When Jesus forgives our sins, He forgets them, period. God gives us a wonderful promise in Micah 7:19. He says He will "*...tread our sins underfoot and hurl all our iniquities into the depths of the sea.*"

This promise paints an awesome word picture. Our sins sink to the depths of the ocean, never to rise again. God not only casts our sins into the deepest sea, I believe He puts a sign there that says, "No Fishing!"

When the Egyptians pursued the Israelites through the Red Sea, there was not one Egyptian left to pursue God's people. They all perished in the sea. Likewise, no sin we have confessed can survive God's forgiveness. Like the Egyptians and their chariots, our sins "*...sank like lead in the mighty waters*" (Exodus 15:10). Our sins are totally forgiven, never to be remembered again. The Lord has forgotten our sins as if they have never been, and He wants us to forget them too. We are totally set free when Jesus forgives our sins. We can trust Him!

22 | We can count on Him!

Our trust in the Lord is a sure hope or confidence that is based on His promises. We can place our confident hope and trust in the Lord who promises not to disappoint us. *And hope does not disappoint us, because God has poured out his love into our hearts by the Holy Spirit, whom he has given us* (Romans 5:5).

The psalmist puts this "trust" and "hope" into perspective in Psalms 146:3-5 when he says, *"Do not put your trust in princes, in mortal men, who cannot save. When their spirit departs, they return to the ground; on that very day their plans come to nothing. Blessed is he whose help is the God of Jacob, whose hope is in the Lord his God."*

We cannot trust mere mortal men, but we can trust our God! We can count on Him to deliver what He has promised. He gives us hope.

I am blessed when my children believe me when I make a promise to them. It would grieve me if they would not trust me. Our heavenly Father feels the same way about us, His children. He has proved Himself faithful to us. We can totally trust Him and His Word. The basis for our trust in God comes from the very nature of God, of Jesus Christ, and His Word. We cannot place our trust in other human beings or material possessions or money or any other thing on this earth. Our abiding trust can only come from the Lord who...*does not disappoint us* (Romans 5:5).

If you trust God, what is His promise (Psalms 146:3-5)?

Tell of times you have trusted in the Lord.

Biblical Foundations for Life

PART 4

Why does the Lord detest spiritual lukewarmness?

_____
_____
_____
_____

In what ways do you resemble the world more than Christ?

_____
_____
_____
_____

Spiritual compromise

2 Corinthians 11:3; 3:14; 10:5

How is it possible to have one foot in God's kingdom and one in the kingdom of darkness?

_____
_____
_____
_____

Why is it important to become enthusiastic about the things of God?

_____
_____
_____
_____

HOT, COLD, OR LUKEWARM?

23 | Neither hot nor cold

If we are apathetic about our relationship with Jesus, we are like a glass of lukewarm water, neither hot or cold. Did anyone ever give you a glassful of warm water on a hot summer day when you wanted a refreshing glass of cold water? What a letdown! You probably spit it out of your mouth in disappointment! In the same way, Jesus detests lukewarmness in us.

The Laodicean church in the book of Revelation was filled with lukewarm Christians who compromised with the world. They professed to be Christians, but they resembled the world more than Christ. Christ said they did not realize it, but they were...*wretched, pitiful, poor, blind, and naked* (Revelation 3:17).

The Lord warns this church about His judgment against their spiritual condition in Revelation 3:15-17. *I know your deeds, that you are neither cold nor hot. I wish you were either one or the other! So, because you are lukewarm—neither hot nor cold—I am about to spit you out of my mouth.*

God hates lukewarmness. He wants our full commitment rather than a compromise with the world resulting in apathy. Our lukewarmness leaves a bad taste in His mouth, and He will vomit us out!

24 | Spiritual compromise

As we just learned, the Lord wants us to completely commit to Him with no compromise. Lukewarmness is repulsive to Him. We cannot try to have one foot in God's kingdom and one foot in the kingdom of darkness. This kind of hypocrisy produces spiritual compromise and displeases God.

One reason that God is so concerned about lukewarmness is because He knows that people are watching our lives. The Bible says that our lives are like a letter that God writes to people who are watching us. *You yourselves are our letter, written on our hearts, known and read by everybody* (2 Corinthians 3:2).

Our lives are the only Bible that many people ever read. Let's examine our spiritual lives today. Are we lukewarm? If we do not find ourselves hot—excited about the things of God—let's follow the prescription of the Lord. It's found in Revelation 3:19...*become enthusiastic about the things of God* (The Living Bible).

It is our choice. I am choosing to be hot! How about you?

25 | A way that seems right

There's a story told of a cruise ship with passengers divided into first-class and second-class accommodations. After a few days at sea, the captain announced that from now on, everyone would be treated first-class, no matter what they paid. There would be lobster and fine cuisine for all. The people were excited and gorged themselves on food and exclaimed that he was the greatest captain in the world. Only the captain knew the real truth behind his offer—the ship was sinking and in a short time all would die.

Biblical Foundations for Life

That's the way the devil lies to us. He says, "You can have it all, don't worry—eat, drink and be merry. You can determine your own truth. God doesn't really require that you live a holy life. Everybody else is doing it." But our own wisdom cannot determine wrong and right. Only God's Word can do that. Only by God's Word can we tell if we are on the right path of life. The devil would prefer that we remain blinded and ignorant because he doesn't want people to know that the Bible says, "*There is a way that seems right to a man, but in the end it leads to death*" (Proverbs 14:12).

In order to determine the right way in life, we must follow God's written revelation in the Bible. Any other path leads us to spiritual death. We cannot allow ourselves to be deceived.

The devil's plan for our lives is to kill us, steal from us, and destroy us. He steals peace, joy, and hope from the lives of those the Lord has created to experience true vibrant life. Jesus Christ came to give us life, abundant life, filled with enthusiasm and joy! Jesus said, "*The thief does not come except to steal, and to kill, and to destroy. I have come that they may have life, and that they may have it more abundantly*" (John 10:10 NKJ).

The Bible tells us that Jesus came to destroy the works of the devil! (1 John 3:8). It seems foolish to not want to be on God's winning team!

26 | Have we turned away from our first love?

When we are spiritually lukewarm, we have turned away from our first love for Jesus. A new love is exciting and vibrant. But love loses its luster when communication wanes. If we no longer communicate in a relationship with our heavenly Father, our love for Him will falter. Perhaps you asked Jesus Christ into your life as your Lord a long time ago, but now you have forsaken your first love for Him.

In Revelation 2:4-5, the Ephesian church had a deep love and devotion to Christ at first, but the Lord warned them that their current relationship with Him was lacking. Although they did a lot of good things and worked hard for the gospel's sake, their heartfelt love for Jesus had died. ...*You have forsaken your first love. Remember the height from which you have fallen! Repent and do the things you did at first....*

Just because we knew the Lord in a personal way in the past does not necessarily mean that we have a close relationship with Him today. I was making a point of this truth while speaking at a public high school one time. I asked the students, "Do any of you still know your first grade teacher?" I was startled when a girl in the back of the room raised her hand and said, "Sure I do. She is my mother!" Her point was well taken. The other students, however, had not maintained a relationship with their first grade teacher so their current relationship with her was nonexistent. Do you have a vital relationship with your heavenly Father today? He is still there, waiting for you and me to come back to Him. *Come near to God and he will come near to you...* (James 4:8).

There is a way that may seem right to you, but where is its destination?

What can you learn from the cruise ship?

What does it mean to forsake your first love for Jesus?

If you turn away from your first love, what does the Lord instruct you to do (Revelation 2:5)?

Biblical Foundations for Life

Open the door to Jesus

John 10:7; Matthew 7:7

What does the Lord promise if you repent from lukewarmness (Revelation 3:20)?

How has He knocked on your heart's door to bring you back in fellowship with Him?

What should you never be ashamed of?

Tell your personal story about how you came to Jesus.

27 | He is knocking at your heart's door

Maybe you knew Jesus Christ in a personal way in the past, but you are far from Him today. You have forsaken your once vibrant love for Jesus. In Revelation 3:20, Christ speaks an invitation for the lukewarm people at the church of Laodicea to come back into fellowship with Him. He is pictured as standing outside the door waiting to be invited in once more.

Jesus is knocking at the door of our lives, waiting for us to repent of our lukewarmness and open the door to invite Him in. Jesus not only warned the Laodicean church of their condition, He immediately invited them to repent and be restored into fellowship with Him again. *…I stand at the door and knock. If anyone hears my voice and opens the door, I will come in and eat with him, and he with me* (Revelation 3:20).

This invitation is spoken outside the door, as Jesus knocks and asks to be readmitted into their presence. He promises that if they repent from their lukewarmness and lack of love for Him, He will completely restore them. What an amazing promise! Jesus wants to have a personal relationship with you today. If you have turned away from God, He wants you to again open the door of your life to Him. And when you open the door, He will come in and again fellowship with you!

28 | The power of your testimony

After you receive Jesus Christ as the Lord of your life, it is important to give your testimony as often as possible to as many people as possible. One of the ways you overcome Satan is by speaking out for Christ. Revelation 12:11 says, *"they overcame him by the blood of the Lamb and by the word of their testimony…."*

There is spiritual power released when we testify how the Lord has changed and is changing our lives! Every Christian has an important personal story to tell of how he or she came to know Jesus Christ as Lord. Never be ashamed to speak for Christ. *So do not be ashamed to testify about our Lord, or ashamed of me his prisoner. But join with me in suffering for the gospel, by the power of God, who has saved us and called us to a holy life—not because of anything we have done but because of his own purpose and grace…*(2 Timothy 1:8-9).

People will listen when we tell our personal stories of how we came to believe in Jesus. They will not be intimidated because they are not forced to agree or disagree with the statements we make. It is our story, and they cannot deny how we were persuaded to follow Jesus. When we share our stories, we should focus on the fact that God loves them and Jesus died for them so they can be forgiven and be made new. We should tell them of the changes the Lord has made in our lives which gives them hope for their lives, too.

29 | Real or counterfeit?

Counterfeit Christianity
Matthew 5:20; 6:1-7
John 3:3-6

To some people, Christianity is based on their outward appearance or on what they do rather than a real love for the Lord. They appear righteous outwardly, but inwardly they are not born of God and the Spirit. Jesus sternly reprimanded the Pharisees and scribes in Mark 7:6 for this kind of hypocrisy. ...*These people honor me with their lips, but their hearts are far from me.*

For years, I was in the same league as the Pharisees. I considered myself a Christian, but I was living a counterfeit Christian life. Here's my story. My family attended church every Sunday during my childhood. When I was eleven years old, we went to a special evangelistic meeting. I really didn't want to go to hell so I stood up when the evangelist gave a call for those who wanted to receive Christ. I was later water baptized to become part of the church.

What I really wanted that night was "fire insurance." I decided that Christianity would keep me out of hell, but that was as far as it went. My commitment to the Lord was incomplete, so it wasn't long before I was living a fake Christian life. I only acted like a Christian when I was with my Christian friends. (This is also called "hypocrisy".) Seven years later, a friend confronted me: "If you were to die tonight, are you sure you would go to heaven?" I honestly didn't know the answer, so I said, "Nobody knows that."

The young lady didn't hesitate with her answer. She said, "Well, *I* know."

I had come face to face with the truth. Sure, I could talk about God and the Bible. However, I couldn't talk about *Jesus* because I didn't *know* Him in a personal way. I had made a type of commitment to the Lord, but I believed that somehow God would accept me if I did enough good things along the way. I didn't realize that eternal life comes only through faith in Jesus *Christ as Lord.*

Later that night, when I opened my Bible at home, everything seemed to be written directly to me. I read where Jesus said, "You hypocrites!" and I knew I was a hypocrite too. My friends considered me to be "the life of the party," but I knew the truth. Loneliness was my companion every evening that I spent at home alone. Even worse, I was afraid that if I died in the night, I would die without God for eternity. I came to the realization I was under a counterfeit conversion. That night I said, "Jesus, I give You my life. If You can use this rotten, mixed-up life, I'll serve You the rest of my life."

God miraculously changed me the moment I reached out in faith to Him. My attitudes and desires changed. Even my thinking began to change. This time, I was clearly born again because Jesus Christ had become my *Lord.* I was a new creation in Christ, and I am eternally grateful to Jesus.

If you are trying to appear righteous but continue to pursue sinful directions in your heart and mind, you may be living a counterfeit Christian life. Now is the time to ask the Holy Spirit to shine God's light on your heart. Come to the cross of Jesus, confess your sin and accept God's forgiveness.

Pray this prayer of confession and repentance and receive God's unconditional love and forgiveness. *Lord, I have been trapped in the web of hypocrisy and long*

How are some professing Christians counterfeit?

How can you know the difference?

Biblical Foundations for Life

for the freedom I can have in You. I confess that I have tried to be righteous without You and have been living a counterfeit Christian life. Please forgive my sin so I can come under the power and control and influence of Your righteousness. Thank You for setting me free, Jesus. I pray for courage and wisdom to live out my new life in Christ and experience the fullness and freedom You desire for me to have.

30 | I am not ashamed of the Gospel of Christ

Jesus said, *"What good is it for someone to gain the whole world, yet forfeit their soul? Or what can anyone give in exchange for their soul? If anyone is ashamed of me and my words in this adulterous and sinful generation, the Son of Man will be ashamed of them when he comes in his Father's glory with the holy angels"* (Mark 8:36-38).

To forfeit our soul is not good. We are made of a body, soul, and spirit. Our soul and our spirit are more important than anything we possess. They live forever. One person's soul is worth more than the entire world!

We should also notice what Jesus says about our future if we are ashamed of Him? If we will be ashamed of Christ, He will be ashamed of us.

Here is some really good news from II Timothy 1:7-9: *"For the Spirit God gave us does not make us timid, but gives us power, love and self-discipline. So do not be ashamed of the testimony about our Lord or of me his prisoner. Rather, join with me in suffering for the gospel, by the power of God. He has saved us and called us to a holy life—not because of anything we have done but because of his own purpose and grace. This grace was given to us in Christ Jesus before the beginning of time."*

Jesus Christ lives in us (Galatians 2:20). He desires to live His life through us. A secret to the Christian life is that Jesus Christ actually lives within us when we invite Him in!

I was a young believer when I learned this. I was struggling to chase pigs on my father's farm, and this scripture rose in my heart. Christ within me was giving me the strength to chase my father's pigs! When I had a hard time forgiving, Christ in me gave me the strength to forgive and move on.

We should have no fear of being ashamed of the gospel because Christ lives in us. He will give us the power to stand for Him in any situation. You can trust Him!

31 | The rich man and the gate

Let's look at two parables Jesus told. First, the "Rich Man" parable in Luke 12:16-21. Jesus said that a rich man who had an abundant harvest decided to build bigger barns to use for storing his surplus grain. Thinking he would have plenty for the coming years, he told himself, *"Take life easy; eat, drink, and be merry."* But the Bible says that his life would be demanded from him that same night. The parable ends by saying, *"This is how it will be with whoever stores up things for themselves but is not rich toward God"* (Luke 12:21).

What good is it for someone to gain the whole world, yet forfeit their soul?

What can anyone give in exchange for their soul?

By saying that he had plenty of grain laid up for many years, he was totally leaving God out of the equation. God called him a fool. We can be caught if we become lukewarm in our faith and trust in things rather than being rich towards God.

The next parable, in Matthew 7:13-14, could be called "Which Gate?" The Bible says,

"Enter through the narrow gate. For wide is the gate and broad is the road that leads to destruction, and many enter through it. But small is the gate and narrow the road that leads to life, and only a few find it."

There are two roads before us, and God allows us to choose which one to follow. The broad road leads to destruction, and many enter it. The small gate leads to life, and only a few find it. We make the choice as to which gate we will enter.

I want to give you another opportunity to enter the narrow gate by receiving Jesus Christ as your Lord. This is a holy moment. Just pray, right where you are:

Jesus, I confess to you I have sinned, I have gone my own way, and I need your forgiveness. I confess with my mouth, "Jesus is Lord," and believe in my heart that God raised Him from the dead, and I know I am saved. My life is completely yours. I receive you into my life and I submit completely to you. In Jesus' name. Amen.

Welcome to your new life in Christ! You have an exciting life ahead.

What did the rich man say to himself?

What did God say?

How might we fall into this same trap?

Biblical Foundations for Life

FOUNDATION 2

The New Way of Living

32 | Introduction to foundation 2

A house we once lived in had a foundation problem. We began to notice cracks in the wall because the foundation was faulty. This same problem plays out spiritually in the lives of believers all over the world who do not have a solid biblical foundation. When they do establish that firm foundation, many of their struggles will disappear. That is why I am so passionate about teaching believers in Christ biblical foundations.

In this next set of Bible teachings we will talk about The New Way of Living, considering two of the six foundational doctrines of the Christian faith found in Hebrews 6:1-2—repentance from dead works and faith toward God:

"Therefore, leaving the discussion of the elementary principles of Christ, let us go on to perfection, not laying again the foundation of repentance from dead works and of faith toward God, of the doctrine of baptisms, of laying on of hands, of resurrection of the dead, and of eternal judgment" (NKJ).

So many believers are trusting their good works to gain right standing with God. It is a dead end. We will learn that we must repent from trying to gain God's acceptance by doing good things (Hebrews 6:2). Good deeds done to impress God or man are "dead works," and they do not get us closer to God. Only true repentance leads to faith in God.

The Bible says in Hebrews 11: 6, *"And without faith it is impossible to please God, because anyone who comes to him must believe that he exists and that he rewards those who earnestly seek him."* In these teachings, we will also study what the Bible says about faith.

What are the two basic foundational doctrines of the Christian faith found in Hebrews 6:1-2?

Biblical Foundations for Life

PART 1

WORKS VS FAITH

33 | An elementary principle: Repentance from dead works

After I received Jesus Christ as the Lord of my life, I realized I had to rebuild my life on a new foundation of the truths found in the Word of God. To grow in my Christian life, I first had to lay down elementary principles of Christianity. Only then could I build upon them to grow in greater maturity.

The spiritual building blocks to build into our lives are basic truths that are found in the Word of God. We will examine each of the six spiritual building blocks found in Hebrews 6:1-2. *Therefore, leaving the discussion of the elementary principles of Christ, let us go on to perfection, not laying again the foundation of repentance from dead works and of faith toward God, of the doctrine of baptisms, of laying on of hands, of resurrection of the dead, and of eternal judgment* (NKJ).

Here, we are urged to move on to maturity, after building on the elementary principles of 1) repentance from dead works 2) faith toward God 3) baptisms 4) laying on of hands 5) resurrection of the dead 6) eternal judgment. The six principles listed in these verses help us build a solid foundation in our spiritual lives.

Let's look at the first foundational stone listed here: "repentance from dead works and faith toward God." We will learn that true repentance always goes before true faith...*the foundation of repentance from dead works and of faith toward God...* (Hebrews 6:1 NKJ).

"Repenting from dead works" means we realize that all the good deeds we do will never get us to heaven. Salvation comes only through saving faith in the Christ. People who hope they can "work" their way to heaven by doing good and avoiding wrong should know that the Bible tells us, "*For whoever keeps the whole law and yet stumbles at just one point is guilty of breaking all of it*" (James 2:10).

The truth is that no one can keep the law of God because even if we stumble in one point (and we will because we have a sin nature), we are guilty. In other words, if I have sinned one time or a million times, I have broken the law. If an airplane crashes 500 feet from the runway or 500 miles from the runway, it still crashes and the casualties are devastating.

Nothing good you do will get you to heaven, but Christ will get you there!

34 | True repentance or false repentance?

We already mentioned that repentance means to change our mind and our actions. Repentance is "an inner change of mind resulting in an outward turning around; to face and to move in a completely new direction."[1]

There is a godly sorrow that accompanies true repentance. We find ourselves truly sorry that our sin has grieved the heart of a holy God. This sorrow will produce true repentance; a willingness to change our actions. When we experience true repentance, we can enjoy the forgiveness and the freedom that Jesus gives us.

Building a solid foundation in your Christian life involves understanding what six principles? What are they?

What does "repentance from dead works" mean?

Repentance
Isaiah 55:6-7
Ezekiel 18:30-32
Acts 3:19; 17:30; 20:21

There is such a thing as *false repentance*, however. False repentance is *repenting for any other reason except that God is worthy of our complete obedience.* For example, children who are caught doing something wrong by their parents may regret they were caught without ever feeling sorry for disobeying their parents. This is false repentance, which in reality, is not repentance at all.

How many times have we been guilty of doing the same thing? If we are only sorry that "we got caught" instead of genuinely being sorry for grieving the heart of God, then we have not truly repented. That means we cannot experience God's forgiveness either. 2 Corinthians 7:10 tells us that, *"godly sorrow brings repentance that leads to salvation and leaves no regret, but worldly sorrow brings death."*

The Bible says that Judas, who betrayed Jesus, repented. But he did not experience true repentance. His "repentance" was only remorse and regret. He did not change his mind and direction like biblical repentance requires. In fact, after he felt terrible remorse, he went and hanged himself. He could no longer find a place of repentance. He could find no way to change his mind.

Just being sorry is not enough. We must trust God to completely change us inside. When we truly repent, Jesus' blood cleanses us from our sin and we can go on to live a new life in a new way. True repentance means that we realize we have sinned against a holy God and our inner change of mind results in a change in our direction.

Although God gives us salvation and forgiveness after true repentance, we may still suffer the consequences of our past sins. Broken relationships and families, loss of trust, sexual diseases, or bad habits are all examples of natural consequences of past sin. But the Lord promises to give us the strength to work through the consequences and to help us live victoriously (Philippians 4:13).

Sometimes we will also have to pay a price for our past sin. For example, a man guilty of murder who later comes to Christ is forgiven of his sin by God, but he still has to pay a price for the consequences of his actions. His sorrow and repentance will not keep him from serving a prison sentence for his crime.

[1] Derek Prince, The Spirit-Filled Believers Handbook (Lake Mary, FL: Creation House, 1993), p. 101.

35 | Good works vs. dead works

Now that we understand the *repentance* part of *repentance from dead works*, what are "dead works?" Our works refer to good deeds or good things that we do. A dead work is any work, or good deed, that we do to try to earn favor with God. No amount of human goodness, human works, human morality, or religious activity can gain acceptance with God or get anyone into heaven.

People in certain parts of Malaysia perform a peculiar ritual to appease their gods and try to gain favor with them. Every year they choose one young man from their tribe and sink hooks into the flesh of his back. Then a rope is attached to the hooks in the young man's back and a cart loaded with a one-foot-high statue of the local god. The people believe they can gain right standing with their god when the blood-covered young man pulls the idol and cart through their town.

What is the difference between true repentance and false repentance?

What must be your only reason for repenting?

What does godly sorrow lead to?

Biblical Foundations for Life

In efforts of trying to gain favor with God, what are some "dead works" people perform?

How can you know your works are good and not dead?

This may sound like a strange and senseless thing for someone to do, yet we are doing a similar thing when we trust in our good works to try to please God. The devil has his hooks in our minds, making us believe that we are accepted by the Lord because of the good things we do. This is entirely wrong thinking and in opposition to what God's Word says in Ephesians 2:8-9. *For it is by grace you have been saved, through faith—and this not from yourselves, it is the gift of God—not by works, so that no one can boast.*

We have been saved through faith. We have favor with God because we have placed our trust in the person and work of Christ. Only Jesus Christ gives us real life. Works are totally incapable of producing spiritual life in us. And yet, we can get caught in the trap of trying to win God's favor by our works. These actions are dead works.

Paul, the apostle, chided the Galatian Christians because they had started out by faith in Christ, but were now trying, through religious dead works, to gain spirituality. *You foolish Galatians! Who has bewitched you? ...Did you receive the Spirit by observing the law, or by believing what you heard? Are you so foolish? After beginning with the Spirit, are you now trying to attain your goal by human effort? ...Does God give you his Spirit and work miracles among you because you observe the law, or because you believe what you heard?* (Galatians 3:1-3, 5).

Dead works can be very religious. If Christians place their faith in their witnessing, or their Bible reading, or attending their church meetings, instead of putting their faith in God, these good deeds become dead works. Involvement in the church, helping the poor, giving offerings, being a good husband or wife, being an obedient child—all these can be dead works if we are trying to gain favor with God through doing them.

I have met people who think that if they break their bad habits, God will accept them. They say, "I'll stop smoking, and then God will accept me." God does not accept us because we have overcome a bad habit. He accepts us because His Son, Jesus Christ, died on the cross two thousand years ago for our sins, and when we receive Him, we become His sons and daughters. When we give our lives to Jesus, He will give us the power and grace to stop smoking or discontinue any other habit that does not bring glory to God. But He accepts us as we are and gives us the grace and desire to change.

Our goodness does not bring us favor with God. We already have favor with God! God has called us to do good works, but we do them because we already have His favor, not to gain His favor.

36 | The futility of our works to save us

So now we know that good works are powerless to help us through the pearly gates of heaven. The Bible tells us that even the best "good works" we do to please God are like filthy rags compared to His goodness. *...All our righteous acts are like filthy rags...* (Isaiah 64:6).

That is why any good deed done to impress God or man is a "dead work." There's a story that is told about a beggar who was walking down the road one day when he saw the king approaching with his entourage. The beggar was awestruck. Then the king looked down on the beggar and said, "Come, sit on my horse with me." The beggar was astounded. "Why would the king do such a thing?" he wondered.

The beggar laid his questions aside and mounted the king's horse. They rode to the palace together and as they entered the royal residence, the king said to the beggar, "Today I have chosen you to live in my palace. I'm going to give you new garments to wear and all of the sumptuous food that you can eat. I will make sure that all of your needs are met."

The beggar thought for a moment. All that he had to do was to receive from the king what he had promised to give him. This was too good to be true. He didn't deserve this royal treatment. It just did not make sense. How could the king accept him and meet all of his needs when he had done nothing to deserve it?

From that time on, the beggar lived by the king's provision. However, the beggar thought, "I think I should hang onto my old clothes just in case the king doesn't really mean what he said. I don't want to take any chances." So, the beggar hung onto his old rags...just in case.

When the beggar was old and dying, the king came to his bedside. When the monarch glanced down and saw the old rags still clutched in the beggar's hand, both men began to weep. The beggar finally realized that even though he had lived his whole life with the king in a royal palace, he had never really trusted the king. Instead, he had chosen to live his entire life under a cruel deception. He should have lived like a royal prince.

Many of us do the same thing. We give our lives to Jesus, but we insist on hanging onto and trusting in our works and the good things we do, "just in case." However, trusting these "dead works," instead of placing our entire confidence in Jesus Christ, is like hanging onto filthy rags from God's perspective. The Lord does not receive us because of our good works. No, we're received by God only because of faith in His Son Jesus Christ and what He has done for us on the cross. We are righteous by faith in Him. Let's not get caught, at the end of our lives, clinging to our old rags, because somehow we found it too hard to believe that the Lord desires to bless us and fill us with His life, even though we do not deserve it at all.

37 | God's perspective on good works

Should we do good works, then? Yes, absolutely! God wants us to do good works. We show our love by actions! We should do millions of good works in our lifetime, but only because God loves us and has accepted us already; we cannot try to earn His favor. Works play no part at all in securing salvation. But after we reach out to the Lord in faith and know that He accepts us and loves us just the way we are, we will find ourselves wanting to obey God. We will want to do good works because God has changed us. Paul told the Ephesians, "*For we are*

Examine yourself—are you hanging onto some ragged dead works "just in case"?

On what condition does God accept you?

Biblical Foundations for Life

God's workmanship, created in Christ Jesus to do good works, which God prepared in advance for us to do" (Ephesians 2:10).

God empowers us to live the Christian life so we will want to act on the great love He has bestowed on us! I don't take care of my children so I can be their father; I take care of my children because I am their father and love them deeply. We don't do good works because we want to become righteous; we do good works because we are righteous.

I once read a story about an eight year old boy who was instructed by his mother to hoe the family garden. His mother told him to hoe two rows of beans. She showed him exactly how she wanted him to do it, and told him, "Now, when you get through, tell me so I can come and look it over." When he finally finished according to her instructions, he called her to inspect it. She took one look at it and shook her head in disapproval, "Well, son, it looks like you're going to have to redo this. For most boys this would be all right. But you are not most boys: you are my son. And my son can do better than this!" Did his mother stop loving him because he did not hoe the garden to perfection? No. She simply expected that he could do better. God's life in us produces good works and changed character. His love for us motivates us to want to reach out to others and do good works for the right reasons—because we love Him with all our hearts.

38 | True righteousness

In Romans 10:2-3, we read about some religious people who had zeal for God, but were trying to gain their salvation by their own merits. They were trying to establish their own righteousness, or *right standing* with God on their own terms. *For I can testify about them that they are zealous for God, but their zeal is not based on knowledge. Since they did not know the righteousness that comes from God and sought to establish their own, they did not submit to God's righteousness.*

These people did not know God's method of saving sinners. They did not realize they are saved only through faith in Jesus Christ. Instead, they tried to establish their own righteousness. They were sincere in their efforts, but sincerely wrong.

This reminds me of the young football player who finally caught the ball and took off with a great burst of speed—toward the other team's goal. This young man had zeal, and he ran as fast as he could, but he was headed in the wrong direction! He had misdirected zeal. Our zeal is misdirected if it is not founded on correct views of truth. Our good works cannot obtain favor with the Lord.

Once, when I was in a Latin American country with a friend, we needed to pay with pesos to get our flight out of the country. We didn't have pesos, so we offered them American dollars which were worth more than the pesos. No matter how hard we tried, they would not accept them. The government had set up their monetary system on pesos and we were using the wrong system. We had zeal, but our way didn't work.

If your own good works are not pleasing to God, how do you explain Ephesians 2:10?

Why does God expect good works from you?

What must be your only motivation for doing good works?

How do people try to establish their own righteousness?

We must be more than sincere: we must know the truth. We have to yield our hearts to Jesus Christ. Right standing with God only comes through faith in Jesus Christ. Satan will tempt us to trust in something—anything—other than the finished work of Jesus Christ for our salvation. Some people accept Jesus as Lord but add on all kinds of good works with hopes of becoming more righteous. God does not accept us because we eat the right foods, read the Bible in the right way, pray the right way or dress the right way. Our acceptance is in Jesus, period! We may do some of the above-mentioned good works, but we do not do them in order to be accepted by the Lord. We do them because we *have* been accepted!

How can you know your "zeal for God" does not result in dead works?

39 | What is like a pile of rubbish?

Paul, the apostle, was of pure Jewish descent, had a prestigious Greek education, and was one of the most influential interpreters of Christ's message and teaching as an early Christian missionary. But he considered all the knowledge and the great things he had done as a pile of garbage compared to knowing Jesus Christ. Paul says in Philippians 3:7-8, *"But whatever was to my profit I now consider loss for the sake of Christ. What is more, I consider everything a loss compared to the surpassing greatness of knowing Christ Jesus my Lord, for whose sake I have lost all things. I consider them rubbish, that I may gain Christ."*

Those who trust in their Christian background or training or credentials to make themselves acceptable to God are trusting in the wrong things. If you grew up in a good Christian home and had the opportunity to get Bible training, thank God for it! However, even these good things are rubbish compared to knowing Jesus as Lord and trusting in His righteousness.

Name some things Paul calls "rubbish" that we often trust instead of trusting in God's righteousness.

Knowing Christ and having an intimate relationship with Him is much more important than what we do or have done for Him. I am thankful that my wife cooks my meals and washes my clothes, but these good works mean nothing compared to our love relationship together. I just enjoy knowing her most of all. The same principle applies to our relationship with Jesus.

If you have been trusting your good works or your background more than your relationship with Jesus, you can repent now. Jesus will fill you with His love, and you will experience His righteousness and His acceptance.

Is knowing Jesus personally the most important thing in your life?

When we repent, we do an "about face"—we are sharply turned around! If we move from one geographical area to another, we need to change schools or change jobs. We go from one to another. True repentance always goes before true faith. So then, in our spiritual lives, we must repent of placing our faith in dead works and do an "about face" by placing our faith in the living God alone!

Biblical Foundations for Life

PART 2

Faith

Acts 20:21
Hebrews 10:22; 11:7; 11:13
Romans 8:24-25; 2 Corinthians

What does faith produce?

_____

_____

_____

_____

According to Romans 12:3, where does faith come from?

_____

_____

_____

Justification by faith alone

Galatians 2:16; 3:11; 5:4-5
Romans 5:1

FAITH IN GOD

40 | An elementary principle: Faith toward God

Previously we learned that we must repent from trying to gain God's acceptance by doing good things (Hebrews 6:2). Good deeds done to impress God or man are "dead works," and they do not get us closer to God. Only true repentance leads to faith in God.

The second part of the verse in Hebrews says that after repentance, we must move on to "faith toward God." Placing our faith in God is another elementary, foundational principle of our Christian lives. *Therefore, leaving the discussion of the elementary principles of Christ, let us go on to perfection, not laying again the foundation of...faith toward God...(Hebrews 6:1 NKJ).*

What is faith? It is something that happens in the heart that produces a transformation in our lives. We cannot just make a profession of Christ in the realm of our minds. Faith toward God produces a change in our hearts. We are moved out of our sin and into His righteousness by our faith. The Bible literally defines *faith* in Hebrews 11:1 when it says, *"Now faith is being sure of what we hope for and certain of what we do not see."*

Faith involves believing first and then seeing. As Christians, we live and act as if we have already seen the Lord because we have confidence in God—we have placed our faith in Him. But, of course, God is not visible to the naked eye. He is visible only to the eye of faith. We believe even though we do not "see" in the physical sense.

God called Abraham "a father of many nations" long before he had a son. The Bible says that Abraham "in hope believed" (Romans 4:18) that this promise would come to pass. He did not wait until he saw the physical evidence before he believed by faith.

Faith is a "gift of God" (Ephesians 2:8) and God uses His divine spoon to give you a "measure of faith" according to Romans 12:3...*in accordance with the measure of faith God has given you.*

Therefore, the question is not, "How do I get faith?" but, "How do I exercise the faith that God has already given me?" All of us have faith in something. We may have faith in our ability to drive our car or faith that the ceiling in our home will not fall down. Some people have faith in their abilities, while others have faith in their philosophies. As Christians, our faith must be focused exclusively on the living God—in Jesus Christ.

41 | We receive Jesus by faith alone

How do we receive Christ as Lord? By faith. How do we live out our Christian life each day? By faith. Hebrews 11:6 tells us, *"and without faith it is impossible to please God, because anyone who comes to him must believe that he exists and that he rewards those who earnestly seek him."*

Faith is our first response to God. We put our trust in Christ by faith and faith alone. We cannot depend on *our* abilities. We must depend on *His* abilities. If the world-renowned evangelist, Billy Graham, would have depended on his own works to be in right standing with God, he'd never have made it, because God's standard is perfection. You see, even a great man of God like Billy Graham had not been perfect. No one is perfect except Jesus Christ. That's why we have to repent from trying to gain acceptance from God by our own morality or good works. Our efforts to "try harder" at being a better student, a better spouse, or a stronger Christian witness can never gain for us more acceptance from God. Placing our faith in God is the only way to please Him. We place our faith in the living God and serve Him for one reason, *because He is God.* He is worthy of our praise and our complete allegiance.

Since we have embraced Christ by faith, we must hold fast and not be sidetracked. When we receive Jesus as our Lord and put our faith in Him, we find that our lives are no longer filled solely with our own thoughts and desires, as our lives had been before we came to Christ. Things have changed! Christ is now actually living in us. Galatians 2:20 says, *"...Christ lives in me. The life I live in the body, I live by faith in the Son of God, who loved me and gave himself for me."*

Why is this so important? Because when I realize that Christ lives in me, I begin to see life from a different perspective. I see it as it really is. Christ lives in me. And the same Holy Spirit that dwelt in Jesus Christ two thousand years ago, that gave Him the power to live a supernatural life, is also in me enabling me to live a supernatural life. His power will lead me on.

42 | Put yourself to the test

Remember, faith is not based on our outward appearance or on what we do, although true faith will result in changed behavior. We may be church members, give money in the offering every week, help other people and even give our lives in service to others. But, as we learned earlier, these good works do not make a person a true Christian, although a Christian will certainly do such things. People who look like Christians on the outside, but have no real spiritual life on the inside, are disappointing counterfeits.

Sometimes counterfeit Christians and genuine Christians look so much alike on the outside that you can hardly tell the difference. God wants us to take stock of our own lives to be completely sure that we are genuine. The scriptures tell us, *"Examine yourselves to see whether you are in the faith; test yourselves. Do you not realize that Christ Jesus is in you—unless, of course, you fail the test?"* (2 Corinthians 13:5).

We must look closely at ourselves and compare what we are to what the scriptures say a Christian must be. Police officers who are trained to spot counterfeit money spend much time in training and studying the real thing. When we study the real thing, the Bible, and allow the Holy Spirit to teach us, we will know the difference between reality and the counterfeit. The Bible tells us that the Holy Spirit will guide us into all truth. *But when he, the Spirit of truth, comes,*

How can you please God?

How can Christ live in you and you in Him?

In what ways is Christ living in you?

The Holy Spirit guides us in truth
John 14:17; Psalms 25:5
John 14:26

What helps you to recognize the difference between the real and the counterfeit Christian?

Biblical Foundations for Life

How will the Holy Spirit guide you into all truth?

What is righteousness?

Describe how you have received righteousness by faith.

he will guide you into all truth (John 16:13). The Holy Spirit convicts us in order to teach, correct and guide us into truth.

One day a friend gave me a candy bar. Little did I know that he had eaten the real candy bar and carefully replaced it with a piece of wood. When I opened the wrapper, I discovered his clever trick! Every Christian must examine himself to determine if his salvation is a present reality or if it is a counterfeit.

43 | We are righteous through faith in God

How do we know we are right with God and not a counterfeit Christian? Romans 3:22 says we are righteous only through faith in Jesus Christ. *This righteousness from God comes through faith in Jesus Christ to all who believe....*

Righteousness is our right standing with God, being right with God. A *righteousness consciousness* means *being constantly conscious, or thinking about, our right standing with God through faith in Jesus Christ.*

Romans 4:3 tells us clearly, "...*Abraham believed God, and it was credited to him as righteousness. The* word *accounted* literally means *credited*." The Lord credits our account with righteousness when we believe Him! Imagine someone depositing money in your account at the bank each week. You say, "I don't deserve this." But your bank account would continue to grow whether you deserved it or not! That is exactly what God does. The Bible says that if we believe God, like Abraham, the Lord puts *righteousness* into our account! So, being right with God does not depend on our performance, it depends on our faith in Jesus Christ—our trust in Him.

When we begin to confess the truth of our righteousness by faith, do you know what happens? The Lord provides for our needs! *But seek first his kingdom and his righteousness, and all these things will be given to you as well* (Matthew 6:33). God provides for our needs because we are His children through faith in Jesus Christ. God makes us righteous through faith in Jesus. God has accepted us. When we seek Him, He will provide for us!

New Christians often make the mistake of relying too much on their feelings. One day they *feel* close to God and the next day they don't *feel* Him. We cannot trust our feelings. We have to trust the truth of the Word of God. When we are tempted to be discouraged or depressed, we must make the decision, in Jesus' name, to replace those thoughts with the thoughts that God thinks about us. See yourself as God sees you. Look at others as God looks at them. Seek first His kingdom and His righteousness, and the Lord will respond by adding all that you need!

44 | Beware of having a sin consciousness

Some people have the opposite mentality of a righteousness consciousness; they have a "sin consciousness." When people have a sin consciousness they constantly are aware of, or thinking about, their tendency toward failure and sin. While it is true that by ourselves, we cannot obey God, the Bible says we can trust His competence (have faith in His strength to see us through). *Such confidence as this is ours through Christ before God. Not that we are competent in ourselves to claim anything for ourselves, but our competence comes from God. He has made us competent as ministers of a new covenant—not of the letter but of the Spirit; for the letter kills, but the Spirit gives life* (2 Corinthians 3:4-6).

It is only by God's competence that we are able to do anything. We have absolutely no chance of obeying God with our own strength. We must have faith in God's strength. Every time we look to ourselves to try to "pull ourselves up by our own bootstraps" we begin to live with a sin consciousness. Sin consciousness turns our thoughts inward. We depend on our own abilities and become proud when we succeed or feel like a failure when we do not succeed. Instead, we must look to Jesus, who gives us strength and peace.

It's like this. If you're in the hospital and they take out your almost-ruptured appendix, what are you going to concentrate on? The pain? The stitches? Or are you going to say, "Praise God! The poison's being removed. I'm being healed in Jesus' name!" We choose to think of one or the other, the pain or the healing. If we keep our eyes on Jesus and on His righteousness, then God is free to allow the abundant life that He promised to permeate our lives.

I can promise you that if you're a child of God, and if there is an area in your life where you are sinning, the Lord will tell you. He loves you that much. He will tell you through His Word or He may bring people into your life to tell you. He will do whatever it takes to make sure that you know the truth. This way, you will look to Jesus and know you are "righteous in Him." When we understand this principle and begin to live in the righteousness of God, we begin to live a life of victory. Whenever we look to ourselves instead of to Jesus for our righteousness, we begin to experience confusion and discouragement.

45 | Plant your righteousness seeds

Did you ever wake up on a holiday and find your alarm ringing in the morning at its normal time? You wake up and tell yourself you have to go to work, then you realize, "This is a holiday! I can sleep in!" You awaken to the truth.

The Bible encourages us to "awake to righteousness:" I can witness! I can be a man or woman of God! I can go to work and enjoy it! I can love my parents! I can raise a family for the Lord, regardless of my present circumstances! I can take a step of faith! I can be victorious! I am righteous through faith in Jesus Christ! You awaken to the God-given truth that you can live righteously and victoriously by the grace of God. *Awake to righteousness, and do not sin, for some do not have the knowledge of God...*(1 Corinthians 15:34a NKJ).

I once heard the story of a rescue operation of two men in a boat that had capsized. A helicopter dropped a rope and the first man held onto the rope to be pulled up into the helicopter. But the second man cried out, "Oh, don't do that! It's extremely dangerous to hang onto a rope tied to the bottom of a helicopter." Both men had a choice. They could either hang onto the rope and be pulled to safety or lose their lives. Either we trust God and receive His righteousness by faith instead of trusting in dead works, or die spiritually. That's how important this truth is. Righteousness through faith in Jesus is the only way out.

Biblical Foundations for Life

What is a "sin consciousness"?

Why is having a negative attitude a sign of weak faith?

Is "pulling ourselves up by our own bootstraps" a biblical idea?

What are some ways you can "awake to righteousness"?

How is your thinking changed?

When you confess the Word of God, what happens?

Again, I want to emphasize that righteousness through faith has nothing to do with the way we feel. It is based on the Word of God and His ability, not on us and our limited ability to "be good." Sometimes it takes time to see the results of living in righteousness by faith. It is like a certain kind of gigantic tropical species of bamboo plant. Initially, the new shoots grow slowly, but suddenly the growth rate increases rapidly and may reach nearly 60 cm (24 inches) per day![1]

So, do not give up. Plant your "righteousness consciousness seeds" and say, "I'm righteous by faith in Jesus." You may not feel any different, but you keep saying it because you know it is true. Faith comes by hearing, and hearing by the Word of God (Romans 10:17). One day the Word of God is going to bear fruit in your life and it's going to grow and completely change your life.

Don't be afraid to talk to yourself. I talk to myself all the time. The Bible says David talked to himself; he...*encouraged himself in the Lord* (1 Samuel 30:6 KJV). Another time, in Psalms 103:1, we see David talking to himself, *"Praise the Lord, O my soul; and all my inmost being, praise his holy name!"* We should be doing the same thing. I encourage you to get up in the morning and say, "I am righteous through faith in Jesus. I am a man or woman of God. I can do all things through Christ who strengthens me today" (Philippians 4:13).

[1] "Bamboo," Microsoft® Encarta® Online Encyclopedia 2001, http://encarta.msn.com © 1997-2001 Microsoft.

46 | Look to Jesus

What are some ways the devil lies to you?

Remember how Satan deceived Adam and Eve in the Garden? He continues to deceive and blind the minds of people today. The devil hates to see people put their trust and faith in the Lord. He knows that if he can get people to look at fear, poverty, disease, and their circumstances, they become defeated and depressed. Some days I don't spend enough time with God even though I know the Lord has called me to seek His face, read His Word, and look to Him. It is often at these times that the devil comes to me to say, "It's all over, because you failed. Now God can't use you."

Instead of listening to his lies, I immediately pray, "Lord, I believe what your Word says about me. I repent of 'missing the mark' today, and by your grace, Lord, I am going to be obedient to You."

When God thinks about you, what is His will for you?

There is a toy that you can find in some department stores. It's a big, tall toy on a heavy base. When you push it over, it always pops back up. That's the way God wants us to be as Christians. We need to say, "I will not listen to the lies of the devil. If I fall, I will get up in Jesus' name, and move on with my God."

A man of God once said, "Look around, and get distressed. Look within, and get depressed. Look to Jesus, and be at rest." We must trust God in faith to truly please Him. The Lord has great plans for our lives according to Jeremiah 29:11. *"For I know the plans I have for you,"* declares the Lord, *"plans to prosper you and not to harm you, plans to give you hope and a future."*

Yes, He is talking about you and me. Our God is thinking of us and cares about our futures!

POTENT MIXTURE: FAITH AND THE WORD PART 3

47 | How do we know the Bible is the true Word of God?

Let's discover how faith and God's Word, the Bible, is a powerful mix to help us live the abundant life Christ wants to give us. But first, let's briefly look at why we believe the Bible is the true Word of God. Some of the many books today that claim to be the Word of God are the Koran, the Book of Mormon, and the Bible. Christians believe the Bible is the Word of God and the source of truth to live by. So what is the evidence proving the authority and divine origin of the Bible?

The Bible proclaims to be the Word of God. *All scripture is inspired by God* (2 Timothy 3:16). *Inspired* means *God-breathed*. The writers of scripture were supernaturally guided to write what God wanted written. *Holy men of God spoke as they were moved by the Holy Spirit* (2 Peter 1:20-21).

Jesus taught that the scripture is God's inspired Word even to the smallest detail. *I tell you the truth, until heaven and earth disappear, not the smallest letter, not the least stroke of a pen, will by any means disappear from the Law until everything is accomplished* (Matthew 5:18).

Although skeptics have tried to destroy the authority of the Bible, the Bible has remained the most well-known book in the history of the world and has proven itself true again and again. The Bible was written over a period of 1,500 years, by over forty different authors from all walks of life, in many different countries, addressing hundreds of issues, and yet remains unified in its message from God. The unity alone is an amazing proof of the divine inspiration and authority of the Bible.

What did Jesus teach concerning the scripture as the inspired Word of God (Matthew 5:18)?

48 | Mixing faith and the Word

We need to take God's Word and mix it with faith. Hearing God's Word alone will not change us, but (by faith) acting on it will! The book of Hebrews tells us that...*the message they heard was of no value to them, because those who heard did not combine it with faith* (Hebrews 4:2).

Combining God's Word with faith is a supernatural mix that causes something powerful to happen. It reminds me of epoxy glue. When the two ingredients of epoxy glue are mixed together, something powerful happens and you can bond together all kinds of materials with it.

When I was a young boy, I really wanted a chemistry set. My parents never got me one. I think they were afraid that I would blow the roof off the house! However, I improvised by making my own experiments. One day I mixed baking soda and vinegar and discovered they make a great explosion! Baking soda and vinegar by themselves are not explosive, but when you mix them, an explosive chemical reaction occurs.

Have you ever experienced a spiritual explosion in your life?

Biblical Foundations for Life

Give an example when you not only heard God's Word but also acted on it in faith.

In the same way, you can trigger a spiritual explosion in your life when you mix the Word of God with your faith and say, "I'm going to believe God's Word and act on it." True faith rises up in your heart and you experience the abundant life that Jesus promised. You are not basing your life on your own righteousness, but instead, on the righteousness that comes by faith in Jesus Christ and His Word.

One day an emotionally depressed woman came to a wise believer for advice. She explained that her daughter was involved in immorality. He gave her simple advice, "You need to start seeing yourself and your daughter as God sees you. Rather than being despondent about her situation, see her behind the cross of Jesus. Confess the truth of God's Word for her life."

A few months later, the woman and her daughter came back, beaming from ear to ear. The woman explained: "I prayed and began to see my daughter from God's perspective. She had been living with a man who was not her husband, and one day she woke up so depressed that she decided to take her own life. But, first, she came home to see me. My family and I received her with joy. She received so much love from our family that she made a decision to give her life to Jesus. Why? Because we saw her behind the cross with the love eyes of Jesus." This family placed their faith in the Word of God instead of their feelings or circumstances. The Lord wants you and me to do the same.

49 | Jesus and His Word are one

The best way to serve Jesus Christ and know His will for our lives is simply to live in obedience to His Word—the scriptures. You see, Jesus and His Word are one. Revelation 19:13 says, "*...his name is the Word of God.*"

How does the Bible lead us into God's will for our lives?

When I travel, my wife often leaves me notes in my luggage. I love to read her notes because it's the same as if she were talking to me. When God's Word tells me He loves me or commands me to do something, it is the same as if Jesus were speaking to me audibly in His own words. We can constantly live under the Lordship of Jesus by listening to what He says—as expressed in His Word. Jesus tells us, "*The words I have spoken to you are spirit and they are life*" (John 6:63b).

How is God's Word renewing your mind today?

True Christians have chosen to live their lives in complete obedience to the Word of God. His words are spirit and life to us! The Bible leads us directly into God's will, and it keeps us from living according to our own desires instead of His desires. We need to read God's Word every day and confess Jesus Christ as our Lord so we can live in victory. God's Word renews our mind. *Do not conform any longer to the pattern of this world, but be transformed by the renewing of your mind. Then you will be able to test and approve what God's will is—his good, pleasing and perfect will* (Romans 12:2).

When we renew our minds daily with the Word of God and obey God's Word and the truth found there, it not only helps us to know Jesus better; it sets us free! When we obey the words that He has spoken to us in the scriptures and the words that He speaks to us by His Holy Spirit, we are obeying God. That is why the scriptures are so important.

If I feel like holding a grudge against someone and yet see in the scriptures that if I do not forgive others, God will not forgive me (Matthew 6:14, 15), I come to a crossroads in my life. Either I choose my way or God's way. We must trust and obey God's Word to renew our minds and change us.

50 | Release your faith by confessing the Word

Explain how you have released your faith in the past week.

You can release your faith by confessing God's Word with your mouth according to Romans 10:9-10. *That if you confess with your mouth, "Jesus is Lord," and believe in your heart that God raised him from the dead, you will be saved. For it is with your heart that you believe and are justified, and it is with your mouth that you confess and are saved.*

We are saved when we believe the truth from the Word of God in our hearts and confess it with our mouths. When we receive Jesus, we receive the gospel or *good news*. God's Word, the Bible, is filled with God's good news.

Being "saved" does not only mean that we go to heaven, as wonderful as that is. It also means we are being healed and set free inside. It means we can be set free emotionally, financially, mentally, and in every other area of our lives. The key is to believe the Word and confess it so faith can mix with God's Word and release mighty miracles in our lives.

I thank God every day that I'm righteous through faith in Jesus Christ. I'm thankful for His Word, and I'm thankful for what He's done in my life. I know that I am right with God, not because of the good works that I do, but because of faith in Jesus Christ.

When I became a new Christian, I began to read the Word of God day by day. I started to think and act differently because my mind was being renewed by the Word of God. Faith rose up in me as a result of God's Word, just like the scriptures promise in Romans 10:17. *Consequently, faith comes from hearing the message, and the message is heard through the word of Christ.*

51 | See faith coming

Describe a time in your life you "saw faith coming."

I have a friend who served as a pastor in India for many years. He said, "In Eastern cultures, we see the Bible differently than you do. We see in pictures. We read in the scriptures that faith comes by hearing and hearing by the Word of God, and we really see faith coming! We confess it because God says it is so, and we see it coming with our spiritual eyes."

I believe the Lord wants us to see what happens when we take the Bible seriously and speak the truth to ourselves. We will "see faith coming." Most of the time, people wait to feel their faith with their emotions, but this is going about it backwards.

Imagine a train running down a track. Let's compare the engine that pulls the train to the *Word of God*. The next car is *our faith*. And the last car, the caboose, is our *feelings* or *our emotions*.

Biblical Foundations for Life

What happens when you place your faith in feelings rather than the Word of God?

When we place our faith in the Word of God, our "feelings or emotions" will always follow like a caboose. However, if we place our faith in our feelings first, we will be frustrated and the enemy will begin to discourage us. We must place our faith in the Word of God first. Then the "feelings of faith" will follow. Faith is not a feeling. It is a mighty, living force released in our lives when we choose to hear and confess God's Word daily. *For the word of God is living and active. Sharper than any double-edged sword, it penetrates even to dividing soul and spirit, joints and marrow; it judges the thoughts and attitudes of the heart* (Hebrews 4:12).

The Word of God causes us to begin to think like Jesus thinks. The Word of God releases the Lord's power so that we can know the difference between our own thoughts (in the soul) and the thoughts the Lord has placed in our spirits.

52 | Meditate on God's Word

What are some ways you meditate on God's Word?

To grow spiritually, we must read and meditate on the Word of God each day. In this way, our minds become renewed. We must fill our minds with the truth of the Word of God, or we will be sidetracked by the philosophies of the world system around us that are completely against the truth of Jesus Christ. Exercising faith in God involves reading God's Word and obeying it.

How do we meditate on the Word of God? To *meditate* simply means *to roll something around over and over again in our minds.* Joshua 1:8 tells us, *Do not let this Book of the Law depart from your mouth; meditate on it day and night, so that you may be careful to do everything written in it. Then you will be prosperous and successful.*

Cows have multiple stomachs. They will fill their stomachs with grass, and then spend the rest of the day laying under a shade tree "chewing their cud." Food is passed from one stomach to the other in stages as they intermittently burp it up and chew it again. We could liken this process to meditating on the Word of God. We need to read the Word, and then write portions of it down and bring it back various times throughout the day to memorize it and meditate on it (chew on it!).

When I gave my life to Christ, I wrote down a verse of scripture that seemed to have special significance to me on an index card. Throughout the day, I pulled out the card to memorize it and meditate on its meaning. I literally "rolled around" God's Word in my mind until it became a part of me. During the first few years as a new Christian, I memorized hundreds of verses of scriptures this way.

There is a big difference between meditation on God's Word and the meditation practiced with some yoga techniques or by Hindu gurus and Buddhist monks. These religious leaders and various modern-day new age cults instruct their followers to meditate with one primary goal: *to empty their minds.* In this disconnection between the body and spirit or altered state of consciousness, a doorway to the occult is opened to the human soul. In sharp contrast, God's Word encourages us to *fill our minds* with (meditate on) the Word of God! As we do so, the Holy Spirit illuminates the Word of God to our minds, and we are changed.

53 | Spiritual sowing and reaping

God has called you and me to sow His Word by praying in alignment with its truth and by speaking it to others. Jesus talked about sowers of God's Word in the Gospel of Mark saying, *The farmer I talked about is anyone who brings God's message to others...the good soil represents the hearts of those who truly accept God's message and produce a plentiful harvest for God—thirty, sixty, or even a hundred times as much as was planted...*(Mark 4:14,20 TLB).

When we sow the seed of the Word of God, God works through it to produce a supernatural spiritual crop. It may not happen the first day, or the first week, but it will happen.

As a young boy, I remember throwing a few watermelon seeds into our garden. Months later we had watermelons everywhere! When we sow the Word of God through prayer and by confessing the truth into our lives and into the lives of others, we will see a mighty crop, a bountiful harvest come forth for God.

You sow dynamic spiritual seeds into lives through prayer and encouragement every time you pray for loved ones or for yourself. Remember that God has promised He will produce a crop through the seeds that we sow.

While traveling with a young man who was not yet a Christian, I began to sow spiritual seeds into his life. I simply told him, "God has a call on your life and I believe you are going to be a man of God. God is going to use you." Months later he told me he received Christ into his life and reminded me of the "seeds of truth" that I sowed into his life months before.

The whole world is God's spiritual garden, and He wants to sow seeds of life everywhere we go. Let's plant spiritual seeds by faith into people's lives. Then we can do what farmers do every year—pray and expect the seeds to grow.

Describe a time you sowed spiritual seeds into someone's life.

Did you see immediate results or not?

Biblical Foundations for Life

PART 4 — WE CAN LIVE VICTORIOUSLY

Describe a spiritual battle you fought and won recently.

54 | There's a battle to be fought

Why do so many people seem to be disinterested in the things of God? Many do not believe in Jesus because they are spiritually blinded by the enemy. *And even if our gospel is veiled, it is veiled to those who are perishing. The god of this age has blinded the minds of unbelievers, so that they cannot see the light of the gospel of the glory of Christ, who is the image of God* (2 Corinthians 4:3-4).

Satan not only tries to hide the truth of the gospel from us, he is ready to do battle with us once we become Christians. The walk of the Christian is described as a spiritual warfare, and we must be equipped to fight. According to Ephesians 6:12, there is a battle being waged for our souls. This battle is not with people, but with the demons of hell. *For our struggle is not against flesh and blood, but against the rulers, against the authorities, against the powers of this dark world and against the spiritual forces of evil in the heavenly realms.*

How did God's Word aid you?

Prayer and the declaration of the Word of God breaks down these demonic hindrances so that we can receive the Word of God and the life-giving conviction of the Holy Spirit. A friend and I went to pray for a man who had cancer. My friend, the man's believing wife, and daughter-in-law had been praying for his salvation for many years, but he was unwilling to receive Christ. After entering his home, I felt impressed to share my testimony with him. About thirty minutes later, he was ready to receive Jesus Christ as the Lord of his life! We rejoiced, knowing that the true battle was won in prayer prior to that day by those who loved him. In prayer, his friend, wife and daughter-in-law had battled the evil forces that had spiritually blinded their loved one, allowing the light of the gospel to penetrate.

Unbelief comes from the devil and from all of his hoards of demonic angels. We live in a spiritual world and must fight spiritual battles. *Therefore put on the full armor of God, so that when the day of evil comes, you may be able to stand your ground...take...the sword of the Spirit, which is the word of God* (Ephesians 6:13a, 17b). The sword of the Spirit that we use to conquer the devil is the Word of God. As we learned earlier in this book, we mix the Word of God with faith and sow the seeds. God promises that we will get a good crop and be victorious in our battles.

55 | Complete in spirit, soul and body

There is another battlefield: it is in our minds. My mind is bombarded with many thoughts every day, some not from God. It is important to understand that temptation is not sin because *every Christian is tempted*. Temptation becomes sin when we think about it and begin to allow it to gain control of our thoughts and our actions. How do we handle the wrong thoughts that come to our minds? We speak the Word of God and rebuke the devil in the name of Jesus. Then we go on, knowing that we are righteous by faith in Jesus Christ.

As Christians, we need to daily purify ourselves from every sin that threatens to contaminate us. The Bible teaches us that we are made up of body, soul and spirit. Before you were a Christian, your body, soul and spirit were polluted by sin. But as a believer, you are made holy. *May God himself, the God of peace, sanctify you through and through. May your whole spirit, soul and body be kept blameless at the coming of our Lord Jesus Christ* (1 Thessalonians 5:23).

If you and I sat down and talked face to face, you would not see all of me. What you would see is my body. My spirit is the part of me that communicates with God. My soul is a composite of my mind, my will, and my emotions.

Like me, you have the three aspects of spirit, soul, and body. When we are born again by the Spirit of God, we receive Jesus as Lord and our spirits are instantly born again. We are brand-new inside. Do our bodies change? Absolutely. Look closely at people who are filled with Jesus, they have a sense of the Lord's peace on their countenance. They "glow" because of the Lord's presence and their faces shine with the glory of God.

What happens to the soul? The soul doesn't change instantaneously. It begins to be renewed as we read, hear and meditate on the Word of God. The Bible tells us to...*be transformed by the renewing of your mind. Then you will be able to test and approve what God's will is—his good, pleasing and perfect will* (Romans 12:2).

To a certain degree, we are all products of our past. We learned to think a certain way (man's way) about the main issues of life. The Word of God renews our minds to see life from *God's perspective* and reap the benefits that come with divine wisdom (Joshua 1:8).

By meditating on the Word of God, we begin to see ourselves from the Lord's perspective instead of from our own. A new Christian will find that his soul (mind, will and emotions) begins to catch up with what happened in his spirit when he received Jesus as his Lord. Gradually, he starts to "think like God" (he thinks according to the guidelines revealed in God's Word), instead of his past way of thinking.

When we lay our past (and present) before the Lord, His peace will stand guard at the door of our hearts and minds and change us. *And the peace of God, which transcends all understanding, will guard your hearts and your minds in Christ Jesus. Finally, brothers, whatever is true, whatever is noble, whatever is right, whatever is pure, whatever is lovely, whatever is admirable—if anything is excellent or praiseworthy—think about such things* (Philippians 4:7-8).

If we fix our minds on the holy things in life, God's peace will prevent the heartaches of this world from wrecking our lives. The Lord knows we are a work in progress, and He will change us daily—body, soul, and spirit!

56 | You are a new creation

As soon as you are born again—you have received Jesus as Lord—a miracle has happened inside of you. You became a brand new person. You are a new creation in Jesus Christ. The Bible says in 2 Corinthians 5:17, "*Therefore, if anyone is in Christ, he is a new creation; the old has gone, the new has come!*"

What do you do when you are tempted to sin?

How is your body, soul, and spirit being renewed?

Biblical Foundations for Life

Explain in your own words what it means to be "in Christ."

_____
_____
_____
_____

What is the evidence of being a new creation?

_____
_____
_____
_____

An elephant becoming a butterfly would be no greater miracle! Yes, there is an indescribable miracle that happens inside of us as we live by faith in Jesus. Remember, putting our faith in Jesus means we cannot trust ourselves or our good works. In 2 Corinthians 1:9-10, Paul was imprisoned and in very dire circumstances. Still, he urged the Corinthian church to not trust in themselves but trust in God who alone has the power to deliver. ...*That we might not rely on ourselves but on God, who raises the dead. He has delivered us from such a deadly peril, and he will deliver us. On him we have set our hope that he will continue to deliver us.*

Faith is believing and trusting in God and God alone. It's not a matter of "turning over a new leaf" or just changing some of our old ways of doing things. No, a miracle has happened inside. We can know it has happened because God's Word says it has. We know by faith in the Word of God that we are new creations in Jesus Christ. Christianity is walking by faith, not by sight! We are righteous only by faith in Jesus Christ, and He makes us new day by day.

57 | Set free!

When we join God's family, we are set free from the power of sin over our lives; we are set free from its guilt. Jesus tells us in John 8:31,32, "*...if you hold to my teaching, you are really my disciples. Then you will know the truth, and the truth will set you free.*"

The first part of that verse says we must continue in God's Word—love it, keep it, and walk in it—and we shall know the truth and experience freedom. No one is truly free until the power of sin has been rendered inoperative as we consider ourselves dead to sin and alive to God. The Bible tells us that we are adopted into God's family. *For you did not receive a spirit that makes you a slave again to fear, but you received the Spirit of sonship. And by him we cry, "Abba, Father"* (Romans 8:15).

Every person living in sin is subject to fear because he is guilty! His conscience will trouble him. But a Christian does not have this fear because he has been adopted as a child into God's family (John 1:12, Ephesians 1:5, Galatians 4:5).

In what ways has "the truth" set you free?

_____
_____
_____
_____
_____
_____

False guilt is something that feels like guilt but it is really just shame. It is the leftover negative feelings from our sinful past. False guilt causes us to hang on to our feelings of being dirty and sinful, even after we have confessed our sins and God has forgiven us. Before I received Jesus as my Lord, I experienced genuine guilt over my sins. Yet even after I received the Lord, the guilt continued although I was totally forgiven from God's perspective. Then I read 1 John 1:9 in God's Word, "*If we confess our sins, he is faithful and just and will forgive us our sins and purify us from all unrighteousness.*"

From that moment on, I stopped living by past experiences, feelings, and fears. I started living by the Word of God, and the guilt left. I knew I was forgiven because the Bible told me so! I remembered that God had "removed my sins as far as the east is from the west" (Psalms 103:12). I was safe from all condemnation for my sins. It was as if they had not been committed at all. That is how freely God forgives when we place our trust in Him!

58 | The devil condemns; God convicts

The devil will tell us that it is a long way back to God when we sin. He will try to make us believe that God will never use us again. But we now know better. If we sin, we must repent (we stop it and we change our direction). The Lord forgives us, and we start with a new, clean slate.

Sometimes restitution has to follow repentance. This is putting things right with people we have wronged. If someone repents from shoplifting, he needs to pay it back. Although he is forgiven the moment he confesses his sin, he needs to take a step of obedience and restore what was stolen. When Zacchaeus repented for running a crooked tax collection agency, he told the Lord he would restore four times what he stole (Luke 19:8-9).

Some time after I received Jesus as my Lord, I was convicted by the Holy Spirit when I remembered I had deceived a classmate in high school. Another friend and I were gambling with him and had "rigged it" so that he always lost. I wrote to the classmate, explained what had happened and asked him for forgiveness, returning the money that I had taken with interest. A few weeks later, I received a return letter saying he forgave me and thanking me for writing. I did not restore what I had taken so that I could be forgiven; I restored it because I *was* forgiven.

The devil condemns us, but God convicts us of our sin. What is the difference between the two? Condemnation brings doubt, fear, unbelief, and hopelessness. Satan condemns us to bring us down and destroy our faith. God convicts us to restore us to righteousness and faith. He always corrects us to build us up, and His conviction always brings hope and a way of escape. *No temptation has seized you except what is common to man. And God is faithful; he will not let you be tempted beyond what you can bear. But when you are tempted, he will also provide a way out so that you can stand up under it* (1 Corinthians 10:13).

Don't accept condemnation from Satan or other people. *Therefore, there is now no condemnation for those who are in Christ Jesus, because through Christ Jesus the law of the Spirit of life set me free from the law of sin and death* (Romans 8:1-2).

Christ has made you free! You are free from the law of sin and death. He has made you righteous by faith in Him.

59 | You can have a full life!

Christ wants to give us a full, abundant life, and He says, "*...I have come that they might have life, and that they may have it more abundantly*" (John 10:10 NKJ).

The term *abundant life* is translated from the Greek word *zoe* which means *the very nature of God and source of life*. The abundant life then, is life filled with the very nature of God inside of us. It is abundant in quantity and quality—overflowing life. That is the kind of life that God has prepared for us as His children.

Christ lives in us to help us live victoriously and fully. *Christ lives in me. The life I live in the body, I live by faith in the Son of God, who loved me and gave himself for me* (Galatians 2:20b). I keenly remember when this truth was made real to me while working on the family farm. I was herding livestock and frustrated by

Think about a time you have felt condemned rather than convicted of a sin.

Explain the difference.

Biblical Foundations for Life

Name some of the things you do that help you to experience an abundant life in Christ.

_____
_____
_____
_____

Can you call God your "Father"?

_____
_____
_____
_____

Are you "reigning in life" through Jesus Christ?

_____
_____
_____

my lack of ability. Then I prayed for God's wisdom rather than trusting in my own strength. As I confessed the truth of "Christ living in me," I was energized to complete my job! I received a clear realization that the Lord lived in me and wanted me to depend on His strength alone!

Do you want to know what the Lord's will is for your life? Of course you do! Trust completely that Jesus is in control of your life and wants to give you the strength you need to persevere. Begin to renew your mind daily with the Word of God, and you will discover the Lord's plans for your life. Our minds are like a painter's canvas, with God's Word the paint. God, the Holy Spirit, is like a paintbrush who wants to paint a clear picture concerning His will for our lives, but we need to have enough paint available for Him to draw us a clear picture.

Here are a few things to do to grow spiritually. We should worship God on a daily basis (John 4:23-24). We need to pray to Him and read the Bible. It is also important to worship with other Christians on a regular basis (Hebrews 10:24-25). We need to find a local church and develop relationships with the people there. In addition, we should share the gospel with others who need to hear (Matthew 28:19-20). When we do these things, we can expect our life-style to change. We will begin to experience the abundant life Jesus came to give us!

60 | You are accepted!

Ephesians 1:6 tells us we are "accepted in the beloved" (God's family). When we are born again, we actually become a part of God's family! The Creator of the universe wants you and me to be in His family! 1 John 3:1 says, *"How great is the love the Father has lavished on us, that we should be called children of God!"*

Think of it! You really are a child of the living God when you receive Jesus by faith. You are righteous! No matter what you have done yesterday, you are right with God as soon as you believe God's Word is true and say, "Lord, I know I'm righteous only because of my faith that You've given me—faith in Jesus Christ. Thank You, God, that I am righteous not by my works but by faith in Christ today!"

We all have a need to be accepted. I have felt misunderstood, left out and rejected many times. In my first year at school, I was one of those kids who was usually the last one picked to play baseball with my schoolmates. It really hurt.

How about you? Can you remember times when you felt all alone? Here is the good news. We are not alone! We can be secure in the fact that God loves us. When I realized that Jesus accepted me just the way I was, a new security came into my life. I can accept others, because I know that God has accepted me!

God has good plans for your life today. He wants you to reign in life through Jesus Christ because…*those who receive God's abundant provision of grace and of the gift of righteousness reign in life through the one man, Jesus Christ* (Romans 5:17b).

Do not allow the enemy to get your focus off of Jesus and His righteousness. Refuse to be controlled by your feelings or circumstances. Rise up in faith and begin to reign in life through Jesus Christ and His righteousness! I have some good news for you: You don't have to wait. You can start today!

FOUNDATION 3

New Testament Baptisms

61 | Introduction to foundation 3

We are going to look at another of the six foundational doctrines of the Christian faith found in Hebrews 6:1-2—the doctrine of baptisms.

Therefore, leaving the discussion of the elementary principles of Christ, let us go on to perfection, not laying again the foundation of repentance from dead works and of faith toward God, of the doctrine of baptisms, of laying on of hands, of resurrection of the dead, and of eternal judgment (NKJ).

This study will cover four different types of baptism:

- **Baptism in water.** This is a sign of cleansing and remission of sin. We are baptized in water out of obedience to God's Word. *"Repent and be baptized, every one of you, in the name of Jesus Christ for the forgiveness of your sins..."* (Acts 2:38).
- **Baptism into the body of Christ.** The Holy Spirit supernaturally places us into the family of God when we accept Christ as Savior and Lord. *"For we were all baptized by one Spirit into one body—whether Jews or Greeks, slave or free—and we were all given the one Spirit to drink"* (1 Corinthians 12:13).
- **Baptism of fire.** This occurs when we face suffering in our lives and persevere through the tests. *John answered them all, "I baptize you with water. But one more powerful than I will come, the thongs of whose sandals I am not worthy to untie. He will baptize you with the Holy Spirit and with fire."* (Mark 8:36-38).
- **Baptism in the Holy Spirit** gives us a new dimension of the Holy Spirit's fire. *He will baptize you with the Holy Spirit and with fire* (Luke 3:16).

It is so important so that we have a solid spiritual foundation built on the truths of God's Word. The higher the building, the deeper the foundation needed. The more God uses you, the deeper the foundation you need in your life.

Have you experienced any of the four types of baptism? Explain.

Biblical Foundations for Life

PART 1

Name the four types of baptisms mentioned in the Bible.

BAPTISM IN WATER

62 | An elementary principle: Doctrine of baptisms

Being baptized is one of the first steps a new Christian should make. Baptism is an essential part of the spiritual foundation of a new Christian's life. When we think of baptism, we normally think of water baptism and its various modes—sprinkling, pouring, immersion. But there really are more kinds of baptisms mentioned in God's Word than water baptism. Let's look at Hebrews 6.

In addition to the previous foundational principles we learned in Biblical Foundation 2, (*repentance from dead works* and *faith toward God*), Hebrews, chapter 6, lists yet another elementary principle—the doctrine of baptisms. *Therefore, leaving the discussion of the elementary principles of Christ, let us go on to perfection, not laying again the foundation of...the doctrine of baptisms...* (Hebrews 6:2 NKJ).

Since this spiritual foundation is listed as plural—baptisms—it indicates that the Christian faith includes more than one kind of baptism. As we read through the New Testament, we discover there are four distinct types of baptisms: baptism in water, baptism into the body of Christ, baptism of fire, and baptism in the Holy Spirit. In this chapter, we will take a look at all four, starting with the Christian baptism in water.

63 | Baptism in water is a demonstration of obedience

Water baptism, sometimes called *believer's baptism*, is for the purpose of identifying with Jesus. In the New Testament, once a person believed in Jesus for salvation, he was then baptized in water. Baptism is a sign of cleansing and forgiveness of sin—an act of faith and obedience. Jesus, Himself, introduces us to water baptism when He was baptized by John the Baptist.

John had been preaching a baptism of repentance for the forgiveness of sins (Mark 1:4). When people repented of their sins, they were water-baptized as the outward evidence that they had repented. Since it was an outward sign, it did not magically save them. The power in baptism was in the power of God, not in the water or the act itself.

"Then why," you may ask, "was Jesus baptized"? Jesus was without sin (1 Peter 2:21-22); He did not need to show evidence of confessing and repenting of sin. John pondered the same question when Jesus came to him to be baptized. Jesus gave John the answer to his question when he said, "Let it be so now; it is proper for us to do this to fulfill all righteousness" (Matthew 3:15).

Jesus was setting an example for Christian believers to follow—not simply as evidence that they had confessed and repented of their sins, but "to fulfill [complete] all righteousness." Christian baptism is an outward act of obedience by which the believer fulfills the inward righteousness he already has through faith in Christ's death and resurrection.

Jesus said that everywhere the gospel is preached, individuals will be saved when they believe. Baptism naturally followed. *Whoever believes and is baptized will be saved...*(Mark 16:16).

The natural succession and pattern of believing first and then being baptized is followed throughout the New Testament. Sometimes people ask, "I was baptized as an infant. Is infant baptism in the Bible?" Infant baptism is not mentioned in the Bible. The record of baptisms in the New Testament are of adults who were previously unbelievers. These believers were baptized after their belief and faith in Jesus. Since infants are incapable of exercising faith, and baptism is the outward sign of faith, it stands to reason that an infant is not eligible for baptism. Although there is not necessarily anything wrong with baptizing a baby as a form of dedication to the Lord, according to scripture, they should be baptized after they believe as an outward sign of faith.

The key question to ask is this: Have you been baptized since you've believed? The Bible teaches us to be baptized in water after we believe in Jesus. It is a sign of our faith.

64 | Baptism in water makes a public announcement

As a sign of our faith in Jesus, water baptism makes several bold statements. Let's look at these statements in the next four sections. First of all, the Bible tells us that water baptism is a public announcement of our decision to turn our backs on sin and live for Jesus Christ...*all should be baptized as a public announcement of their decision to turn their backs on sin* (Mark 1:4 TLB).

Baptism is a public announcement that we have taken a clear stand for Jesus Christ. In the early church, it was taken for granted that when someone turned his life over to Jesus Christ, his first step of obedience was water baptism...*Repent and be baptized, every one of you, in the name of Jesus Christ for the forgiveness of your sins...*(Acts 2:38).

When I was a youth worker, there were times when dozens of young people gave their lives to Jesus during a given week. We often baptized them the same day they were born again. Some were baptized in swimming pools, others in rivers and ponds, and still others in bathtubs. These water baptisms were very meaningful, spiritual times. Baptisms can take place in varied settings, large or small. Some baptisms can be planned ahead and attended by friends and family so they can be a part of the celebration.

No matter what method or in what setting, new Christians are making a public statement by participating in the physical, outward sign of their salvation by being baptized. This act of faith is a decision that empowers Christians to fulfill the Great Commission to wholeheartedly make and baptize disciples. *Therefore go and make disciples of all nations, baptizing them in the name of the Father and of the Son and of the Holy Spirit, and teaching them to obey everything I have commanded you. And surely I am with you always, to the very end of the age* (Matthew 28:19-20).

If you have been water-baptized, recall your experience.

If you have been water-baptized, what does it mean to you, to Jesus, to your friends?

Biblical Foundations for Life

What is the spiritual explanation of going under and coming back up out of the water?

Can you truly say that your "old self" is dead?

New Testament circumcision

Romans 2:29

65 | Baptism in water shows we are dead to sin and alive to Christ

A second reason why water baptism is so important is that it shows we are dead to sin and alive to Christ, according to Romans 6:4. *We were therefore buried with him through baptism into death in order that, just as Christ was raised from the dead through the glory of the Father, we too may live a new life.*

Water baptism is a sign of being buried to sin and resurrected to new life. Jesus was buried and resurrected two thousand years ago. We are buried with Him by baptism in a spiritual sense. We must be dead to ourselves before we can have new life. When we come to the cross, we die to our old way of living so that we can have the new resurrected life that God has promised.

When you go to a funeral and see a dead man, you know that he cannot respond to anything. He cannot be hurt physically or emotionally. He cannot feel pain. He is dead! When we are buried in Christ, our old nature no longer can do its own thing; it is dead. So then, spiritually speaking, our old life is dead.

Here's an example: Joe was a former gangster with the Mafia, who gave his life to Jesus. His life was permanently changed. A few weeks after he gave his life to the Lord, one of his Mafia brothers called him on the phone and said, "Hey, is Joe there?"

Joe answered, "No, Joe died," and hung up the phone. The truth is, Joe *had* died. He was a brand new Joe and was living a brand new life. The old Joe was dead, a new Joe had come, and Jesus Christ now lived in him. Water baptism is a sign that we have died to self and, with the power of God's glory, now walk in a new life.

Sometimes people ask, "How should a person be baptized?" The Greek word for *baptize* is *baptiso*, which means *to immerse*. We encourage people to be immersed in the water. Going into the watery grave of baptism is symbolic of dying to self, being buried and then resurrected as we come up out of the water.

You have been crucified with Christ. Your old "man" (evil nature) is dead. Through water baptism, you become dead to sin and alive to Christ.

66 | Baptism in water illustrates a New Testament circumcision

This brings us to a third statement that water baptism makes. Water baptism is a type of New Testament circumcision. In the Old Testament circumcision, when an infant boy was eight days old, his foreskin was cut away as a sign of God's covenant to His people. It was a sign of faith just as it is in the New Testament. Colossians 2:11-12 says that submitting to the watery grave of baptism, just like circumcision, shows that our old sin nature has been cut away, supernaturally. *In him you were also circumcised, in the putting off of the sinful nature, not with a circumcision done by the hands of men but with the circumcision done by Christ, having been buried with him in baptism and raised with him through your faith in the power of God, who raised him from the dead.* The power of the sin nature that is inside you and me—that old nature that says, "I want to do what I want to do"—is symbolically cut away when we're baptized in water. It's a New Testament circumcision.

I once read about a man who had a very mean landlord who was always causing problems. One day, the landlord sold the property to a new landlord, a wonderful man. Sometime later, the first landlord came back and demanded that the tenant pay him. The tenant said, "What do you mean? You don't own this anymore. Go talk to my new landlord." When your old landlord, the devil, comes and tries to tell you that you are still under bondage to the old habits of the past—lying, criticism, lust, hatred, anger, or whatever—you can tell the devil you have a new landlord. His name is Jesus. Tell the devil, "Go talk to Jesus!"

When we are baptized in water, we are making a statement that the bondage of the past is broken. It's a supernatural work of God. Moses and the children of Israel were in bondage to the Egyptians, but when they came through the Red Sea, God's people were baptized and set free after coming through the water. *For I do not want you to be ignorant of the fact, brothers, that our forefathers were all under the cloud and that they all passed through the sea. They were all baptized into Moses in the cloud and in the sea* (1 Corinthians 10:1-2).

Having trusted God, by faith in Jesus, for freedom from the bondage of our past, we are then baptized. We don't always feel that we are freed from bondage. That's why it's important that we know it by faith. We live by the truth of His Word, not by our emotions. I remember flying into my hometown of Lancaster, Pennsylvania, one time and feeling sure we were going the wrong way. But we came into the right airport. The pilots were flying by the navigation equipment—and it was right. We should live our lives, not by every whim of our emotions, but according to God's navigation instrument, the Bible, which gives us the will of God.

Romans 6:14 says, *"For sin shall not be your master...."* Instead of seeing this scripture as a law, see it as a promise. God says that sin shall not have power over me because I am buried with Him in baptism. The old me is dead. I am a brand new person!

Our old, evil nature is rendered inoperative and through water baptism, we experience New Testament circumcision. Romans 6:6 states, *"For we know that our old self was crucified with him so that the body of sin might be done away with, that we should no longer be slaves to sin."*

The old has been cut away! We are living a new life with Christ inside of us.

67 | Baptism in water shows we are obeying God

A fourth statement water baptism makes is that it shows we are obeying God. The Word of God instructs us to be baptized in water. We are exhorted to "believe and be baptized" (Mark 16:16). Water baptism symbolizes a spiritual cleansing, according to 1 Peter 3:21. *And this water symbolizes baptism that now*

As we pass through the water, we are symbolizing our freedom from our past bondage to ____(fill in the blank).

Why is it important not to rely on our feelings?

What brings a clear conscience toward God?

saves you also—not the removal of dirt from the body but the pledge of a good conscience toward God. It saves you by the resurrection of Jesus Christ.

It is the cleansing of the heart, not the outward ceremony that saves. Washing with water does little more than removing dirt. But being baptized shows that we are living with a clear conscience. We have an unwavering confidence in Jesus Christ. We are obeying the Lord in all that He has asked us to do, and it brings a tremendous freedom into our lives.

Sometimes people ask, "What about a deathbed conversion? If someone gives his heart to Jesus and dies two minutes later and there is no time to baptize him, where does he spend eternity?" Remember, baptism does not save us. The blood of Jesus Christ saves us. Baptism is simply an act of obedience. After his profession of faith, the thief on the cross could not be water baptized but Jesus said He would see him in paradise (Luke 23:40-43).

According to the examples given in the scriptures, and if we have the opportunity, we should be baptized as soon after conversion as possible. When Paul was in jail, the Philippian jailer gave his heart to Jesus. The jailer's whole household was baptized that night with water (Acts 16:33). While Philip was walking down a road one day, he met an Ethiopian official sitting in his chariot and reading the scriptures. Philip explained the good news about Jesus to him, and he was baptized as soon as they found some water (Acts 8:38). Crispus and his household, and many other Corinthians (Acts 18:8), believed and were baptized immediately.

Every believer, even a young child who has faith to be baptized should be encouraged to be baptized...*According to your faith, let it be to you* (Matthew 9:29 NKJ). It should be noted, however, that a child should never be pressured into water baptism; he or she must desire it and be ready for it.

68 | Be baptized in water!

If you have never been baptized in water, what are you waiting for? Do it today! We mentioned already that when Jesus hung on the cross between two thieves, one of them was saved but there was no opportunity for him to come down from the cross and be baptized.

However, you and I have that opportunity. Although baptism does not save us, let's be obedient to the Word of God and take the opportunity to show we are dead to sin and alive to Christ. If you have any doubts about your baptism in water, I encourage you to be rebaptized. Doubts can cloud your faith and cast a shadow of condemnation on your life. Romans 14:23 says that, "...*everything that does not come from faith is sin.*"

It's important that you are living and walking in faith. If you're not sure, be baptized in water so that you can be certain and the enemy cannot sow seeds of doubts in your mind. Water baptism is a physical act which reminds you of your faith and freedom in Jesus. You can point to it if the devil tries to lie to you and put doubt in your heart. You can say with assurance, "I was baptized in water and I know that I'm free. The old man, the former sinful nature, is cut off and has no power. Jesus Christ lives strong in my life." Talk to a pastor or small group leader to arrange for your water baptism.

In my opinion, any believer in Christ can baptize another believer in water. You do not have to necessarily be a pastor or elder to perform a baptism. Paul, the apostle, often left water baptism to other believers in the church. He did it simply because they could help out this way. Paul knew his primary calling was to preach the gospel and to train others. *I am thankful that I did not baptize any of you except Crispus and Gaius…For Christ did not send me to baptize, but to preach the gospel…*(1 Corinthians 1:14, 17).

To summarize, water baptism is a sign of an inner cleansing of the heart. It is a public declaration that I have turned from sin to serve Jesus Christ as Lord. It shows that I am dead to sin and alive to Christ. It is a type of New Testament circumcision where the power of my old nature has been cut off. And most important of all, baptism in water is important because the Lord, in His Word, commands me to be baptized, and I want to be obedient to Him.

If you have doubts about your conversion and baptism, what can you do about it?

PART 2

MORE BAPTISMS

69 | Baptism into the body of Christ

Baptism into the body of Christ is another kind of baptism mentioned in the New Testament. We learned earlier that the word *baptize* literally means *to put into*. When we're baptized in water, someone places us into the water. When we're baptized into the body of Christ, the Holy Spirit supernaturally places us into the "body" or "the family of God." *For we were all baptized by one Spirit into one body—whether Jews or Greeks, slave or free—and we were all given the one Spirit to drink* (1 Corinthians 12:13).

We are united by one Spirit as members of the body of Christ. God gives us other people in the body of Christ for support and encouragement. As we learn from each other, and get to know Jesus better, we are made complete by His Spirit. Jesus is the head of the body, and each believer makes up a part of His spiritual body on earth. We are here on earth to become Christ's hands, feet and tongue, and other parts of the body with various functions, abilities, and callings.

When a young man is newly married, he leaves his old family and is placed into a new family. As a new husband, he and his wife start a new unit of their own. Likewise, a new believer is supernaturally placed in the new family of God to begin life anew. Being baptized into the body of Christ is a supernatural work of God. We are placed, spiritually, into the body of Christ the moment we receive Jesus Christ as Lord. Because we belong to Christ, we are members and belong to each other.

Who baptizes you into the body of Christ?

70 | God's wonderful family

When you are born again into God's family, you become a brother or sister in Christ to every other believer in the world. Being a part of the Lord's family is a wonderful blessing. You can meet a Christian brother or sister for the very first time from another nation and it seems like you have known them forever. You are a part of the same family!

Years ago, I visited the largest church in the world in Seoul, Korea. It was a beautiful experience meeting dozens of Korean believers, and although we did not speak the same language, we were able to sense that we were a part of the same spiritual family.

When John, the apostle, saw the throne of heaven in Revelation 5:9, he saw "living creatures and elders" (representing followers of Christ or the church in all nations and among all kinds of people), giving honor to Jesus. *And they sang a new song: "You are worthy to take the scroll and to open its seals, because you were slain, and with your blood you purchased men for God from every tribe and language and people and nation."*

God's wonderful family is made up of people from every nationality, race, and culture. We are all brothers and sisters through faith in our Lord Jesus Christ!

Think about a time you experienced kinship with a believer from a different culture. What did you have in common?

The Lord's family is awesome. Each of us has been born again by the Spirit of God. We are sons and daughters of the King of the universe, according to 2 Corinthians 6:18. *"I will be a Father to you, and you will be my sons and daughters," says the Lord Almighty.*

71 | Baptism of fire

Yet another kind of baptism mentioned in the New Testament is the *baptism of fire.* John the Baptist mentions this baptism in Luke 3:16. *John answered them all, "I baptize you with water. But one more powerful than I will come, the thongs of whose sandals I am not worthy to untie. He will baptize you with the Holy Spirit and with fire."*

Baptism with fire

Isaiah 48:10; Philippians 1:29
2 Corinthians 5:7

We learned earlier that the baptism with water signifies repentance. Here we see that the coming of the Holy Spirit is proof of the presence of God. Fire is a biblical symbol of purification and power. John the Baptist said that Jesus will baptize us with the Holy Spirit and fire.

What is some "chaff" in your life that God is cleaning away?

Let's talk about the baptism of fire first, specifically in the way it can purify us. Trials or difficult times that we go through are a type of baptism of fire. After John said Jesus would baptize us with the Holy Spirit and fire, he explains it more fully in the next verse. *His winnowing fork is in his hand to clear his threshing floor and to gather the wheat into his barn, but he will burn up the chaff with unquenchable fire* (Luke 3:17).

A fan or winnowing shovel was used to throw grain into the air so that the chaff would blow away, while the clean kernels fell back to the threshing floor. The Lord tells us that He will "clean out His threshing floor, and gather the wheat into His barn, and burn the chaff." In other words, our God is committed to cleaning out of our lives all of those unwholesome things (chaff) that may still be clinging to us. This could be habits from our past or old ways of thinking that are contrary to God's Word.

This cleaning process is not always easy! Sometimes new Christians are shocked when they have to face trials in their lives. They assumed that the Christian life was going to be a life of ease.

I grew up on a farm, so I clearly understand the importance of the chaff being separated from the wheat in order to get a clean product. When wheat harvest came each year, we had a large vibrating screen that the wheat was poured onto which literally shook the chaff free as it was separated from the wheat. God is looking for good fruit (wheat) in our lives. Sometimes He allows us to be in circumstances to "vibrate" us a bit until the "chaff" in our lives can be blown away.

On the family farm, I also learned a similar lesson while welding. I remember taking a torch and heating metal until it was very hot. When it was hot, the impurities came to the top. We called it *slag.* When the slag surfaced, we would scrape it off, or it could keep the two pieces of metal from being properly welded together. Again, this is a picture of a separation of the good from the bad so that we can find purity.

Biblical Foundations for Life

There are times when we need the *slag* skimmed out of our lives in a baptism of fire. When we go through these fiery trials and hard times, the impurities will "come to the top" in our lives. The wrong attitudes, those things that irritate us, the critical spirit, lack of love, lack of joy, lack of patience, fear—all "come to the top." When the "spiritual slag" is revealed in our lives, we can receive from Jesus the ability to repent and get rid of the impurities.

72 | Drinking the cup

Can you see how God is molding you through the baptism of fire to become the person He needs for the task He wants you to accomplish?

James and John, two of the disciples, had some *chaff* or *slag* in their lives that needed to be eradicated so they could become stronger. They sincerely loved Jesus and wanted to be close to Him, but they seemed to be focusing mainly on the benefits Jesus could give them when they sent their mother to ask a favor of Jesus on their behalf. When their mother asked if her sons could sit on the right and left side of Jesus in His kingdom, Jesus asked the following hard question, *"...Are you able to drink the cup that I am about to drink, and be baptized with the baptism that I am baptized with?" They said to Him, "We are able." So He said to them, "You will indeed drink My cup, and be baptized with the baptism that I am baptized with..."* (Matthew 20:22-23 NKJ).

Were they willing to be baptized with the baptism that He was to be baptized with—namely, to go to the cross? Were they willing to suffer in order to build the kingdom? Were they willing to face the impurities in their lives and allow Jesus to change them? They thought they were ready, so they said, "We are able." However, a few days later, they deserted their Master when He was arrested. The benefits of following Jesus just became less desirable to them when it involved suffering for Him!

Of course, the disciples later returned to Jesus after they had betrayed and abandoned Him. They witnessed His love and forgiveness in their lives. Jesus knows and understands our weaknesses. When the impurities come out of our lives, He reaches out with forgiveness and love. His power strengthens us so we can be victorious the next time we are faced with life's difficulties.

73 | Count it all joy

You may say, "Man, I'm having some hard times! Why me?" It is never easy when God allows us to go through the fire. It can make us feel like giving up when God doesn't make sense to us. What God really wants us to do is keep trusting Him. This is why James 1:2-5 tells us, *"Consider it pure joy, my brothers, whenever you face trials of many kinds, because you know that the testing of your faith develops perseverance. Perseverance must finish its work so that you may be mature and complete, not lacking anything. If any of you lacks wisdom, he should ask God, who gives generously to all without finding fault, and it will be given to him."*

When we understand that the trials of life can be used by the Lord to work His character in our lives, it really changes our perspective. We can rejoice, because the Lord is using it for our good! And He promises to give us wisdom right in the middle of the trials if we just ask Him! He can be trusted, in spite of the pain.

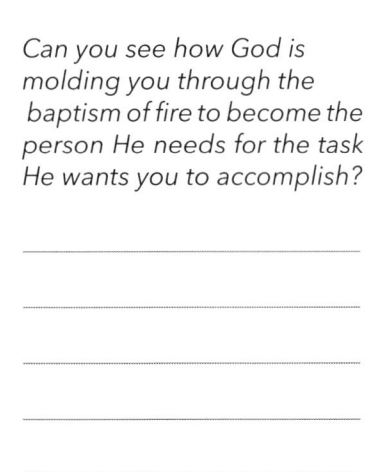

I took a course in high school learning how to make certain metal tools. In order for the tools to be hardened, we were taught to take a hot molten piece of metal and dip it in and out of water in order to temper it. This process gave the tool the proper strength to be useful.

Our Lord allows us to go through the baptism of fire in order to make us useful in His service. An attitude of pride will not hold up under pressure. When we go through some fiery trials in life, we learn to trust in the Lord and in His Word. His character is built into our lives. Without His character built into our lives, we will break under pressure when the Lord really begins to use us.

74 | Persevering in our trials

Yes, the Lord will use us, even when we are going through hard times! For example, did you ever have a brother or sister "sandpaper" in your life—someone who rubbed you the wrong way? Maybe the Lord allowed this person in your life for a reason. Perhaps He wanted to see if you would respond in a Christ-like way. So you reached out to the Lord for His strength to love this person unconditionally. It was not easy, and life was unpleasant for awhile, but you came through this baptism of fire with a new love and awareness of God's grace and mercy. Today you have a great relationship with this former "sister sandpaper"! Trusting Him and persevering really made you strong and cleaned out some bad attitudes in your own life.

Did you ever pinch your finger causing a painful blood clot to form under the fingernail? You will probably have to go to the doctor so he can use a sterile needle to drill a little hole in the nail, releasing the pressure. The Lord wants us to release spiritual pressure in the lives of others. But, He can only use us effectively if our attitudes are pure and we trust Him.

When we persevere in our trials, we are purified by the Word of God so we can be the pure bride of Christ. The Bible calls the church "the bride of Christ." Did you ever see a dirty bride? I haven't. The Lord is cleaning us up. The book of Ephesians 5:25-27 says, *"Husbands, love your wives, just as Christ loved the church and gave himself up for her to make her holy, cleansing her by the washing with water through the word, and to present her to himself as a radiant church, without stain or wrinkle or any other blemish, but holy and blameless."*

The Lord uses His Word to wash us. However, if we never look into the mirror, we tend to forget how dirty we can be. The Word of God is our mirror and our cleanser. As a little boy, I hated to take baths. But my parents made sure that I took a regular bath, whether I liked it or not! And now, I'm glad they did. You, too, will look back later and really appreciate your "spiritual bath."

Don't be afraid of the baptism of fire. Jesus will give you the strength to persevere. Trials can make you strong if you respond to them the right way.

In what ways are you different after going through trials and tribulations?

Persevering in our trials
James 1:2-4
1 Corinthians 10:13
Romans 8:18,28

Have you seen spiritual growth in your life after coming through a trial?

How did God's Word help you?

Biblical Foundations for Life

75 | On fire for Jesus

Are you enthused about what God is doing in your life?

Previously we said that fire is a symbol of purification and power, and we have examined how we can be purified by "fiery" trials. Another side to the baptism of fire is the *power* aspect of it. We should live in such a way that our lives are "on fire for Jesus Christ." We need to be earnest and enthusiastic in our love for God, according to Revelation 3:19. "...*Turn from your [our] indifference and become enthusiastic about the things of God*" (TLB).

If we are not enthusiastic about the things of God, we are commanded to turn from our indifference or apathy. We have been created to experience His "fire" burning inside of us, baptized with fire. The early disciples "burned" with a zeal for God. Ask the Lord to baptize you with His fire and His zeal. God is looking for zealous men and women. Numbers 25:11-13 speaks of such a zealous man. *Phinehas son of Eleazar, the son of Aaron, the priest, has turned my anger away from the Israelites; for he was as zealous as I am for my honor among them, so that in my zeal I did not put an end to them. Therefore tell him I am making my covenant of peace with him. He and his descendants will have a covenant of a lasting priesthood, because he was zealous for the honor of his God and made atonement for the Israelites.* The Lord honored Phinehas because he was zealous for his God. Are you zealous for your God today? Are you experiencing this type of *baptism of fire*?

Are you full of zeal for Jesus?

Those who are baptized with fire are men and women of prayer who have a holy hatred for sin, and a holy love for the Lord with a compassion for the lost and for the church of Jesus Christ. The psalmist in Psalms 69:9 reveals his righteous zeal for God's house and kingdom...*zeal for your house consumes me....* When we are truly on fire for God, all the desires of our body and soul are wrapped up in His desires. We are absorbed in who God wants us to be and what He wants us to do. We will have a godly zeal to see His house (His church) be all that it was created to be in our generation. "Lord, baptize us in your fire!"

BAPTISM IN THE HOLY SPIRIT I PART 3

76 | The promise of the Holy Spirit

So far we have covered three baptisms: baptism in water, baptism into the body of Christ, and baptism of fire. Next we will look at the *baptism in the Holy Spirit*. It is important to realize how the Holy Spirit desires to use us and flow from our lives. The subject of the baptism in the Holy Spirit is sometimes a controversial one in today's Christian church, so let's carefully look at this experience to help us understand it better.

Let's look again at Luke 3:16. *John answered them all, "I baptize you with water. But one more powerful than I will come, the thongs of whose sandals I am not worthy to untie. He will baptize you with the Holy Spirit and with fire."* When we previously mentioned this verse, we covered the *baptism of fire* part of it. Now we want to look at what John the Baptist meant when he said Jesus would baptize us *with the Holy Spirit*.

All genuine believers have the Spirit of God dwelling in them. I Corinthians 3:16 says, *"Don't you know that you yourselves are God's temple and that God's Spirit lives in you?"* The Holy Spirit lives within each child of God. The Holy Spirit is a person, not a doctrine or merely an influence or power. This is very important. The Holy Spirit is God and has the personal characteristics of God. God is the Father, Son, and Holy Spirit—often referred to as the Trinity (see Biblical Foundation 7 for more on the Trinity). The Holy Spirit is the third person of the Trinity.

The divine person of the Holy Spirit comes to dwell in you when you give your life to Jesus and receive Him into your life. He cares about you and has the power to help you. However, this does not mean you have been *baptized* in the Holy Spirit.

77 | The Holy Spirit lives within every believer

At the time of our salvation, the Holy Spirit comes to live within us. He leads and motivates us to live holy lives and delivers us from the bondage of sin. Romans 8:9 says, *"You, however, are controlled not by the sinful nature but by the Spirit, if the Spirit of God lives in you. And if anyone does not have the Spirit of Christ, he does not belong to Christ."*

During Jesus' last talk with His disciples before His trial and crucifixion, He promised them they would receive the Holy Spirit (John 14:17). Subsequently, after His resurrection, Jesus visited the disciples and breathed on them saying, *"...Receive the Holy Spirit"* (John 20:22).

At that moment, the disciples were born again by the Holy Spirit. Although the disciples had already confessed Jesus as Lord and were saved according to the old covenant provisions, they could not have been born again before Jesus was raised from the dead. Jesus had to come and give them His resurrection

---

The Holy Spirit has characteristics of God

- Thinks: Romans 8:27; 1 Corinthians 2:10-11
- Feels: Romans 15:30; Ephesians 4:30
- Wills: 1 Corinthians 12:11
- Has the capacity to enjoy our fellowship

Who is the Holy Spirit?

How can you be sure you have the Holy Spirit living in you?

Biblical Foundations for Life

When do Christians receive the Holy Spirit?

power according to the new covenant. Now they also believed that Jesus was raised from the dead, and their salvation was completed.

When God took a hunk of clay in the Garden of Eden and breathed on it, Adam was formed and received physical life. Here, God breathed on the disciples and gave them spiritual life. When you were convicted of your sin before you received Christ, the Holy Spirit was outside of you bringing conviction. When you received Jesus, the Holy Spirit then came *inside* to live within you. But there's more! The New Testament depicts *two* distinct yet complementary aspects of receiving the Holy Spirit—the experience of the disciples receiving the Holy Spirit on "Resurrection Sunday" that we just described, and the experience they later received on "Pentecost Sunday." Let's compare the two experiences in the next section.

Baptism in the Holy Spirit
Luke 24:49-51
John 16:7-14, Acts 1:4

78 | You shall receive power!

After the disciples' encounter with the Holy Spirit when Jesus breathed on them and told them to "receive the Holy Spirit," He made it clear that their experience was still incomplete. In His final words to them before His ascension, He commanded them not to go out and preach immediately, but to go back to Jerusalem and wait there until they were baptized in the Holy Spirit and thus given the power they needed to be effective witnesses. *Do not leave Jerusalem, but wait for the gift my Father promised, which you have heard me speak about. For John baptized with water, but in a few days you will be baptized with the Holy Spirit...you will receive power when the Holy Spirit comes on you; and you will be my witnesses in Jerusalem, and in all Judea and Samaria, and to the ends of the earth* (Acts 1:4-5, 8).

Have you experienced the power of the Holy Spirit?

So the disciples prayed and waited. During the festival of Pentecost, 120 of His disciples were gathered together in one place, and it happened! *When the day of Pentecost came, they were all together in one place. Suddenly a sound like the blowing of a violent wind came from heaven and filled the whole house where they were sitting. They saw what seemed to be tongues of fire that separated and came to rest on each of them. All of them were filled with the Holy Spirit and began to speak in other tongues as the Spirit enabled them* (Acts 2:1-4).

Describe your experience.

Here, the disciples experienced the mighty baptism in the Holy Spirit. Although they had received the life of the Holy Spirit only a few weeks before when Jesus breathed on them (John 20:22), this time they received the *baptism* in the Holy Spirit. They received a new dimension of the Holy Spirit's power.

This distinction between receiving the Holy Spirit at rebirth and receiving the *baptism in the Holy Spirit* is significant. We need to recognize the difference between having the Holy Spirit living within us and being baptized in the Holy Spirit. The baptism in the Holy Spirit is the Lord's provision for releasing the power of the Holy Spirit into the believer's life.

The story is told of a Christian man who lived in a poor village in the interior of his nation who had the opportunity to come to a big city. Having never experienced the use of electricity before, he was fascinated when he saw electric light bulbs for the first time. He asked his host if he could have one to take back to his home. When he got back to his village, he hung the light bulb on a string in his hut. He was frustrated because it wouldn't work, until a missionary explained to him that it must be plugged into a power source. That's the way it is with us. To enter into the fullness of what God has planned for our lives, we have no greater need than to be plugged into the power source. We need the mighty baptism in the Holy Spirit. It is the gateway into a new dimension of the Spirit's presence and power in our lives, and it empowers us for ministry.

79 | We receive by faith

Just like salvation comes by faith, so the baptism in the Holy Spirit comes by faith. We receive the baptism in the Holy Spirit by faith in the Word of God and by faith in Jesus Christ. Faith is always a prerequisite for receiving the baptism in the Holy Spirit. Galatians 3:14 tells us explicitly, *"…that by faith we might receive the promise of the Spirit."*

Not everyone's experience will be the same. We can pray and receive the Holy Spirit baptism on our own or have someone pray for us to receive the power of the Spirit. Some believers have a dynamic, emotional experience at the time of their Holy Spirit baptism. They may begin to sing a new song that God gave to them in an unknown language or speak in tongues. Others simply take God at His Word and experience the reality of the baptism in the Holy Spirit as a process over the days and weeks that follow.

The type of experience that we have is not of primary importance; the key is that we know by faith in the Word of God that we've been filled and baptized with the Holy Spirit. We need to *know* we are baptized with the Spirit just as we need to *know* we have been born again.

It is possible to be baptized in water and in the Holy Spirit at the same time. Or, some may be baptized in the Holy Spirit before they are water-baptized. It happened in Acts 10:44-46. Peter was preaching the gospel to the Gentiles in Cornelius's home when an amazing phenomenon occurred. *While Peter was still speaking these words, the Holy Spirit came on all who heard the message. The circumcised believers who had come with Peter were astonished that the gift of the Holy Spirit had been poured out even on the Gentiles. For they heard them speaking in tongues and praising God.* The people at Cornelius' house received the Word and were saved. The Lord immediately poured out the Holy Spirit on them in power, thus paralleling the disciples' experience at Pentecost. The Holy Spirit baptism brings the personal boldness and power of the Spirit into our lives that we need to be effective.

Regardless of our personal experience, the baptism in the Holy Spirit is received by faith. A pastor and his wife came to me and said, "We're not sure we've been baptized in the Holy Spirit." I assured them they can know for sure as I laid my hands on them and prayed. This time, they chose to "receive the promise of the Spirit through faith," and they were gloriously baptized with the Holy Spirit! From that time on, they knew it. Their spiritual thirst led them to yield to and receive the baptism in the Holy Spirit.

Biblical Foundations for Life

By what means do we receive the baptism in the Holy Spirit?

Describe a time you have experienced a greater effectiveness because of the baptism in the Holy Spirit.

80 | Want to be effective? It's your decision

Some might ask, "Do I really have to be baptized in the Holy Spirit?"

My reply would be, "Do you really need to have all of God's power so you can help other people find God?" People all around us are going to hell. We *need* God's power so He can fulfill His purpose in us and through us!

I often explain the power of the Holy Spirit like this. If you mow a lawn, you can do it with a scissors or with a lawn mower. It's your decision. You don't have to be baptized in the Holy Spirit to be a Christian, but like using the mower, God wants us to be effective. In fact, the early disciples of Jesus made being filled with the Holy Spirit a requirement for anyone who was to be set apart for special responsibilities in the church. *Brothers, choose seven men from among you who are known to be full of the Spirit and wisdom. We will turn this responsibility over to them (Acts 6:3).*

The baptism in the Holy Spirit increases the effectiveness of a Christian's witness because of a strengthening relationship with the Father, Son and Holy Spirit that comes from being filled with the Spirit. The Holy Spirit makes the personal presence of Jesus more real to us, and it results in wanting to love and obey Him more.

A survey was taken in the Philippines some time back which found that each Christian who had received the baptism of the Holy Spirit brought 36 people to Christ compared to the 1 person led to the Lord by each Christian who had not received the Holy Spirit baptism. Why? The spirit-baptized Christians simply had the power of God in their lives to witness with greater effect.

You may say you know of Christians who are being used by God who are not baptized in the Holy Spirit. So do I. But think how much more effective they would be if they were baptized in the Spirit.

Explain the difference between receiving the Holy Spirit and being baptized in the Holy Spirit.

81 | Saul's experiences with the Holy Spirit

Saul was a devout Jew who was playing havoc with the Christians in the book of Acts. He was on his way to Damascus to persecute the early Christians when the Lord met him and did something supernatural in his life. *"Who are you, Lord?" Saul asked. "I am Jesus, whom you are persecuting," he replied. "Now get up and go into the city, and you will be told what you must do." Then Ananias went to the house and entered it. Placing his hands on Saul, he said, "Brother Saul, the Lord—Jesus, who appeared to you on the road as you were coming here—has sent me so that you may see again and be filled with the Holy Spirit"* (Acts 9:5, 6, 17).

Ananias called Saul "brother" because Saul was now a Christian. However, Saul still wasn't filled with the Holy Spirit. Many people say that when you're saved, you are also automatically baptized in the Spirit. Although it is possible to receive and be baptized in the Holy Spirit at conversion, it is not always so. Saul, who became Paul, was baptized in the Holy Spirit three days after he received Christ into his life. It happened when Ananias laid his hands on Saul and prayed.

Biblical Foundations for Life

The difference between receiving the Holy Spirit at salvation and being baptized in the Holy Spirit can be explained like this: You can be led to a pool of water and drink from it (receive the Holy Spirit at salvation), or you can jump fully into the water (be baptized with the Holy Spirit). It's the same water (Holy Spirit) but you have a completely different experience.

During the late 1800's, evangelist Dwight L. Moody was preaching and saw the same two ladies sitting in the front row night after night. Nearly every night, they came up to him after his meetings and said, "Mr. Moody, you need to be filled with the Holy Spirit." At first he resisted their remarks. However, months later, as he walked down a street in New York City, he had an experience with God and was filled with the Holy Spirit.

The results were amazing! He preached the same sermons, but instead of two or three people getting saved at his services, hundreds and thousands came to know Jesus. In his lifetime, a million people were kept out of hell because of the power of God on his life. What made the difference? The mighty baptism—infilling—of the Holy Spirit. He had received power.

82 | Experiencing His power for yourself

I was baptized in the Holy Spirit seven years after I received Jesus Christ as my Lord. I could have been baptized in the Holy Spirit sooner, but I was ignorant of the Holy Spirit's work. Although I loved the Lord and was part of a youth ministry, I realized there was something missing in my life. I needed the power of the Holy Spirit. I sometimes attended Christian ministries where people were set free from drugs or other life-controlling problems, and I realized these people had a spiritual power that I didn't have.

After studying the scripture and being convinced this experience was based on the Word of God, I went out into the woods one day and prayed, "God, I want You to baptize me in the Holy Spirit." I prayed, but nothing happened. In retrospect, I can see that I had pride in my heart. I wanted to receive the baptism in the Holy Spirit alone, on my own terms. I didn't really want anything too radical to happen! So, I humbled myself and went to a pastor who laid hands on me and prayed for me. That night I received the baptism of the Holy Spirit.

After I was baptized in the Holy Spirit, my life immediately took on a whole new dimension of power. It wasn't me—it was God—the baptism in the Holy Spirit gave me an intense desire to please Him. Before I was baptized in the Holy Spirit, I was involved in a ministry where a few people had given their lives to the Lord. However, after I was baptized in the Holy Spirit, everything seemed to change. Hundreds of young people gave their lives to Christ during the next few years. I knew that it certainly wasn't anything that I was doing in my own power and strength. It was the Holy Spirit's power.

I must admit, that at first, I was not sure if I should share this experience with others because it was so controversial in the church at that time. I changed my mind when a young lady reprimanded me by saying, "Why didn't you tell me about the baptism in the Holy Spirit? Last Saturday night I was baptized with

Why do you think every person's experience is a bit different?

The baptism in the Holy Spirit is for whom?

Biblical Foundations for Life

the Holy Spirit, and now I have experienced His power in my life." If you filled a kerosene lantern with oil, you would still have to strike a match and light the lantern so its power could be released. The same principle applies to the truth of the Holy Spirit. We can have the Holy Spirit living in us but lack the power He can release in our lives. God spoke to me through this young lady, and from that time on, I told people the truth I had discovered. It was a joy to serve as a "spiritual midwife" when Jesus baptized them in His precious Holy Spirit!

Although it took me *several* years from the time I was saved to the time I was baptized in the Holy Spirit, I believe it is God's will that we are born again and immediately receive the baptism in the Holy Spirit and the power of God in our lives. Acts 2:38-39 says the baptism in the Holy Spirit was not just for those at Pentecost, but for all who would believe in Christ throughout this age…*and you will receive the gift of the Holy Spirit. The promise is for you and your children and for all who are far off….*

BAPTISM IN THE HOLY SPIRIIT II — PART 4

83 | Receive God's good gift

Some sincere believers have told me they heard negative things about Spirit-baptized people. So have I. But, we live by the Word of God, not by other people's experiences. We may see something happen in the name of the Holy Spirit that may not be the Holy Spirit at all and think, "If that's the Holy Spirit, I want nothing to do with it." But we cannot throw out the baptism of the Holy Spirit because of what we saw or experienced that was not authentic.

Others may say, "If I'm supposed to be filled with the Holy Spirit, well, that's up to God...I'm open to whatever the Lord wants to do." This sounds like a noble response, but in reality, it may be a statement of unbelief because they do not really want to be filled. A young man told me once that he felt he did not deserve to be baptized with the Holy Spirit. I told him, "You're right. I don't deserve it either. We don't deserve salvation or anything else, but God wants to give it to us as a free gift."

God has already initiated His part in our receiving Christ and being baptized with the Holy Spirit. It's now up to us to receive by faith what He has freely offered. To be baptized with the Holy Spirit is a personal act of faith, a decision that we make. Our heavenly Father wants to give us the gift of the Holy Spirit. *If you then, though you are evil, know how to give good gifts to your children, how much more will your Father in heaven give the Holy Spirit to those who ask him! (Luke 11:13).*

Have you been baptized in the Holy Spirit? If you are not sure, ask! Jesus wants to baptize you with the Holy Spirit. You only need to ask Him in faith, in the same way that a child would ask his father for a gift.

Your heavenly Father wants you to receive the Holy Spirit, and He offers the baptism in the Holy Spirit to you freely! Suppose I gave you a Christmas gift and you took it home and opened it and found many gifts wrapped up inside. One of these gifts is a tool you needed, a pliers. But you must take the pliers out and use it in order for it to be effective. The same principle applies to the Spirit of God. We need to receive the gift of the baptism in the Holy Spirit by faith, and then begin to use all the wonderful individual spiritual gifts that accompany it.

84 | What about tongues?

In Ephesus, some of the believers had never even heard of the Holy Spirit. So Paul instructed them, telling how they could receive the Holy Spirit. When he prayed for them, the Holy Spirit came upon them and they spoke with tongues. *When Paul placed his hands on them, the Holy Spirit came on them, and they spoke in tongues...(Acts 19:6).*

There are nine supernatural gifts of the Holy Spirit listed in 1 Corinthians 12:7-10. (For more about *using* these gifts, see Foundation 4.) The gift we want to look at here is the gift of tongues. *Now to each one the manifestation of the*

Gifts must be accepted, opened and used in order to really experience them. How do we accept the spiritual gifts God offers to His children?

According to Acts 10:46, what is the purpose of tongues?

Spirit is given for the common good. To one there is given through the Spirit the message of wisdom, to another the message of knowledge by means of the same Spirit, to another faith by the same Spirit, to another gifts of healing by that one Spirit, to another miraculous powers, to another prophecy, to another distinguishing between spirits, to another speaking in different kinds of tongues, and to still another the interpretation of tongues.

Often, when believers are baptized in the Holy Spirit, they begin to speak in *tongues* or a new heavenly language. The Bible says they magnify God (Acts 10:46). This personal prayer language is understood by God because it is my spirit speaking to God. Speaking in tongues is a direct line of communication between me and God.

In the book of Acts, speaking in tongues was often the initial outward sign accompanying the baptism in the Holy Spirit (Acts 2:4; 10:45-46; 19:6). Should every Spirit-filled believer speak with tongues, then? No, you don't have to, but you may! It's like going into a shoe store and getting a pair of shoes and saying, "Must I have tongues in my shoes?" No! But you take the tongues because they are part of the shoes! Praying in tongues is a blessing from God. Let's imagine that you came to my home and I gave you a meal. You say, "Must I eat this steak?" or "Must I eat this salad?" Well, no, you don't have to, but it is available for you as part of the whole meal deal!

God wants us to have and use spiritual gifts so that we may be a blessing to others. We need to exercise them so they can be used in our lives to build us up spiritually to give us supernatural strength and ability to be effective in our Christian lives. 1 Corinthians 14:1 says, "*...eagerly desire spiritual gifts....*"

And Jude 20 tells us to, "*...build yourselves up in your most holy faith and pray in the Holy Spirit.*"

God wants us to build ourselves up in faith so we may be the powerful witnesses. In Acts 1:8 we read that when the Holy Spirit comes upon us, we will receive power to be His witnesses. That's why we receive power—to be His witnesses. Praying in tongues builds us up spiritually. It's like charging your spiritual battery. You can, with power, pray for the sick, and minister to people and help them as you continue to build up yourself spiritually by praying in other tongues.

85 | I wish you all spoke in tongues

Speaking in tongues has been controversial in some parts of the church of Jesus Christ. One of the first times that I went to a public meeting where I was told that some of the people spoke in tongues, I sat near the back of the building. I wanted to make a quick exit if I became too uncomfortable! Although some believers hesitate because they have heard or seen misuses of the gift of tongues or other gifts of the Spirit, we have no need to be afraid.

It seems funny to recall now, but one of the fears that I had when I was considering being baptized in the Holy Spirit was that I would be in a place like a department store and the Spirit of God would come on me. I was afraid I'd begin to speak in tongues uncontrollably. I pictured myself being so embarrassed! Then one day I read this scripture, *The spirits of prophets are subject to the control of prophets* (1 Corinthians 14:32).

Your spirit is subject to you. It's like a water spigot. You turn it off and on. The water is always there, but it's under your control. You choose to pray or not to pray in tongues at any given time, but it's God who gives you the gift and the power to speak.

How important then is it for us as Christians to speak in tongues and exercise other spiritual gifts? Paul the apostle wished that every person spoke in tongues and stressed that the gift of tongues was an important part of his spiritual life. *I would like every one of you to speak in tongues...I thank God that I speak in tongues more than all of you (1 Corinthians 14:5a; 14:18).*

Is someone a second-rate Christian if they don't speak in tongues? No, of course not! But God wants us to be blessed and use these blessings so we can fulfill His call on our lives. Some say they believe it is selfish to pray in tongues. Is it selfish to pray? Is it selfish to read the Bible? Why do we pray and read the scriptures and speak in tongues? We do it to communicate with God and in order to be built up spiritually so we can be effective in helping other people.

86 | Bypassing the devil!

We pray two ways—with our mind and with our spirit. Both are needed, and both are under the influence of the Holy Spirit, according to 1 Corinthians 14:14-15. *For if I pray in a tongue, my spirit prays, but my mind is unfruitful. So what shall I do? I will pray with my spirit, but I will also pray with my mind; I will sing with my spirit, but I will also sing with my mind.*

The first way we pray is with our mind. When we pray, "Our Father in heaven..." it's coming from our mind. We understand it. We are using our intellect to pray in a learned language.

The second way we pray is with our spirit. When we pray with our spirit (in tongues), it's unfruitful to our mind. Our spirit is praying directly to the Father without having to accept the limitations of our human intellect.

In other words, when you and I pray with our spirit, we have no idea what we are saying, but our heavenly Father knows what we're saying. We come in simple faith and trust God to provide the form of the words and their meaning to Him. Using our new language, we edify ourselves (1 Corinthians 14:4) or "build ourselves up" spiritually. It is like a direct phone line to God.

I walked into a hardware store one night soon after I was baptized in the Holy Spirit and there were two men conversing in "Pennsylvania Dutch," a language many people of German descent use in my community. I cannot understand this language at all. Even though I didn't understand, those men understood one another clearly. The Spirit of God spoke to me and said, "In the same way that these two men understand one another, I understand exactly what you are saying when you pray in tongues. Continue to praise Me and magnify Me in this

Why are some Christians afraid to receive the gift of tongues?

How can the gift of tongues help me to pray?

Do I know what I am saying when I pray in tongues?

Biblical Foundations for Life

Does the devil know what I am saying when I pray in tongues?

new language I've given to you." I was set free to pray in tongues from that day on without the nagging thoughts of unbelief and doubt from the devil.

Today, I pray in tongues daily, because when I pray in tongues, I bypass the devil. He has no idea what I'm saying. I'm speaking the "language of angels" and "mysteries" according to God's Word...*I speak with the tongues of men and of angels...*(1 Corinthians 13:1).

For anyone who speaks in a tongue does not speak to men but to God. Indeed, no one understands him; he utters mysteries with his spirit (1 Corinthians 14:2).

87 | Kinds of tongues

To clarify some common misconceptions of tongues, let's look at two different kinds of tongues mentioned in God's Word. The kind of tongues we have mentioned so far is for personal prayer and intercession. This is the type of tongues that magnifies God and is a direct line of communication between us and God. It is God speaking through us. *In the same way, the Spirit helps us in our weakness. We do not know what we ought to pray for, but the Spirit himself intercedes for us with groans that words cannot express. And he who searches our hearts knows the mind of the Spirit, because the Spirit intercedes for the saints in accordance with God's will* (Romans 8:26-27).

Can you have and use your prayer tongue even if you do not use it publicly?

P. C. Nelson, founder of the Southwestern Bible Institute, was a Greek scholar. He told his young ministers that the Greek literally reads, "The Holy Spirit maketh intercession for us with groanings which cannot be uttered in articulate speech" (articulate speech is the ordinary kind of speech). He pointed out that the Greek bears out that this not only includes "groanings" in prayer, but also "other tongues."[1] The Bible tells us that the Holy Spirit helps us to pray. Many times I have felt unable to put into words the desires of my heart when I pray. And sometimes, situations are so complex that I just do not know how to pray. But the Holy Spirit does!

The second type of tongues is mentioned in 1 Corinthians 12:28-30 after God says He has appointed some in the church for various tasks and responsibilities. *And in the church God has appointed first of all apostles, second prophets, third teachers, then workers of miracles, also those having gifts of healing, those able to help others, those with gifts of administration, and those speaking in different kinds of tongues. Are all apostles? Are all prophets? Are all teachers? Do all work miracles? Do all have gifts of healing? Do all speak in tongues? Do all interpret?*

What is the purpose of tongues when the church meets together?

Because this scripture states, "Do all speak in tongues?" many think this means that not all can speak in tongues as a personal prayer language. However, this scripture is really asking, "Are all appointed to speak with the gift of tongues *to the church*?"

You see, there is a gift to be used *in the church* which is a type of speaking in tongues. It is different from the type of speaking in tongues that we experience when we pray in our prayer language. When this gift of tongues is used in the church, someone who has the gift gives a message in tongues, and someone with the *gift of interpretation* gives the meaning, thus building up the body of Christ.

Biblical Foundations for Life

To summarize, although all Christians may speak in tongues so we can be built up spiritually to serve God better, He also sometimes gives a special gift of tongues to be used to build up His church. These scriptures are clear that not all will be used by God to speak in tongues in a church meeting. However, we can still pray in tongues as a personal prayer language to the Lord. The same goes for the other gifts listed here. You and I may not have the gift of administration in the church, but we all must administer our checkbooks. We may not have the gift of healing, but we are all called to pray for the sick in our own families.

[1] *Seven Vital Steps To Receiving the Holy Spirit* by Kenneth E. Hagin, p. 10.

88 | Eagerly desire

What is the best gift?

After Paul lists the ministry gifts of the Holy Spirit to the church, in 1 Corinthians 12:28-30, he says in verse 31, "*But eagerly desire the greater gifts. And now I will show you the most excellent way.*"

What is the greater gift? The greater gift depends on the situation you're in. If you need healing, you believe God for the "greater" gift of healing because that is what you need.

What is the "most excellent way?" It is love. 1 Corinthians, chapter 13, tells us all about it! Some say they don't need all these gifts; they just need love. That's not what Paul was trying to communicate. He is emphasizing that to possess spiritual gifts without love amounts to nothing. We need to use these gifts in love according to 1 Corinthians 13:8-13. *Love never fails. But where there are... tongues, they will be stilled...For we know in part and we prophesy in part, but when perfection comes, the imperfect disappears. When I was a child, I talked like a child, I thought like a child, I reasoned like a child. When I became a man, I put childish ways behind me. Now we see but a poor reflection as in a mirror; then we shall see face to face. Now I know in part; then I shall know fully, even as I am fully known. And now these three remain: faith, hope and love. But the greatest of these is love.*

What is the more excellent way?

This passage of scripture reveals that tongues will cease when "that which is perfect is come." Some people believe that this means tongues are no longer needed today. They believe that "that which is perfect" refers to the Bible. However, they fail to realize that the same passage says we shall see "face to face." We will not see the Bible face to face. We will see Jesus face to face. At that time, at the end of the age, there will be no need for the gift of tongues. But until we see Jesus face to face, the Lord has given us the gifts of tongues and prophecy and other supernatural gifts of the Holy Spirit to use for His glory here on earth.

89 | Continue to be filled with the Spirit

Do you know for sure that you are baptized with the Holy Spirit? Do you pray in tongues? Are the spiritual gifts becoming evident in your life? If you are not sure, ask Jesus to fill you with His precious Holy Spirit today. Ask another Spirit-filled believer to pray for you. Sometimes it takes someone else to agree with us in faith to experience the Holy Spirit's filling. Paul went to Ananias. The Samaritans waited for Peter and John. I went to a pastor friend.

Biblical Foundations for Life

Why did the believers in Acts 4:31 have to be filled with the Holy Spirit again?

Is there evidence of power in your life that you have been baptized in the Holy Spirit?

What is the work that the Holy Spirit does in our lives?

We must reach out and receive the promise of the Spirit by faith. By faith we receive, and then are continually filled, day by day! Dwight L. Moody, the famous evangelist, used to say, "I need to be filled with the Holy Spirit every day, because I leak!"

The early believers knew this, too, according to Acts 4:31. *After they prayed, the place where they were meeting was shaken. And they were all filled with the Holy Spirit and spoke the word of God boldly.* Many of these believers were already filled with the Holy Spirit at Pentecost in Acts chapter 2. But they needed to be filled again. We, too, must experience constant renewal. Paul warns the believers that to maintain the fullness of the Spirit, they must live lives separate from sin. *Do not get drunk on wine, which leads to debauchery. Instead, be filled with the Spirit* (Ephesians 5:18).

The New Testament baptism in the Holy Spirit happens in the context of committed discipleship to Jesus Christ. Our hearts must be right with God so He can pour out His Spirit on us. As we live in obedience to Christ, there will be a greater awareness and presence of the Holy Spirit in our lives. We will deepen our relationship with the Father and grow in our love for others.

God wants to use you to see change come into people's lives. But it takes the Holy Spirit's power to "break through." The Lord wants to use you to touch others' lives for eternity. People in your family will be changed when you are baptized in the Holy Spirit. It may not happen immediately, but it will happen! It won't be through your natural ability, but by Christ who is at work in you through the Holy Spirit. God bless you as you live by the power and the authority of God and experience the Holy Spirit flowing through your life.

90 | The Spirit of Truth

We read in John 16:13-14, *"But when he, the Spirit of truth, comes, he will guide you into all the truth. He will not speak on his own; he will speak only what he hears, and he will tell you what is yet to come. He will glorify me because it is from me that he will receive what he will make known to you."*

These verses tell us of the work that the Holy Spirit does in our lives. Let's list them.

1. He guides us into all truth. That which the Spirit of God reveals always lines up with the truth of His Word.

2. He will only speak what He hears from the Father and the Son. The three persons in the trinity: Father, Son, and Holy Spirit are in complete unity. They are one.

3. He will tell you of what is yet to come. The Spirit of God can show us things that will happen in the future.

4. He will glorify Jesus. The Spirit always brings glory to Christ.

Does the Holy Spirit ever speak to you? How can you know it is He? He can speak in so many ways: a whisper… a still small voice… through another person… and many more. I have found at least fifty different ways He speaks to us. We just need to learn to listen.

91 | Rivers of living water and joy and the Holy Spirit

Jesus promised that when believers receive the Holy Spirit, He would flow out of their hearts like great rivers of life-giving water. John 7:38-39 says, *"Whoever believes in me, as Scripture has said, rivers of living water will flow from within them. By this he meant the Spirit, whom those who believed in him were later to receive."*

When I was baptized in the Holy Spirit I was changed forever. I thought differently. I acted differently. I suddenly loved to worship Jesus. I loved to pray for miracles in people's lives, even though I was just an ordinary chicken farmer.

But God loves to use ordinary people. Smith Wigglesworth was a plumber, but saw more than twenty people raised from the dead. He had an encounter with God and experienced rivers of living waters flowing from his life.

The Holy Spirit also gives us joy. Let's read Acts 13:49-52.

The word of the Lord spread through the whole region. But the Jewish leaders incited the God-fearing women of high standing and the leading men of the city. They stirred up persecution against Paul and Barnabas, and expelled them from their region. So they shook the dust off their feet as a warning to them and went to Iconium. And the disciples were filled with joy and with the Holy Spirit.

If you have received Christ as Lord, you are one of His disciples. As we follow in the footsteps of the early disciples—even though persecution or trials may come—we will nonetheless experience the joy of the Lord when we are filled with the Holy Spirit.

Nehemiah 8:10b says, *"This day is holy to our Lord. Do not grieve, for the joy of the Lord is your strength."*

Do not allow the devil to steal your joy. Be filled and refilled with the Holy Spirit. The joy of the Lord is our strength!

Who wants to steal our joy?

What does the joy of the Lord give to us?

Biblical Foundations for Life

FOUNDATION 4

Building for Eternity

92 | Introduction to foundation 4

As we continue to study the basic biblical foundations that we need in our lives, we will look at the final three of the six foundational doctrines of the Christian faith found in Hebrews 6:1-2—the laying on of hands, the resurrection of the dead and eternal judgment:

> *"Therefore, leaving the discussion of the elementary principles of Christ, let us go on to perfection, not laying again the foundation of repentance from dead works and of faith toward God, of the doctrine of baptisms, of laying on of hands, of resurrection of the dead, and of eternal judgment"* (Hebrews 6:1-2 NKJ)

Laying on of hands is an act in which one person imparts or conveys blessing, healing and/or authority to another for a specific spiritual purpose. We will learn that the laying on of hands has a vital connection with many aspects of our Christian lives.

The hope of the resurrection is another biblical foundation that is so important to a Christian's faith because those who believe in Christ will share in His resurrection and have eternal life!

Another foundation stone that is linked to the resurrection of the dead is eternal judgment. Every man and woman who has ever lived will be judged by God for all of eternity. The reality of an eternal judgment should cause all believers to hate sin and diligently seek the lost to tell them of God's wonderful plan for mankind!

The few years we will live on this earth are so small compared to the billions of years of all eternity. That's why it is so important that we live every day in fellowship with Jesus, and then help as many people as possible find life through Jesus Christ.

Why is it important that we live every day in fellowship with Jesus?

Biblical Foundations for Life

PART 1

What is supernatural about the laying on of hands?

Have you ever asked another Christian to impart a blessing to you by the laying on of hands?

Describe what you asked for.

IMPARTING BLESSING AND HEALING

93 | An elementary principle: The laying on of hands

A few years ago, I visited a Bible School where I met an elderly gentleman. He had experienced God moving in miraculous ways during his lifetime, and I asked him if he would be willing to come to my dormitory room to pray for me. I knew that he had something I needed. As he laid his hands on me and prayed, I sensed the Lord giving me His blessing through this precious man of God. I knew that according to the scriptures, something happens when one believer lays his hands on another believer and prays for him. He *gives* or *imparts* something, through his teaching or influence, that the other person needs.

In Leviticus 16:21-22, Aaron laid his hands on a live goat and confessed the people's sins which were imparted from his hands to the goat. This supernatural transference happened through the laying on of hands.

What happens in this supernatural transference? The Bible tells us there is a clear impartation of power and God's blessing that is transferred from one person to another through the laying on of hands. "The laying on of hands" is another one of the important foundation stones that we need to place in our Christian lives from Hebrews 6:1-2. *Therefore, leaving the discussion of the elementary principles of Christ, let us go on to perfection, not laying again the foundation of... the laying on of hands...(NKJ)*

The Lord's purpose for the foundation stone of *the laying on of hands* is for us to experience the Lord's blessing and to be a blessing to others. In the Old Testament, the laying on of hands was an accepted practice for imparting blessing to be transmitted to future generations. Jacob imparted the blessing of God to his children by laying hands on them before he died (Genesis 48:14).

A friend of mine tells the true story of a Christian man who realized that he was close to the end of his life and was soon going to go to be with his Father in Heaven. He gathered his children around and imparted God's blessings to each of them. He then went into his bedroom, lay down and went home to be with the Lord. This is a true, modern-day example of imparting the blessing of God.

We don't have to wait until we come to the end of our lives to impart our blessing through the laying on of hands, however! Next we will examine how *the laying on of hands* is for imparting not only blessing, but also healing, spiritual gifts and authority.

94 | Imparting life to one another

There is a tremendous power in our lives to bless, encourage and help people just by touching them. I believe this especially applies to children. Those who serve in a children's nursery are able to bless children by holding them in their arms and speaking God's Word over them. One night there was a child in our home who continued to cry. I took the crying child in my arms and prayed in the Spirit as I imparted the blessing of God to him. After a few minutes, the child became peaceful. What a privilege it was to impart a spiritual blessing of peace to that child. Jesus Himself did this. *And he took the children in his arms, put his hands on them and blessed them* (Mark 10:16). When my children were young, I laid my hands on them and blessed them each night before they went to bed. As I prayed for them, I was imparting the Lord's health, healing, grace, and anointing into their lives. Why? Because there is power released as we impart spiritual blessings to others.

I love to shake people's hands for the first time. As a believer in Jesus Christ, we can shake someone's hand and impart, through a type of laying on of hands, faith, conviction, the grace of God, and the Lord's anointing into their lives. The Lord wants us to be a blessing to others so we may inherit a blessing from Him according to 1 Peter 3:8-9. *Finally, all of you, live in harmony with one another; be sympathetic, love as brothers, be compassionate and humble. Do not repay evil with evil or insult with insult, but with blessing, because to this you were called so that you may inherit a blessing.*

Something supernatural happens when we understand the principle of the laying on of hands and participate in this life-giving truth. When Spirit-filled Christians lay their hands on others and pray a prayer of faith, the power of God that is in them will also be received by the person for whom they are praying. Did you ever hug someone who had strong perfume on, and then for the next few minutes, you continue to smell that perfume or cologne? When someone lays their hands on you, they impart to you something that the Lord has given them. Something that is on them gets on you. We can lay our hands on others and impart the blessings of God to them and they can do the same for us.

95 | Imparting the power of the Holy Spirit

In both the Old and New Testament, there are numerous examples of the laying on of hands, where one person laid hands on another person for a very specific purpose. Let's take a few moments and look at some distinct purposes that we see in the scriptures for the laying on of hands. Notice first of all how the power of the Holy Spirit is imparted through the laying on of hands. In Acts 8:14-15, 17, we observe that the laying on of hands helped those who were seeking the baptism in the Holy Spirit. *When the apostles in Jerusalem heard that Samaria had accepted the word of God, they sent Peter and John to them. When they arrived, they prayed for them that they might receive the Holy Spirit...Then Peter and John placed their hands on them, and they received the Holy Spirit.*

Peter and John went down to Samaria, laid their hands on the new believers and they received the baptism in the Holy Spirit. You may ask, "Must I have someone lay hands on me to be baptized with the Holy Spirit?" No, you don't have to. However, something supernatural happens when a Spirit-filled believer in Jesus Christ lays hands on another person and prays a prayer of faith. God supernaturally works through His people and gives them the divine ability to impart the mighty power of the Holy Spirit as they pray in faith.

How does the Lord impart a blessing to us and through us?

Can you receive the Holy Spirit without the laying on of hands?

Has God used you to impart the Holy Spirit to someone through the laying on of hands? Describe.

Biblical Foundations for Life

Many years ago, a friend laid his hands on me and prayed, and I began to pray in a new language. (I spoke in tongues.) Now I have the same privilege of laying hands on people and seeing them baptized with the Holy Spirit and praying in tongues. And so do you. The laying on of hands to impart the baptism in the Holy Spirit is not just for the believers in the book of Acts, it is also true for us today.

Jesus Christ is the same yesterday, today, and forever (Hebrews 13:8). He desires to use you to pray for others to be baptized in the Holy Spirit as you lay your hands on them and pray a prayer of faith. Expect the Lord to use you!

96 | Imparting spiritual gifts

List the nine spiritual gifts found in 1 Corinthians 12.

Another purpose for the laying on of hands is for the imparting of spiritual gifts. Paul said in Romans 1:11-12 that he wanted to impart spiritual gifts to them so they would be strengthened in their faith. *I long to see you so that I may impart to you some spiritual gift to make you strong—that is, that you and I may be mutually encouraged by each other's faith.*

Jesus wants us to not only impart the baptism in the Holy Spirit through the laying on of hands, but also to impart spiritual gifts that the Holy Spirit gives. 1 Corinthians 12:8-10 speaks of nine of these supernatural spiritual gifts. *To one there is given through the Spirit the message of wisdom, to another the message of knowledge by means of the same Spirit, to another faith by the same Spirit, to another gifts of healing by that one Spirit, to another miraculous powers, to another prophecy, to another distinguishing between spirits, to another speaking in different kinds of tongues, and to still another the interpretation of tongues.*

List seven more spiritual gifts found in Romans 12. Do you have any of these gifts?

As we receive particular spiritual gifts from the Lord and learn how to use and exercise them, we can then lay hands on others and impart these gifts to them. These are not the only gifts the Holy Spirit gives to the body of Christ to be used among His people. Other gifts mentioned in Romans 12:6-8 are the gifts of prophecy, serving, teaching, encouraging, giving, leading, and mercy. These gifts are inward desires or motivations we have that enable us to build up God's people and express His love to others.

There are many supernatural and very practical spiritual gifts that God gives us. When God gives them to us, He then gives us the power and ability to lay our hands on others so they also can see these gifts begin to blossom in their own lives. The Lord wants to use you to impart to others what He has given you.

Have you imparted any of these gifts to others?

Maybe you need a gift of *discerning spirits* or a *gift of faith*. Find someone who has this gift operating in his or her life. Ask him or her to lay hands on you and pray for you. Many times I have asked others to lay their hands on me and pray for me, and I have received supernatural ability and spiritual strength. Other times I have had the privilege of laying my hands on others and imparting a gift of faith, and they received spiritual strength and a renewed faith.

97 | Associate with those who can impart gifts to you

The anointing and gifts of God are enhanced by associating with people who have these kinds of gifts operating in their lives. This gives us a greater opportunity to get these gifts transferred or imparted to us. When we rub shoulders with those who have certain spiritual gifts, they can lay their hands on us to impart that gift to us. In 1 Timothy 4:14, Paul said, *"Do not neglect your gift, which was given you through a prophetic message when the body of elders laid their hands on you."*

The leaders of the church laid their hands on Timothy, and God gave him the spiritual gifts that he needed to fulfill his responsibilities. Paul told Timothy to not neglect the gifts he had received from the Lord through the laying on of hands. He also told Timothy that he needs to stir up these gifts. *For this reason I remind you to fan into flame the gift of God, which is in you through the laying on of my hands (2 Timothy 1:6).*

If you have the gift of prophecy, serving or mercy, you can stir up these gifts as you pray in the Spirit and exercise these gifts. As you confess the truth of the Word of God, and thank God that He has given you these gifts, you stir them up within you so that you can be a blessing to those around you.

98 | Imparting health to the sick

The laying on of hands is also associated with the ministry of physical healing. The Lord wants us to be open to His Spirit's prompting, pray for others and have others pray for us to see God's healing power released. The Bible tells us in Mark 16:17-18 that *...these signs will accompany those who believe: In my name... they will place their hands on sick people, and they will get well.*

This promise is for every believer. The scriptures tell us that those who believe in Jesus will lay their hands on the sick and they will recover. God has called you and your family to lay hands on those who are sick. For many Christians, the first thing they will do when someone is sick is to call the doctor or go to the drugstore. The first thing we should do when someone is sick is to lay our hands on that person and pray. God tells us that they will recover! The healing power of God goes from one believer to another through the laying on of our hands. There's nothing wrong with going to the doctor, but we need to go to Jesus first.

We read in the book of Acts, chapter 9, that Ananias, who understood the power that is released through the laying on of hands and prayer, laid hands on Saul for healing...*Placing his hands on Saul, he said, "Brother Saul, the Lord—Jesus, who appeared to you on the road as you were coming here—has sent me so that you may see again and be filled with the Holy Spirit." Immediately, something like scales fell from Saul's eyes, and he could see again...*(Acts 9:17-18). Saul had given his life to Jesus Christ on the road to Damascus. Three days later Ananias prayed for Saul, and two things happened. First of all, Saul had been blind for three days, and there were scales on his eyes. The scripture says the scales fell from his eyes when Ananias laid his hands on him and prayed for him. Secondly, Saul was filled with the Holy Spirit.

Jesus constantly imparted health to others as He touched them. We see it in Mark 1:41-42 when Jesus healed a man with leprosy. *Filled with compassion, Jesus reached out his hand and touched the man...Immediately the leprosy left him and he was cured.*

Biblical Foundations for Life

Explain in your own words, "anointing comes by association."

According to 2 Timothy 1:6, how can you stir up the gifts God has given you?

What usually happened when Jesus touched people or they touched Him?

Can we do the same today?

We again see Jesus' healing impartation in Mark 6:56. *And wherever he went—into villages, towns or countryside—they placed the sick in the marketplaces. They begged him to let them touch even the edge of his cloak, and all who touched him were healed.*

Jesus lives in each of us today. As we take a step of faith and believe God's Word, we will also be vessels of healing. When we lay our hands on the sick and pray a prayer of faith, the Bible says that they will recover.

99 | Any believer can impart a blessing

The laying on of hands is not just for leaders to practice. Every believer can transmit spiritual blessings to others in this way. As God's people, we are the church. When we read the New Testament, we do not see the church as a group of believers who only met together in a building on a Sunday morning; they had interactive relationships with each other daily. They were an integral part of each others' lives. *Every day they continued to meet together in the temple courts. They broke bread in their homes and ate together with glad and sincere hearts, praising God and enjoying the favor of all the people. And the Lord added to their number daily those who were being saved* (Acts 2:46-47).

These believers were experiencing true church. They knew how to impart God's blessing to each other as they related closely together as God's people. The same thing is happening all over the world today. People are getting excited about their relationship with Jesus Christ. People are tired of dead religion. They want the real thing. When Jesus Christ saves them and baptizes them in the Holy Spirit, these believers do not want to just sit around and "play church." They want relationships—with Jesus and with each other! They open up their homes and minister to people right in their own homes.

Small, interactive groups that meet together from house to house and also in larger meetings to receive teaching and experience times of worship are springing up—small groups, house churches, life groups, micro churches—no matter what you call them, they have the purpose of raising mature Christians and giving every Christian a job to do. Small groups give everyone an opportunity to bless others and impart their lives to others. In small spiritual family groups, the next generation of believers can be nurtured and blessed.

There are times when I feel like I am totally depleted of faith. Since faith comes by hearing the word of God (Romans 10:17), I know that meditating on God's Word is the first step to experiencing renewed faith. But many times I have also been renewed in faith when someone who is "full of faith" prays for me and imparts faith and the healing power of Jesus to me. God has made us in such a way that we need each other. We are His body, and each part of the body is important. When we have a need, the Lord often chooses to use others to impart into our lives what we need. The Lord also wants to use us to impart into others' lives what He has given to us.

Give some examples of ways the Lord may want to use you to impart spiritual blessings to others.

IMPARTING AUTHORITY · PART 2

100 | To acknowledge a specific ministry

Another purpose for the laying on of hands is for publicly acknowledging that someone has received authority from God for a specific ministry and sending them out to fulfill it. The book of Acts 13:2-3 gives an account of the spiritual leaders at the church in Antioch acknowledging and sending out two apostles by laying hands on them. *While they were worshiping the Lord and fasting, the Holy Spirit said, "Set apart for me Barnabas and Saul for the work to which I have called them." So after they had fasted and prayed, they placed their hands on them and sent them off.*

The church leadership imparted to Barnabas and Saul, through the laying on of hands, the blessing and the grace that the Holy Spirit had given them. They were commissioned for a specific ministry which acknowledged the call of God already on their lives. Barnabas and Saul were sent out as one of the most powerful missionary teams that ever walked on the face of the earth!

In Acts, chapter six, a group of men were set apart to distribute food to the widows and to those who were needy. These men were brought before the apostles, who laid their hands on them and imparted to them authority and responsibility for the specific work of food distribution. Because of their history of godliness and faithfulness to the Lord, these "deacons" were set apart for ministry in serving the church in this way. *They chose Stephen, a man full of faith and of the Holy Spirit; also Philip, Procorus, Nicanor, Timon, Parmenas, and Nicolas from Antioch, a convert to Judaism. They presented these men to the apostles, who prayed and laid their hands on them* (Acts 6:5-6).

The scriptures teach us that those who have received authority from God (they already have a proven ministry) should be set apart or consecrated for this specific ministry in the church by the laying on of hands by their church leaders. When I was a young pastor, the spiritual leaders to whom I was accountable laid their hands on me and appointed me to a new role of leadership. The Lord used them to establish this new leadership appointment in my life.

Why is it important to receive impartation from leaders before being sent out in a specific ministry?

101 | An Old Testament example of imparting authority

An Old Testament example of the laying on of hands for authority in a specific ministry is mentioned in the story of Moses and Joshua. Moses faithfully led the children of Israel in the wilderness. When he came near the end of his ministry, he asked the Lord to appoint a new leader over Israel who would take his place. Joshua, whom Moses had trained for forty years, took his place in leadership among God's people. Let's see what happened during that time of transfer of leadership. We can see clearly the principle of the laying on of hands in Numbers 27:18, 20. *So the Lord said to Moses, "Take Joshua son of Nun, a man in whom is the spirit, and lay your hand on him...Give him some of your authority..."*

Why was it important for Moses to impart his authority to Joshua?

This happened, of course, when Moses realized the need for Joshua to become the next leader. Joshua already was trained by Moses and called by God, but Moses acknowledged his call by laying hands on Joshua and imparting some of the power and authority that the Lord had given him to lead God's people. Joshua was filled with the spirit of wisdom (Deuteronomy 34:9) after Moses imparted his authority to him. This impartation gave Joshua what Moses had been given. Moses imparted to Joshua the spiritual ability and blessing that he received from the Lord.

102 | Spiritual leaders have the authority to impart

The Bible teaches us that spiritual leaders the Lord places in our lives have been given godly authority and responsibility for us. The Lord commands them to watch out for our souls. Hebrews 13:17 tells us, *"Obey your leaders and submit to their authority. They keep watch over you as men who must give an account. Obey them so that their work will be a joy, not a burden, for that would be of no advantage to you."*

First of all, in the body of Christ, we have God's authority because we are sons and daughters of the Lord through faith in Jesus Christ. But as we become involved in the church in areas of ministry, we not only receive authority from God directly, but also receive authority as we are commissioned by the spiritual leaders the Lord has placed in our lives.

In whatever area of service we find ourselves, we would be wise to ask these questions, "Lord, have you placed one or more spiritual leaders in my life who are watching out for my soul?" And the second question to ask is, "Lord, is there someone with whom I can share some of my responsibility?" When the timing is right, the Lord may ask us to lay our hands on someone else to impart the blessings and spiritual gifts the Lord has given to us.

Spiritual leaders lay their hands on new pastors, leaders and missionaries and commission them to new areas of service. Hands are laid on them to impart the spiritual blessings and gifts that God gives. Something supernatural happens when we lay hands on others and set them apart for a particular ministry. Those who lay their hands on new Christian leaders are responsible to the Lord to "watch out for the souls" of those they are commissioning.

103 | A word of caution: Don't be hasty

A few years ago, I read about a major revival in southeast Asia where a young man came to know Jesus, and God started to use him in a mighty way. The elders of the church came together, laid their hands on him, and prayed, giving him authority and responsibility to be sent out as an evangelist. Nearly everywhere he went, people were saved and healed. The church started to grow and miraculous things happened. After a while, this young man got puffed up with pride and eventually fell into immorality.

Do you desire to have someone lay hands on you to impart a blessing and spiritual gifts? Ask!

When the leaders of the church lovingly confronted him, the young man said, "Look, miracles and healings are happening, who are you to tell me what to do?" He was not willing to be accountable for his actions and refused to repent of his sins. The same leaders, who had laid their hands on this young man a few years earlier commissioning him into this work, informed the young man that they felt responsible.

"Here's what we're going to do," they told him. "We care about you as a person, but we believe your disobedience to the Lord has caused you to misuse the power of God. We are going to pray and receive back that anointing, that empowering that we gave you when we laid hands on you." Do you know what happened? After they had their time of prayer of "decommissioning," the young man no longer received the power of God to heal the sick, and the miracles stopped happening. From that day on, the evangelist did not see the kinds of miracles that he was accustomed to experiencing.

The leaders of the church realized they had laid hands on this young leader giving him responsibility and authority as an evangelist too soon. They learned the hard way what the scripture warns us about in 1 Timothy 5:22. *Do not be hasty in the laying on of hands....*

Church leaders need to be careful not to lay hands on new elders, pastors and ministry leaders prematurely. A person set apart for ministry must have a history of faithfulness to the Lord.

When spiritual leaders lay hands on someone, they stand as God's representatives and give that person authority in Christian service. There is spiritual power released through the laying on of hands when the Lord's people are set apart for specific ministry. In the same way, this authority can be received back.

104 | Another word of caution: Keep yourself pure

After 1 Timothy 5:22 mentions that we should not be hasty in laying hands on someone, it continues to say, "*...and do not share in the sins of others. Keep yourself pure.*"

We can "share in" or be a part of another person's sin if we lay hands on him and he has known sin in his life. This verse may be speaking mainly about commissioning someone in the church into specific service, but I believe it can relate to any person for whom we pray.

For example, one evening a young lady in our cell group asked us to pray for her because she was having severe back problems. Someone discerned that she needed to forgive a family member first. When asked about it, she was quick to say she could not forgive the person who had hurt her. We encouraged her to first forgive so she could fully receive the prayer of faith for her healing, which she did. It is important to first pray with others and help them find freedom by confessing their sin, repenting of it, and receiving God's Word and forgiveness before we impart God's blessing or authority to them. Only then will the laying on of hands be truly fruitful.

Name some valid reasons for refusing to lay hands on someone.

Explain in your own words what "abstaining from an appearance of evil" means in the context of laying on of hands.

Biblical Foundations for Life

God wants to use you to lay hands on others to impart His blessing and authority. Everywhere you go, God wants to give you opportunities to impart the authority of God to people. We need, of course, to use wisdom in doing it. For instance, men should minister to men as much as possible. Women need to minister to women. The scriptures seem to imply that older men should be reaching out to younger men, and older women should be reaching out to younger women. Paul gives Titus this guideline, *Likewise, teach the older women...then they can train the younger women...Similarly, encourage the young men...*(Titus 2:3-4, 6).

If I'm going to impart the blessing or authority of God to a woman, I will have someone else join me for this time of ministry. We need to use discretion. Proper boundaries should always be maintained between a man and a woman, especially as we lay our hands on them for prayer, so there are no misunderstandings. The scripture tells us to *"abstain from all appearance of evil"* (1 Thessalonians 5:22).

105 | We have delegated authority to minister to others

The principle of the laying on of hands reminds me of going to the bank. Let's imagine that I go to the bank and take my father's checkbook with a check signed by my father. I would have his delegated authority to get money out of the bank. Let's ask the Lord, "How can I impart Your blessing and authority to people today?" The scriptures tell us that we are priests. We are a royal priesthood, according to 1 Peter 2:9. *But you are a chosen people, a royal priesthood, a holy nation, a people belonging to God, that you may declare the praises of him who called you out of darkness into his wonderful light.* Remember what the priests did in the Old Testament before Jesus came? They stood between the Lord and His people.

Today, in a new way, we are able to take the blessings of God through the laying on of hands and impart them to people, even to people who aren't yet Christians. The Bible says in 2 Corinthians 3:6 that we are *"ministers of the new covenant."* You and I are ministers today and can minister to people through the laying on of hands. When they are sick, we minister healing in Jesus' name. When there is a lack of peace, we minister His peace. When they are weak, we minister His strength. When they need to be filled with the Holy Spirit, we minister the precious Holy Spirit.

If you are a part of a group of believers in a small group or house church, you know you can do the *"work of ministry."* You do not have to wait for your small group leader, pastor or elder to pray for others—you can do it yourself. So there are times when you need to go to the hospital to pray for someone who is sick. At a time like this, you should ask the others in your small group to lay hands on you and pray for you. They will impart God's blessing and anointing into your life so that you can be more effective as you pray for the sick and minister in the name of Jesus Christ at the hospital.

If you are a parent, lay your hands on your children and minister to them. You minister the authority of God, the grace of God and the anointing of God to your children through the laying on of hands. I have often had the privilege of

Give examples of how you have ministered to others through the laying on of hands.

imparting His peace, His wisdom, and His strength to people. I have also been privileged to have had many people lay their hands on me and impart these same blessings to me. That is what God wants us to do: minister to one another.

106 | Receiving authority from others

If you are involved in a specific area of ministry, have you ever had someone lay hands on you and commission you into this area of service? Maybe you have a ministry to children in the church or in the community. Receive the Lord's blessing and authority through the laying on of hands. Ask those whom the Lord has placed in your life as spiritual overseers to lay their hands on you and pray for you. The scriptures tell us in Hebrews 13:7, *"Remember your leaders, who spoke the word of God to you. Consider the outcome of their way of life and imitate their faith."* Your spiritual leaders have something you need—you can copy their faith and practices because they are strong in the faith. In doing so, you receive an impartation from them.

Perhaps your local pastor or small group leader could lay their hands on you and commission you to serve in a particular way. This way you will have God's authority, as well as the authority and blessing of His church to do those things that the Lord has called you to do.

Have you ever had someone lay hands on you and commission you into an area of service? If not, ask!

PART 3

WE WILL LIVE FOREVER

107 | An elementary principle: The resurrection of the dead

What fact is central to the gospel of Jesus Christ?

In this part, we will also examine the important foundation stone of the "resurrection of the dead," and "eternal judgment." and then—"eternal judgment." *Therefore, leaving the discussion of the elementary principles of Christ, let us go on to perfection, not laying again the foundation of...resurrection of the dead, and of eternal judgment* (Hebrews 6:1-2 NKJ).

Why is the resurrection of the dead so important to our faith? The difference between Christianity and all other religions is that at the very center of Christianity is this truth: Jesus Christ is alive today! Mohammed is dead. Buddha is dead. All these "great prophets," who founded various world religions, are dead, but Jesus Christ is alive! The early church proclaimed clearly, "Jesus Christ is alive from the dead." It was the foundation of their faith that Jesus Christ had risen from the dead and was alive and well!

Why is it so important?

The fact of His resurrection is at the center of our faith. He is alive from the dead—this is central to the gospel of Jesus Christ. Jesus was raised from the dead and those who believe in Christ will share His resurrection. We will live forever! In fact, at the end of time, everyone will be resurrected, including the wicked who will be judged and punished. Jesus, Himself, spoke of the resurrection of the dead, both the godly and ungodly, in John 5:28-29. *Do not be amazed at this, for a time is coming when all who are in their graves will hear his voice and come out—those who have done good will rise to live, and those who have done evil will rise to be condemned.*

108 | Hope arises from knowing we will be resurrected

There is an incredible amount of hope that comes from knowing there will be a resurrection of the dead. For one thing, without eternal life, there are no lasting relationships. Since relationship is so important to God, He created us as eternal beings. He wanted to fellowship with us forever. Christians will have relationships (with God and each other) throughout eternity because we will live forever!

Why do Christians have hope?

When Jesus was walking on this earth, His own brother, James, did not realize He was the Son of God (John 7:5) until Jesus arose from the dead and appeared to him. James became an instant believer. Wouldn't you? ...*Christ died for our sins according to the Scriptures...he was buried...he was raised on the third day according to the Scriptures...After that, he appeared to James, then to all the apostles* (1 Corinthians 15:3, 4, 7).

I have gone to many funerals. For those who are true Christians when they die, there is hope. They go on to be with the Lord. Hope surrounds the entire funeral because the resurrection of the dead assures that you will see them again in the future.

Those who don't believe in eternal life have no hope of the future resurrection of the dead. Thomas Paine, known widely by his connection with the American and French revolutions, was also a noted infidel who died miserably in rebellion to the God he turned a deaf ear to. When Christians tried to share with him during his last days on this earth, his response was, "Away with you, and your God too! Leave the room instantly!" Among the last utterances that fell upon the ears of the attendants of this dying infidel, and which have been recorded in history, were the words, "My God, My God, why hast thou forsaken me?" He died without hope.[1]

Everyone lives forever because they are eternal beings. Jesus speaks of a resurrection of life for the believer and a resurrection of judgment for the wicked in John 5:24. *I tell you the truth, whoever hears my word and believes him who sent me has eternal life and will not be condemned; he has crossed over from death to life.*

Christians will live forever with the Lord, because they have heard God's Word and believed, but unbelievers will be condemned to live in eternal damnation (hell) forever.

[1] Compiled by John Myers, *Voices From the Edge of Eternity*, p. 133.

Do you know for sure if you died tonight, you would go to heaven?

109 | Death is abolished!

The resurrection of Jesus is a triumph over death. Jesus defeated the devil when He rose from the dead. In 1 Corinthians 15:25-26, we read that the last enemy to be abolished is *death. For he must reign until he has put all his enemies under his feet. The last enemy to be destroyed is death.*

I have a book in my home that is filled with hundreds of stories telling what happened in the last moments of peoples' lives before death. Some are wonderful stories about Christians who, during the last moments on this earth, catch a glimpse of heaven and peacefully go on to be with the Lord.

However, there are horrible stories told of the end for atheists or agnostics or those who cursed the name of God. Nurses in the same room with these infidels were horrified because these unbelievers were literally seeing the fires of hell before they died.

Friends of ours had their mother living with them for the last years of her life. This elderly Christian woman who loved the Lord with all of her heart, had cataracts in her eyes for years. The day that she passed away and went on to be with the Lord Jesus, the cataracts fell from her eyes. The blue eyes she had in her youth again sparkled. She looked to the corner of her room and reported that she saw Jesus.

While I was in the nation of Zambia, I met a young lady who told an amazing story of heaven. She had just been in a serious car accident and while she was unconscious, she saw a bright light coming into the back of the van. She found herself carried away up into the heavenlies where glorious beings were singing in an angelic language. As she got closer to the most beautiful place she had ever seen, she began to descend back to the earth. She sensed disappointment

Whom has been defeated because of Jesus' resurrection?

How does that affect your life?

Biblical Foundations for Life

when she realized that she was not continuing on toward the glorious city she had seen. The next thing she saw was the top of the bed rails in a hospital room and the voice of a family member saying, "You'll be OK."

"But I want to go on," she told the angelic being at her side.

"It's not your time yet," the angel responded. Then she awoke on the hospital bed. The Lord had given her a small taste of heaven!

Christians will live forever with the Lord, because they have heard God's Word and believed, but unbelievers will be condemned to live in eternal damnation (hell) forever.

110 | Our names are in the Book of Life

Are any of your sins recorded in the Book of Life?

Why or why not?

Did you know the Lord has every believer's name written in a book called the Book of Life? When we receive Jesus Christ as the Lord of our lives, our names are entered in His book. He will give us the strength to overcome sin and the temptations of this world until the end. *He who overcomes will, like them, be dressed in white. I will never blot out his name from the book of life, but will acknowledge his name before my Father and his angels* (Revelation 3:5).

Picture this Book of Life containing a complete record of every person's life on electromagnetic recording tape that was used 20 years ago. Modern technology allowed an error to be simply and completely erased in a few moments by running the recording head past that particular stretch of tape a second time. There was even a "bulk eraser" which could, in a few seconds, completely erase the whole recorded contents of an entire tape. One man of God said, "So it is with the heavenly record of the sinner's life. When a sinner comes for the first time in repentance and faith to Christ, God applies His heavenly "bulk eraser." The whole record of the sinner's former sins is thereby instantly and completely erased, and a clean tape is made available, upon which a new life of faith and righteousness may be recorded. If at any time thereafter the believer should fall again into sin, he needs only to repent and confess his sin, and God erases that particular section of the record, and once again the tape is clean."[1]

When you stand before God, and Jesus Christ is seated at the right hand of the Father, He will say, "I gave my life for you." Your sins have been completely cleansed and taken away, two thousand years ago! That is why I love Jesus Christ so much! He paid the price for my salvation on the cross!

1 Derek Prince, Foundation Series, p. 579.

111 | We graduate to heaven!

Our resurrected bodies
Romans 8:29
1 Corinthians 15:20,42-44,49
Philippians 3:20-21
1 John 3:2
2 Corinthians 5:7

When you are saved and come to know Jesus, your spirit is saved. When you die and pass on to eternal life, your spirit goes directly into the presence of Christ in heaven. Immediately, you will be *absent from the body and present with the Lord* (2 Corinthians 5:8 NKJ).

When Jesus comes again for His people, both those who have died in Christ and the faithful who are still alive are going to receive new, resurrected bodies adapted for heaven. Our spirit, soul, and body will come together at that time into a new resurrected body as we live for God throughout eternity—a body possessing an identity with the body of this life and recognizable (Luke 16:19-31), a body adapted for heaven, free from decay and death (1 Corinthians 15:42), a powerful body not subject to disease (1 Corinthians 15:43), a body not bound by the laws of nature (Luke 24:31; John 20:19; 1 Corinthians 15:44), a body that can eat and drink (Luke 14:15; 22:14-18,30; 24:43). So then, for the Christian, death is like graduation. We are passing on from one phase of life to the next phase of life!

How is death like a graduation?

Heaven is going to be a wonderful place. Worshiping God in His presence will be the best experience of all. Just think for a moment about the most wonderful things that you enjoy doing on this earth, and then realize that heaven will be a billion times better than that. Revelation 21:1-4 speaks of heaven. *Then I saw a new heaven and a new earth, for the first heaven and the first earth had passed away, and there was no longer any sea. I saw the Holy City, the new Jerusalem, coming down out of heaven from God, prepared as a bride beautifully dressed for her husband. And I heard a loud voice from the throne saying, "Now the dwelling of God is with men, and he will live with them. They will be his people, and God himself will be with them and be their God. He will wipe every tear from their eyes. There will be no more death or mourning or crying or pain, for the old order of things has passed away."*

What do you think heaven will be like with a new and perfect body, soul, and spirit?

Heaven will be a place of total relief. We'll be totally caught up in the presence of God.

Augustus Toplady, author of the immortal song, "Rock of Ages," was dying at age thirty-eight, but he was ready for graduation day. About an hour before he died, he seemed to awaken from a gentle slumber. "Oh, what delights! Who can fathom the joys of the third heaven? What bright sunshine has been spread around me! I have not words to express it. All is light, light, light—the brightness of His glory!" [1]

[1] Compiled by John Myers, *Voices From the Edge of Eternity*, pp. 23,24.

112 | What about children?

Sometimes people ask, "What about children? Are children going to be in heaven?" Yes, heaven will be filled with children! When children are born into this fallen world, they are born with a fallen nature. However, a young child is not old enough to know the difference between God's laws and the cravings of his fallen nature. When a child comes to the "age of accountability," he has to make the decision to choose right from wrong. He eventually chooses God or chooses his own way which would lead to eternal separation from God.

What qualifies a person for entrance to heaven, according to Matthew 18:3?

Children are without guilt and spiritual accountability until they sin against God's law. *Once I was alive apart from law; but when the commandment came, sin sprang to life and I died* (Romans 7:9). Paul says he was "once alive apart from the law," showing us that a child is "alive" until he understands the difference between right and wrong. Only God knows when that time is. However, after a child knows the law, then sin revives and they die. In other words, when

Biblical Foundations for Life

we come to the realization that we are sinning against the law of God, we are spiritually dead. That is why we need to give our lives to Jesus Christ. We need to be born again.

Each of our four children were convicted of their sins at a young age and received Jesus Christ as their Lord and Savior. When they were babies, they had no understanding of conviction of sin. However, the day came (their "age of accountability") for each of them to respond to the Holy Spirit's conviction.

Every person must come to a place of decision and respond to Jesus Christ and His offer of salvation in order to secure their place in heaven. Jesus said in Matthew 18:3, *"Assuredly, I say to you, unless you are converted and become as little children, you will by no means enter the kingdom of heaven."*

113 | Preparing a place for us

What is Jesus preparing for us, according to John 14:1-3?

At this very moment, the Lord is preparing a place for us to live throughout all of eternity. Jesus tells us in His Word, *Do not let your hearts be troubled. Trust in God; trust also in me. In my Father's house are many rooms; if it were not so, I would have told you. I am going there to prepare a place for you. And if I go and prepare a place for you, I will come back and take you to be with me that you also may be where I am* (John 14:1-3).

Can you imagine it! Jesus is preparing a special place just for you in heaven! Jesus Christ is coming back for us! Those of us who are still alive on this earth when He returns will meet Him in the air. Those who are dead, whose spirits are with the Lord, will return with the Lord and He will give them new bodies. It is going to be an exciting day! *Brothers, we do not want you to be ignorant about those who fall asleep, or to grieve like the rest of men, who have no hope. We believe that Jesus died and rose again and so we believe that God will bring with Jesus those who have fallen asleep in him. According to the Lord's own word, we tell you that we who are still alive, who are left till the coming of the Lord, will certainly not precede those who have fallen asleep. For the Lord himself will come down from heaven, with a loud command, with the voice of the archangel and with the trumpet call of God, and the dead in Christ will rise first. After that, we who are still alive and are left will be caught up together with them in the clouds to meet the Lord in the air. And so we will be with the Lord forever* (1 Thessalonians 4:13-17).

When is Jesus coming back for us?

Jesus Christ is coming back for His church—His people. It is going to be the most historic event since His visit to this planet two thousand years ago. As Christians, we should live each day as if He is coming today! If He doesn't come back for a few years yet, that's okay. We will just keep looking up, expecting His return, as we live in fellowship with the Holy Spirit each day.

D. L. Moody, an evangelist from the nineteenth century, knew a place was being prepared for him in heaven. On his deathbed, he seemed to see beyond the veil as he exclaimed, "Earth recedes, heaven opens before me. It is beautiful. If this is death, it is sweet. There is no valley here. God is calling me, and I must go. This is my triumph; this is my coronation day! I have been looking forward to it for years." [1]

[1] Compiled by John Myers, *Voices From the Edge of Eternity*, pp. 23, 24.

GOD JUDGES ALL   PART 4

114 | An elementary principle: Eternal judgment

Previously we examined the principle of the "resurrection of the dead." In this part of the section, we will look at another basic foundation stone of the Christian faith that is linked to the resurrection of the dead—"eternal judgment." *Therefore, leaving the discussion of the elementary principles of Christ, let us go on to perfection, not laying again the foundation of eternal judgment* (Hebrews 6:1-2 NKJ).

What is judgment? The word *judgment* literally means *verdict*. When a judge sentences someone, he passes the verdict. Judgment is pronounced. There is no reversal. The scripture says that judgment is eternal. Eternal judgment is a verdict given that will last forever.

What is eternity? Imagine one little bird coming to the seashore every one thousand years. This bird then takes one grain of sand and carries it from the seashore and drops it somewhere into the ocean. After all of the sand on all of the seashores along all of the oceans of the world would be totally depleted of sand, eternity would have just begun! It is *that* hard to fathom the length of eternity!

Every man and woman who has ever lived will someday be judged by God for all of eternity. *Just as man is destined to die once, and after that to face judgment* (Hebrews 9:27). The faithful do not need to fear God's judgment because they will receive eternal life in heaven with Jesus. The wicked, however will be eternally punished. *Then they will go away to eternal punishment, but the righteous to eternal life* (Matthew 25:46).

Voltaire was a noted French infidel who spent most of his life ridiculing Christianity. When Voltaire had a stroke which he realized would terminate his life, he was terrified and tortured with such agony that at times he gnashed his teeth in rage against God and man. At other times, he would plead, "O Christ! I must die—abandoned of God and of men!" Voltaire's infidel associates were afraid to approach his bedside. His nurse repeatedly said that for all the wealth of Europe she would never want to see another infidel die. It was a scene of horror that lies beyond all exaggeration.[1]

While heaven is a place of unimaginable beauty where God's people will fellowship with each other and their God forever, hell is a place of endless suffering and punishment for those who reject Christ.

[1] Compiled by John Myers, *Voices From the Edge of Eternity*, p. 22.

115 | The judgment seat of Christ

Someday we will all stand before the living God in judgment. For believers in Jesus Christ, our sins were judged on the cross two thousand years ago, so it will not be a judgment of condemnation. However, those who have not received the Lord Jesus Christ into their lives will await sentencing. There is no escape. *For we must all appear before the judgment seat of Christ, that each one*

What is eternal judgment?

Where do the wicked go and where do the righteous go, according to Matthew 25:46?

Biblical Foundations for Life   93

Imagine standing before God on judgment day. How can you be sure you will gain eternal life?

may receive what is due him for the things done while in the body, whether good or bad. Since, then, we know what it is to fear the Lord, we try to persuade men... (2 Corinthians 5:10-11).

Now is the time to tell people the good news that will set men and women free. Today, as I write this, I had the privilege of assisting a young couple as they gave their lives to Jesus Christ. Because of their decision for Christ, their sins are forgiven and they will not have to face eternal punishment. They will live forever in God's kingdom!

Praise God for Jesus, who paid the price on the cross to save us from eternal damnation! When we receive Jesus as Lord, He says, " I love you, I will cleanse you, and I will make you a brand new person, as a part of My family. You will live with Me forever." It is God's plan for us to be saved. *For God did not send his Son into the world to condemn the world, but to save the world through him* (John 3:17).

116 | Christians will have to give an account at judgment

What will be "brought to light" in a believer's life on judgment day according to 1 Corinthians 3:12-15?

Although believers are free of God's judgment of condemnation and will go to heaven, the Bible does say we will have to give an account as to the degree of our faithfulness to God, according to 1 Corinthians 3:12-15. *If any man builds on this foundation using gold, silver, costly stones, wood, hay or straw, his work will be shown for what it is, because the Day will bring it to light. It will be revealed with fire, and the fire will test the quality of each man's work. If what he has built survives, he will receive his reward. If it is burned up, he will suffer loss; he himself will be saved, but only as one escaping through the flames.*

On that Day, at the judgment seat of Christ, God will examine openly our character, secret acts, good deeds, motives, attitudes, etc. If we have not lived holy and godly lives and shown mercy and kindness, our foundation is weak—one of "wood, hay or stubble, rather than gold, silver, or precious stones." Although we will receive salvation, we will experience great "loss." A careless believer suffers loss in the following ways: by feeling shame at Christ's coming (1 John 2:28), loss of his life's work for God (1 Corinthians 3:13-15), loss of glory and honor before God (Romans 2:7), loss of opportunity for service and authority in heaven (Matthew 25:14-30; 5:15; 19:30) and loss of rewards (1 Corinthians 3:12-14; Philippians 3:14; 2 Timothy 4:8).

When our attitude and motivation reflects the fruit of the Spirit and a Christ-like love, our works will be built with precious stones with many rewards from God. If we are motivated more by selfish ambition than by the leading of God's Holy Spirit, those works will be destroyed—burned up. These solemn words should motivate us to live faithful, self-sacrificing lives for the Lord.

A well-known Bible teacher who has spent dozens of years proclaiming the gospel throughout the world writes the following to describe the moment when God will judge every Christian's works: "In the fiery rays of those eyes, as each one stands before His judgment seat, all that is base, insincere and valueless in His people's works will be instantly and eternally consumed. Only that which is of true and enduring value will survive, purified and refined by fire. As we consider this scene of judgment, each of us needs to ask himself: How may I serve Christ in this life, so that my works will stand the test of fire in that day?"[1]

[1] Derek Prince, *Foundation Series*, p. 583.

117 | The judgment of the wicked—a literal hell

Although everyone, living or dead, throughout the ages will be judged, the Bible portrays a different picture of the final destiny of the lost as they stand before the living God. Revelation 20:11-15 says, "*Then I saw a great white throne and him who was seated on it. Earth and sky fled from his presence, and there was no place for them. And I saw the dead, great and small, standing before the throne, and books were opened. Another book was opened, which is the book of life. The dead were judged according to what they had done as recorded in the books. The sea gave up the dead that were in it, and death and Hades gave up the dead that were in them, and each person was judged according to what he had done. Then death and Hades were thrown into the lake of fire. The lake of fire is the second death. If anyone's name was not found written in the book of life, he was thrown into the lake of fire.*"

What is the *second death* mentioned here? The *second death* is an eternal hell that burns with fire for ever and ever. This terrible picture of hell is almost too horrible to think about, but according to the Bible, there is a real, burning hell. The scriptures tell us, *The Son of Man will send out his angels, and they will weed out of his kingdom everything that causes sin and all who do evil. They will throw them into the fiery furnace, where there will be weeping and gnashing of teeth. Then the righteous will shine like the sun in the kingdom of their Father. He who has ears, let him hear* (Matthew 13:41-43).

The destinies of both the Christian and the unbeliever are irreversible at death. In Luke 16:19-31, we read the story of the rich man and Lazarus. The rich man spent his life consumed in self-centered living and found himself in hell after he died. Lazarus was a beggar, a poor man who lived in the rich man's neighborhood, and was fed by the crumbs that came from the rich man's table. His heart was right with God, and when he died, he was immediately taken to paradise. The rich man cried out because of his torment in hell, but it was too late.

Some people say sarcastically, "I'm not afraid of hell. I'll just be having a party with all my friends." Hell will not be a party. It will be an eternal fire—a place of horrible torment.

118 | Hell is prepared for the devil and his angels

Jesus did not make hell for people. He made hell for the devil and his angels. *Then he will say to those on his left, "Depart from me, you who are cursed, into the eternal fire prepared for the devil and his angels"* (Matthew 25:41).

The worst thing about hell is the lack of the goodness of God. Everything good that we know of is from God. Can you imagine being in a place where there is nothing good? That is what hell is going to be like, in the midst of all the

---

Hell, the final destiny of the lost
Romans 2:9; Matthew 13:42,50; 22:13 25:30,46; Mark 9:43; 14:11 2 Thessalonians 1:9; 2 Peter 2:4 Hebrews 10:31

If a person's name is not found in the Book of Life, what is his or her final destiny, according to Revelation 20:11-15?

_____

_____

_____

_____

Is this destiny reversible? (see Luke 16:19-31)

_____

_____

_____

_____

Biblical Foundations for Life

Did God create hell for bad people?

What is hell like, according to Mark 9:43?

How will God be a fair judge, according to Romans 2:14-15?

torment from the fires of hell.

Just like there are degrees of reward in heaven, there are degrees of punishment in hell, according to the Bible. *That servant who knows his master's will and does not get ready or does not do what his master wants will be beaten with many blows. But the one who does not know and does things deserving punishment will be beaten with few blows. From everyone who has been given much, much will be demanded; and from the one who has been entrusted with much, much more will be asked* (Luke 12:47-48).

In other words, those persons who have heard the gospel and know about the Truth (Jesus), and simply continue to turn away from Him, are under a much worse judgment than those who have never heard. I used to think that the people who have been involved in all kinds of "gross sin"—like murder, adultery and witchcraft—would have the worst punishment in hell. However, here the Bible tells us that people who know the truth and do not obey will have a stricter punishment in hell than those who didn't know or obey. The sobering truth, however, is that hell is hell. Whether it is a million degrees or ten million degrees, it is hell—a "fire that never goes out" (Mark 9:43), a place of endless torment and pain, a terrifying reality for those condemned.

119 | What about people who have never heard of Jesus?

Jesus Christ is the only way that we can get to God and live eternally with Him. Jesus, Himself, said in John 14:6, "*...I am the way and the truth and the life. No one comes to the Father except through me.*"

So what about people who have never heard of Jesus Christ? We can be assured that God is a fair judge. The Bible says He is righteous (1 John 2:1). When someone questions the fairness of God's judgment concerning those who have not heard, my initial response often is, "But *you* have heard; what is *your* response to Jesus?" Romans 2:14-15 says, "*Indeed, when Gentiles, who do not have the law, do by nature things required by the law, they are a law for themselves, even though they do not have the law, since they show that the requirements of the law are written on their hearts, their consciences also bearing witness, and their thoughts now accusing, now even defending them.*"

Here we see that the Lord judges according to what someone has learned, what their conscience tells them. Everyone has a measure of knowledge of right and wrong, and we need to trust God to be a fair judge. God is a faithful and just God (1 John 1:9). He is more fair than any human being could ever be. It is those of us who *do* know the truth of Jesus Christ that have no excuse. Galatians 6:7-8 says, "*Do not be deceived: God cannot be mocked. A man reaps what he sows. The one who sows to please his sinful nature, from that nature will reap destruction; the one who sows to please the Spirit, from the Spirit will reap eternal life.*"

That is why we need to sow into our lives spiritually. We must read and meditate on the Word of God, and share its truth with others. We need to develop an intimate relationship with our Lord Jesus. Whatever we sow spiritually, we will reap spiritually. Whenever we sow from the flesh (our own evil nature), we will reap that kind of eternal destiny. Let's sow to the Spirit, and live for Him throughout all of eternity. *But seek first his kingdom and his righteousness, and all these things will be given to you as well* (Matthew 6:33).

What *things*, you ask? All the blessings of God including eternal life in heaven. People live forever. What is the kingdom of God? It is God and His people. It's a relationship with God and relationships with one another that will last forever.

120 | We must tell them the Good News

An atheist in England made a statement that I never forgot. He said, "I am an atheist, because if I believed what Christians preach, I would crawl on my hands and knees on broken glass to tell one person how he could escape the punishment of which they speak." Christians know that Christianity is real and an eternal destiny awaits both the saved and the unsaved.

Back in the early days of our church, God gave a vision to a young man: "I saw in my vision the fires of hell. And I saw many, many people walking toward the fires of hell, falling over the cliff into hell. Then I saw another group of people, an army. I saw people joining together hand in hand, and they were going down to the brink of the fire and pulling people up at the last moment before they went plunging over. People were being literally snatched from hell. That is what God has called us to do as a church." We need to do whatever we can to see people snatched from the fires of hell to live for God eternally.

When Christians see themselves as spiritual soldiers in His army, we will be motivated to pull people out of the fires of hell because we know the truth that will set them free. The truth will set those free who respond to the name of Jesus.

Jesus Christ is coming back soon. We have a job to do! Jesus admonished believers to remember all the lost souls that will spend eternity in hell if the gospel is not presented to them. The fields are ready and white for harvest now, and we must tell them the good news. Jesus said, *"Do you not say, 'Four months more and then the harvest?' I tell you, open your eyes and look at the fields! They are ripe for harvest"* (John 4:35b).

The reality of an eternal judgment should cause all believers to hate sin and diligently seek the lost to tell them of God's wonderful plan for mankind.

People who joke about hell have no idea how real hell will be. After an individual dies there will be no more opportunity to escape (Hebrews 9:27). There is an old saying, "The road to hell is paved with good intentions." If you have not done so already, now is the time to accept God's provision of His Son, Jesus Christ, for you to live forever! Don't delay.

How can you snatch someone from the brink of hell? Have you ever done this?

121 | We are being changed and have been redemed

1 Corinthians 15:51-52 says, *"Listen, I tell you a mystery: We will not all sleep, but we will all be changed—in a flash, in the twinkling of an eye, at the last*

How have we been bought back?

trumpet. *For the trumpet will sound, the dead will be raised imperishable, and we will be changed."*

When Jesus comes again, we will be changed in a flash. Instantly. What must we do to be prepared for His coming? The Word says that we must repent and confess Jesus Christ as Lord.

We have been redeemed by the blood of Jesus. This means we have been "bought back." When Jesus died on the cross, He purchased us back from the enemy, who had stolen us away.

Now let's read Isaiah 43:25. *I, even I, am he who blots out your transgressions, for my own sake, and remembers your sins no more.* Isaiah 44:22 also says, *"I have swept away your offenses like a cloud, your sins like the morning mist. Return to me, for I have redeemed you.*

I leave you with this question to consider: How does God see you when He looks at you? Why is that so?

FOUNDATION 5

Living in the Grace of God

122 | Introduction to Foundation 5

As we continue to look at the basic biblical foundations we need in our lives to be strong spiritually, we will focus on the foundational truth of Living in the Grace of God. We will discover that it is grace that motivates God to offer us salvation. We get right with God by His grace, not because we somehow earned it. And we also live for Christ each day by God's amazing grace.

Grace is a gift; we cannot do anything to earn it. Our salvation comes as a gift of God's grace, and it can be accessed by our response of faith.

The Bible says in Ephesians 2:8-9, *"For it is by grace you have been saved, through faith—and this is not from yourselves, it is the gift of God—not by works, so that no one can boast."*

We are totally dependent on the grace of God for everything. When we apply the truth of God's grace to our daily lives, we can live as victorious Christians.

The other aspect of God's grace can be defined as *"the power and desire to do God's will."* The grace of God is literally divine energy that the Holy Spirit releases in our lives. God has given us supernatural provision to live a victorious life.

Romans 5:17 tells us, *"For if, by the trespass of the one man, death reigned through that one man, how much more will those who receive God's abundant provision of grace and of the gift of righteousness reign in life through the one many, Jesus Christ!"*

God gives us an abundance of grace! We do not deserve any of it, but the Lord pours it on us anyway! He is the God of all grace! A biblical clear understanding of the grace of God will revolutionize your life.

Is it possible to earn God's grace?

How do we experience God's grace?

PART 1   WHAT IS GARCE?

123 | Grace affects everything

A famous zoo in Germany purchased a great brown bear from the traveling circus. Up until this point, this magnificent, but abused creature had lived in misery. For the duration of its life the bear had been locked up in a tiny circus cage about twelve feet long. Every waking hour of the day, with its massive head swaying back and forth in rhythm, he took twelve steps forward and twelve steps backward in his narrow prison. The water given to him was stagnant slop; the food was rotten garbage.

Finally he was sold and transferred from his tiny little cage to the beautiful German Zoo. The zoo had a bear compound consisting of acres of lush, green grass. There were trees to climb and sparkling pools of fresh drinking water. The bear would be fed three meals each day and have other bear companions.

Like the bear in the cage, are you held captive to any old habits or deceptions?

The zoo-keepers wheeled the bear's cage into the compound of the zoo and opened the door to freedom. The bear continued his march—twelve feet forward and twelve feet backward. They called out to him, but he would not respond. They offered him food. They offered him freedom, but he still would not respond.

Finally, they lit a stick on fire and place the burning stick through the bars. This scared the bear enough to jump from the cage onto the ground. The bear looked around, and to the zoo attendant's amazement, he started pacing twelve feet forward and twelve feet backward—the exact dimensions of his cage!

Suddenly it dawned on the attendants—the bear's prison was not a *metal* one, but a *mental, invisible* one! They could do nothing to help him out of his prison.

Some Christians find themselves in a similar dilemma. Having become so accustomed to certain thought patterns of defeat and failure in some areas of their lives, they convince themselves things will never change and are locked in an invisible, mental prison.

Precious, born again, Spirit-filled Christians who love Jesus with all of their hearts are susceptible to this kind of mental trap. Some, upon facing incredible obstacles in their lives, become weary and settle for far less than the Lord intended for them.

Years ago, I received a revelation from the Lord about the grace of God that has literally revolutionized my life. Although I was in love with Jesus and filled with the Holy Spirit, I was still living in a mental prison. It seemed like some things would never change. Then one day someone vividly described the "grace of God" to me in a way that literally changed my life! God's grace offered in the scriptures goes far beyond what is offered by other world religions. Many religions say that man gets what he deserves. Others add that man does not get all that he deserves (mercy). Grace goes way beyond that idea, however. Grace is God's unimaginable and total kindness! We receive it freely and do not deserve it, and our hearts cannot but change because of it! We cannot fully describe it, but we can experience it. Grace affects everything we do in life. When I finally began to understand the grace of God, it changed the way I thought, acted and responded to difficulties that arose in my life.

Grace is mentioned more than 125 times in the New Testament. Since "grace" is mentioned so often, we need to understand what the grace of God is really about and how it affects our lives. Paul, the apostle, while writing to the church, often began his letters speaking about grace. He would also close his letters with, "The grace of the Lord Jesus be with you." He continually emphasized *grace* throughout the New Testament. *Grace and peace to you from God our Father and the Lord Jesus Christ. I always thank God for you because of his grace given you in Christ Jesus* (1 Corinthians 1:3-4).

124 | God's free gift of grace is the basis of salvation

Grace is sometimes defined as *the free unmerited favor of God on the undeserving and ill-deserving*. God loves us and does not want us to be separated from Him by sin. So our first glimpse of grace occurs when God offers salvation to us even though we do not deserve it or work to earn it. He gives a measure of grace as a gift to unbelievers so they may be able to believe in the Lord Jesus. Ephesians 2:8-9 says, *"For it is by grace you have been saved, through faith—and this not from yourselves, it is the gift of God—not by works, so that no one can boast."*

How does grace first impact our lives according to Ephesians 2:8-9?

We come to God initially because He is the One who has drawn us. Jesus says in John 6:44, *"No one can come to Me unless the Father who has sent me draws him."* I've met people who have said, "I found God." We do not find God; He finds us! He has been drawing us to Himself all along. The reason that we are Christians is simply because of God's grace and God's goodness on our lives. Grace is dependent on the infinite goodness of God. Because of the grace of God—because of His love, goodness and caring as He draws us to Himself, we are saved. We don't deserve to be saved but God freely extends His grace to us. Romans 11:6 says, *"And if by grace, then it is no longer by works; if it were, grace would no longer be grace."*

Describe the two sides of grace.

It is grace that motivates God to offer us salvation even though we did not earn it. We cannot earn it; it is a gift. So we see that our salvation comes as a gift of God's grace, and it can be accessed by our response of faith.

Grace could be described as a coin with two distinct sides to it. We just described the one side of the coin that is characterized by the saving grace of God—"the free unmerited favor of God on the undeserving and ill-deserving." The other side of the grace coin is the grace God gives to believers to give them the "desire and the power to do God's will." We will look at this aspect of grace a bit later in this book. Both aspects of grace encompass the whole of the Christian life from the beginning to the end. We are totally dependent on the grace of God!

125 | Mercy vs. grace

There is a difference between God's grace and mercy. Sometimes we get these two terms confused. God's *mercy* is "God not giving us what we deserve" and God's *grace* is "giving us those things that we do not deserve."

Biblical Foundations for Life

What are some things God gave you because of His grace?

_____
_____
_____

What are some things He did not give because of His mercy?

_____
_____
_____

The law came through Moses, but what came through Jesus Christ according to John 1:17?

_____
_____

How do we escape the law and come under grace?

_____
_____
_____

We deserve hell, sickness, disease and troubles because our sin places us in darkness. Yet, even though we do not deserve it, God offers us forgiveness, peace, eternal life, hope, healing, the Holy Spirit: the list goes on—all because of His wonderful grace!

A few years ago, I was traveling through a small town in the Midwest with my family. I was not aware the speed limit was 25 miles per hour and I was traveling 35 miles per hour. As I got to the other side of the town, I heard a shrill siren behind me. Sure enough, it was a policeman, signaling me to pull off to the side of the road. He then proceeded to write up a traffic ticket as he fulfilled his responsibility as a police officer. Now, if the policeman would have been exercising mercy he would have said, "Look, I understand you didn't realize you were going 10 m.p.h. over the limit. I'll allow you to go free." If he would have been operating in a principle of grace, he would have said, "You are a really nice guy. In fact, I like you so much I'd like to give you a hundred dollars just for traveling on our streets." Unfortunately for me, he did not operate in mercy or grace, but he did allow me to receive *justice*—he gave me a ticket with a fine to pay!

I can remember, early in my Christian life, that I felt like God somehow owed me a nice family and a prosperous life, complete with a paycheck each week. After all, I thought, I had worked for it. I didn't realize how arrogant I was. If it wasn't for the grace of God, I would not have the physical strength or health to work in the first place. God didn't owe me anything. First He had shown mercy to me and saved me, then He showered His grace on me, giving me those things I did not deserve—God's wonderful presence in my life through Jesus Christ. *Christ Jesus came into the world to save sinners—of whom I am the worst. But for that very reason I was shown mercy so that in me, the worst of sinners, Christ Jesus might display his unlimited patience as an example for those who would believe on him and receive eternal life* (1 Timothy 1:15-17).

126 | No longer under the law but under grace

God gave Moses moral laws to follow (the Ten Commandments) that were given to show men their sinful condition. The law showed the human race the difference between right and wrong. Through attempting to obey the law, mankind sought to earn the blessing of God by what they did.

Then Jesus came and changed all that. Through Him we are offered grace—the free, undeserving favor of God that comes through faith in Jesus, who is the Truth. When a person trusts Christ for salvation, his righteousness no longer depends on keeping the law. Since the Christian is under grace, he cannot be under the law. The Bible says that grace and truth came through Jesus Christ. *For the law was given through Moses; grace and truth came through Jesus Christ* (John 1:17).

Those under the law are always conscious of the power of sin within themselves, frustrating them to live victoriously. Those observing the law must observe all its requirements at all times because if they break even one point, they break the whole law (James 2:10). We cannot become righteous from keeping the law, in fact, it is impossible to keep the law. We all stand self-condemned because we fall short of obeying the law. The only escape is to come out from under the law. That is why we are righteous only by faith in Christ. To escape the dominion of sin, a Christian comes out from under the law and comes under grace. *For sin shall not be your master, because you are not under law, but under grace* (Romans 6:14).

127 | The Ten Commandments show how important grace is

Let's take a brief look at the Ten Commandments (Deuteronomy 5:6-21) to see how far every person falls short of keeping the law. The law helps us to see how important grace is to our lives.

The Ten Commandments

1. *You shall have no other gods before me.*
   We break this law every time we give something or someone other than God complete first place in our affections. No man has ever kept this commandment.

2. *You shall not make for yourself a graven image.*
   It is impossible for an image or picture of God to truly represent God and all His glory. If we approach God with our lips, but not our hearts, we have a false image of Him and are far from Him (Mark 7:6).

3. *You shall not take the name of the Lord your God in vain.*
   Most times we think of using the Lord's name in a profane utterance as "taking His name in vain." But if we call Him *Lord* and disobey Him, we are taking His name in vain. If we are filled with fear and doubts, we deny His name.

4. *Remember the sabbath day, to keep it holy.*
   God's plan was to give man a day of rest so he could worship, undistracted. Christ takes our burdens and gives us a spiritual rest or "Sabbath-rest" (Hebrews 4:10) but often we fail to enter into that rest.

5. *Honor your father and your mother.*
   Parents represent God's authority to their children. Yet children are often disrespectful and ungrateful to their parents.

6. *You shall not kill.*
   Jesus said that to be angry with another without a cause, and to be insulting, are just as serious as murder (Matthew 5:21-22). We can murder others by gossip, neglect, cruelty or jealousy.

7. *You shall not commit adultery.*
   This commandment not only includes sex outside of marriage, but such sin as entertaining adulterous thoughts, looking at pornography, submitting to impure fantasies, selfish demands in marriage, flirting, etc. (Matthew 5:27-28).

Think about your life and your inability to keep the ten commandments.

How important is grace to your life?

Biblical Foundations for Life

8. ***You shall not steal.***
   Evading income tax is stealing. Working short hours for an employer is stealing. An employer who underpays his workers steals from them.

9. ***You shall not bear false witness against your neighbor.***
   This is not only referring to what could happen in a court of law, but includes all kinds of idle talk, lies, exaggerations, gossip or even making jokes at another's expense.

10. ***You shall not covet.***
    Covetousness happens in the heart and mind. When we are jealous of someone's house or life-style or spouse or car, we are enslaved to covetousness.

The Ten Commandments convince us of our sinfulness and inability to keep the righteous law of God. As important as the Ten Commandments are, we simply cannot keep these rules on our own. We need a Savior. Jesus came as the remedy for our sin! Sin does not have dominion over Christians because we are not under the law! We are under grace!

128 | Grace is more powerful than sin

What increases with sin, according to Romans 5:20?

God's moral law, the Ten Commandments, are important because they show mankind the true nature of sin. When we see the extent of our failure to obey God's laws, the more we see God's abounding grace forgiving us! The Bible says, *"...but where sin increased, grace increased all the more"* (Romans 5:20).

Grace is much more powerful than sin! Verse 21 goes on to say that sin used to rule over all men and bring them to death, but now God's kindness rules instead, giving us right standing with God and resulting in eternal life through Jesus Christ. Wherever you find sin and disobedience, you will find God's grace available.

The Holy Spirit works within believers to allow them to live lives of righteousness. This is a fulfillment of God's moral law. We cannot do it on our own, but only by God's grace. So grace and obedience to God's law are not in conflict. They both point to righteousness and holiness. We are able to live holy lives and keep God's moral codes only by His grace!

How have you experienced this in your life?

Many years ago, I drove a little Volkswagen "bug." One day, the car stopped running. I decided I had enough of a mechanical background to enable me to take the motor out and fix it. I soon realized that I was getting nowhere fast. I certainly was trying, but I knew I needed help. I towed it to a garage where a mechanic fixed it! Without the grace of God, we cannot fix ourselves. Did I deserve to have the Volkswagen fixed? No, but it ran again because of God's grace and because of the grace on the mechanic who fixed it. It is God's grace that saves us from sin and puts us back together.

If we make a mistake, we confess it to God and move ahead by the grace of God, knowing that it's His grace that gives us the strength to go on. Why did God forgive us? He forgave us because of His gift of grace. Why does God fill us with the Holy Spirit? We're filled because of the grace of God. Even if we have made a mess of our lives, we can find forgiveness and move on because of the grace of God.

129 | Cheap grace?

If God is willing to forgive sin, and since Christians are under grace and not the law, does this mean we can continue to tolerate sin in our lives and yet remain secure from judgment? After all, God's grace pardons sin. We can sin because God will always forgive us, right? Wrong! This is the very issue the early church ran into. Paul challenges this train of thought that "cheapens" God's grace. *What shall we say, then? Shall we go on sinning so that grace may increase? By no means! We died to sin; how can we live in it any longer?* (Romans 6:1).

It is a distortion of God's grace to think we can continue to live in sin and God's grace will cover it. The Bible tells us in 1 John 3:4 that *everyone who sins breaks the law, in fact, sin is lawlessness.* When we came to Christ, we made a separation from sin—we died to sin's power and control over our lives. As Christians, we are freed from sin's power to walk in newness of life (Romans 6:4-5,10). We are no longer slaves to sin.

Yet, every believer must be careful to daily reaffirm his decision to resist sin and follow Christ (Romans 8:13; Hebrews 3:7-11). Known sin in our lives grieves the Holy Spirit and quenches His power (Ephesians 4:30; 1 Thessalonians 5:19). If we keep returning to sin and cease to resist it, eventually our hearts will grow hard and unyielding. It is possible (because of the hardening that can take place in our hearts because of sin—see Hebrews 3:8), we could reach a place in the downward spiral of rebellion and disobedience when we no longer really believe in anything. We become sin's slave again with death as its result. *For the wages of sin is death...* (Romans 6:23).

Although God's grace gives us power to resist sin, it is true that while living our day-to-day lives, we will not always consistently resist sin. When we fail, our God of grace and mercy is willing to forgive us. When we mess up our lives and go back to God, God's grace is freely extended. However, we should be cautioned against thinking we can sin *because* we are under grace. Remember, there may be a point of no return.

Since grace increases with sin, can we continue to sin because God will always forgive us?

What can happen if we keep returning to sin, according to Romans 6:23?

Biblical Foundations for Life

PART 2 — RESPONDING TO GOD'S GRACE

130 | Totally dependent on God's grace

Paul, the apostle, went through years of theological training and had an impeccable background of pure Jewish descent. Yet he says that all his advantages of birth, education and personal achievement can be attributed to the grace of God. *But by the grace of God I am what I am, and his grace to me was not without effect. No, I worked harder than all of them—yet not I, but the grace of God that was with me* (1 Corinthians 15:10).

If we think we are strong spiritually or a fantastic husband or a good student or a mature single, we must remember our strength is not in ourselves, but in Jesus Christ. Like Paul, we are totally dependent on the grace of God. Everything that we have, everything that we will ever do, everything that we are, is simply by the grace of God.

When we understand how grace works in our lives, we will find ourselves living with a new freedom in our daily relationship with Jesus. Every good thing in our lives is a result of the grace of God. You and I really do not deserve anything. If you have good health today, it is because of the grace of God. Any gift or ability you have can be credited to the grace of God. If you are an excellent parent, it is not because you are so talented with children, but it is the grace of God that enables you to be a good parent. If you are a fantastic basketball player, it's because of the grace of God. You may say, "But I practice." Who gave you the ability and health to practice? God did. Good students are recipients of the grace of God. If you are a financially secure businessman, the grace of God is the reason that you are successful. When we get this truth into our spirits and live out the grace of God, it totally revolutionizes us. It changes us from the inside out.

The devil cannot puff you up with pride if you understand the grace of God. People who are proud are really saying, "I am the reason things are working so well" and they look to themselves instead of to God. People who are living in the grace of God are always looking to Jesus. They are living with a sense of thankfulness, knowing that He's the One who has given them every good gift and every good thing they have.

131 | God gives us unlimited grace to change

Sometimes people confuse the grace of God with fatalism. Fatalism is the idea that we cannot change our circumstances despite what we do, so we just allow fate to take its course. Although we are totally dependent on the grace of God, it does not mean we sit passively and do nothing to utilize grace. Grace must be diligently desired and accepted.

Imagine yourself lying in the sunshine on a grassy hill on a warm summer's day. A huge rock begins to roll down the hill towards you. Fatalism says, "There's nothing I can do about it. Being crushed by this rock must be my destiny." The grace of God says, "I do not have to just lie here and be crushed by a rock. I will accept and utilize the strength God has given me, and I will get out of its way!"

Can you honestly agree with the following statements?

_____
_____
_____
_____

I am totally dependent on the grace of God. I am what I am by the grace of God. Explain.

_____
_____
_____
_____

Of course, there are things in life that we cannot change, but we must realize that if it wasn't for the grace of God, things could be much worse. Many undesirable things that happen in our lives can be avoided when we take God at His Word and trust His grace to give us the wisdom and strength to see things changed. God wants to give us more and more of His grace to live victorious as Christians on this earth...*he gives us more grace*...(James 4:6). At every turn, God is on the lookout to offer grace to us!

Responding in the grace of God always brings more freedom, hope, refreshment and peace so we can move ahead with God. Paul, the apostle, told a church of new believers to continue on in the grace of God even when they had opposition. *Now when the congregation had broken up, many of the Jews and devout proselytes followed Paul and Barnabas, who, speaking to them, persuaded them to continue in the grace of God* (Acts 13:43).

Paul knew that this recently established church of new believers had to have a clear understanding of grace in order to continue to move ahead in His purposes. Otherwise they would succumb to the tactics of the devil and forget that God's grace was sufficient.

132 | Falling short of God's grace

Jesus told a parable one day about a landowner who had a vineyard (Matthew 20:11-15). The grapes were ready to pick, so the landowner found some willing workers and sent them out at 9:00 AM to pick grapes. Later, he hired some more men and sent them out at 12:00 noon. Later still, he employed other workers and sent them out at 3:00 PM. The grape crop was still not completely picked, so at 5:00 PM he sent some final laborers out to complete the harvest for the day. At the end of the day, he called all of the laborers in and gave them exactly the same amount of money because that is what he had promised each group at the start of their job. When the workers who worked the longest hours discovered that the workers who worked only a few hours were paid the same, they complained to the landowner.

If this doesn't sound fair to you, you do not yet understand the grace of God. God loves us unconditionally, just the way we are. When we are secure in His love and acceptance, we no longer are concerned if someone else "gets a better deal" than we do. We live by grace, completely satisfied. When we understand that God's love and acceptance can't be earned or deserved, we live in the blessing of His grace each day.

Did you know that we will never be jealous and become bitter if we understand and live in the grace of God? Hebrews 12:15 says it like this, *See to it that no one misses the grace of God and that no bitter root grows up to cause trouble and defile many.* Bitterness starts out like a small root. Did you ever see a sidewalk where roots had pushed up and cracked the concrete? It started with just one little root. Many times, people get bitter at God. They say, "God, why is that person prosperous and I am struggling financially?" They have fallen short of the grace of God.

Describe a time you received grace to live victoriously.

What is a "root of bitterness," according to Hebrews 12:15?

Does it ever cause trouble in your life? How so?

Biblical Foundations for Life

1 Corinthians 10:12 says, *"So, if you think you are standing firm, be careful that you don't fall!"* If we are at the place where we think we are strong and we're going to be okay and we're not going to fall, the Bible says, *"Be careful."* Any of us can fall short of the grace of God in our lives.

133 | Grace to the humble

There is tremendous spiritual power released when we begin to experience the grace of God. Years ago, I was involved in a youth ministry. I remember coming home one day, and discovering that someone had taken a big rock and thrown it through our window. I knew the rock-thrower was someone we cared about and to whom we had ministered. God was teaching us about His grace, so the Lord helped us to take the attitude that it was only by His grace that our whole house did not have every window broken! We could have cried and complained, but God's grace gave us the power to move on so that we could continue to build His life in the people that He had placed in our lives. 1 Peter 5:5-6 says, *"...God opposes the proud but gives grace to the humble. Humble yourselves, therefore, under God's mighty hand, that he may lift you up in due time."*

Humility is an attitude of total dependence on Jesus Christ. Pride is the opposite of a healthy understanding of the grace of God. The scripture makes it clear that if we humble ourselves under the mighty hand of God, He will exalt us in due time. God wants to exalt you. He wants to honor you. When are we honored by God? When we humble ourselves before Him. If I try to do God's job, if I try to exalt myself, then God would have to do my job. He would have to humble me. I would rather humble myself and allow God to exalt me rather than have God humble me, wouldn't you?

Humility places us in a position to receive this grace. True humility is constantly acknowledging that without Jesus we can do nothing, but with Jesus we can do all things. Humility isn't walking with your head bowed down, trying to look humble. True humility is understanding and living out the principle of the grace of God.

134 | Season your speech with grace

We will not gossip if we understand the grace of God. The reason people gossip is because of false humility. Those who gossip try to elevate themselves on a pedestal as they look down on others. When someone is going through a difficult time or is involved in sin, we may be tempted to gossip about them. We will quickly stop gossiping when we remember that it is only by the grace of God that we are not going through the same things they are experiencing.

The words we speak are very powerful! Words are like dynamite. They can either be used powerfully for good, or they can be used powerfully for evil. Colossians 4:6 says, *"Let your conversation be always full of grace, seasoned with salt, so that you may know how to answer everyone."*

How can we speak with grace, seasoned with salt? When I was growing up, I never liked eating beef liver, but when I got married, I discovered I had a beef-

According to 1 Peter 5:5-6, how can we humble ourselves?

Tell about a time you spoke words "full of grace, seasoned with salt" into someone's life.

liver-eating wife! One day she served a beautiful meal. The meat smelled and tasted delicious. I said, "Honey, what is this? This meat is really good."

My wife, LaVerne, grinned from ear to ear. "It's liver!" She had seasoned it with the right kind of seasoning, and I liked it.

If you feel like you need to share correction with a struggling person that will help him or her to get back on the right course, season your speech with grace. In other words, say it in a way he or she can receive it. How we say it (with the right attitude) can be as important, if not more important, than what we actually say. Even a word of correction seasoned with grace will tell someone, "I care about you, and you can make it." The Bible tells us to speak the truth in love (Ephesians 4:15).

135 | God's grace through suffering

Down through the ages, man has asked the question, "How can God be good and allow us to suffer?" I like the simple answer given by a Nazi concentration camp inmate: "When you know God, you don't need to know why." The important issue is that God is involved in our sufferings. He came and entered our condition—became sin for us, so we might become the righteousness of God (2 Corinthians 5:21).

In fact, God tells us we are to expect suffering (John 16:1-4, 33; Titus 3:12). There are many reasons why we suffer—sometimes it is a consequence of our own actions, or because we live in a sinful world, or demonic affliction. If we allow Him, God will use suffering as a catalyst to spiritual growth in our lives.

Being faithful to God does not guarantee we will be free from trouble or pain in this life. Job, Joseph, David, Jeremiah— the list goes on—all suffered for a variety of reasons. Paul experienced many trials: he was put in chains, and experienced storms and shipwreck. Yet he still proclaimed that no tragedy could "separate us from the love of God" (Romans 8:35-39).

In addition, the Lord will not allow us to be tempted beyond what we can bear (1 Corinthians 10:13). He will provide a way out so that we can stand up under our trials. Our suffering actually opens us up to Christ's abundant grace, according to 2 Corinthians 12:9. *My grace is sufficient for you, for my power is made perfect in weakness....*

In our weakness or suffering, we can count on His strength to make us strong. In our times of tears, troubles, sickness, weaknesses and fears, we can be strong because we have exchanged His strength for our weakness. Our strength comes from His strength, and His alone.

Often, during times of trials and struggles, we find God's grace is very real to us. The Israelites found grace even in the desolate desert. *The people who survived the sword found grace in the wilderness...*(Jeremiah 31:2 NKJ).

God promised to bring good out of our sufferings (Romans 8:28). If we continue to love and obey Him, He will give us the grace necessary to bear our affliction. The Bible says Christians are like "jars of clay" who sometime experi-

What were the results?

How does suffering and grace work together, according to 2 Corinthians 12:9?

Biblical Foundations for Life

ence sadness and pain, yet because of the heavenly treasure (Jesus) within, they are not defeated. *But we have this treasure in jars of clay to show that this all-surpassing power is from God and not from us. We are hard pressed on every side, but not crushed; perplexed, but not in despair* (2 Corinthians 4:7-8).

In the midst of all the sufferings and pressures of life, we are sustained by an inner life that cannot be defeated! I have found Jesus to be very close in my life during periods of greatest darkness. Jesus' abundant grace comes in troubled times.

136 | Allow His grace to motivate you

What can happen when we "receive God's grace in vain"?

How are we reconciled back to God (2 Corinthians 5:20)?

I used to grumble and think, "God, why do You allow me to experience bad days? I'm serving You. It just doesn't seem right." The Bible tells us, "*In everything give thanks, for this is the will of God in Christ Jesus concerning you*" (1 Thessalonians 5:18). The Lord is teaching us to give thanks to Him in the midst of bad days. We need to "count our blessings." By God's grace, we have so much for which to be thankful.

One day I was replacing a window in our home. I got frustrated, became careless and broke the window. I realized then that I was trying to put the window in on my strength. I was frustrated and uptight and had moved out of the grace of God. When I admitted, "God, I cannot even put a window pane in without Your grace," do you know what happened? The next window went in with no problem. The grace of God affects even the practical day to day areas of our lives.

Some people love to go shopping. They may get a bargain and think, "This is great. It used to be $35 and I got it for $10! Man, wasn't I lucky?" Not really. It was the grace of God. The world system calls it luck. If you got a bargain while you were shopping, it was simply because of the grace of God on your life. The Lord wants us to thank and glorify Him for His grace to receive bargains! "Good luck" is the world system's replacement for the grace of God.

As a new Christian, I used to wonder why God would let my car break down so often. Now I realize that it was only by the grace of God my old car did not completely quit years earlier! You may ask, "Does God want our cars to break down?" No, of course not, but God wants us, in every situation, to allow His grace to motivate us.

Paul firmly believed that if we receive God's grace and later, by deliberate sin, abandon the faith, we can again be lost. *As God's fellow workers we urge you not to receive God's grace in vain. For he says, "In the time of my favor I heard you, and in the day of salvation I helped you." I tell you, now is the time of God's favor, now is the day of salvation* (2 Corinthians 6:1-2). The grace of God affects us every day! We need to be sure to never take it for granted! As the comic strip character Pogo once stated, "We have met the enemy, and he is us." Only we can block the grace of God from flowing through our lives. If we find ourselves outside the grace of God, we are urged to be reconciled to God (2 Corinthians 5:20). Now is the time to receive His grace and allow it to make a difference in our lives. Let's start today!

SPEAKING GRACE TO THE MOUNTAIN   PART 3

137 | Grace releases divine energy

Previously in this section on grace, we described how God's grace is present in our lives to save us—"the free unmerited favor of God on the undeserving and ill-deserving." Let's focus now on another side of the "grace coin." The other side of God's grace is defined as "the power and desire to do God's will." The grace of God is literally "divine energy" that the Holy Spirit releases in our lives.

Here is a clear example from the scriptures. Zerubbabel was faced with a formidable challenge. When Cyrus the king allowed the Jews to return to their own land, he appointed Zerubbabel to be the governor of the colony. One of Zerubbabel's first responsibilities was to lay the foundation for the new temple. However, due to opposition from the enemies of the Jews, the work on this project soon ceased.

Doesn't that sound familiar? We get a vision from the Lord or begin to take a direction in life and before long we receive opposition and become discouraged and quit. Or maybe we don't quit, but we seem to find it impossible to complete the task that we believe the Lord has laid before us. This is where grace comes in!

One day Zechariah the prophet has a vision from the Lord. As he describes his vision in Zechariah chapter 4:6-7, an angel of the Lord gives Zechariah a prophetic message for Zerubbabel. *"Not by might nor by power, but by my Spirit,"* says the Lord of Hosts. *"Who are you, O great mountain? Before Zerubbabel you shall become a plain! And he shall bring forth the capstone with shouts of Grace, grace to it!"* (NKJ)

The work on the temple was resumed and completed four years later. The Lord gave them "divine energy," and the circumstances supernaturally changed for them to complete the entire project! That which seemed impossible literally happened before their very eyes. They no longer trusted in their own ability, but in the grace of God. As they released divine energy by shouting, "Grace, grace," the *mountain* before them became a *great plain*. They were convinced that the temple was built not by military might, or by political power or human strength, but by the Spirit of the Lord. They had experienced the grace of God!

We can only do God's work if we are enabled by the Holy Spirit. I dare you to apply this scriptural principle to your life. The next time a mountain of impossibility stares you in the face, shout "Grace, grace" to it. See the mountain leveled as you take an act of simple faith and shout "Grace, grace" in the face of the devil. You will find your focus changing from your ability (or lack of ability) to His ability.

Some time ago, I ministered to a group of university student leaders. We stood together and proclaimed "Grace, grace" over every university campus represented at the conference. Faith arose in our hearts as our dependency was no longer in our own strategies and abilities but in the living God.

Explain "divine energy." How is it at work in your life?

I find it refreshing to walk into our offices and hear staff persons declaring "Grace, grace" in the midst of deadlines that seem impossible to meet. My faith is increased when fathers proclaim "Grace, grace" over their families. Striving is replaced by a sense of peace and rest in the Lord.

When the children of Israel shouted "Grace, grace" to the temple, they did not sit around and wait for the walls to be built by an angel. They had a renewed sense that, as they worked together fulfilling the plan of God, it was not by their own might or power, but by the Spirit of the Lord that the walls were being built. As we proclaim "Grace, grace" over our lives and situations, we do not receive a license to be lazy. Instead, we receive divine energy to fulfill the purposes of God for our lives.

138 | Speak grace to impossible situations

How does God respond to our shouting "grace, grace" to the mountains of impossibility that stare us in the face?

Do you feel foolish doing that?

Why is it important to do it?

Skeptics may say, "What does shouting 'Grace, grace' have to do with God acting on our behalf? It seems so foolish." The truth is that the wisdom of God and the wisdom of the world are at odds. *For the message of the cross is foolishness to those who are perishing, but to us who are being saved it is the power of God* (1 Corinthians 1:18).

The wisdom of the world is a wisdom that excludes God and emphasizes our ability to take care of things ourselves. God's wisdom emphasizes a complete dependency on God and His grace. God honors this dependency and obedience to Him.

Why did the army advance only when Moses held up his arms in the battle with the Amalekites? It made absolutely no sense to the natural mind, but Moses was being obedient to his God (Exodus 17).

Jehoash, the king of Israel, came to Elisha, the prophet, for help because the Israelite army faced a massive Aramean army. It seemed like an impossible situation. Elisha instructed King Jehoash to take a bow and some arrows and open the east window. Then Elisha told him to shoot and declared that they would have victory. In addition, the prophet told Jehoash to "strike the ground." The king struck the ground three times and stopped. The prophet Elisha was angry with the king, "You should have struck the ground five or six times; then you would have defeated Aram and completely destroyed it. But now you will defeat it only three times" (2 Kings 13:19). It happened just as the prophet said. King Jehoash showed that he lacked the commitment and faith necessary for the Lord to fulfill His promise. Consequently, he could not completely defeat the Arameans.

What does striking the ground with arrows have to do with winning battles? Nothing, unless the Lord instructs us to do it. In the same way Elisha instructed King Jehoash to strike the ground with arrows, I believe the Lord is calling His people to be obedient and shout "Grace, grace" to situations that seem impossible to them.

139 | We receive grace to reign in life!

A king reigns in a nation, and as God's children, we are promised to reign in life! How do we reign? We can reign, or be victorious, only by His grace. We receive grace to reign in life...*those who receive God's abundant provision of grace and of the gift of righteousness reign in life through the one man, Jesus Christ* (Romans 5:17).

This promise is for all of us! Those who receive God's overflowing grace and the free gift of righteousness will reign as kings in life. We are called to live above the circumstances, difficulties and problems because reigning comes from understanding the grace of God.

We can be victorious in every area of life—in our homes, in school, in our cell groups and churches and in our places of business. God has given us supernatural provision to live an overcomer's life. God gives us an abundance of grace! We do not deserve any of it, but the Lord pours it on us anyway!

Are you struggling with a habit that you have tried to break free from? Speak "Grace, grace" to it! Receive the divine energy that is needed to break free forever. Are you struggling in business, school or family relationships? Speak "Grace, grace" to the area of your life that seems like an impossible mountain to cross.

I had the privilege of addressing the students of Lifeway School in New Zealand where a proposed building project had come to a halt due to a lack of finances. Along with the students and the leadership of the school, we positioned ourselves toward the plot of land that was undeveloped and shouted, "Grace, grace." Within the next eight weeks, the school experienced a series of financial miracles, and the expansion of the facilities got underway. The only explanation was the grace of God!

There are times when I'm speaking or counseling someone, and after I leave, I'll feel discouraged. Satan often tries to place condemnation on us so he can defeat us by capitalizing on the way we feel or the blunders we made. We must live by faith, not by our feelings. When things go bad, whether in our business, school, community, home, or church, we must never forget that God's grace gives us divine energy to push on through. When things are fine, we must not forget that it is only by God's grace that we are experiencing victory to reign in life!

140 | God gives gifts according to grace

God's grace is so rich and multifaceted that a different aspect of it can be manifested through every believer. God gives gifts, inward motivations and abilities to believers so they may use them to benefit the rest of the body of Christ. These "grace gifts" are given to enable us to minister to others. *Having then gifts differing according to the grace that is given to us, let us use them...*(Romans 12:6a NKJ)

...If a man's gift is prophesying, let him use it in proportion to his faith. If it is serving, let him serve; if it is teaching, let him teach; if it is encouraging, let him encourage; if it is contributing to the needs of others, let him give generously; if it

---

According to Romans 5:17, how do we get the power to reign as kings in this life?

List struggles you are having, and shout "grace" to them.

What do you expect to happen?

Biblical Foundations for Life

What gifts has God given you to minister to others?

_____
_____
_____
_____

What gifts from God do others use to minister to you?

_____
_____
_____
_____

Do you feel better than other people you know? Worse?

_____
_____
_____
_____

When we compare ourselves to others, what happens?

_____
_____
_____
_____
_____

is leadership, let him govern diligently; if it is showing mercy, let him do it cheerfully (Romans 12:6b-8).

Have you ever witnessed to somebody and sensed the Holy Spirit moving through you as the right words came flowing from your mouth? This was simply the grace of God on your life as you shared the gospel. Do you enjoy serving? God has given you the desire and ability to give practical assistance to others. Teaching is the ability to examine God's Word and proclaim its truth so people grow in godliness. We should use the gift(s) to go about fulfilling God's purposes for our lives according to what He has given us. Each gift and ability that we have is a result of God's grace. He has given us these gifts and blessings in order to be a blessing and to serve others. *Each one should use whatever gift he has received to serve others, faithfully administering God's grace in its various forms* (1 Peter 4:10).

The gifts the Lord gives to us are divine abilities that we use to help and bless others. If you have the gift of prophecy, use it to speak encouragement and conviction in someone's life. If you have an inward motivation to give, those around you will be blessed by your financial help. When you operate in your gift(s), you are being used of the Lord to express His grace to others.

141 | Comparing is not wise

Remember the grape-picking laborers in Matthew 20? They complained and wondered why everyone got paid the same for varying hours of labor because they didn't understand the grace of God. If we question why God gives some people greater talents and abilities than others, we have not understood the grace of God. If we think we are a better worship leader than Jim or a better teacher than Sally, we are falling short of God's grace.

It is so important to refrain from comparing ourselves with others. We should only compare ourselves with the Word of God and allow the Word to dwell in us so we can live out the principles of grace in our lives. If we feel like we are doing better than others, we fall into pride. If we feel like we are doing worse than those around us, we can suffer from feelings of inferiority. When we compare ourselves to others, we are not wise, according to God's Word in 2 Corinthians 10:12. *We do not dare to classify or compare ourselves with some who commend themselves. When they measure themselves by themselves and compare themselves with themselves, they are not wise.* Neither pride or inferiority are grace-filled responses.

When God uses someone else for a certain ministry or responsibility and we are not called into action, how do we respond? When we begin to compare ourselves to other people, we are falling short of the grace of God. God is God. He knows best what we need. He may give somebody one gift and another a different type of gift. Understanding and walking in the grace of God will permeate our total being and way of thinking. It changes our attitudes, causing us to want to grow up spiritually so that we can help and serve those around us.

142 | Impart grace to others

God has called you to impart His grace everywhere you go— work, school, home or to other believers in your small group. He has called you to impart grace to people and see them built up. *Do not let any unwholesome talk come out of your mouths, but only what is helpful for building others up according to their needs, that it may benefit those who listen* (Ephesians 4:29).

When we speak, we should say things that build people up so that we can impart grace (divine energy) into their lives. Words of encouragement will minister to others the grace that God has placed in our lives. When you thank your spouse, your parents or another family member, you are ministering the grace of God to them. Thank your boss for his oversight at work. You are ministering the grace of God. Maybe you are a boss. You need to give encouragement to the people who work for you. You are ministering the grace of God to them.

Why not encourage your small group leader and minister grace to him or her? Encourage your leaders and thank them for what they have done. The grace of God should be the underlying attitude in everything we do. The book of Acts tells us that "much grace" was on the apostles. *With great power the apostles continued to testify to the resurrection of the Lord Jesus, and much grace was upon them all* (Acts 4:33).

We need a dose of God's "much grace" each day. John, the apostle, tells us that grace and truth come through Jesus Christ (John 1:17). Jesus has already granted us grace for our salvation. He is waiting for us to acknowledge Him and His grace so that we can experience His divine energy in our everyday living!

Why should we be careful not to allow discouraging words to come out of our mouths? Think of some people to whom the Lord may be asking you to minister His grace today, and do it!

Describe a time you imparted grace into someone's life.

Did you see immediate results or not?

143 | All credit to God

We will never take credit for what God does if we understand His grace. For example, I have had the privilege of ministering to many people throughout the world in the past few years. It has been such a blessing to see people's lives changed by the power of God. I could never take credit for that. I know it is only by the grace of God I can minister the good news of Jesus Christ.

The Bible tells us we are all competent ministers (2 Corinthians 3:5); we are called to help other people and minister in Jesus' name. It's not us ministering to others in our own strength, but God who lives inside of us ministering through us. You and I are called to be channels of God's love.

Electric wire is a channel for electric power. We don't see an electric line and think, "What a beautiful wire." No, we are just thankful for the power that comes through the wire. Likewise, we are channels of the Holy Spirit, and we can never take credit for anything that God does. We must allow His grace and power to flow from our lives. We have been chosen as heirs of Christ to carry His banner because...*having been justified by his grace, we might become heirs*

Biblical Foundations for Life

List areas of your life that need grace applied to them.

having the hope of eternal life (Titus 3:7). What an awesome privilege—of all the people in the world, He has chosen you and me!

I encourage you to begin to shout "Grace, grace" to the mountains in your life. Remember Zerubbabel? He knew that the grace of God would be released and the people would get the job completed quickly, effectively and efficiently if he was obedient. So the people shouted, "Grace, grace" to the temple, and it was completed, causing great excitement among the people. They realized that it wasn't their strength but the strength of God's grace working through them.

No matter what situation you find yourself in, you need to learn to speak "Grace, grace" to it. If you have a habit you want to conquer, but have repeatedly fallen flat on your face, begin to speak "grace" to that situation. Maybe you are a business person and struggling financially. Begin to speak grace to your business. Perhaps you are encouraging a new believer who is dealing with some area of his or her life. Begin to speak grace to that area. Is there a conflict in your marriage? Maybe you are a single person and have a special need. Begin to speak grace to your life. Maybe your prayer life needs revitalizing. Speak grace to your prayer life.

The commander in chief of the armies of heaven is waiting for us to declare "Grace, grace" over our families, our churches, our cities and our nations. The kingdoms of this world shall become the kingdoms of our Lord and of His Christ, and He shall reign forever and ever! (Revelation 11:15).

"Grace, grace!"

GRACE FOR EVERYDAY LIVING   PART 4

144 | Grow in grace

When I was young in the Lord, I did not understand grace at all. I thought God really owed me something. "Look, God," I said, "I've given you my life. I've given you everything. I've given you my family. It all belongs to you." I was working sixty hours on a job in addition to being involved with a full-time youth ministry. I thought, "God, you have to take care of my family. You have to take care of my relationship with my wife. After all, I'm serving you; I'm giving you my life." I later realized that God didn't owe me anything. God did not owe me a strong marriage or a healthy family. But even though I did not deserve it, God wanted to give me a strong marriage and family because of His awesome grace.

Does God owe us anything because we serve Him?

The grace of God will affect every area of your life. We can do absolutely nothing except by the grace of God. Do we deserve a bright, sunny, summer day? No. But we receive the sunshine because of the grace of God. We stand in a position for the sun to shine on us, and when we see the sun, we receive it. As Christians, we need to get into a position to receive the grace of God in our lives. However, growing in grace is a process. It doesn't just happen overnight. *But grow in the grace and knowledge of our Lord and Savior Jesus Christ. To him be glory both now and forever! Amen* (2 Peter 3:18).

Tell of ways you have grown in the grace of God.

God gives us grace to grow every step of the way if we walk in obedience to Him. We were saved because of God's grace through faith (Ephesians 2:5, 8) and we continue to receive grace to live the Christian life. Now let's look at several areas in our daily lives that God wants to invade and keep permeating with His grace.

145 | The fruit of the Spirit

How, then, do we grow in grace? The Spirit and our sinful nature are at war with each other. Since the sinful nature remains within us after our conversion and is our deadly enemy (Romans 8:6-8, 13; Galatians 5:1, 21), it must be resisted and put to death in a continual warfare that we wage through the power of the Holy Spirit (Romans 8:4-14). If we do not fight a battle against our sinful nature and continue to practice the acts of the sinful nature, the Bible says we cannot inherit God's kingdom (Galatians 5:21). According to Galatians 5:19-21, our sinful nature causes us to fall into things as sexual immorality, impurity, debauchery, idolatry, witchcraft, hatred, discord, jealousy, fits of rage, selfish ambition, dissensions, factions, envy, drunkenness, and orgies.

What happens to our sinful nature when we begin to fellowship with God (Galatians 5:22-26)?

Thank God for His grace because this list of the acts of our sinful nature in Galatians continues on to say that when we fellowship with God, He produces the fruit of the Spirit in our lives. *But the fruit of the Spirit is love, joy, peace, patience, kindness, goodness, faithfulness, gentleness and self-control...Those who belong to Christ Jesus have crucified the sinful nature with its passions and desires. Since we live by the Spirit, let us keep in step with the Spirit* (Galatians 5:22-25).

Biblical Foundations for Life

How does the fruit of the Spirit cause us to grow in grace?

The contrast between the life-style of the Spirit-filled Christian and one who is controlled by his sinful nature is clear. Our human nature with its corrupt desires is our "sinful nature."

When we depend on God's grace to live a life-style of love, joy, peace, patience, kindness, goodness, faithfulness, gentleness and self-control, we will experience these virtues or "fruits" in our lives. When we allow the Holy Spirit to direct our lives, sin's power is destroyed. We can then walk in fellowship with God, and by His grace, He will produce the fruit of the Spirit to help us live victoriously in every area of our lives.

146 | Grace to live sexually pure

Standards for sexual morality are clear in God's Word. Believers must live morally and sexually pure lives, according to Hebrews 13:4. *"Marriage should be honored by all, and the marriage bed kept pure, for God will judge the adulterer and all the sexually immoral."* The word pure in the Greek means to be free from all that which is lewd. It suggests refraining from all acts and thoughts that incite desire not in accordance with one's virginity or one's marriage vows. It stresses restraint and avoidance of all sexual actions and excitements that would defile our purity before God. It includes controlling our own bodies *"in a way that is holy and honorable"* (1 Thessalonians 4:4), and not in *"passionate lust"* (4:5). This scriptural instruction is for both those who are single and those who are married.

Why is it important to live a sexually pure life (Hebrews 13:4)?

Sexual intimacy has boundaries. It is reserved for the marriage relationship when a man and a woman become one. In that arena, God blesses the relationship with the physical and emotional pleasures that result.

Premarital sex is condemned in the Bible. Self-control is a fruit of the Spirit that contrasts with getting involved in sexual gratification with someone who is not one's marriage partner...*Do not arouse or awaken love until it so desires* (Song of Songs 2:7). This phrase occurs two more times in the Song of Songs (3:5; 8:4) where the Shulammite woman says she does not want physical intimacy until she and Solomon are married. Virginity until marriage is God's sexual standard of purity for men and women.

Sometimes Christians struggle with same sex attraction. Understanding and wise guidance can make the difference in helping those attracted to the same sex to avoid homosexual activity altogether. Those who are caught in sin (according to Galatians 6:1) need to be restored in a spirit of compassion and gentleness. As Christians, we must be ministers of God's transforming grace toward those living a gay lifestyle and those struggling with its temptations. The Bible provides hope for all of us. We have all been sinners, and have missed the mark. Everyone is equally in need of God's grace. We must love people as we point them toward the victorious life that is possible through Jesus Christ.

Those living a homosexual lifestyle have sometimes been excluded and persecuted by a culture that hypocritically glorifies other forms of sexual sin. A gay person who sins should not be treated differently from those who have fallen victim to other types of sin. Homosexual practice is called sin (Romans 1:26-27;

1 Timothy 1:9-10), but sin is by no means unique to those who practice sin as homosexuals. We are all sinners. Paul's words in 1 Corinthians 6:9-11 describes homosexuality as a sin, but he calls upon Christians to treat the homosexual as a person who is in need of God's grace, forgiveness, and transformation.

Or do you not know that the unrighteous will not inherit the kingdom of God? Do not be deceived: neither the sexually immoral, nor idolaters, nor adulterers, nor men who practice homosexuality, nor thieves, nor the greedy, nor drunkards, nor revilers, nor swindlers will inherit the kingdom of God. And such were some of you. But you were washed, you were sanctified, you were justified in the name of the Lord Jesus Christ and by the Spirit of our God. (1 Corinthians 6:9-11 ESV). Remember, temptation is not sin. We are all tempted to sin, but it is only when we dwell on it or act on it that it becomes sin. God's grace is available for everyone!

147 | Grace for marriage

Marriage is God's idea. Genesis 2:24 implies that marriage is an exclusive relationship (a man...his wife), which is publicly acknowledged (leaves his parents), permanent (cleaves to his wife), and consummated by having sexual relations (they will become one flesh). The marriage bond is a divine covenant that is intended to last for life. Fidelity, support and mutual sharing as the husband and wife build the life of Christ in each other are at the center of the relationship.

God gave man rulership over every living creature (Genesis 1:28). He then placed man in the Garden of Eden to care for His creation (Genesis 2:15). He created order so that things would not be in chaos in the world. The same is true of marriage. The scriptural basis for order in Christian marriage is found in Ephesians 5:21-33. *Submit to one another out of reverence for Christ. Wives, submit to your husbands as to the Lord. For the husband is the head of the wife as Christ is the head of the church, his body, of which he is the Savior...In this same way, husbands ought to love their wives as their own bodies. He who loves his wife loves himself. After all, no one ever hated his own body, but he feeds and cares for it, just as Christ does the church—for we are members of his body. "For this reason a man will leave his father and mother and be united to his wife, and the two will become one flesh." This is a profound mystery—but I am talking about Christ and the church. However, each one of you also must love his wife as he loves himself, and the wife must respect her husband.*

Husbands and wives need to submit to each other in love. This scripture says that the husband is positionally the "head" of the wife which means he is the responsible one. Responsibility, however, does not mean control. In today's world where domestic violence is a huge problem, we can never think that physical or verbal abuse is about a lack of submission. Selfishness and control is not a form of headship. Any kind of abuse in marriage, including physical, emotional, spiritual or sexual is wrong. If physical abuse occurs, a spouse should seek a safe place.

Marriage is instituted by God so that men and women can mutually complete each other. Marriage takes two people, working hard at nourishing this bond. Sadly, in today's world, the incidence of divorce has reached epidemic proportions.

How much should a husband love his wife, according to Ephesians 5:21-33?

Biblical Foundations for Life

What about a marriage that has failed? Read the next section for some answers.

148 | Grace when a marriage fails

Reconciliation lies at the very heart of Christianity. Although scripture cites two biblical grounds for divorce, every effort should be made to restore a marriage. Paul, the apostle wrote to the Corinthian church, *"Are you married? Do not seek a divorce..."* (1 Corinthians 7:27a).

When the Pharisees asked Jesus about the grounds for divorce, He referred them to the original institution of marriage (Matthew 19:3-8) stressing that marriage is intended for life. God hates divorce (Malachi 2:13-16). Divorce is devastating. It has an effect, not on just two people, but their children and families. Reconciliation in marriage is God's desire (1 Corinthians 7:12-14). However, sometimes reconciliation is not possible. In this case, God's Word cites two reasons when divorce is permitted—for marital unfaithfulness (Matthew 5:31-32; 19:9) or abandonment (1 Corinthians 7:15-16).

Failure in marriage often has *selfishness* as its roots. We want what we want! Regardless of the reasons, we have to face the facts: today's world is full of broken marriages. We must minister with compassion to those facing a failed marriage.

Those going through a divorce have experienced a breakdown in trust. At this crucial and heartbreaking time, a person going through a divorce needs prayerful accountability with trusted church leadership or counselors. They will need to deal with trust and fear issues. (How can I ever trust a spouse again? What will keep another marriage from failing?)

Some of the most heroic people are those who have been sinned against by having to experience abandonment, separation, and/or divorce unwillingly. These persons have not sinned, but feel rejected by many in the church today. Jesus does not abandon, separate from (reject), or divorce those who are His. During these times, His grace will increase! *Marriage should be honored by all, and the marriage bed kept pure, for God will judge the adulterer and all the sexually immoral...God has said, "Never will I leave you; never will I forsake you." So we say with confidence, "The Lord is my helper; I will not be afraid. What can man do to me?"* (Hebrews 13:4-6).

149 | Grace for singles

We said earlier that sex is for marriage only. What does the Bible say about singleness? The world may say that a human cannot live without sexual experience but the Bible disagrees. A single person can be fulfilled and live without sexual experience. Jesus referred to singleness as a divine vocation in Matthew 19:12. *Others have renounced marriage because of the kingdom of heaven. The one who can accept this should accept it.*

The apostle Paul said that one of the blessings of singleness is that it releases people to give their undivided devotion to Jesus. *I would like you to be free from concern. An unmarried man is concerned about the Lord's affairs—how he can please the Lord. But a married man is concerned about the affairs of this world-*

How can we minister with compassion to a person going through a divorce?

Who will never leave us, according to Hebrews 13:4-6?

how he can please his wife—and his interests are divided. An unmarried woman or virgin is concerned about the Lord's affairs: Her aim is to be devoted to the Lord in both body and spirit. But a married woman is concerned about the affairs of this world—how she can please her husband. I am saying this for your own good, not to restrict you, but that you may live in a right way in undivided devotion to the Lord (1 Corinthians 7:32-35).

He also says that both singleness and marriage are a gift of God's grace. *I wish that all men were as I am. But each man has his own gift from God; one has this gift, another has that* (1 Corinthians 7:7). Both the married person and unmarried will receive grace for the state in which they find themselves.

Unmarried people may be quite lonely at times, but God always gives the grace to live in obedience to Him. If you're single, you are not half a person. You are whole in Christ. He wants you to be fulfilled as a single person, and He will give you the grace.

150 | Grace is available; don't miss it!

The writer of Hebrews 12:15 warns believers that they should not miss God's grace. *See to it that no one misses the grace of God....* We can miss God's grace when we try to live the Christian life by our own efforts. In Galatians 5:3-4, Paul says the Galatians had moved from a faith in Christ to legalistic observances of the law. Thus, they had...*fallen away from grace* (v.5).

Sometimes people say of someone who hurt them, "He really hurt my feelings." If we allow our hurt feelings to control our lives, we are not living in the realm of God's grace. Who says everyone should be nice to us? If we are misunderstood, the only reason it is not much worse is because of the grace of God. If we are hurt, we are demanding our own rights. But we do not have rights. They were nailed to the cross two thousand years ago. We no longer have a *right* to not get hurt. However, we do have *privileges* whereby we can live for God and experience a victorious life. These privileges we have are the result of the grace of God.

Let it be clear that as Christians we do have rights against the devil. The Bible teaches us that we have spiritual rights as we stand against the devil to rebuke him in the name of Jesus. We have the right to use the name of Jesus and the blood of Christ and the Word of God. But we need to realize that even that right is available because of the grace of God.

Often when I meet parents who have raised godly families, I ask them, "How did you do it?" I have not been surprised by their answer. They tell me it was simply the grace of God. If we think we deserve godly children, a good job and good friends because we have done all the right things, we are simply wrong!

I am thankful that God has given me a wonderful family and marriage. But it is not because of anything that I have done. I am simply a recipient of the grace of God that I have received from Him as a free gift. From start to finish, we must live our lives in God's grace. God's grace through faith brings salvation to us at the start of our Christian lives and continues giving us the ability to resist sin. Grace is a wonderful gift that God gives because He loves us!

Biblical Foundations for Life

What is an advantage of being single, according to 1 Corinthians 7:32-35?

How can we miss the grace of God?

Explain the difference between having rights and privileges.

151 | Let's talk about being dead to sin

Romans 6:1-2, 11-12 explains, *"What shall we say, then? Shall we go on sinning so that grace may increase? By no means! We are those who have died to sin; how can we live in it any longer? In the same way, count yourselves dead to sin but alive to God in Christ Jesus. Therefore do not let sin reign in your mortal body so that you obey its evil desires."*

Since sin is rampant in the world, and since grace is greater than sin, should we sin so that God pours out more grace? Of course not!

Grace and humility are related. Romans 12:3 tells us, *"For by the grace given me I say to every one of you: Do not think of yourself more highly than you ought, but rather think of yourself with sober judgment, in accordance with the faith God has distributed to each of you."*

Paul is writing to the church at Rome and admits that it is only through God's grace that he instructs them in humility.

As Christ increases in you, you will decrease. This is the opposite of pride, which elevates self over God. How do you judge yourself to be in relation to others? The Lord wants us to see ourselves in a sober way, recognizing that we are only products of God's grace.

Have you died to sin or are you still a slave to sin? What does the Bible tell us to do about sin that would try to creep into our lives?

Should we sin so that God pours out more grace?

152 | Receiving God's grace in your life

You can completely trust God's power to defeat your enemies. The Word of God says, *"The God of peace will soon crush Satan under your feet. The grace of our Lord Jesus be with you"* (Romans 16:20).

Receive God's grace when it is spoken over you, and, in turn, speak it over the lives of others. The grace of God will affect every area of your life. We can do absolutely nothing except by the grace of God. Do we deserve everything to go right in our lives? No. But we receive His blessings because of the grace of God. We stand in a position for the grace of God to shine on our lives, and we receive it by faith.

As believers in Christ, we need to get into a position to receive the grace of God in our lives. Growing in grace is a process. It doesn't just happen overnight. The scriptures tell us, *"But grow in the grace and knowledge of our Lord and Savior Jesus Christ. To him be glory both now and forever! Amen"* (2 Peter 3:18).

God gives us grace to grow every step of the way as we walk in obedience to Him. What is the biggest struggle you are currently facing in your life? God has given you an abundance of grace to live victoriously in this area of your life today! Receive His grace and declare "grace, grace" over this area of your life and watch what the Lord does!

What is the biggest struggle you are currently facing in your life that needs God's grace?

FOUNDATION 6

Freedom from the Curse

153 | Introduction to foundation 6

In this sixth Biblical Foundation teaching, Freedom From the Curse, we learn that when Adam and Even chose to believe the lies of the devil in the Garden of Eden and disobeyed God, we now live in a "cursed" or "fallen" world. In the fall of Adam, sin gained entrance into the human race. The Bible tells us in 1 John 3:8 that *"...the reason the Son of God appeared was to destroy the devil's work."*

We will take a closer look at all that is involved in the curse and how to be freed spiritually, physically, and emotionally from its bondage. Although sin has cursed mankind, Christ provides everything we need to defeat both sin and the devil! Jesus came to give us an abundant, victorious life (John 10:10).

God never intended for murder, starvation, poverty, wars, or disease to be a part of His plan. God does not cause the evil that happens to us in this world. However, God is sovereign and allows the evil in the world to happen under His permissive will. At times He directly intervenes, but often He allows bad things to happen even though He does not desire it. Evil often continues in this world because the devil continues to operate through individuals who do not serve God and have no power over the devil to resist evil.

The Lord gives us authority over the devil who has come to steal, to kill, and to destroy. Jesus has come that we may have life, and that we may have it more abundantly.

We are going to continue to learn from the Word of God how we can find freedom over the works of darkness and help others find this same freedom.

How did sin gain entrance into the human race?

Biblical Foundations for Life

PART 1

We are born with an impulse toward sin

Romans 5:19; 1:21;7:24
Genesis 6:5,12; 8:21
Psalms 14:1-3; Jeremiah 17:9
Mark 7:21-22
1 Corinthians 2:14
Galatians 5:19; Ephesians

How did sin curse this world (Romans 5:12)?

_____
_____
_____
_____

Why was the ground cursed in Genesis 3:17?

_____
_____
_____
_____

What happened as a result (Romans 6:23)?

_____
_____
_____
_____

WHAT IS A CURSE?

154 | Sin enters a perfect world and changes it forever

God had a perfect plan for this world. His plan for the human race, starting with Adam and Eve, was that all of creation would be blessed. There would be no sickness, disease or poverty. There would be only beauty, health, and abundance. However, Adam and Eve disobeyed the commandment God gave them about the tree of the knowledge of good and evil, and sin entered the world. They trusted in themselves and in their own ability to make a decision that seemed right in their eyes instead of obeying God, and they made a fatal mistake. This mistake has affected all of us. *Therefore, just as sin entered the world through one man, and death through sin, and in this way death came to all men, because all sinned* (Romans 5:12).

Due to Adam and Eve's disobedience to the Lord when they chose to believe the lies of the devil, we now live in a "cursed or fallen" world. In the fall of Adam, sin gained entrance into the human race. All humans are now born into the world with an impulse toward sin and evil. Each of us comes into the world with a sinful nature and has the natural tendency to go our own selfish way with little concern for God or others (Romans 8:5-8).

155 | Satan now causes havoc in the world

Because of what Adam and Eve did by breaking the law God gave them, the ground (nature) was cursed. God told Adam, "*...cursed is the ground because of you; through painful toil you will eat of it all the days of your life*" (Genesis 3:17b). Adam would now have to work with sweat and toil in order to provide for himself, and eventually death would come to him and his offspring.

Sin and its curse began to increase in the world, and the world experienced the "wages" of this sin. *The wages which sin pays is death* (Romans 6:23 Amplified). This "death" includes all the heartaches and miseries that come from sin. Sin brings destruction into every area of our human existence.

We can see sin's destruction evidenced in the misery people experience in today's world—hundreds die from AIDS every week, and hundreds more are infected by this killer virus...a relative or friend may suddenly have a heart attack...another may die of cancer...brutal gang rapes, murder, violence...there seems to be an upsurge of atrocious crimes being committed daily. Who is responsible for these horrors? If God really cares, some people ask, why are people starving in parts of the world? I believe it all boils down to the fact that we are constantly faced with the power and activity of Satan in this world in one way or another. From the beginning of time, he has caused havoc in the world. Satan intends to afflict us with his lies and treachery. Down through the ages, Satan and his demons have continued to plague mankind as a result of the initial curse.

In this book, we will take a closer look at all that is involved in the curse and how to be freed from its bondage(s). Although sin has cursed mankind, praise God, Christ provided everything we need to defeat sin and Satan!

156 | Jesus reigns over the devil

Satan is the father of sin and the god of this world system. He brought sin into the world and tries to entice people to all sorts of evil. He controls this present evil age because the world is in rebellion against God's rule and enslaved to Satan (2 Corinthians 4:4; Luke 13:16; Galatians 1:4; Ephesians 6:12; Hebrews 2:14). But the glorious, good news is that Jesus came to destroy the works of the devil! He came to dissolve the power, influence and connection of sin in our lives. The Bible tells us in 1 John 3:8 that *"...the reason the Son of God appeared was to destroy the devil's work."*

Jesus has undertaken a holy war against Satan who wants to ruin the work of God in this world. This was Jesus' purpose for coming to the earth two thousand years ago. Jesus' plan is to destroy the works of the devil in our lives! He came to establish God's kingdom in our hearts and deliver us from Satan's dominion. By his death and resurrection, Christ initiated the defeat of Satan which will eventually culminate in complete and total victory over Satan at the end of this age. Because of Jesus, we do not have to fear the curse and its effects. Jesus is more powerful than Satan! Jesus acknowledges His supreme power over the devil, the ruler of this world, in John 14:30 when He says, *"...the prince of this world is coming. He has no hold on me."*

Jesus also says, *"You, dear children, are from God and have overcome them, because the one who is in you is greater than the one who is in the world"* (1 John 4:4).

The Holy Spirit, who lives in every Christian, is greater and more powerful than the devil and his demons who are in the world. He will fight our battles and give us the victory. We can overcome the devil and his evil schemes in this world because we have been given the victory through Jesus!

157 | Jesus became a curse for us

We can be completely free from the curse of breaking God's law. We can be free from the devil's lies over our lives because of what Christ did on the cross. The Bible says He redeemed us from the curse. *Christ redeemed us from the curse of the law by becoming a curse for us, for it is written: "Cursed is everyone who is hung on a tree"* (Galatians 3:13).

When the mob called for Jesus to be crucified, they wanted Him identified as a cursed person because according to Jewish law, anyone who hung on a tree was under God's curse (Deuteronomy 21:23). So Jesus, in our behalf, was crucified and became a curse for us. He was crowned with a crown of thorns, the very symbol of sin and guilt, because he is the Lamb of God that takes away the sin of the world! Every curse over our lives was placed on Jesus when He hung on the cross nearly two thousand years ago! We are redeemed and set free of the curse!

The word *redeemed* means *to buy back*. I've heard the story of a young boy, who after spending many hours constructing a little boat, took it out on the lake to sail it. With a long string attached to the boat, the boy was having a great time

---

God provides what we need to defeat sin and Satan

1 John 4:4; 5:4-5; Revelation 3:21
Romans 6:1-14; Colossians 2:6-15
Hebrews 2:14-15; Ephesians 6:10

Why did Jesus come, according to 1 John 3:8?

How does Jesus destroy the works of the devil in our lives?

How can we be free of the curse of the law (Galatians 3:13)?

Biblical Foundations for Life

What does it mean to be redeemed?

as the boat floated and bobbed. Suddenly, the string tore. In an instant, he lost his prized possession and could only watch as the boat headed downstream where it eventually exited into the river. He thought it was gone forever.

Several years later, this lad entered a pawn shop in a town downstream from where he grew up. He spotted the boat that he had built years before. The young man approached the storekeeper and said, "This is my boat. My initials are carved on the bottom."

The owner said, "Well, I'm sorry, but somebody brought that boat into my store and I bought it from him. You'll need to pay me for it." The young man immediately paid the shopkeeper so he could buy back his cherished boat.

This is a picture of what God did for us. First of all, God made you and me. We went our own way, He redeemed us and bought us back again. By the blood that Jesus shed on the cross two thousand years ago, we have been redeemed (or bought back) from the curse of breaking God's law (sin) that was over our lives.

Jesus broke the curse, but we must seek the freedom. The devil can keep the curse over people's lives when they do not know that Jesus has given them authority to break the curse or when they do not walk in the authority of Christ who sets them free.

158 | People suffer because our planet was turned over to the powers of darkness

If we have been redeemed and set free, why then, along with the rest of mankind, do Christians suffer financial loss, serious illness, emotional upheaval and other problems? The reason people suffer varies greatly. In this section, we are going to take a look at the first of three general reasons why people suffer in this world.

Jesus once healed a man who was blind from birth (John 9:1-3). The disciples asked Jesus, "Who sinned, this man or his parents, that he was born blind?" Jesus answered that neither the man nor his parents had sinned. Why had he suffered then? It was through no fault of his own that he was born blind. Why do people often find themselves afflicted in some way or another with no apparent fault of their own?

We have to go back to the fact that there is a curse in the world. We learned earlier that sin entered the world through the "curse of the law." The curse of the law is God's label for all the distresses experienced as a result of mankind's initial sin. Since the time that Adam and Eve disobeyed God (broke His law or sinned), *we live on a planet that was turned over to the powers of darkness.* Ever since that time, the world has suffered under Satan's rule. Believers along with nonbelievers experience suffering as an ongoing consequence of the fall of Adam and Eve. Much of what happens often is simply the result of life in a fallen world. For example, cancer and other diseases may be the result of an unhealthy diet of highly processed foods, foods that have lost their food value due to pesticides, preservatives, and chemicals.

Imagine this scenario. A beautiful garden is given to an evil landlord. What was once filled with beautiful flowers, plants, and food, is soon filled with thistles and thorns. One day a kind and caring man pays a great price and purchases the garden. He gives it back to the former caretakers and gives them clear instructions to make it beautiful and profitable again. Bit by bit, with much hard work, the garden becomes alive. This is what Jesus did for mankind! He paid the great price of His own life in order to purchase back the world. Jesus went to the cross to initiate the defeat of Satan and destroy Satan's power in our lives. We have been given the authority as followers of Jesus on this earth, to replace evil with love, health, forgiveness, peace and blessing for all.

God never intended for wars, disease, cancer, murder, starvation, and poverty to be a part of His plan. God does not cause the evil that happens to us in this world (James 1:13). However, God is sovereign and allows the evil in the world to happen under His permissive will. At times He will directly intervene, but often He allows bad to happen even though He does not desire it. Evil often continues unabated in this world because the devil continues to operate through individuals that do not serve God and have no power over the devil to resist evil.

God permits evil to continue for the time being. But at the end of the age, Satan will experience His final demise when God throws him into the lake of fire forever (Revelation 20:7-10).

Until that time, says Romans 8:23, believers groan inwardly, because of the effects of living in a sinful world. *We ourselves, who have the firstfruits of the Spirit, groan inwardly as we wait eagerly for our adoption as sons, the redemption of our bodies.*

Although we have the Spirit and His blessings, we still groan inwardly because we live in a sinful world and experience its imperfections, pain, and sorrow. We are groaning for the complete redemption that will be given at the resurrection when the glory of God will be revealed (2 Corinthians 5:4). Until that time, we must walk in God's grace, strength, and comfort which brings spiritual victory in our lives.

159 | People suffer because humans make wrong choices

A second reason why people (both believers and unbelievers) suffer on our planet is simply this: *People make wrong choices.* God created mankind to have fellowship with Him. He did not create robots who were programmed to make perfect choices. God wants us to fellowship with Him and obey Him because we want to, not because we have to. God made us in His image with the ability to choose. And sometimes our choices are bad. What happens then?

There is a law in this universe set up by God called "the law of sowing and reaping." The Bible says in Galatians 6:7 that, "...*a man reaps what he sows.*" In other words, if we make wrong choices in life, we will have to reap the consequences. If we drive recklessly, we will probably have an accident. If we mistreat

In light of the suffering caused by Satan on this earth, what is our responsibility as Christians?

How do our choices make a difference in the way our lives are lived?

Is it possible to be affected by the sins of our ancestors?

our bodies, we may have serious health problems. If we refuse to work, we may have to go without food and clothing. The sin of immorality and adultery often results in the breakdown of a marriage.

Wrong choices not only affect an individual, it may affect his family and those around him and even future generations. An alcoholic father not only ruins his own life but his life-style has a devastating effect on his whole family. The Bible says that the sins of parents can follow their children to the third and fourth generations (Exodus 20:5; Deuteronomy 5:9).

A young man I was counseling once told me he didn't want to end up like his father. His father's life-style and example was deplorable and undesirable. Sometime later, this man chose to turn away from Christ, and the most astonishing thing happened during the next few years. The young man's life-style and characteristics became like those of his father. Since this young man was no longer living in obedience to Jesus Christ as his Lord, he was unable to break the curse that was passed down from his father's generation to his generation. In fact, this curse had been passed down to his life from many preceding generations and caused him to continue to live in bondage. This is why Jesus gave His life on the cross. He became a curse for us so that we no longer need to fear reaping what was sown by our ancestors. (For more on breaking generational curses or strongholds, see Day 180.)

As Christians, we must act in accord with God's Word and avoid whatever will remove us from God's protection. We must confess known sin and examine our lives to see if we are displeasing the Holy Spirit. However, when we do make bad choices, even innocently, God may allow hardships and suffering in our lives as a means of discipline so we again submit to His will and walk in faith. When God disciplines us, He does so because He loves us, according to Hebrews 12:5-6. *My son, do not make light of the Lord's discipline, and do not lose heart when he rebukes you, because the Lord disciplines those he loves, and he punishes everyone he accepts as a son.*

God wants us to live holy lives as His children. Suffering is sometimes a tool God uses to get our attention. He wants to accomplish His purposes for our lives and get us to trust Him completely. Sometimes we must endure hardships because they can serve as a catalyst to spiritual growth. *No discipline seems pleasant at the time, but painful. Later on, however, it produces a harvest of righteousness and peace for those who have been trained by it* (Hebrews 12:11). Suffering forces us to trust in God rather than ourselves.

160 | People suffer because of satanic attack

Direct satanic attack is a third reason people suffer in this world. The New Testament is filled with people who suffered because demons tormented them, and it continues to happen today.

Demonic curses are sometimes placed on a person so that he or she is crippled emotionally, spiritually, and even physically. The word *curse* means *to call evil down, or to bring evil on, or to afflict.* Those involved in satanic cults sometimes attempt to place curses on others. People who have had curses placed on them may have an unexplained accident or go through specific kinds of problems.

Balak, king of the Moabites, tried to place a curse on the Israelites who were coming in his direction. Balak had heard the stories of how the God of the Israelites had destroyed their enemies, and he was scared. So he called a prophet named Balaam and asked him to put a curse on the people of Israel. His plan did not work. The children of Israel had chosen to follow God's plan for their lives, and no enemy could defeat them (Numbers 22).

Believers are not always immune to Satan's attacks and bondages. Even though Job was a righteous man who walked with God, the Lord allowed Satan to attack him. Paul was a spirit-filled godly man, yet he experienced a "thorn in the flesh" that he described as a messenger of Satan. Both men suffered, but God used their afflictions to teach them important spiritual lessons. These men learned to live victoriously because they knew they ultimately had authority over the power of Satan and his demons just as we do today.

Usually direct satanic attack occurs for two reasons:

1. We are not walking under the protection of Christ or fail to walk in His power, therefore opening our lives up to demonic attack.

2. In the case of Paul, he was walking in such a great revelation that Jesus allowed Satan access to him so he would not become proud (2 Corinthians 12:7).

We must break the power of Satan by waging intense spiritual warfare. We live in a spirit world. The enemy is out to destroy us any way he can. The devil has come to steal, kill and destroy (John 10:10). When Satan can attack, he will. As Christians we must be alert to Satan's schemes. *Be self-controlled and alert. Your enemy the devil prowls around like a roaring lion looking for someone to devour. Resist him, standing firm in the faith, because you know that your brothers throughout the world are undergoing the same kind of sufferings. And the God of all grace, who called you to his eternal glory in Christ, after you have suffered a little while, will himself restore you and make you strong, firm and steadfast* (1 Peter 5:8-10).

Although, as Christians, we do not have to walk in fear of Satan and his demons. Satan is our enemy. We have been delivered from his power, but as a roaring lion, he remains a threat to us and seeks to destroy us. We must stand firm in the faith. No matter what kind of suffering he inflicts, or how he tries to influence our emotions, our thoughts or our actions, God will see us through.

Are believers immune to Satan's attacks?

How can we be alert to Satan's schemes (1 Peter 5:8-10)?

Biblical Foundations for Life

PART 2

WE CAN RECLAIM WHAT THE ENEMY STOLE

161 | We can be victorious!

If we have the power of God living in us and are set free from the curse of the law, then why are some Christians living as if they have not been redeemed and set free? Yes, even Christians may find themselves in areas of bondages. Even though we have given our lives to Jesus Christ and are filled with His Holy Spirit, there may be areas of bondage in our lives we continue to deal with.

First of all, as Christians, we need to realize that **we can have victory in every area of our lives!** This victory is promised in the first book of the Bible when God promises to redeem the world, giving us the victory over Satan.

The devil is the most cursed being in the entire universe, and his demise is certain. That's why he wars so relentlessly against God and His people. But his fate was already sealed in the third chapter of Genesis. God tells the serpent that there would be a spiritual conflict between the offspring of the woman (Jesus Christ) and the offspring of the serpent (Satan and his demons). *So the Lord God said to the serpent, "Because you have done this, cursed are you above all the livestock and all the wild animals! You will crawl on your belly and you will eat dust all the days of your life. And I will put enmity between you and the woman, and between your offspring and hers; he will crush your head, and you will strike his heel"* (Genesis 3:14-15).

God promises that Christ would be born of a woman and be "struck" through His crucifixion. But even though He was struck, He would rise from the dead to completely crush Satan, sin, and death. Jesus came to earth to deliver us from Satan's dominion and establish God's kingdom in our hearts. He came to give us life and victory!

Tragedies are not a part of God's plan for your life—they have not originated in heaven. The Bible tells us clearly that every good gift comes from above (James 1:17). One of Satan's most subtle schemes is to try to cause us to blame God for the bad things that happen in our lives. We have already discussed that the trials and sufferings in our lives have various causes—because we live in a sinful world, because we make wrong choices or due to direct satanic attack. If we look at the root of all of these causes, notice that they have Satan at their core! So we can never blame God.

God is the One who provides a way out of our bondage to sin and suffering. He has a plan for our lives. It is a plan that is filled with hope. God can take the most negative circumstances and turn them around for good. No matter how dark our circumstances seem at the moment, we can be full of hope. Jesus helps us to come through every obstacle victoriously. His plans for you are plans of peace and not of evil. He wants to give you a future and a hope (Jeremiah 29:11).

Jesus understands suffering, because He was willing to suffer more than anyone ever has, by taking our sins upon Himself when He died on the cross.

What is Satan's fate (Genesis 3:14-15)?

What is God's plan for our lives (Jeremiah 29:11)?

There, he broke the powers of darkness and provided forgiveness for us, setting us free from the curse.

162 | We live in a covenant relationship with God

We must realize, like Abraham did, that we have a covenant with God. In a covenant made with Abraham in Genesis 17:7, God promised, *"I will establish my covenant as an everlasting covenant between me and you and your descendants after you for the generations to come, to be your God..."*

With this Old Testament covenant, God promises Abraham to bind Himself to His faithful people to be their God. God continued this relationship in the New Testament where He made a new covenant with us in Jesus Christ. The new covenant is a promise to bestow divine protection and blessing on those who, through faith, accept Christ and receive His promises. Galatians 3:6-9 says, *"Consider Abraham: 'He believed God, and it was credited to him as righteousness.' Understand, then, that those who believe are children of Abraham. The Scripture foresaw that God would justify the Gentiles by faith, and announced the gospel in advance to Abraham: 'All nations will be blessed through you.' So those who have faith are blessed along with Abraham, the man of faith."*

All who believe, as Abraham believed, share in Abraham's blessings. We have inherited the blessing of Abraham through faith in Jesus Christ. Faith brings blessing.

Our relationship with God is secured by His blood, but the depth of our fellowship with Him may fluctuate. It depends on our obedience to God. We must maintain a close fellowship with God so we can be blessed according to Deuteronomy 28:1-3.

But if we do not heed the voice of the Lord, we will be under a curse (v. 15). A curse is the absence of a blessing. The consequences of turning away from fellowshipping with God results in a curse on our lives. We cannot expect God to bless us if we have turned away from Him.

Nevertheless, believers are assured that if they love Jesus and depend on Him, He will never leave or forsake them. He will be their helper through any difficulties. Jesus Christ has come to set us free, to be whole, in every area of life.

It is not the will of God for evil to come upon our lives. It's not God's will for sickness, confusion, depression, fear, insecurity or inferiority to come upon us. However, as we learned before, we will not always be exempt from suffering. That does not negate the fact that God wants us to be free from all of these afflictions. They are a part of the original curse, and God wants us to be free. He has created us to be whole!

When I was a child, I had a heart murmur. Some of my relatives also had heart problems. I believe it was a product of a curse genetically passed down from generation to generation. When my schoolmates were having fun playing sports, I had to stand on the sidelines and watch. Often, to make matters worse, the teachers recruited me to be the umpire. Every time I had to call a close play,

What does our covenant with Christ depend upon?

Name some areas that are a part of the original curse. How can we be set free?

Biblical Foundations for Life

the team that didn't agree with me let me know in no uncertain terms they thought I was a lousy umpire.

But, praise God, today I have been set free and healed of not only those memories but of the heart murmur as well! Today I can play baseball, basketball, and football and enjoy every minute of it. It is all because Jesus Christ became a curse for me. I am reaping the benefits of my relationship or covenant with Him!

163 | We cannot allow the enemy to lie to us

It is true that Christians get sick and depressed. Christians sometimes struggle with temper tantrums in the same way their parents and grandparents struggled with hot tempers. Even Christians may be susceptible to a curse that has been passed down through the family line, continuing unchecked for generations. The beautiful truth for us to know is that we can be set free from those curses in Jesus' name! We do not have to wallow helplessly in a life-controlling habit, sin or curse.

Because of our disobedience to the Lord before we came to know Jesus, we deserve to experience the curse on our lives. However, because of faith in Jesus and the grace of God, we can rise up and walk in the freedom that comes from knowing Jesus Christ.

The devil has lied to many of us. He is the father of all lies (John 8:44). Probably the devil has lied to you. Maybe he told you that you can't help yourself because the problems that you deal with are the same kind of problems and tendencies that you see in your parents. The truth is this: You may not have been able to help yourself before you received Jesus into your life, but when you were born again, things changed. You have a new Father in heaven. Your new daddy is not under the curse. Your new father in heaven does not have temper tantrums. Your new Father in heaven has not been struggling with cancer or migraine headaches or heart problems or whatever else may have "grown" into your family tree. Your new Father in heaven will set you free from every curse.

Many times people "prophesy" over us in negative ways. Parents tell their children, "You're just like your dad; you have his bad temper." Or, "You'll never amount to anything." We can break these negative "prophesies" in the name of Jesus Christ. They are a part of the curse. God loves you. He cares about you. That is why He went to the cross, so that all of our insecurities and fears and all those curses from past generations can be broken (see Day 180).

God wants to give you and me good gifts. James 1:17 tells us, *"Every good and perfect gift is from above, coming down from the Father of the heavenly lights, who does not change like shifting shadows."*

164 | We must stake our claim!

We know that Jesus came to set us free from every curse the enemy wants to place in our lives. Romans 5:15, 19 tells us that Adam brought sin and death, but Christ brought grace and life. *For if the many died by the trespass of the one man*

Has the devil lied to you about an area of your life in which you do not seem to have victory?

What can you do about it?

[Adam], how much more did God's grace and the gift that came by the grace of the one man, Jesus Christ, overflow to the many! For just as through the disobedience of the one man [Adam] the many were made sinners, so also through the obedience of the one man [Jesus] the many will be made righteous.

Christ reclaimed what Satan tried to take from us. We need to take back the areas of our lives that our enemy, the devil, has stolen from us.

The children of Israel went into Canaan, the new land that God promised to them. This new land was legally their land. God had told them clearly, "I'll give it to you." However, they had to go in and receive it, step by step. They had to walk in and claim it. Joshua 1:3 says, "*I will give you every place where you set your foot, as I promised Moses.*"

In other words, God told Joshua, "Joshua, the land is yours, but you have to go in and claim it. You must take it back from your enemies." If the devil has stolen your peace, your joy, your health, or your hope, today is your day to claim it back from the enemy!

The children of Israel went to the city of Jericho, marched around seven times, shouted, and the walls came down. Even though it was theirs for the taking, they had to physically go in and claim it. You may say, "Well, I'm a Christian. Doesn't this all happen automatically?" Legally, yes, it's yours. But practically, in order to experience it, you need to go in and claim back from the devil the specific areas that he has stolen from you.

165 | We apply God's Word to our lives

Christians have been delivered from the power of darkness and are now in Christ's kingdom (Colossians 1:13). It is faith that unlocks the door. It is faith that makes the difference in our lives. Joshua was a man of faith. That's why he marched around the city of Jericho for seven days. As a man of faith, he obeyed God's Word and claimed the inheritance that the Lord had promised him. When we believe what God says in His Word, we will find ourselves being freed from depression, inferiority, insecurities, fears of mental illness, sickness, and disease. It is faith that unlocks the door. Romans 5:17 tells us clearly, "*For if, by the trespass of the one man, death reigned through that one man, how much more will those who receive God's abundant provision of grace and of the gift of righteousness reign in life through the one man, Jesus Christ.*"

God has called us to reign in life, to live a victorious life in Christ. If I give you a gift certificate for one thousand dollars, that gift certificate is worthless until you cash it in. The same is true of the Word of God. In order to walk victoriously in our spiritual lives, we have to seek, learn and grow in the knowledge of God through His Word. We cannot grow without God's Word and we cannot change without it. God's Word motivates us to obedience and fellowship with Him. We need to take the Word of God and begin to apply it to every area of our lives so that we can experience the wholeness that God has promised. By doing so, we reclaim what the devil has tried to steal from us. God's Word is an

---

What does the Lord promise to those who want to reclaim what Satan has taken from them (Joshua 1:3)?

God's Word is likened to what offensive weapon (Ephesians 6:17)?

Biblical Foundations for Life

How can we attack the powers of darkness and put them to flight (Romans 10:17)?

indispensable weapon in Christian warfare against the devil. *Take the…sword of the Spirit, which is the word of God* (Ephesians 6:17).

In Ephesians 6, we see there are other items of Christian armor—the belt, the breastplate, the shoes, the shield, and the helmet—all intended for defense. The Word of God is the only weapon of attack. We must know God's Word and apply it to our lives so we can attack the powers of darkness in our lives and put them to flight.

This may or may not happen overnight. God is a God of miracles and may move supernaturally and quickly to alter or heal a problem in our lives. But many times, He changes us through a more gradual process of growth and change. It takes more faith and character to persevere through problems, and God wants us to use His Word to overcome in this way.

To overcome life-dominating patterns in our lives or any other trial or temptation that confronts us, we need to be honest with God and confess our weakness and dependency on Him. As we confess the truth of God's Word, faith is built in our hearts (Romans 10:17). And as faith is built, we begin to experience the Lord's wholeness.

For example, if we struggle with depression, we should pray, *"Father in Jesus' name, this depression and despondency has no hold on me. I am set free by the blood of Jesus and the power of His Spirit. Soul, be encouraged in Jesus' name!"*

166 | We guard our tongues

How can the words you say condemn you?

We must be careful how we speak. Matthew 12:34 says, *"For out of the abundance of the heart the mouth speaks."* In other words, we believe with the heart, and what we speak is often what we really believe. The Bible also says we will be judged by our words. *But I tell you that men will have to give account on the day of judgment for every careless word they have spoken. For by your words you will be acquitted, and by your words you will be condemned* (Matthew 12:36-37). Life and death are in the power of the tongue.

By our speech, we can pronounce either a blessing or a curse. If we continually say, "I think I'm going to get sick," we can begin to pronounce a curse of sickness on our lives. Instead we need to say, "I feel like I'm getting sick, but I know that God desires for me to be a whole person, and I can receive His healing." By speaking words of faith, we pronounce a blessing on our lives.

Give examples from your life.

Sometimes people say, "My mother had a miscarriage, maybe I'll have a miscarriage too." By believing these words, we can begin to open the door for the devil to lay what we speak on our lives. The enemy will attempt to use these words to place fear in our lives, and the things that we fear can come upon us. Job 3:25 tells us, *"For the thing I greatly feared has come upon me, and what I dreaded has happened to me."* Fear is destroyed as we speak the Word of God to ourselves and to others around us. God tells us in 2 Timothy 1:7, *"For God has not given us a spirit of fear, but of power and of love and of a sound mind."*

134 Biblical Foundations for Life

You may ask, "Why does it matter what we say, as long as our hearts are right?" Imagine walking into a bank with a toy water pistol and saying, "I'll take ten thousand dollars, please." The teller, seeing the gun, activates the alarm. The police rush in and arrest you. "I'm only kidding," you say. "It's only a water pistol. I was just joking. I didn't really mean it." Maybe you did not mean it, but you will end up in jail for the words you said and the action you took! The same principle applies to spiritual things. The devil is a legalist. He will use our words against us. We need to be careful how we speak. We need to speak the things that God says in His Word. We need to speak life-giving words that release hope in people's lives.

167 | We release our inheritance

Our God promises us wholeness and health and victory in every area of our lives. *If you belong to Christ, then you are Abraham's seed, and heirs according to the promise* (Galatians 3:29).

The Spirit himself testifies with our spirit that we are God's children (Romans 8:16).

We are God's children through faith in Jesus Christ! God speaks to us by the Holy Spirit and tells us we are heirs of His promises. He is the God who said He would bless Abraham, and by faith you and I are also the children of Abraham. You may ask, "If I am really an heir of God, then why do I still deal with depression?" We must remember, the New Testament is the new covenant or will that our Father in heaven has left for us. If your uncle dies, and wills you his inheritance, you must sign the proper documents to release the inheritance before you can receive it. Spiritually, we must receive our inheritance from God in order to be set free.

We are free from the curse when we realize what the Word of God, the Lord's will and our inheritance says, and we act on it. For example, if you are feeling weak today, claim the strength the Lord promises in His Word. The Bible says, "*I can do everything through him who gives me strength*" (Philippians 4:13). Confess this promise and receive His strength today!

I was driving down the road in my car one day when a spirit of fear came on me like a cloud. I was paralyzed with fear. Immediately I was aware of what was happening. The enemy was trying to cause me to live by my feelings of fear rather than doing the things I knew God was calling me to do. I said boldly, "In Jesus' name, I renounce this spirit of fear and command it to leave." And guess what? It left! When we resist the devil, he has to flee! (James 4:7).

A few years ago, I was in Europe and experienced a similar spirit of fear. Again, this spirit of fear had to leave when confronted with the name of Jesus. Jesus Christ became a curse for us. We do not have to put up with a spirit of fear or any other affliction that the devil will try to bring against us. Jesus Christ has come to set us free!

When we realize what our inheritance is, how do we release it?

Speak Philippians 4:13 aloud.

Biblical Foundations for Life

PART 3

RECIEVING FREEDOM IN JESUS' NAME

168 | Free spiritually!

In the next sections we will look at seven areas of freedom that we can experience as believers in Jesus Christ. First of all, let's take a look at *spiritual freedom*. 1 John 1:9 says, *"If we confess our sins, he is faithful and just and will forgive us our sins and purify us from all unrighteousness."*

After we have given our lives to Jesus, the devil may try to paralyze us spiritually by telling us that we are not really saved. He is a liar! The Bible tells us in Romans 8:1-2, *"Therefore, there is now no condemnation for those who are in Christ Jesus, because through Christ Jesus the law of the Spirit of life set me free from the law of sin and death."* There is no condemnation to those who are in Christ. And remember, there is a big difference between God's conviction and the enemy's condemnation. God's conviction always brings hope. But the devil's condemnation brings hopelessness.

The Bible tells us, *"For God is not a God of disorder but of peace…"* (1 Corinthians 14:33). If your heart is turned toward the Lord and you are still experiencing spiritual doubts and confusion in your life, it is not from God. The devil is the author of confusion and condemnation. Jesus paid the price for this curse to be broken. I dealt with times of intense guilt after I gave my life to Jesus. One day, I got tired of it. I opened my Bible to 1 John 1:9, and declared to the devil, "I'm believing the Word of God, instead of what I feel in my emotions." Do you know what happened? I was set free. I later realized that the enemy had placed a curse over me. That curse of false guilt was trying to push me into depression, confusion and frustration, but it was broken that night in Jesus' name.

I am reminded of the story of a farmer who was battling with false guilt and confusion in his life. He wasn't sure he was saved. Finally, he went to the back of his barn, took a big stake and hammered it into the ground. He confessed, "Jesus, you are the Lord of my life." He believed in his heart that Jesus was alive from the dead (Romans 10:9). Then He made a bold statement. "It happened right here at this stake. I gave my life completely to God. The next time the devil lies to me, I'm going right back here to this stake as proof. From this moment on, I will know, that I know, I am saved!" How could he know? Because he knew the curse of false guilt and confusion was broken because of Jesus Christ. He had made a decision to believe the truth, the Word of God. His life was different from that day on.

169 | Free from sickness and disease

A second area of freedom has to do with *freedom from sickness and disease*. Physical healing is sometimes controversial in the body of Christ. Let's see what the Bible has to say. Matthew 8:16-17 tells us, *"When evening came, many who were demon-possessed were brought to him, and he drove out the spirits with a word and healed all the sick. This was to fulfill what was spoken through the prophet Isaiah: 'He took up our infirmities and carried our diseases.'"*

How do you get rid of feelings of guilt and condemnation (Romans 8:1-2)?

What is the difference between conviction and condemnation?

According to the new covenant, the New Testament, it is God's will that you and I are healed and healthy. When Jesus Christ went to the cross two thousand years ago, He provided forgiveness for sin, eternal and resurrection life for death, and *healing for sickness!* Freedom from the curse also includes the area of physical healing.

Jesus healed people who came to Him for healing. Matthew, chapter eight, tells us that when the people came to Him, He healed them. He was fulfilling the prophecy in the Old Testament from the book of Isaiah 53:4-5 that says, "*Surely he took up our infirmities...and by his wounds we are healed.*" 1 Peter 2:24 says similarly, "*He himself bore our sins in his body on the tree, so that we might die to sins and live for righteousness; by his wounds you have been healed.*"

While Jesus was teaching in a synagogue one Sabbath, He called a woman forward who was crippled by a spirit of infirmity which was a direct result of demonic activity. We should note here that although Jesus healed many diseases, not all of them were attributed to demonic causes. However, in this case it was. Jesus laid His hands on her and immediately she was made straight, and glorified God (Luke 13:13). The ruler of the synagogue was indignant. He was not accustomed to this kind of thing happening in his religious meetings. Sometimes religious people have problems believing that we can be free from the curse of sickness and disease. Nevertheless, it could not be denied, Jesus Christ set the woman free. The same can happen today. The Bible tells us, Jesus Christ is the same yesterday, today, and forever (Hebrews 13:8).

Every sickness, every type of cancer, every case of heart failure, every migraine headache has been hung on the cross through Jesus Christ. We need to take God's Word seriously and place our faith in the Word of God instead of on the symptoms we see in our body. We must seek the presence of Jesus in our lives and saturate our lives with God's Word. We should expect a miracle (Matthew 7:8; 19:26).

I mentioned earlier in this book that I had a heart murmur as a young man. But a short time after coming to know Jesus Christ as Lord, my doctor found I had been made completely whole. By the grace of God, I am completely free from any heart murmur today. Jesus Christ is our healer because He is the same yesterday, today, and forever.

170 | Hindrances to healing

Sometimes people say, "I know Jesus heals spiritually, but I'm not sure that He heals physically." The truth is that God wants to bless us with both.

Sometime back, a friend who owns a restaurant decided to treat our family to a meal. He told us we could have anything we wanted on the menu, absolutely free. I had a choice to make. I did not deserve this free meal, yet, I was told I could not pay for it. As I looked at all of the sumptuous food I could think, "I don't want to ask for too much. I don't want to take advantage of my friend." My friend would have been disappointed if I had responded that way, and it would have been pride keeping me from receiving a blessing. I believe the Lord

Put your name in place of the words "our" and "we" in 1 Peter 2:24. Do you believe God wants you to be free of every sickness and disease?

Biblical Foundations for Life

As an heir of all the promises in the Bible, why wouldn't you want to take all you can have?

What should you do if your prayers for healing are not answered (Philippians 4:4)?

responds to us the same way. God's only Son, Jesus Christ, went to the cross so that you and I could take advantage of the precious gift of wholeness that He has given to us. The entire bill has been paid!

Jesus Christ came to set you and me free from every curse including the curse of sickness, disease and all types of physical infirmities in our bodies. I have a friend who was miraculously healed of rheumatic fever. His parents decided to trust the Word of God to see their son healed, and although he was very sick, they chose to believe the Word of God instead of the symptoms they saw. And he was healed! Jesus Christ came to set my friend free from the curse. The Bible says, *Praise the Lord, O my soul, and forget not all his benefits—who forgives all your sins and heals all your diseases* (Psalms 103:2-3).

God wants to heal all our diseases, but sometimes there are hindrances to receiving divine healing, such as, unconfessed sin (James 5:16), demonic oppression or bondage (Luke 13:11-13), fear or acute anxiety (Proverbs 3:5-8; Philippians 4:6-7), past disappointments that undermine present faith (Mark 5:26; John 5:5-7), unbiblical teaching (Mark 3:1-5; 7:13), failure of the leaders to pray the prayer of faith (Mark 11:22-24; James 5:14-16), failure of the church to seek and obtain the gifts of miracles and healings as God intended (Acts 4:29-30; 6:8; 8:5-6; 1 Corinthians 12:9-10,29-31; Hebrews 2:3-4), unbelief (Mark 6:3-6; 9:19,23-24), or self-centered behavior (1 Corinthians 11:29-30). At other times, the reason for the persistence of physical affliction in godly people is not readily apparent (Galatians 4:13; 1 Timothy 5:23; 2 Timothy 4:20). In still other instances, God chooses to take His beloved saints to heaven during an illness (2 Kings 13:14).[1]

If our prayers are not answered for healing, we cannot give up. We should rejoice if healing comes immediately and rejoice if it does not come (Philippians 4:4). God promises to never forsake us or forget us. Sometimes God's purposes for us are for our greater good that we cannot understand.

If we believe the Lord wants us to go to a doctor, then, by all means, we should go to a doctor. But let's go to our Great Physician first! The power of medical science is limited, but the power of God and His Word is unlimited! In the end, it is always Jesus, our Great Physician, who ultimately heals, anyway.

We are learning to live out the promises of God's Word in our Christian lives. We are learning to apply the promises of the Lord's inheritance to our lives. So we must choose to live by what God says in His Word even though we may not see the expected results. Sometimes God tests our hearts to see if we really fear Him. He tested Abraham when He asked him to sacrifice Isaac. Job was tested, too, but in the end he prospered (Job 42:10). God wants to set us free, but He also wants to know that we love Him more than any covenant blessing.

God is getting His church to a place where we will walk in wholeness and victory as we grow in applying the Word of God to our lives. There are times when we need to do something specific like calling for the elders of our church to pray for us and anoint us with oil. *Is any one of you sick? He should call the elders of the church to pray over him and anoint him with oil in the name of the Lord. And the prayer offered in faith will make the sick person well; the Lord will raise him up...*

(James 5:14-15). The Bible tells us if we obey this scriptural mandate, the Lord will "raise us up," heal us and make us completely whole by their prayer of faith.

[1] Full Life Study Bible, (Grand Rapids, Michigan: Zondervan Publishing House, 1992), p. 1421.

171 | Free from painful memories

Many Christians long for a deeper and closer relationship with the Lord. But they continue to struggle with the same fears and hurtful memories from their past, unable to break free. Crippled emotionally, they need to be set free from the curse of painful memories and hurts in their lives. It is not God's will for people's hearts to be broken. He wants to heal us emotionally according to Luke 4:18-19. *The Spirit of the Lord is on me, because he has anointed me to preach good news to the poor. He has sent me to proclaim freedom for the prisoners and recovery of sight for the blind,* **to release the oppressed**, *to proclaim the year of the Lord's favor.*

A young man and his fiancée came to me for premarital counseling. The young man had experienced many hurts in his life. For one, his father had constantly blamed him for the problems in his marriage because the son was conceived out of wedlock. The young man was hurting and needed healing. I asked him if he was willing to forgive his dad. He was willing. We laid hands on him and prayed for him to be healed of the painful memories he received while growing up.

The young man had a wonderful wedding a few months later. His father attended and there was no longer a wall between them. The pain was gone. God supernaturally healed him because Jesus took that pain on the cross two thousand years ago. Jesus Christ became a curse for that young man.

Sometimes the term, "inner healing" is used for explaining emotional healing. To receive inner healing means to be healed of lie-filled memories or to have our broken hearts healed. Sometimes our present emotional pain comes from the misinterpretations (lies) embedded in our memories and not from the memories themselves. For example, an incest victim feels shame not because she was molested but because she may believe it was her fault (lie). When the lie is exposed, she can receive freedom!

Inner healing, or the healing of memories, is a very valid ministry in the body of Christ today. If we believe someone has hurt us and continue to remember those hurts and the memories of what has happened, we need to be healed emotionally. We can be made whole! Jesus wants to heal us and set us free in His name.

The healing of memories does not mean that we no longer remember what has happened. We may remember what happened, but the pain has been healed through Jesus revealing the truth to us. We can look back and now give praise to God for His healing on our lives and His grace and strength to go on.

173 | Forgive, forgive, forgive

An important scriptural key to being healed and set free is found in Matthew 6:14-15. *For if you forgive men when they sin against you, your heavenly Father will also forgive you. But if you do not forgive men their sins, your Father will not forgive your sins.*

Do you have painful memories of past hurts?

Why do you think you are unable to break free?

Biblical Foundations for Life

What is the first step in receiving healing of memories (Matthew 6:14-15)?

What happens if we do not forgive (Matthew 18:34-35)?

This is important! **We must forgive those who have hurt us in order for God to heal us.** In Matthew 18, Jesus tells a parable about a servant who owed his king one million dollars. He begged the king for extra time to pay the debt, and the king had pity on him and canceled the whole debt. The servant then went out and found one of his fellow servants who owed him two thousand dollars. He grabbed him by the shirt and demanded immediate payment. The fellow servant pleaded for more time, but the servant refused and had him thrown into prison. The king discovered what happened and called the servant in. "I forgave you a million dollars and you couldn't forgive someone a few thousand dollars? I showed you mercy but you could not show mercy to another?" Then the scripture makes an interesting statement, *"In anger his master turned him over to the jailers to be tortured, until he should pay back all he owed. This is how my heavenly Father will treat each of you unless you forgive your brother from your heart"* (Matthew 18:34-35).

The king had the man thrown into prison for not showing forgiveness to another. Jesus says that if we don't forgive someone who has hurt us or "ripped us off," God will deliver us to the *torturers* or *demons of hell*. Even Christians at times can be tormented with confusion, frustration, depression, etc. brought on by the demons of hell if they choose not to forgive. Unforgiveness leaves the door wide open for the devil!

Forgiving those who have hurt us is the first step to being set free. We may not feel like it, but because God forgave us, we need to forgive others in Jesus' name. God will bring emotional healing into our lives as we obey His Word and forgive in faith from our hearts.

173 | And forgive some more!

In addition to "forgiving the person who has hurt us," we must also "ask God to forgive the person." Asking God to forgive them, is a vital second step of forgiveness we need to take so that we can be set free. Stephen, when he was being stoned, said, "Father, forgive them." Jesus, on the cross, said, "Father, forgive them, they don't know what they do."

A third step is to "ask God to forgive us for any wrong attitudes or attempt to hide our sin." Proverbs 28:13 says, *"He who conceals his sins does not prosper, but whoever confesses and renounces them finds mercy.* The word *prosper* means *to break out of bondage."* If we hide our sin and are not honest about it, we cannot break out of the bondage in our lives. If we don't ask God to heal us for wrong attitudes, then we cannot prosper in this area of our lives.

A fourth step is to "confess our faults to someone" and have him or her pray for us so that God will heal us. The scripture says in James 5:16, *"Therefore confess your sins to each other and pray for each other so that you may be healed. The prayer of a righteous man is powerful and effective."*

Ask someone to lay hands on you and pray for emotional healing. This is why it is so important to be connected to the rest of the body of Christ through a local church. As you meet together with other believers, ask the Lord to show you someone whom you can trust to pray for you. The Lord wants to heal you and set you free from the curse in Jesus' name.

Corrie ten Boom, who experienced life in a Nazi concentration camp and whose life story inspired the movie, "The Hiding Place," often spoke about "the bell theory." A church bell rings ding-dong, ding-dong, ding-dong after someone pulls the long chord attached to the ringer. The ding-dong begins very loud and then grows softer and softer until it finally stops ringing. Corrie said that when you ask the Lord to heal you, the devil may try to bring some of those old emotions of hurt and pain back to you again and again. That is the time for you to say emphatically, "In Jesus' name, I know He took my pain on the cross." As you declare the truth, the emotions of hurt feelings will dissipate as you focus on Jesus your healer instead of on the pain. In the same way that the sound from the big church bell rings loudly at first and then less and less, the memories of hurt will become less and less as you declare the truth that Jesus has healed you. In a very short time, you will get to the place where the devil cannot even tempt you anymore in this area. You will be completely and totally healed.

After the first step of forgiving those who hurt us, write down the next steps for healing as mentioned.

174 | Free to have a sound mind

We live in a day of extreme stress. Many of us face mental anguish. Jesus came to set us free from this curse on our minds that has its root based in unwholesome fear. The scriptures tell us in 2 Timothy 1:7, *"For God has not given us a spirit of fear, but of power and of love and of a sound mind"* (NKJ).

God's purpose for your life is for you to have a sound mind. Perhaps your ancestors had some type of mental problems. God says that you can be free from that curse in Jesus' name. As I was growing up, I can vividly remember various members of my extended family who had a history of mental illness. I feared that I would spend periods of my life mentally ill in a mental hospital like some of my family members. One day I came to the realization that I didn't have to fear mental illness because Jesus Christ became a curse for me. By the grace of God, I have been freed from that curse in Jesus' name.

The Lord's will for each of us is to have peace of mind. Isaiah 26:3 says, *"You will keep in perfect peace him whose mind is steadfast, because he trusts in you."*

Since I have been set free from the curse in Jesus' name, the Lord has delivered me from the fear of mental illness. We serve a good God! We can trust Him! He has promised us perfect peace as we continue to focus on our heavenly Father, the author of all peace (1 Corinthians 14:33).

You and I are in a brand new family, the family of God, through faith in Jesus Christ. We have a brand new household, the household of God. Our new Father in heaven does not have any mental problems at all.

We need to break every curse that is over our lives in Jesus' name. By the grace of God, I have broken every curse over my life in the name of Jesus. I am a free man! Today is your day of freedom. Today is the day for any curse over your life to be completely broken in Jesus' name.

If you are fearful, stressed out and worried all the time, 2 Timothy 1:7 gives the solution. What is it?

Biblical Foundations for Life

PART 4   YOU CAN BE COMPLETELY FREE

175 | Financial freedom

To summarize the previous section, we learned we are redeemed from the curse in every facet of our existence. The curse is still in the world, but it has no right to be on us as Christians. We are redeemed from the curse! The curse on our spiritual, physical, emotional and mental lives is removed by the blood of Jesus.

A fifth area of freedom we can experience is financial freedom. 2 Corinthians 8:9 says, *"For you know the grace of our Lord Jesus Christ, that though he was rich, yet for your sakes he became poor, so that you through his poverty might become rich."* God wants to prosper us in every way, including financially, so we can give financially in order for the good news of Jesus to be taken throughout the whole world. Some people think it is godly to be poor. What they don't understand is that poverty is a part of the curse. If poverty is godly, then we should never be giving money to the poor. We would be hindering them from living in this godly state!

Is it godly to be poor?

If you are struggling financially, I have good news for you. You don't have to be poor. God wants to prosper you. God wants to bless you and give you hope. Some people think that money is the root of evil. That's not exactly what the scripture says in I Timothy 6:10. It says that the *love* of money is a root of evil. If we love money more than God, it is idolatry and leads us away from God.

It is wise to remember that prosperity and material things can never make us happy. Only Jesus can give us fulfillment and the abundant life. At the same time, the Lord desires to bless us. God wants to prosper us so we can give to our families, the church, the poor, and give to see His kingdom built throughout the whole world.

Who does God want to use to spread the gospel and meet the needs of millions in the world?

A lady who was experiencing deep financial problems in her home, came to her pastor for help. Both her husband and her son were out of work. The pastor told her, "You need to read Galatians 3:13." He opened his Bible and read, *"Christ redeemed us from the curse of the law by becoming a curse for us, for it is written: 'Cursed is everyone who is hung on a tree.'"*

"Jesus became a curse for you," he explained, "so that you can be financially free." She came often for counsel but didn't really listen.

Then about a year after she had first sought the pastor's advice, she came to his office again. She said, "Guess what happened? I am finally prosperous. I was reading the Bible one day and I received a revelation from God." She said, "It's Galatians 3:13." (This was the same truth that the pastor had been telling her over and over again, but this time she herself received a revelation from God.) She said, "Here's what happened. I realized God wanted to prosper me. This poverty was a curse over my life. So, I went and got a job at a restaurant. The joy of the Lord was in my life, and I knew the financial curse had been broken. Later I bought the restaurant." She is a prosperous woman today, because the favor of God is on her. In fact, people come back just because of the godly atmosphere in her restaurant. The scriptures tell us in Ephesians 4:28, "*He who has been stealing must steal no longer, but must work, doing something useful with his own hands, that he may have something to share with those in need.*"

Jesus wants to bless us so we can give to others. As we work with an attitude of freedom and joy, we will experience the Lord's blessing. The curse has been broken. The Lord desires to prosper you as you obey Him.

176 | Social freedom

A sixth area of freedom from the curse is social freedom. God wants us to have good success in every realm and area of our life, including the way in which we relate to people socially. Growing up, I had a hard time looking people in the eye because I felt inferior. It was a curse that had to be broken. Today, by the grace of God, I love to meet people. The curse of being afraid to face people is gone in Jesus' name! According to the Bible, being afraid of people is a trap! When we really trust the Lord, we can find safety in our relationships. *Fear of man will prove to be a snare, but whoever trusts in the Lord is kept safe* (Proverbs 29:25).

A social snare is what, according to Proverbs 29:25?

Jesus had great favor with the people of His day. Wherever Jesus went, "*the common people heard Him gladly*" (Mark 12:37 NKJ). I believe Jesus was really fun to be with. Children loved to be with Jesus (Matthew 18:2-5).

God wants you and me to be able to relate to other people in a positive way. A curse that may be over you from generations past will hinder you from relating to people in a sociable and loving way. Jesus has liberated us from that horrible harvest of sin that can affect generations. That curse needs to be broken today in the name of Jesus. Jesus Christ became a curse for you!

This does not mean that we will escape persecution or that everyone will like us. Persecution may take many forms. In some countries today, Christians are tortured and imprisoned for their beliefs. I was recently in such a nation, meeting with Christian leaders, most of whom had been in prison for their faith. Other times, Christians may be deprived of a job for which they are eligible or held up to ridicule at work or school, all because of their religious persuasion. 2 Timothy 3:12 tells us we will all experience some kind of persecution if we truly live godly lives. *In fact, everyone who wants to live a godly life in Christ Jesus will be persecuted.*

What does Psalms 5:12 say God wants to surround us with?

Jesus instructed us to rejoice when others say all kinds of evil against us falsely for His sake (Matthew 5:11-12), and yet, the Bible tells us that people in the early church had favor with all the people, and people were coming to know Jesus Christ every day (Acts 2:47). Are you finding God's favor on your life? The Lord's desire is for you to experience the favor of the Lord. Take a close look at Psalms 5:12, "*For surely, O Lord, you bless the righteous; you surround them with your favor as with a shield.*"

God desires to surround you with His favor today. Declare your freedom from the curse through Jesus. The price of redemption is paid. Receive it for yourself. Today is your day of freedom.

Biblical Foundations for Life

177 | Freedom from demonic activity

What does it mean to be demonized?

What sets us free, according to Revelation 12:11?

A seventh area of freedom is freedom from demonic activity. The word "demon possessed" in New Testament Greek is the word *demonized* which means *to have a demon*. People throughout the New Testament often suffered from Satan's oppression and influence because of an indwelling evil spirit. Jesus and the New Testament Christians cast demons out of people. *When evening came, many who were demon-possessed were brought to him, and he drove out the spirits with a word and healed all the sick* (Matthew 8:16).

In our modern society, people often are too sophisticated to believe that individuals can have demons. Some people don't even believe in demons. The Bible tells us, however, that demons are evil spirit beings who are enemies of God and humans (Matthew 12:43-45). In addition, they can live in the bodies of unbelievers to enslave them to immorality and evil (Mark 5:15; Luke 4:41; 8:27-28; Acts 16:18) and they can cause physical illness (Matthew 4:24; Luke 5:12-13) although not all illness is the result of evil spirits.

Whether people want to believe it or not, the truth is, many people today are tormented by demons. Those involved in magic or spiritism using Ouija boards, seances, tarot cards, or horoscopes are dealing with evil spirits and can be led into demonic bondage. Demonic activity in their lives may express itself in fits of anger, confusion, violence, immorality, depression…the list goes on and on.

People sometimes ask me if Christians can have demonic activity in their lives. Yes, they can, but it doesn't mean that they are demon possessed or under the complete control of a demon. However, demons may have influence in Christians thoughts and emotions and actions when they fail to submit to the Holy Spirit's leading in their lives.

A Christian leader told me he had a demon of anger cast out of his life. He had gone through times of uncontrollable anger and didn't understand why. Finally one day, he confided in a pastor who took authority over the demon and cast it out in Jesus' name. He has not been the same since. Today he is one of the most gentle men I have ever met. Jesus Christ set him free.

Although Satan constantly wars against God's people, trying to draw them away from loyalty to Christ, Jesus promised believers authority over the power of Satan and his demons. He became a curse for us so that we can be free from any type of demon spirit influencing our lives. We do not have to fear the powers of darkness. Years ago, a man said to me, "Larry, I want you to know that I have used a voodoo doll and have placed a curse on you." There was no fear in my heart when he said that. Do you know why? Because I knew that Christ became a curse for me. A curse could not be placed on me, because I was protected by the blood of Jesus. *They overcame him by the blood of the Lamb…*(Revelation 12:11).

As Christians, we live by faith in the Word of God. We are living under His grace and are protected with God's law of protection from the enemy through Christ! As Christians, we have power over Satan because of what Jesus did on the cross. He shattered the power of Satan's realm when he died and rose again. He disarmed Satan.

The Bible says, *For God has not given us a spirit of fear...* (2 Timothy 1:7 NKJ). If we have a paralyzing fear of Satan and his evil intentions, we are not just fearful; we have a spirit of fear. A spirit of fear can be a demonic spirit of deception. Satan is the author of fear and wants us to walk in fear. Demonic spirits of all kinds must be resisted and commanded to leave in Jesus' name. We can break the power they attempt to exert over us. If we are dealing with a violent temper, depression, a sudden compulsion to commit suicide, or other life-dominating problem, these very well may be demonic spirits that are controlling our lives. We cannot be oblivious to their deception. We must be alert to Satan's schemes and temptations and desire to be set free.

178 | Resist the devil, and he will flee

To be set free from demonic bondage we must resist the devil by prayer and proclaim God's Word as we call upon the mighty name of Jesus. A friend told me he once sensed a strange, evil presence at a friend's house. Calling upon the name of Jesus Christ, a few Christian believers prayed and took authority over a curse that needed to be broken over that home. The evil presence left. James 4:7 says, *"Submit yourselves, then, to God. Resist the devil, and he will flee from you."*

What two things must we do to make the devil flee?

Smith Wigglesworth was an evangelist in Great Britain years ago. He compared the devil to a stray dog that is barking at our heels. He taught that unless we resist the dog, he will continue with his "yelping" and aggravation. But if we boldly tell him to leave us alone, he will flee. The devil has no choice when we resist him in Jesus' name. He must flee.

As Christians, we can call upon Jesus to defeat Satan and his demonic powers. Matthew 12:29-30 says we can tie up the strong man (Satan) and rob his house (set free those who are enslaved to Satan). *Or again, how can anyone enter a strong man's house and carry off his possessions unless he first ties up the strong man? Then he can rob his house* (Matthew 12:29-30).

How do we defeat demonic powers, according to Matthew 12:29-30?

We can drive demons out in the name of Jesus by "tying up" the demonic spirit that is influencing our lives or someone else's life. Only then can we be free. As believers, we can provide deliverance for those who have been held captive by Satan's power. *And these signs will accompany those who believe: In my name they will drive out demons; they will speak in new tongues* (Mark 16:17).

Casting out demons is a ministry that the Lord has given to those who believe in Him. Christians are called to minister deliverance to those bound by Satan. If you believe the Lord is calling you to set people free from demon spirits, I encourage you to follow the example of Jesus. He sent His disciples out two by two to minister, and they came back excited! Why? *...Even the demons submit to us in your name!* (Luke 10:17).

We should note that Jesus gives His disciples a word of caution, *"...do not rejoice that the spirits submit to you, but rejoice that your names are written in heaven"* (v. 20). Jesus cautioned the disciples to not make the power over the demons the source of their joy but rejoice because of their relationship with Him.

Biblical Foundations for Life

The fact remained—demons could not stand in the presence of the disciples commissioned by Jesus to cast them out. The Lord has also commissioned us to cast demons out of people and be set free from demonic activity in our own lives in Jesus' powerful name!

179 | Renounce demonic spirits

Sometimes people get involved innocently with the demonic by dabbling in paranormal energies in order to gain knowledge of the future or uncover secrets—reading tarot cards, demonic games like Dungeons and Dragons, and the ouija board, water witching, seances to contact the dead, use of drugs to produce "spiritual experiences"—all these practices are associated with the occult. Attempting to communicate with the supernatural through these kinds of methods is actually communication with demons (1 Samuel 28:8-14; 2 Kings 21:6; Isaiah 8:19).

Getting involved in these kinds of occult practices are dangerous and can lead to demonic bondage. The Bible gives these warnings:

...Do not practice divination or sorcery (Leviticus 19:26).

Do not turn to mediums or seek out spiritists, for you will be defiled by them. I am the Lord your God (Leviticus 19:31).

As a young boy, I participated in a type of *divination* by trying to "smell for water" on our family farm. We believed that by holding a rod, we could locate underground streams of water, thus knowing where to drill a well. Although I was completely unaware of it at the time, I was dabbling in the occult. Trying to uncover the unknown forces of nature by using superstitious practices like this is really opening ourselves to demonic spirits. After I received Jesus Christ as Lord, I claimed my freedom from the curse the enemy tried to place over my life through my involvement in this occult practice. Years ago, I also played with an ouija board, a game that attempts to uncover secret things by submitting to unknown spiritual forces. Again, I broke that curse over my life in the name of Jesus Christ.

There are two supernatural powers—the power of God through Jesus Christ, and the power of the enemy. A curse can be placed over our lives if we are involved in any type of occult practices. I have ministered to people who had an intense desire to commit suicide or fell into depression because the devil held them in bondage due to their involvement in the occult. The good news is this! You can be set completely free. If you or your ancestors have been involved in any type of occult activity, you can be set free. When you renounce those demonic spirits in the name of Jesus, the demons can no longer have any control of your life.

A friend of ours had migraine headaches for over eight years. In her case, this physical ailment was tied into her involvement in the occult. In desperation, she went to some Christians for help. They rebuked the devil in Jesus' name, and she was set free from the curse of constant headaches.

Occult practices

Leviticus 19:31; 20:6
Deuteronomy 18:10-11
Revelation 9:21

What dangers must we be aware of when someone is involved in the supernatural?

How do occult practices affect the lives of those involved?

Our lives are like an onion with many layers of skin. Maybe you have been set free from demonic spirits in your life. There may be little layers that God has already peeled off. However, the Lord may take you through other areas of freedom in the future.

He loves us and takes us step by step. He knows what we can handle. As the Lord reveals other areas of bondage in our lives, we receive His freedom. Then another layer comes off. The Lord continues this process until we are completely clean and are the people God has called us to be. He is committed to seeing us set completely free. This process may take days, months, or even years.

180 | Free from family curses

Earlier in this book (Day 159 and Day 163) we mentioned generational (family) curses that may be passed down through the generations. Unrepented sin can leave a spiritual weakness toward a particular sin in a family line. For example, a sexual sin may produce a curse. The curse then causes a generational weakness to that sin to be passed down in the family line. If the sin is not made right before God, it continues its pattern and strongly influences our lives.

Identify any generational sins in your family line. Write them down and walk through the steps of repentance and forgiveness mentioned above.

Generational sins cause spiritual *strongholds* or thinking in our minds that cause us to say, "Even God cannot change this circumstance in my life. It's hopeless." We begin to accept this lie and fall into sin that produces a stronghold in our lives. There are multitudes of strongholds that can be passed through family lines: addictions like alcohol, food, compulsive spending; mental problems like depression, rage, worry; sexual problems like homosexuality, fornication, pornography; heart issues that include bitterness, greed, rebellion, legalism, gossip.

First, it is important to identify the strongholds that afflict our family lines because we can demolish these strongholds in our lives. *The weapons we fight with are not the weapons of the world. On the contrary, they have divine power to demolish strongholds. We demolish arguments and every pretension that sets itself up against the knowledge of God, and we take captive every thought to make it obedient to Christ* (2 Corinthians 10:4-5).

Next, we should repent of our own sin. Even though we have inherited a spiritual weakness to a particular sin in our family, it is no excuse for the sin we have committed. Then, we forgive our ancestors for bringing the sin into the family line. *If you forgive anyone his sins, they are forgiven; if you do not forgive them, they are not forgiven* (John 20:23). We cannot have unforgiveness in our hearts. Finally, we need to repent of (or renounce) the sin. By doing so, we break the power of that sin in our generation. We remove Satan's legal right to continue plaguing us and our children in that particular area.

181 | Our spiritual weapons

As Christians, we are engaged in a spiritual conflict with evil. Although we have been guaranteed victory through Christ's death on the cross, we must wage a spiritual warfare by the power of the Holy Spirit using our spiritual armor (Ephesians 6:10-18). For more on spiritual warfare, see Biblical Foundation 12, Part 2.

Biblical Foundations for Life

Name the three spiritual weapons explained here.

_____

_____

_____

How powerful is your testimony against demonic powers?

_____

_____

_____

One time, the disciples could not cast out a demon in a young boy, and Jesus said, "...*this kind can come out only by prayer ["and fasting," in some translations]*" (Mark 9:29).

Jesus implied that if His disciples had maintained a life of prayer, like He did, they could have successfully cast this demon out. When we recognize we are in conflict against spiritual forces and powers of evil, we will live fervently before God and be equipped by faith to see others delivered from demonic spirits.

To overcome evil, God has given us weapons. The first weapon is the "name of Jesus Christ." The scriptures tell us, "*That at the name of Jesus every knee should bow, in heaven and on earth and under the earth, and every tongue confess that Jesus Christ is Lord, to the glory of God the Father*" (Philippians 2:10-11).

Some time ago, I was awakened in the night and sensed an evil presence in my room. I was away from home, and no one else was in the house where I was staying. I felt like I was frozen to my bed. I could only call out the name of "Jesus." The evil presence left and I was able to go back to sleep. There is power in the name of Jesus.

The second weapon the Lord has given to us against the enemy is the "blood of Jesus Christ." I have actually witnessed demons in people who have shrieked in fear at the mention of the blood of Jesus. On one occasion, a man with demons held his hands over his ears and screamed when the blood of Jesus was mentioned. The blood of the Lamb has freed us from the power of the enemy. The scriptures tell us in Revelation 12:11, "*they overcame him by the blood of the Lamb and by the word of their testimony; they did not love their lives so much as to shrink from death*" (Revelation 12:11).

The third weapon the Lord has given to us against the curse of the enemy is the "word of our testimony." Our testimony is simply confessing what the Lord has done in our lives and what God is saying about us. We know what God says about us by believing His Word. The truth of God's Word sets us free.

In closing, I am going to ask you to pray the following prayer aloud. We will confess the Word of God and our testimony, and find freedom from the curse in Jesus' name.`

Freedom Prayer

In the name of Jesus Christ, I renounce any involvement that I or my family has ever had with the occult back to the third and fourth generation in Jesus' name. I declare that I am a child of the living God through faith in Jesus Christ.

Jesus Christ is the Lord and King of my life. His blood has cleansed me from every sin and from every curse that the enemy would have tried to place against my life. The Bible says, 'whom the Son sets free is free indeed' (John 8:36). I am free today in the mighty name of Jesus. I declare my freedom from spiritual bondage and false guilt in Jesus' Name. I declare freedom today from any type of physical illness or disease in the name of Jesus. I declare I am emotionally whole in the name of Jesus Christ. I forgive anyone who has ever hurt me in Jesus' name. I declare that I am free mentally in the name of Jesus.

I declare that I am free financially, and I shall prosper in Jesus' name. I declare in the name of Jesus that I am free socially, and the favor of God is on my life. I declare that I am free from every demonic stronghold and strategy of the enemy in the name of Jesus. The strong man has been bound in Jesus' name and Jesus Christ has set me free. I declare the blood of Jesus Christ has set me free!

I claim my inheritance according to the Word of God that Jesus Christ has become a curse for me. I thank you for it in Jesus' name.

Amen.

If you feel you need to have another person pray with you and take authority over any demonic spirit or influence in your life, do it! He will be faithful to lead you to the right person. This Spirit-filled believer in Jesus Christ who has an intimate relationship with Jesus can pray for you, and the Lord will set you free.

182 | Coming to simple faith

Mark tells the story of a man with leprosy who came to Jesus on His knees, begging Jesus to heal him. He declared, *"If you are willing, you can make me clean"* (Mark 1:40-42). Jesus responded as He reached out His hand and touched the man. "I am willing," Jesus said. "Be clean!" Immediately the leprosy left the man, and he was cleansed.

Place yourself as the leper in this story. Ask Jesus to help you with any curse or bondage in your life. Repeat aloud what Jesus said to the leper in verse 41: *"'I am willing,' he said. 'Be clean!'"*

Let's read a second story in Mark 2:3-12a. *Some men came, bringing to him a paralyzed man, carried by four of them. Since they could not get him to Jesus because of the crowd, they made an opening in the roof above Jesus by digging through it and then lowered the mat the man was lying on. When Jesus saw their faith, he said to the paralyzed man, "Son, your sins are forgiven." Now some teachers of the law were sitting there, thinking to themselves, "Why does this fellow talk like that? He's blaspheming! Who can forgive sins but God alone?" Immediately Jesus knew in his spirit that this was what they were thinking in their hearts, and he said to them, "Why are you thinking these things?" Which is easier: to say to this paralyzed man, "Your sins are forgiven," or to say, "Get up, take your mat and walk?" But I want you to know that the Son of Man has authority on earth to forgive sins. So he said to the man, "I tell you, get up, take your mat and go home." He got up, took his mat and walked out in full view of them all.'*

Jesus saw the faith of those who were bringing the paralyzed man to Jesus: "Jesus saw their faith." Jesus responds to faith by running towards it. He is excited to answer our prayers when He sees our faith.

When Jesus was on this earth, He healed those who came to him in simple faith. He does the same today.

Ask Jesus to help you with any curse or bondage in your life. Repeat aloud what Jesus said to the leper in Mark 1:41: "I am willing," he said. "Be clean!"

FOUNDATION 7

Learning to Fellowship with God

183 | Introduction to foundation 7

In this seventh book of the Biblical Foundation Series, Learning to Fellowship with God, we will see that God wants to know us personally, and learn how that is possible through meditating on His Word and praying and worshiping Him. We will discover how to develop a close, intimate relationship with God through Jesus Christ as we learn to hear His voice.

John 5:17, 19 tells us, *"Jesus said to them, 'My Father is always at his work to this very day, and I too am working.' Jesus gave them this answer: 'Very truly I tell you, the Son can do nothing by himself; he can do only what he sees his Father doing, because whatever the Father does the Son also does.'"*

Jesus had an intimate relationship with His heavenly Father. He told His disciples that the Son could not do anything by Himself, but only what He saw His Father doing. This is because whatever the Father does, the Son also does.

It is so important to learn how to pray. I have found that Christians struggle with their prayer lives more than any other area of their walk with God. Yet, our time alone with our heavenly Father in prayer should be a source of great joy in our lives. Isaiah 56:7 tells us, *"These I will bring to my holy mountain and give them joy in my house of prayer."*

In this series of teachings from the scriptures we will talk about what I have learned regarding how to pray and about hearing the voice of God.

What was the key to Jesus life while He was on this earth?

PART 1

KNOWING GOD THROUGH HIS WORD

184 | How can we get to know such an awesome God?

Let's imagine that you are going for a run down a street in Washington D.C. and the President of the United States jogs by. You hail him with a greeting, "Hello, Mr. President." Does the president know you? Do you know him? Probably not. You may know all about the president, but it's one thing to know a lot of facts about him; it's a different thing to actually know him personally.

In the same way, many people know all about God, but they don't really know Him in a personal way. God is infinite, the creator of the universe, the original being, the sovereign ruler of all that is. No one created Him (Acts 17:23-25), He has always been around and will continue eternally unchanged (Hebrews 13:8). How can we get to know this infinite God when we are but finite humans? How can our minds even begin to comprehend Him?

We can get to know God through Jesus Christ. God has made Himself known through Jesus. He is made real to us through a relationship with His Son whom He sent to earth to do His will. Jesus came to personally encounter us and die for our sins so we can live forever. *Now this is eternal life: that they may know you, the only true God, and Jesus Christ, whom you have sent* (John 17:3).

According to the Bible, eternal life involves getting to know, commune, and fellowship with our God who is made known through His Son Jesus Christ whom He sent. God wants to know us personally! Let's learn how to fellowship with God through meditating on God's Word and praying and worshiping Him. We will discover how to develop a close, intimate relationship with God through Jesus Christ.

Beforehand, however, it is important to understand who God is. We believe in and worship one God. When God spoke to Moses in the ancient days, He revealed Himself as One. Centuries later, when Jesus was asked to choose the greatest commandment, Jesus quoted those same words of long ago...*Hear, O Israel, the Lord our God, the Lord is one*...(Mark 12:29).

The Bible clearly teaches there is only one God. Yet we know from scripture that God is Father, God is Jesus and God is Spirit. That does not mean that God is three. There is only one God whom we love and worship. So how can He be one and yet three?

185 | When three equals one

According to the Bible, God is one God who is three persons. The term *Trinity* is used to describe this concept. When Jesus said we should go into all nations making disciples, the three persons of the Trinity are linked together... *in the name of the Father and of the Son and of the Holy Spirit* (Matthew 28:19).

The Bible also tells us in the book of Genesis, *"Let Us make man in Our image"* (Genesis 1:26). When the world was created, God the Father, God the Son,

---

There is one God
1 Corinthians 8:4
Ephesians 4:6; James 2:19

According to John 17:3, how can we get to know God?

Do you know God or only know about Him?

The Trinity
God is one essence existing in three distinct persons who share a divine nature: Father, Son and Holy Spirit: Matthew 3:16-17; 28:19
2 Corinthians 13:14
Ephesians 4:4-6
1 Peter 1:2; Jude 20-21

and God the Holy Spirit worked together to create the earth and all that is on it. God the Father, God the Son, and God the Holy Spirit always were in existence.

The Father, Son and Holy Spirit are coequal, coeternal members. Although this concept is not easy for us to understand, our God is one essence existing in three distinct persons who share a divine nature—God our Father who is in Heaven, God the Son whom He sent to earth, and God the Holy Spirit who dwells in every believer who has been born again through faith in Jesus Christ.

The three are not three gods, or three parts or expressions of God, but are three persons so completely united that they form the one true and eternal God.[1] To fathom this, our minds and hearts must be stretched to hold a greater God than we can even imagine! God is so great—our finite minds cannot easily understand. It sometimes helps to look at the things He has created. In nature, we find things that take different forms and have different effects on our senses, yet are still one.

For example, water takes on three different forms. Water is converted into an invisible vapor or gas (steam) by being heated. Ice is the crystalline form of water made solid by cold temperatures. No matter what its form (water, steam or ice), it is still water.

Another example from nature is the sun. According to scientists, no one has actually seen the sun because it is so powerful. When we look at the sun, we do not see the star itself, but we can clearly see the rays of sun that shine on the earth. From the sun itself, through its rays, we have light and heat, and something mysterious makes plants grow (through the process of photosynthesis). We can conclude that the sun is the sun—one entity. Yet, the sun is light; the sun is heat; the sun is growth-life. All of this is true without contradiction. It is still the sun.

Although these illustrations from what has been created may help us to understand the idea of God being One—Father, Jesus, Spirit—they are not enough. We cannot decide who God is and what He is like based on what our eyes see, our ears hear or our hands touch. We must put our faith in God Himself. We must choose what to believe about Him based on His Word.

We must spend our lives seeking Him and getting to know Him better. We must read the Bible and do what it says. How can we understand Him without knowing and loving Him? How can we see Him without believing and obeying Him? No one person can fully explain God to another. We must each seek Him and know Him. *And without faith it is impossible to please God, because anyone who comes to him must believe that he exists and that he rewards those who earnestly seek him* (Hebrews 11:6).

[1] *Full Life Study Bible*, NIV, Life Publishers International, 1992, p.1479.

Name the three persons of the Trinity.

According to Hebrews 11:6, how can we really get to know God?

186 | Jesus is God

When we earnestly seek God, we find Him through Jesus Christ. Let's look briefly at the claims of Jesus. As Christians, we must believe He is who He said He is, because it persuades us of His deity.

Biblical Foundations for Life

Write down the four reasons confirming that Jesus is who He said He is.

_____

_____

_____

_____

Did Jesus ever deny that He is One with God?

_____

_____

_____

_____

Very few people will say that a man called Jesus of Nazareth never existed. There are many ancient writings, both religious and secular, that confirm to His place in history. There are many, however, who will say that He was just a good man or a prophet. Many believe that He was just a man, flesh and blood, like the rest of us. The religious leaders of Jesus thought the same, and they wanted to stone Him. The things Jesus said made them furious (see John 10:24-38) because Jesus boldly claimed that He was God. They accused him of blasphemy because only God has the right to say He is God.

How can we know that Jesus is who He claimed to be? Jesus' answers to the stone-throwers pointed to four reasons we can be certain:

Scripture: Jesus continually pointed to and affirmed the scripture. He knew the scriptures and obeyed them. He fulfilled all the prophecies of the Messiah.

Sonship: According to prophecies, Jesus was born of a virgin in Bethlehem. Jesus called God "Father" and stressed his unique relationship as His only begotten Son.

Actions: Jesus told His accusers not to believe Him unless He did what His Father does. Jesus' whole life was characterized by a constant awareness of the Father's will. He said and did what the Father said and did. Though many tried to accuse Him, they never were able to because He had done no wrong.

Miracles: If none of that will persuade us to believe, the miracles should. He restored sight to the eyes of a man born blind. He made the deaf hear and speak. He made the lame walk, cured lepers and made many other sick people well. Demons obeyed Him without hesitation, knowing who He was. He had authority over nature, calming a storm with a word. He changed water to wine and multiplied one boy's lunch to feed thousands. He walked on water. He made accurate predictions about what people would do and what events would take place. Greatest of all, Christ rose from the dead. Death could not rule over Him! Jesus' resurrection is the real proof and demonstration of His deity.

It is interesting to see that with all Jesus' claims and with all His power, He never denied that God is One. He simply said that He and the Father are One. Jesus was not merely a man or prophet. Jesus is who He claimed to be. He is God's Son. He is One with the Father. Because of who He is, Jesus was able to reconcile the world to the Father.

187 | God's Word is life to us

God wants us to get to know Him. The scriptures say in Revelation 3:20, *"Here I am! I stand at the door and knock. If anyone hears my voice and opens the door, I will come in and eat with him, and he with me."* This is an invitation! When we receive Jesus, we are invited to sit down to a friendly meal together. This is a picture of the intimacy that God wants to have with us.

How can we build a relationship with Him? First of all, we build a relationship with the Lord by meditating on the Word of God. John 6:63 teaches us, *"the Spirit gives life; the flesh counts for nothing. The words I have spoken to you are spirit and they are life."* Many Christians today find themselves dried up spiritually because they have not taken God's Word as spirit and life. The Bible is not just a set of good principles and historical facts; it is life to us! As we meditate on His Word, we build a relationship with Him. He speaks to us through His Word.

A friend of mine stepped onto an elevator many years ago, and to his surprise, there stood Billy Graham the renowned evangelist. He only had a split second to ask one quick question, "Mr. Graham, if you were a young man like me, what word of advice would you have?"

The evangelist looked at him with the sincerity that has marked his life and said, "Read the Bible and get to know the Word of God." The evangelist had learned that the best way to know God is to know His Word.

In reality, Jesus and His Word are one. *In the beginning was the Word, and the Word was with God, and the Word was God* (John 1:1). To know Jesus is to know His Word. To love Jesus is to love His Word. You cannot separate the Word of God and Jesus Christ. Revelation 19:13b says...*his name is the Word of God.*

Some years ago, I read a survey that produced some startling findings. It said that one-quarter of Protestant church leaders are not born again Christians and only half of all church leaders (53%) believe that there are moral truths that are absolute.[1] That's one of the reasons why spiritual power has gone from many churches today! If we don't believe that the Bible is the Word of God—that it is actually Jesus speaking to us as His people—we are bankrupt of spiritual power. God will not be able to move supernaturally in our lives. Unbelief will hinder God's supernatural work. Even Jesus could not do many miracles in His hometown because of the unbelief of some of His own family members (John 7:1-5).

[1] Barna Research Online, www.barna.org, "Leadership" statistics and analysis in this archive come from national surveys conducted by Barna Research, 1997.

What does the Word of God do in our lives, according to John 6:63?

188 | God's Word renews our minds

Romans 12:2 says, *"Do not conform any longer to the pattern of this world, but be transformed by the renewing of your mind...."*

What does it mean to not be conformed to the pattern of this world? The *world* mentioned here refers to our present age or world system. This *world* is subject to the devil—the god of this world (2 Corinthians 4:4) and is consequently filled with sin and suffering.

In this age, Satan uses the world's ideas, morality, philosophies, mass media, etc. to oppose God's people and His Word. The world's system is one of selfishness that is under Satan's rule. In contrast, God's kingdom is a kingdom of love.

One translation of this verse in the Bible says we should not be "put into the world's mold." Have you ever taken a box of gelatin, mixed it with hot water, and poured it into a mold? After it has time to chill, the gelatin is shaped like the mold. The Bible says that if we do not separate ourselves from this world's system, we will end up molded like the world.

Renewing our minds is like taking a car with an old engine to a mechanic. After the mechanic puts in new parts, greases and adjusts them correctly, the engine runs like new. If we do not renew our minds by the Word of God by get-

How do you know when your mind needs to be renewed?

Biblical Foundations for Life

According to Ephesians 5:25-26, what does God use to cleanse us?

ting "greased and adjusted," we will begin to think and act like the world's system around us. The Word of God actually cleanses our minds from the thoughts and mindsets of the world system around us. It is like taking a spiritual bath on a regular basis. Living in this world causes us to get spiritually dirty. The Word of God cleanses us and renews our minds. Ephesians 5:25-26 tells us, *"Christ loved the church and gave himself up for her to make her holy, cleansing her by the washing with water through the word."*

In the book of Acts, we read that Paul, the apostle, was impressed when he met a group of people called the Bereans (Acts 17:10-11). Whenever Paul preached, the Bereans checked it out to see if Paul's teaching coincided with the scriptures. Whenever you hear the Word of God preached, regardless of who says it, realize that it must line up with what God says in His Word. Men and women are fallible, but God's Word can always be trusted. It is always the final authority. We need to study God's Word so we know the truth (2 Timothy 2:15).

189 | God's Word gives us power to live

Some years ago, a friend went to visit one of his neighbors who had been sick for a long time. The neighbor was in a subconscious state and couldn't respond to anyone who came into his room. My friend took his Bible along and began to read the Word of God. An amazing thing happened. For the first time in weeks, the man began to stir. The Word is full of living power...*whatever God says to us is full of living power* (Hebrews 4:12 Living Bible).

How much power does God's Word have?

Jesus realized that the key to His life was in knowing the Word of God and communing with His Father in Heaven. God has given us the Bible so that we can know the Word of God, apply it to our lives and defeat the devil. Taking time each day to commune with God and to read His Word protects us from the lies of the enemy. When Jesus was tempted in the wilderness, He said to the devil, in Matthew 4:4, *"...It is written: Man does not live on bread alone, but on every word that comes from the mouth of God."*

If I receive an email from a person, it is a direct communication from that person. When we read the Word of God, God speaks to us clearly. Jesus and His Word are one (John 1:2).

How do you feed your spirit so that it may grow?

A common problem many Christians experience is finding time to read and meditate on the Word of God each day. The devil and the demons of hell will do everything they can to keep a Christian from studying the scriptures and communing with the Lord through His Word. God wants us to set aside a specific time to pray and read His Word each day. Take that time seriously and plan for it. It will not just happen.

Reading a scripture with your cereal in the morning and then praying for two minutes as you drive to work or school does not really add up to a time of communing with Jesus! However, it is important to start somewhere. Begin by reading a few verses each day and expect the Lord to speak to you. Take time to be with your friend, Jesus. As you grow in the Lord, you will want to spend more time with Him.

I have found that by reading one or two chapters from the New Testament and two or three chapters from the Old Testament each day, I can read through the entire Bible each year. But that is not where I started as a young Christian. I started with what I could handle—several minutes each day.

Those who do not spend time in the Word of God each day become weak. What happens if you do not eat food for a few days? You become physically weak. If we do not meditate on the Word each day, we become spiritually weak.

When we are born again and receive Jesus Christ through faith, our spirit has been reborn by the Spirit of God. Our soul, mind, will and emotions are being renewed each day by the Word of God as we meditate on His Word.

190 | Meditate on God's Word

We need Jesus and His Word in our lives each day. Without Him, we can do absolutely nothing, but with Him, we can do all things (Philippians 4:13). Whenever I do not have the Word of God flowing through my life by daily prayerful study of the Word of God, I find myself growing weak spiritually. I cannot do the things that God has called me to do. Jesus promises in John 15:4-5, *"remain in me, and I will remain in you. No branch can bear fruit by itself; it must remain in the vine. Neither can you bear fruit unless you remain in me. I am the vine; you are the branches. If a man remains in me and I in him, he will bear much fruit; apart from me you can do nothing."*

As we allow the life of God to come into us when we commune with Him daily by His Word, our lives will bear spiritual fruit. And that is exactly what the Lord has called us to do—bear fruit.

The Living Bible tells us, "the backslider gets bored with himself, but the godly man's life is exciting" (Proverbs 14:14). Our lives will be filled with excitement as we get to know God and experience His Word helping us overcome obstacles in our lives. People around us should say, "What do you have? I want it." As we meditate on the Word of God, He builds faith in our lives to do what He has told us to do. We should meditate on His Word day and night. *But his delight is in the law of the Lord, and on his law he meditates day and night. He is like a tree planted by streams of water, which yields its fruit in season and whose leaf does not wither. Whatever he does prospers* (Psalms 1:2-3).

The word *meditate* literally means *to roll something around over and over again in our minds*. Memorizing the Word is a part of the meditating process. When you and I eat physical food, that food becomes bone, blood and tissue in our bodies. When we meditate on the Word of God, it spiritually becomes a part of our lives. We begin to act and react the way Jesus does because of the power that is in His Word. Those who live in the Word of God will produce spiritual fruit. The Bible says in Galatians 5:22-23, *"But the fruit of the Spirit is love, joy, peace, patience, kindness, goodness, faithfulness, gentleness and self-control...."*

All of the fruit of the Holy Spirit will become a very active part of our lives when we meditate on the Word of God each day and commune with Him. Are you meditating on God's Word each day? If not, today is your day to begin.

Biblical Foundations for Life

> What qualities of Galatians 5:22-23 are produced in your life by meditating on God's Word?

PART 2 — KNOWING GOD THROUGH PRAYER AND WORSHIP

191 | Prayer, our communication line with God

Besides meditating on God's Word, another way we can fellowship with the Lord each day is through prayer. The Lord wants to communicate with us! Ephesians 6:18 says, *"And pray in the Spirit on all occasions with all kinds of prayers and requests. With this in mind, be alert and always keep on praying for all the saints."*

Prayer is our communication line with our God. During war, if a battalion loses contact with headquarters, the soldiers are in serious trouble, becoming much more vulnerable to the enemy. It often works the same way in our Christian lives. We are in a spiritual war. The devil is constantly trying to break down our communication line with God.

Prayer is only as complicated as we make it. God has not asked us to pray fancy prayers. Prayer is simply communication with Him. It is talking with God, sharing our hearts and listening. God wants us to talk to Him in the same way we talk to our closest friend. I often write down my prayers and then I can give praise to God when I see these prayers answered. When we know that God is answering prayer, it builds our faith.

Prayer can take various forms. We can pray in the language we speak (English, Spanish, Swahili, French, etc.) or speak in tongues (our prayer language between us and God used to build up our spiritual life). Paul is referring to both when he describes how he prays in 1 Corinthians 14:15, *"...I will pray with my spirit, but I will also pray with my mind...."*

Paul prayed with his spirit and he prayed with his mind. In other words, a believer can pray with his spirit (in tongues) as the Holy Spirit gives the utterance (1 Corinthians 12:7, 11; Acts 2:4) or pray with his mind (in a known language) also under the impulse of the Holy Spirit.

When our spirits are praying in our heavenly language (in tongues), we are bypassing the devil by using a direct prayer line that God has given to us (1 Corinthians 14:2). It is equally important to pray prayers directed by God in our own language. Both are needed!

192 | Lord, teach us to pray

Jesus lived a life-style of prayer. He was constantly in communication and fellowship with His Father in heaven.

But Jesus often withdrew to lonely places and prayed (Luke 5:16).

...Jesus went out to a mountainside to pray, and spent the night praying to God (Luke 6:12).

The disciples witnessed Jesus' prayer life and wanted it for themselves. *One day Jesus was praying in a certain place. When he finished, one of his disciples said to him, "Lord, teach us to pray..."* (Luke 11:1).

Describe prayer in your own words.

According to 1 Corinthians 14:15, what two things can a believer pray with?

Why did Jesus withdraw from the world to commune with God?

To my knowledge, the only thing that the disciples actually asked Jesus to teach them was "to pray." They saw how Jesus prayed in secret. Whenever Jesus was involved with people, they saw miracles and wonderful events take place through Jesus' life and ministry. They knew there was a direct correlation between His communing with His Father and the supernatural occurrences. Jesus set the example of listening to the voice of the Holy Spirit to direct Him in every situation. His heavenly Father gave Him the ability to always know just where to go and who to talk and minister to.

John Wesley, the founder of the Methodist church, once said, "Give me one hundred preachers who fear nothing but sin and desire nothing but God, and I care not a straw whether they be clergymen or laymen, such alone will shake the gates of Hell and set up the kingdom of Heaven on earth. God does nothing but in answer to prayer." Wesley knew that God uses prayer in our lives to fulfill His purposes.

Why did the disciples want to learn to pray as Jesus did?

193 | A model prayer

Jesus gave His disciples a model prayer, which we call *The Lord's Prayer*. The purpose of this prayer was to teach us how to pray. Jesus said in Matthew 6:9-13, *"in this manner, therefore, pray: Our Father in heaven, Hallowed be Your name. Your kingdom come. Your will be done On earth as it is in heaven. Give us this day our daily bread. And forgive us our debts, as we forgive our debtors. And do not lead us into temptation, but deliver us from the evil one. For Yours is the kingdom and the power and the glory forever. Amen"* (NKJ).

This prayer has helped my more than 50 years of walking with Jesus. When Jesus says, *"Our Father in Heaven, hallowed be Your name,"* He is simply saying, *"Father, Your name is holy. We lift up Your name."*

Jesus declares, *"Your kingdom come."* We also should declare His kingdom to come and His will to be done on earth as it is in Heaven. We can declare that God's kingdom will come and His will be accomplished in our families, our communities, our church, our schools, our places of business, our small groups, and literally everywhere we go. When we pray, *"Give us this day our daily bread,"* we are asking for the things that we need. God wants us to ask. He tells us that "we have not because we ask not" (James 4:2).

When Jesus prayed, *"Forgive us our debts as we forgive our debtors,"* He reinforced the truth that we must forgive anyone who has sinned against us. If we do not forgive, God cannot forgive us (Matthew 6:14-15).

When we declare, *"Do not lead us into temptation, but deliver us from the evil one,"* we are reminded of the truth that the Lord has called us to stand against the powers of darkness in Jesus' name. That is why the Word of God tells us we should resist the devil and he will flee from us (James 4:7). Jesus closes this model prayer by declaring, *"For Yours is the kingdom and the power and the glory forever. Amen."* The Lord's Prayer starts and closes by giving honor and glory to our God through Jesus Christ. We can follow His example.

What have you learned about prayer through studying this model?

Biblical Foundations for Life

What are three possible answers to our prayers?

How can we eliminate anxiety from our lives, according to Philippians 4:6?

194 | Let your requests be known

The Bible teaches us to pray without ceasing (1 Thessalonians 5:17). We need to be in a constant attitude of prayer all day long whether we are at work, home, school, or spending time with friends. We can pray on the way to the office or while cutting the grass. Jesus gives us this advice in Luke 11:9-10. *...Ask and it will be given to you; seek and you will find; knock and the door will be opened to you. For everyone who asks receives; he who seeks finds; and to him who knocks, the door will be opened.* If you lost a check with a whole week's wages, how long would you search for it? You probably would search until you found it. We need the same tenacity as we pray. We need to continue to ask and thank God for His answers until we experience an answer to our prayers. God may answer, "yes," "no," or "wait."

It amazes me how God will answer almost any prayer that a new Christian prays. When babies are born into a family, they get constant attention every time they cry. When they begin to grow up and mature, they do not always get their own way. As we begin to grow in the Lord, we may not always get our prayers answered the same way. The Lord wants to give us what is best for us, not always what we want.

God instructs us to refuse anxiety as we talk to Him and walk with Him in a constant attitude of thanksgiving. Philippians 4:6 tells us to, "*...not be anxious about anything, but in everything, by prayer and petition, with thanksgiving, present your requests to God.*"

Years ago my family had a financial need. We were living on a very small budget and obeying God in every way that we knew. One day, I was praying for the Lord to provide for us financially. I opened the door of our home so I could go to work and I saw the most amazing phenomenon. Money was lying all over the place! It was on the front lawn, the porch, and all around the house—even on the back lawn! You may ask, "How did it get there?" I have no idea. Did it ever happen again? No, but I will never forget it. All I know is that God did it, and it was a blessing to us. God is a supernatural God who answers prayers in a supernatural way.

195 | Praise and worship brings us to the Father

Fellowship with God not only includes meditating on His Word and praying but also *worshiping and praising* the Lord. To *praise* God means *to respond to God for what He has done*. Praise God for specific things He has done in your life.

Worship focuses more on *who God is*—on His person. We thank Him because He is God. Everyone worships something. Some people worship themselves. Some people worship their jobs, a motorcycle, sports or a spouse. We have been chosen to worship only God. The word *worship* comes from an old Anglo-Saxon word, *weorthsceipe*, which means *to ascribe worth to our God*. Only God is worthy of glory and praise. The Bible says in John 4:23-24 that we must worship with our heart, it cannot be merely form because *...true worshipers will worship the*

Father in spirit and truth, for they are the kind of worshipers the Father seeks. God is spirit, and his worshipers must worship in spirit and in truth.

I must admit, I don't always feel like worshiping God. Praising or worshiping the Lord is not to be dependent upon our emotions, but instead a *decision* we make. God is worthy of all glory and praise. The Bible says that we should offer Him a sacrifice of praise. *Through Jesus, therefore, let us continually offer to God a sacrifice of praise—the fruit of lips that confess his name* (Hebrews 13:15).

The tabernacle of David in the Old Testament was known as a place of freedom in praise and worship. God is going to rebuild the tabernacle of David again in the last days (Acts 15:16). That is why God is bringing the freedom to worship to His church today.

Music is a basic form of worship. Music was so important in David's day that he appointed people with instruments to praise and worship the Lord (1 Chronicles 15:16;16:5-6). God is restoring praise and worship to His church today. God's original intention of unbridled praise and worship will be restored to His church.

We need to be involved privately in praise and worship to our God in our time alone with Him. In the same way that the moon reflects the glory of the sun, we will reflect the glory of God in our lives as we spend time worshiping Him. The book of Psalms is filled with songs of praise to our God. I encourage you to take the book of Psalms and begin to sing those psalms and make up your own songs and to use them to give worship to God.

196 | He is worthy to receive praise

Heaven is a place that will be filled with praise and worship! Revelation 5:11-12 describes a scene of heaven. *Then I looked and heard the voice of many angels...They encircled the throne and the living creatures and the elders. In a loud voice they sang: Worthy is the Lamb, who was slain, to receive power and wealth and wisdom and strength and honor and glory and praise!*

Some people think that worship should be quiet. There is a place for quietly worshiping God, but the Bible also encourages us to worship God with a loud voice (Psalm 47:1). You can go to a football game and see thousands of people get emotionally charged by a little pigskin being thrown around a field. Think how much more exciting it is because Jesus Christ went to the cross and gave His life for you! That's why we shout unto God and praise and bless Him—He is worthy to receive the praise due only to Him!

We worship God here on earth in preparation for heaven. I certainly do not want to be a spiritually dead person who cannot praise the Lord. *It is not the dead who praise the Lord, those who go down to silence* (Psalms 115:17).

Although I am not an exceptionally emotional person, when I realize what Jesus Christ did for me, my spirit, soul, and body begins to get caught up in praise and worship to my God. According to the scripture, the demons of hell can be bound (tied up spiritually) through praise and worship to our God. Psalms

Explain the difference between praise and worship.

What is a true worshiper, according to John 4:23-24?

What happens when we praise God, according to Psalms 149:6-8?

Biblical Foundations for Life

149:6-8 says, *"May the praise of God be in their mouths and a double-edged sword in their hands, to inflict vengeance on the nations and punishment on the peoples, to bind their kings with fetters, their nobles with shackles of iron."*

Whether we are alone or with two or three others or with one thousand people, the demons tremble when God's people commune with Him through praise and worship.

God inhabits, actually lives in, the praises of His people. *But You are holy, who inhabit the praises of Israel (Psalms 22:3 NKJ).*

How does God live in our praises?

197 | Expressing worship

There are many ways that we can express worship and praise to our God. Here are just a few of the ways mentioned in the scriptures. First of all, we can kneel before the Lord. *Come, let us bow down in worship, let us kneel before the Lord our Maker* (Psalms 95:6).

We can stand and worship our God like the multitude of people in Revelation 7:9-10. *A great multitude that no one could count, from every nation, tribe, people and language, standing before the throne and in front of the Lamb. They were wearing white robes and were holding palm branches in their hands. And they cried out in a loud voice: "Salvation belongs to our God, who sits on the throne, and to the Lamb."*

The scripture also says there are times God has called us to lift up our hands to the Lord. *I want men everywhere to lift up holy hands in prayer...*(1 Timothy 2:8).

Other scriptures teach us we should be still before the Lord. *Be still, and know that I am God...*(Psalms 46:10).

We are also exhorted to praise Him with instruments. *Praise him with the sounding of the trumpet, praise him with the harp and lyre...praise him with the clash of cymbals, praise him with resounding cymbals* (Psalms 150:3,5).

We can also worship the Lord in dance. The word *dance* in Hebrew means *the lifting of the feet.* David danced before the Lord in the Old Testament. The devil has taken the dance and made it sensual, but God is restoring dance to His church in purity through praise and worship to our King Jesus. Psalms 149:3 says, *"Let them praise his name with dancing and make music to him with tambourine and harp."*

God has also called us to sing new songs to our God. Singing a new song is simply asking God to give us a tune or a melody and then allowing the Holy Spirit to give us the words. Or we can take the words directly from the scriptures and sing them to Him. *Praise the Lord. Sing to the Lord a new song, his praise in the assembly of the saints* (Psalms 149:1).

The scripture also speaks of clapping and shouting unto the Lord. Remember the time God's people marched around Jericho day after day? On the seventh day, they shouted and the walls came tumbling down. Demons tremble when we shout because of what Jesus Christ has done and because of who He is. The

List the physical ways we can express our worship to God.

How many do you use when worshiping God?

Bible says we should clap and shout with cries of joy. *Clap your hands, all you nations; shout to God with cries of joy* (Psalms 47:1).

Ephesians 5:19 says that we should be speaking to one another in psalms and hymns and spiritual songs and making melody in our hearts to the Lord. When a couple gets married, the greatest desire they have is to be in a relationship together, to spend time together. This involves both speaking and listening. Our God wants us to have communion with Him and relationship with Him. Sometimes we express that relationship by being quiet and listening. Sometimes we shout unto our God. Other times we talk or weep. We've been created to praise and commune with our wonderful, heavenly Daddy.

PART 3

HOW CAN WE HEAR GOD'S VOICE?

198 | "Is that you, God?"

One evening after I taught at a church, a young man came to me and shared his struggle. "I feel the Lord is calling me to go to the mission field, but I'm not sure if I should quit my job or not. I keep hearing different voices. How do I know whether or not I am hearing God's voice clearly?"

Another time, a young man in his late teens stopped by our house and declared he had heard God's voice. He had a strange expression on his face and then spelled it out. "The Lord spoke to me today…and He told me to kill myself." I was momentarily stunned! But I knew from the Word of God the Lord would never tell someone to kill himself. It was clear the young man was hearing some other voice.

One time I was driving down a rural road when I passed a hitchhiker. I sensed a voice telling me to go back and pick him up. I thought the Lord wanted me to share my faith with him. When I turned around, he was nowhere in sight. I was confused. I thought the Lord had spoken to me.

Christians sometimes find themselves in situations where they struggle to hear God's voice. We really want to do what the Lord wants us to do. We know that we serve a living God who wants to speak to us, and yet we struggle with the fact that we often do not hear as clearly as we would like to. Sometimes we may think we have heard the Lord's voice and respond to it, only to find out that we were wrong. Instead of pressing in to find out why we "missed it," we hesitate to step out in faith the next time. Other times, we get so involved in the affairs of this natural world that we forget to listen to the voice of the Lord and receive His instructions for our daily living.

You probably know this already, but the Lord does not speak to us in reverb. Granted, in the movie, *The Ten Commandments*, the Lord spoke to Moses in a deep, booming voice, but that was only sound effects! How does He really speak to us? How can we hear His voice?

Let's see what God's Word says about hearing His voice. One day, Jesus made an interesting statement, *The one who sent me is with me; he has not left me alone, for I always do what pleases him* (John 8:29).

Jesus does only what the Father in heaven has told Him to do. If it is important for Jesus to hear from His Father in heaven, how much more important is it for each of us to hear His voice clearly? Read on to discover how to hear God's voice more clearly.

199 | Acknowledge God's voice

For those who are willing to check in with their heavenly Father about decisions of life, Proverbs 3:5-6 promises, *"Trust in the Lord with all your heart and lean not on your own understanding; in all your ways acknowledge him, and he will make your paths straight."*

Why did Jesus have to speak often with His heavenly Father (John 8:29)?

Have you ever obeyed what you thought was God's voice and later found it was not? Explain.

After serving the Lord for more than three decades, I am totally convinced that it is a whole lot harder to get out of His will than we think. If we do get off course, He will reach out in love and nudge us back on track, if we are really trusting and acknowledging Him in our lives.

What does *acknowledge* mean? The Webster dictionary says it is *to admit the existence, reality, or truth of or express gratitude for*. So then, if we acknowledge a new friend, we talk to him, express our appreciation for him, and recognize his presence in our lives.

Imagine your friends not acknowledging your presence when you are together. You try to talk to them, and they completely ignore you. In fact, they talk right over you as if you were not even there. That is how we treat the Lord if we are not acknowledging Him moment by moment in our lives. If we are not recognizing His presence in our lives, we are probably not hearing the voice of the Lord as we should.

The Lord desires to speak to us in many ways, and we need to allow Him to do so. I spend much of my time traveling throughout the world teaching the Bible. One of the things that I miss most when I travel is communicating with my family. I really miss spending time with my wife, LaVerne. However, because of the technologically advanced age we live in, I can usually communicate with her regardless of where I am in the world. I don't care whether the message comes by phone, text, email, letter, or by a note. I just want to hear from her.

Let's not get too selective about how the Lord speaks to us. We need to get to a place where we want to hear His voice desperately. This desire comes out of a love relationship with Him. The Lord may speak to us at times in dreams, visions, or by His audible voice, but these are not the ways that He usually speaks to us. Usually, the Lord speaks to us either by His Word or by His Spirit speaking to our spirits. Jesus tells us that if we continue in His Word, we shall know the truth...*If you hold to my teaching, you are really my disciples. Then you will know the truth, and the truth will set you free* (John 8:31-32). He speaks to us by His Word! We will never go off track if we obey the Word of God!

200 | God's voice is compatible with God's Word!

We need to saturate ourselves with God's Word. We must have a full reservoir of the Word of God to draw from so we do not become deceived by the enemy. Any dream, prophecy, vision or audible voice that does not line up with scripture is not the voice of God. Scripture is given as a standard so that we will never get off track. 2 Timothy 3:16-17 describes God's Word this way. *All Scripture is God-breathed and is useful for teaching, rebuking, correcting and training in righteousness, so that the man of God may be thoroughly equipped for every good work.*

A man asked me one time if I could give my "stamp of approval" on his decision to divorce his wife and marry another woman in the church whom he felt could be more compatible with him in his ministry. I told him that no matter how right it felt to him, his plan was in direct disobedience to the Lord. How did I know? I knew from the scriptures, in Mark 10:11-12, that he would be committing adultery.

Biblical Foundations for Life

What happens when we acknowledge God (Proverbs 3:5-6)?

How does God give us truth and how does it set us free (John 8:31-32)?

What is the first step in determining if some thought or word is from God (2 Timothy 3:16-17)?

How does God's Word benefit you (Hebrews 5:12-14)?

What are some ways the Lord has spoken to you through the Holy Spirit?

Do you always recognize the voice of your Shepherd?

If we want to mature in our Christian lives, we will learn to renew our minds with God's Word so we can distinguish between good and evil. We will practice doing right. *You will never be able to eat solid spiritual food and understand the deeper things of God's Word until you become better Christians and learn right from wrong by practicing doing right* (Hebrews 5:12-14, Living Bible).

God's Word never changes. Many times, however, the area in which we need guidance is not in direct conflict with the scriptures. We may need to know the answers for some of the following questions: What is the Lord's plan for my career? Do I need to consider further training? Where should I live? Should I buy a house or a car? Where should I go to college? Which group of believers has the Lord called me to serve with? This is the time to learn to listen to the voice of the Holy Spirit speaking to our spirits.

201 | Allow the Holy Spirit to enlighten your spirit

The Lord desires to speak to us by His Spirit. Romans 8:16 says, "*The Spirit himself testifies with our spirit that we are God's children.*" Proverbs 20:27 says, "*The lamp of the Lord searches the spirit of a man; it searches out his inmost being.*"

Your spirit along with your soul dwell inside your body. Your spirit and soul live forever. Your soul includes your mind, will and emotions and your spirit communicates with the Holy Spirit.

We are learning on this earth how we can communicate with the Holy Spirit. Many times, we hear a voice deep within us but excuse it as "just us." The Lord wants to teach us to trust the Holy Spirit to speak to our spirit. Our spirit is like a lamp that the Lord will "light" and use to give us clear direction.

We often think that hearing God's voice is complicated. It is really not as hard as we think. When my wife and I were preparing to become missionaries as a young couple, we had two choices. Our mission board told us there was an opening in the states of Connecticut and South Carolina. As we prayed, the Lord placed a burden on our hearts for the people on an island off the coast of South Carolina. We didn't hear God speak in an audible voice, but the feeling kept getting stronger. We knew it was the right place.

We need to expect an answer from the Lord when we are really serious about listening to Him. The scriptures tell us, *In his heart a man plans his course, but the Lord determines his steps* (Proverbs 16:9). Look back at your life and see how the Lord has directed your steps. Sometimes God speaks to us by putting a desire or burden in our hearts that we know would not be from anyone else but God.

You can trust God. He speaks to those whose trust is completely in Him. As a boy growing up, I trapped muskrats every winter. Early every morning before dawn, I would follow the trap line to inspect my traps. Whenever I saw moving shadows or heard strange sounds, I would freeze in my tracks with fear. On those dark, cold, wintery mornings, the most comforting sound I could hear was the voice of my father, who would finish his morning chores and meet me on the trap line. Just the sound of his voice calling my name gave me a sense of peace and security.

Jesus is teaching us to hear His voice. He tells us, in John 10:4, that the sheep hear the shepherd's voice. *When he has brought out all his own, he goes on ahead of them, and his sheep follow him because they know his voice.* There are various voices that the sheep hear; however, they will not follow the voice of a stranger. The sheep have been trained to only follow the voice of the shepherd.

202 | Beware of other voices

When I first became a Christian, I thought that, from that day on, I was only going to hear the voice of God. Wow, was I ever in for a shock! I actually heard all kinds of voices inside my head. I soon realized that some of those voices most certainly were not the voice of the Holy Spirit. As time went on, experience taught me that there are at least four different kinds of voices a person may hear. If we are not hearing God's voice, we are hearing our own voice, the voice of others, or even the devil's voice at times. How can we know which voice is resounding inside of us?

Our own voice Let's talk about our own voice first. Remember, our soul is our mind, will, and emotions. So, then, the decisions that we often want to make originate from our beliefs, which are manifested in our feelings and emotions. This includes our personal preferences and desires, such as whether or not we like pizza, who our favorite football team is, or if we like shopping, fishing, or cherry pie. These things are not wrong, but they are personal preferences, not the voice of God. Many times, Christians confuse their own desires with the voice of the Lord.

Other people's voices Instead of God's voice, we may also hear other people's voices vying for our attention. 2 Corinthians 10:5 tells us, "*We demolish arguments and every pretension that sets itself up against the knowledge of God, and we take captive every thought to make it obedient to Christ.*"

Many times, the voices we hear have been placed inside us by those who try to sell us their products or philosophies. Whenever these thoughts and opinions are hostile to the Word of God, we are told to demolish them.

Sometimes it is difficult to know if we have heard from God correctly and to know if others have also heard correctly. We are told in 1 John 4:1 to test the "spirits." If another believer speaks out a word from God for you, test it. Ask God to confirm to you if this is really from Him. If you have any doubts, go to your pastor or other Christian leader. Ask them to pray about it with you.

203 | Enemy talk vs. the still small voice

The voice of the enemy A third voice that we may hear instead of God's voice is the voice of the enemy. The devil does not appear to us in a red jumpsuit with a long tail. He comes very slyly as an angel of light (2 Corinthians 11:14). He may use well-meaning people to speak words that could water down our faith. Or, he could place thoughts into our minds that are contrary to God's Word.

How do we "take captive every thought to make it obedient to Christ"?

Biblical Foundations for Life

Name some ways you resist the devil and his lies.

_____
_____
_____
_____
_____

Give examples of times God led you by His still, small voice.

_____
_____
_____
_____
_____
_____
_____

How often have you decided to get serious about studying the scriptures and a voice informs you that there are chores that need to be completed immediately? Tell the devil the same thing that Jesus told him, "It is written." Resist him in Jesus' name, and he will flee!

For a time in my life, while driving in my car, the enemy would attempt to place a cloud of depression around me. One day, I boldly spoke the Word to myself and the powers of darkness in the car. I shouted...*the one who is in [me] is greater than the one who is in the world* (1 John 4:4). Within minutes, the whole atmosphere in the car changed. The presence of the Lord replaced the presence of the enemy. I had silenced the enemy's voice by proclaiming the truth of the Word of God.

The voice of God The real voice we want to hear and obey is the voice of our God speaking to our spirit. We often call the Lord's voice a "still, small voice." This phrase comes from the story of Elijah in 1 Kings 19:11-13, when God spoke to him in a *"still, small voice."* Often, we are looking for the Lord to speak to us in an earth-shattering way. But the Lord usually speaks to us by His Spirit, deep within our spirits.

Psalm 46:10 says, *"Be still and know that I am God."* It is important to take time to be quiet and listen. If you get together with a close friend and do all the talking without listening, the relationship is one-sided. In our prayers, we should talk to God, but we need to listen, too.

Most of the major decisions in my life have come as a result of that "still, small voice." When the Lord spoke to me about being involved in church planting through small groups, He asked, "Are you willing to be involved in the underground church?" It was not a booming voice in an earthquake, but a "still, small voice." The "voice" was very clear—it changed the direction of my life.

There are times when I am picking up something for my family at the grocery store and a "still, small voice" tells me to purchase an extra item, not on the list. Nearly always, when I get home, the item that I chose was needed. If we are sensitive to the Holy Spirit, we will hear when He speaks. On one occasion, the Holy Spirit asked me to give some money to a missionary family. I was later informed that they had no money for food, and this gift was an answer to their prayers.

Ask God to communicate to you during your times with Him, and all throughout the day. You will learn more and more to discern what is your voice and what is the Holy Spirit's. You will learn how to hear the voice of God and obey Him.

204 | Tuning in to God's voice

Did you ever experience a verse almost leaping off the pages of the Bible? You may have read it one thousand times, but this time it really "grabs" you. God is speaking to you!

A husband may be relaxing and feel impressed to help his wife with some of the maintenance around the house. He should not be too quick to rebuke that thought! It is probably the Lord speaking to him. A teenager is listening to her favorite song or talking to one of her friends on the phone. A voice inside tells her to clean her room. It is probably God!

We learn to hear the voice of the Lord through practice and obedience. Sometimes we may feel discouraged trying to discern between the Lord's voice, the enemy's voice, others' voices, and our own voice. Sometimes it seems like we are listening to a radio station with a weak signal, while a few other stations continue to fade in and out. But, as we continue to listen to the voice of our Shepherd, we will learn the difference between the voices.

Loren Cunningham, the founder of *Youth With A Mission,* says that he has found three simple steps that have helped him and thousands of YWAMers to hear God's voice:

SUBMIT to His Lordship. Ask Him to help you silence your own thoughts, desires, and the opinions of others which may be filling your mind (2 Corinthians 10:5). Even though you have been given a good mind to use, you want to hear the thoughts of the Lord who has the best mind (Proverbs 3:5-6).

RESIST the enemy in case he is trying to deceive you. Use the authority that Jesus Christ has given you to silence the voice of the enemy (James 4:7; Ephesians 6:10-20).

EXPECT an answer. After asking the question that is on your mind, wait for Him to answer. Expect your loving heavenly father to speak to you, and He will (John 10:27; Psalms 69:13; Exodus 33:11).

Years ago, we were shopping with our two younger children. In one split second our then four-year-old daughter was missing from view. I instantly called out her name. Thankfully, she quickly responded to the voice of her father. I was so relieved to see her! Our heavenly Father wants His children to heed His voice. *Lord, teach us to hear Your voice and to obey it.*

Remember times when you had to discern between your own voice, others, the enemy, and the Lord's. What can you learn from your past that will keep you from making the same mistakes in the future?

Biblical Foundations for Life

PART 4

HEARING HIS VOICE CLEARLY

205 | The struggle to stay on track

Sometimes hearing the voice of the Lord is like driving down the road through intense fog late at night. It is really a struggle. The painted line in the center is our guide, and if we can see a car in front of us, we can follow its taillights. The painted line in the center of the road is symbolic of the Word of God. The most basic way that God speaks is through His Word, and we cannot go wrong by following it. The taillights from the car that we are following are symbolic of the Holy Spirit who guides us and helps us to stay on track.

There are times, however, when it seems like we have entirely lost our way. We really want to obey the Lord and fulfill His will for our lives, but somehow we can no longer see the taillights of the car in front of us or the painted line on the road. What do we do then? There is a story in the Old Testament that gives us some insight. A man was cutting down a tree by the river when his iron ax head fell into the water. An ax head was a very expensive tool, and the man desperately wanted to retrieve it because it was borrowed. He went to Elisha, a man of God, for help. Elisha asked where he had last seen it fall, threw a stick in the water, and it miraculously floated to the surface! (2 Kings 6:1-6). At the same place that it was lost, the ax head reappeared!

We can learn an important lesson from this. Whenever we have problems with finding direction in our lives, it is often helpful to go back to where we were certain we last heard the voice of the Lord clearly. If we do not go back, we may continue to flounder and be distressed. If we believe that we've lost our way spiritually, the Bible is very clear...*Remember the height from which you have fallen! Repent and do the things you did at first...*(Revelation 2:5).

We must go back to where the ax head fell, and remember the "height from which we have fallen"—where our love and obedience for the Lord declined. We need to acknowledge the Lord when we get off track and then repent (turn around) and go back to the last time we heard the clear, sharp, cutting-edge voice of the Lord. Then obey.

The Lord called a young man to go far from home to a Bible school. After spending a few weeks in the school, he found himself having second thoughts about his decision. He hated the discipline, the climate—you name it. He stayed, however, when he remembered the time the Lord had clearly called him to go to that school. By being obedient, he was a recipient of the benefits, and the Lord did a tremendous work in His life.

206 | Go back to where you lost your way

In 1992, I began to question whether or not I was called to church leadership. Anything else looked much better than to continue on in a leadership role. However, I remembered the initial call when God called me to start a new church in 1980. This was the place the ax head had fallen for me, and I was convinced the Lord had spoken to me and given me a mandate to start the church. Know-

---

Give examples of "ax heads" in your Christian walk.

What does Revelation 2:5 advise us to do?

ing this gave me the confidence to go on. I knew He had not yet completed the work He had begun.

Do you get tired of your job sometimes? Perhaps you are tired of going to school or of your involvement in the church. Go back to the last time you knew you heard clearly from the Lord on the subject, and allow the Lord to take you from there. If you made a mistake, there is hope. That is why Jesus came in the first place, to forgive us as we acknowledge our sin and cleanse us and give us a brand-new start.

Remember Jonah? He refused to obey the Lord, who told him to preach the gospel in the city of Nineveh. God got his attention by using ungodly sailors to push him into the ocean, and the Lord prepared a great fish to swallow him alive to give him some time to think. I believe Jonah thought back to where "the ax head fell" (he went off-track) and quickly repented! The Lord gave him another chance and the fish spit him out on dry land. The Bible says in Jonah 3:1, *Then the word of the Lord came to Jonah a second time: "Go to the great city of Nineveh and proclaim to it the message I give you." Jonah obeyed the word of the Lord and went to Nineveh* (Jonah 3:1-3a).

As we repent before God, we can receive the word of the Lord a second time. A key question to ask ourselves is this, "Have I obeyed the last thing the Lord asked me to do?"

Before we had navigation systems one thing that used to cause stress in our marriage was the fact that I was constantly trying to find shortcuts whenever my wife, LaVerne, and I were driving somewhere. To make matters worse, I usually got lost! To backtrack over and over again was embarrassing! I usually needed to go back to the last road I was familiar with before I could find the way.

If you find yourself on the wrong path, it is not the end of the world. The Lord is able to "restore the years that the locusts have eaten" (Joel 2:25), but going back to the place where we last heard from God is often the way to get to our destination.

207 | The Word of God should "align"

I learned a principle from a man of God once that has helped steer me in the right direction as I have attempted to hear God's voice. This man told a story of three lighthouses that were built to warn ships of the monstrous rocks which were below the surface of the water as they sailed into the harbor. To avoid getting snagged on these huge rocks, the captain had to be sure that the three lighthouses were aligned as he sailed into the harbor. If the captain could see two or three lighthouses at the same time, he knew he was in the danger zone.

In order to avoid shipwreck in our lives, we need to be sure that three different "lighthouses" are aligned before we begin to move in a new direction.

The first lighthouse to align is the Word of God. There is no substitute for God's Word. Paul, the apostle, tells us in 1 Corinthians 14:37, *If anyone thinks himself to be a prophet or spiritual, let him acknowledge that the things which I write to you are the commandments of the Lord.* God told Joshua in Joshua 1:8

Have you had an experience where you struggled to repent, like Jonah?

What did you do? What should you have done?

What are we promised if we obey God's Word (Joshua 1:8)?

Biblical Foundations for Life

What happens if we listen to something other than God's Word for direction?

to be faithful to God's Word. *Do not let this Book of the Law depart from your mouth; meditate on it day and night, so that you may be careful to do everything written in it. Then you will be prosperous and successful.*

When we obey the Word of God, we are promised to have good success. When we disobey the Word of God, it will cause shipwreck in our lives. Things may be okay for a period of time, but eventually disobedience to God's Word will take a toll on our lives.

If anyone claims to have supernatural revelation from God, it must line up with the Word of God. The whole Mormon cult was started by Joseph Smith, a man who claimed he had a visitation from an angel. We know this was really a fallen angel or demonic spiritual being, because the message did not line up with the Word of God. It was a perversion of the true gospel. Paul, the apostle, urges the Galatian believers to not be persuaded by false teachers in Galatians 1:6-8. *I am astonished that you are so quickly deserting the one who called you by the grace of Christ and are turning to a different gospel—which is really no gospel at all. Evidently some people are throwing you into confusion and are trying to pervert the gospel of Christ. But even if we or an angel from heaven should preach a gospel other than the one we preached to you, let him be eternally condemned!*

Remember, the Bible says Satan comes to us like an angel of light (2 Corinthians 11:14). Check everything against the Word of God. If you are not sure, go to a mature believer or leader of your church. The Word of God is our standard to be sure that the revelation we are getting is in line with the perfect will of God.

208 | The peace of God should "align"

The second spiritual lighthouse that needs to line up is the peace of God. The scriptures tell us in Colossians 3:15, *"Let the peace of Christ rule in your hearts, since as members of one body you were called to peace. And be thankful."* The word *rule* literally means *to be an umpire*. In other words, the peace of God in our hearts is an umpire to alert us as to whether or not we should make a certain decision.

How does the "peace of God" feel and how does it affect your life?

A man was offered a job by a large company where he would make much more money than he ever made in his life. He thought of all the wonderful things he could do with the money—use it to help friends who needed to buy an apartment, give money to the poor, help the homeless. However, he did not have peace from God about taking the job, so he turned it down. The president of the company thought he was crazy, as did some friends. It seemed like a once in a lifetime opportunity. But He could not take it without the blessing of God. A short time later, he found out that the president of the company had done many illegal things, and the whole company was in trouble. If he had taken the job, he might have been implicated just because he worked there. At the very least, he would have had to choose between being honest and keeping the job. God kept this man from getting involved in a very messy situation.

Several years ago, a friend told me he wanted to give me his car. It was a beautiful car, but my wife, LaVerne, and I did not have the peace of God in our hearts to receive it. So we graciously declined. Some time later, the Lord provided our family with a van, and this time we had the peace to receive it from the benefactor. Obeying the peace of God in our hearts allows us to carry on with a sense of His acceptance and favor in our lives.

209 | Circumstances should "align"

The third lighthouse to align is *circumstances*. Sometimes we can be so sure that something is God's will, but it is not the right timing for us. If you feel this way, it is best to let the desire die. If it is really from God, He will resurrect it (bring it back to life) in the future when the timing is right.

We have counseled countless young men and women who were sure the Lord had shown them whom they should marry, but the other person wasn't getting the same message. Our advice is to let the desire die for now, and if the Lord has really spoken it to you, it will happen sometime in the future.

If you believe the Lord wants you to buy a certain house or car, and it is not available, either you have missed the timing or it is not the Lord's answer for you. Timing is so important. You may have the right *direction* from the Lord, but the wrong *timing* as you try to fulfill it. Moses had the right vision from the Lord—deliver the Lord's people from the slavery of the Egyptians. The only problem—he initially missed the timing of God (by forty years!) when he killed an Egyptian. Someone may feel called to start a business or be a missionary, and the vision is a genuine vision from the Lord. Often the problem comes when they jump into it too fast. When the Lord is in it, the circumstances will work out.

The Lord clearly opened up a door for Paul in 1 Corinthians 16:8-9. The circumstances lined up with the Word of God and with the peace of God. Although Paul faced many adversaries, he knew that the Lord had opened up the door for him. *But I will stay on at Ephesus until Pentecost, because a great door for effective work has opened to me, and there are many who oppose me.*

Jeremiah gives an interesting account of heeding the voice of the Lord through circumstances. *Then this message from the Lord came to Jeremiah: "Your cousin Hanamel (son of Shallum) will soon arrive to ask you to buy the farm he owns in Anathoth, for by law you have a chance to buy before it is offered to anyone else." So, Hanamel came, as the Lord had said he would, and visited me in the prison. "Buy my field in Anathoth, in the land of Benjamin," he said, "for the law gives you the first right to purchase it." Then I knew for sure that the message I had heard was really from the Lord* (Jeremiah 32:6-8, Living Bible). After the circumstances lined up, Jeremiah knew that the message was from the Lord. If the Lord is asking you to do something, He will make it clear. You can trust Him.

210 | God will make it clear

George Mueller was a man of faith from Bristol, England, who fed hundreds of children in his orphanages in 19th-century England. The following relates his valuable insights on hearing from God:

"I seek at the beginning to get my heart in such a state that it has no will of its

Describe a situation when you had the right direction from the Lord but missed His perfect timing. How did you know?

Biblical Foundations for Life

What does George Mueller mean by "the Spirit and the Word must be combined"?

own in regard to a given matter. Nine-tenths of the trouble with people generally is just there. Nine-tenths of the difficulties are overcome when our hearts are ready to do the Lord's will whatever it may be. When one is truly in this state, it is usually but a little way to the knowledge of what His will is.

"Having done this, I do not leave the result to feeling or simple impression. If so, I make myself liable to great delusions.

"I will seek the will of the Spirit of God through, or in connection with, the Word of God. The Spirit and the Word must be combined. If I look to the Spirit alone without the Word, I lay myself open to great delusions also. If the Holy Ghost guides us at all, He will do it according to the scriptures and never contrary to them.

"Next, I take into account providential circumstances. These often plainly indicate God's will in connection with His Word and Spirit.

"I ask God in prayer to reveal His will to me aright.

"Thus, through prayer to God, the study of the Word, and reflection, I come to deliberate judgment according to the best of my ability and knowledge, and if my mind is thus at peace, and continues so after two or three more petitions, I proceed accordingly. In trivial matters and in transactions involving most important issues, I find this method always effective.[1]

"I never remember, in all of my Christian course, a period now (in March 1895) of sixty-nine years and four months, that I ever sincerely and patiently sought to know the will of God by the teaching of the Holy Ghost, through the instrumentality of the Word of God, but I have always been directed rightly. But if honesty of heart and uprightness before God were lacking, or if I did not patiently wait upon God for instruction, or if I preferred the counsel of my fellow man to the declarations of the Word of the living God, I made great mistakes."[2]

That is good advice. Let us look for the three lighthouse beacon lights (the Word of God, the peace of God, and circumstances) to line up in the days ahead. If the lights do not line up, we are in danger of running into the rocks. I'm heading for the three beacon lights. How about you?

[1] *Answers to Prayer from George Mueller's Narratives,* Compiled by A.E.C. Brooks.

[2] From the classic biography of George Mueller, *George Müller of Bristol,* by A. T. Pierson.

211 | Listen and communicate!

Describe the relationship Jesus desires to have with His bride—the church.

My wife, LaVerne, has learned the importance of communing with God and having a real love relationship with her Father in Heaven. Sometime back, she shared these thoughts with a group of believers:

"We as a church are engaged to Jesus, the bridegroom who is coming back for us—the bride. What do engaged couples do to have an effective relationship? They spend time together, not just talking, but listening to each other's heart, sharing each other's dreams. As they listen and talk together, they understand each other. If they just talk and do not listen, they have an ineffective relationship. So it is in our relationship with Jesus. It is Jesus' desire that we listen to

Him and commune with Him. We need to see that we are engaged to Him and the Word of God needs to be powerful in our lives. When the Word of God is in us, we understand and know who God is. We understand that He wants to speak to us. The Word of God is spirit and life within us. As we drive down the road, as we wash dishes, as we sit at the desk, we are aware of His presence and are willing to listen to that 'still, small voice' based on the Word of God, because the Word of God is in us. God desires to speak to us all day long. It is up to us to listen to Him."

Just as a husband and wife learn to communicate, growing in their love relationship, the Lord teaches us to grow in our love relationship with Him. Jesus, our bridegroom, is coming back for us. Nothing is more important or has more eternal significance. *Husbands, love your wives, just as Christ loved the church and gave himself up for her to make her holy, cleansing her by the washing with water through the word, and to present her to himself as a radiant church, without stain or wrinkle or any other blemish, but holy and blameless* (Ephesians 5:25-27).

Jesus gave His life for us on the cross. He paid the price for us to experience a loving relationship with our heavenly Father. He desires to guide and lead us as we build a relationship with Him. He is worthy of our fellowship and worship.

212 | Your Personal House of Prayer

The disciples of Jesus watched their Master getting up early each morning spending time alone with his Father in heaven. They watched Him in the remaining part of His days speaking words of wisdom. They saw miracles literally flowing from His life. At one point they asked Him, "Lord, teach us to pray" (Luke 11:1). Jesus answered by giving them a pattern of prayer, which we have come to identify as "The Lord's prayer." This can be our pattern for prayer, as well.

Mark 11: 17 tells us; *"Is it not written, 'My house shall be called a house of prayer for all nations?'"* Is this an actual building that will be a house of prayer?

This can be answered if we look at Acts 17:24: "God does not live in temples made with hands." I Corinthians 3:16 further explains that "Our bodies are the temples of the Holy Spirit." When God talks about a house of prayer, He is talking about each of us personally becoming a house of prayer.

God is a God of patterns and plans. He gave Moses plans to build the tabernacle and Solomon plans to build the temple. He gave us the plan for salvation through his Son Jesus. Matthew 6: 9-13 can serve as a manual to teach us to pray according to the pattern given by Jesus. Believers around the world and church fathers through church history have used Jesus' prayer as a guide for prayer.

God has called us to become a house of prayer. Most houses have rooms. I have found there are twelve rooms—or twelve focal points of prayer—in the Lord's Prayer.

In Jesus' model prayer, He enumerated twelve topics and instructed: "After this manner therefore pray" (Matthew 6:9-13). This prayer is not a legalistic pattern, but a statement of truth to guide us we are led by the Holy Spirit in prayer.

Biblical Foundations for Life

Describe your relationship with Jesus.

Ask someone to pray with you to have a more intimate relationship with Jesus.

Are you becoming a house of prayer?

213 | Twelve Rooms in Your House of Prayer

The Lord's prayer gives us twelve rooms in our house of prayer: twelve different focal points of prayer (Matthew 6:9-13). Take His Word with you into each room. Enter each room with thanksgiving and praise (Psalm 100:4).

Room 1: Family Room *Our Father which are in heaven* You are loved by your Daddy in heaven. He is our Father.

Room 2: Adoration Room *Holy is your Name* The name of the Lord is above every name. His name is above sickness, depression or pain. His name is greater.

Room 3: Declaration Room *May your Kingdom come* Many Bible characters made declarations. Joshua declared, "As for me and my house, we will serve the Lord." Jesus declared: "I will build my church." Paul declared: "I can do all things through him who gives me strength."

Room 4: Surrender Room *May your will be done, on earth as it is in heaven.* To surrender means "to yield ownership, to relinquish control over what we consider ours." Surrender everything in your life to God. Jesus said in the garden: "Lord, not my will but yours be done."

Room 5: Provision Room *Give us this day our daily bread.* God desires to provide for us but He wants us to ask Him daily. He is El Shaddai, the God who is more than enough.

Room 6: Forgiveness Room *And forgive us our debts* Forgiveness is a gift from God. We receive forgiveness because of the cross as we confess our sins (I John 1:9).

Room 7: Freedom Room *As we forgive our debtors* Why do we need to forgive every day? Hebrews 12:15 explains, "See to it that no one misses the grace of God and that no bitter root grows up to cause trouble and defile many." Bitterness starts out like a small root that can destroy us!

Room 8: Protection Room: *And lead us not into temptation* Ask God to protect you from falling into temptation (Matthew 26:41).

Room 9: Warfare Room *But deliver us from evil.* We need to battle against the forces of darkness. The Word promises, "Resist the devil and he will flee from you" (James 4:7).

Room 10: Kingdom Room *For yours is the Kingdom* Christ is the King, and we are His servants. "The Kingdom of God is righteousness, peace and joy in the Holy Spirit" (Romans 14:17).

Room 11: Power Room *And the power* Pray in the Holy Spirit. "Not by might, nor by power, but by my Spirit, says the Lord!" (Zechariah 4:6). We desperately need the power of the Holy Spirit operating in our lives.

Room 12: Exaltation Room *And the glory forever. Amen* We give Him all the honor and praise that only He deserves! We worship Him and exalt Him!

Some days you may stay longer in one room than another as the Holy Spirit leads. Obey the Holy Spirit! Let's receive a renewed passion for prayer today and become the house of prayer the Lord has called us to be.

How can you enter into your house of prayer more often?

FOUNDATION 8

What is the Church?

214 | Introduction to foundation 8

We see from Scripture the importance of being a part of a spiritual family united under Christ. The local church is a spiritual family that gives us a place to grow and learn from spiritual leaders and other believers how to live our Christian lives. We need this input from spiritual leaders and fellow believers. We need one another. We are not supposed to live the Christian life alone. It is God's will for every believer to be connected to a local church where he or she can be trained, protected, and available to serve others.

The church is not a building or a meeting or a program. The church of Jesus Christ is simply people. As believers, we are the church. The word church means "called out ones." The church is a group of people who have been called out of spiritual darkness into the light of God's kingdom. They are a spiritual family with a mission to extend the kingdom of God.

Sometimes people call a building on the street corner the "church," But in reality, the true church is people. The Bible calls us "living stones." Each believer has been made alive through faith in our Lord Jesus Christ. The Lord builds us together with other Christians into a type of spiritual house or community. *You also, like living stones, are being built into a spiritual house to be a holy priesthood, offering spiritual sacrifices acceptable to God through Jesus Christ* (1 Peter 2:5).

When we are committed to other believers in a local church and have regular fellowship with them, we become a part of a spiritual family that is united under Christ. This spiritual family gives us a place to walk with other believers and learn how we can live our Christian lives effectively. We need this input from others. God loves His church and so do we! The church is far from perfect, but Jesus, the perfect one, is the one we worship as we grow in Him.

What is the church?

Why is the church so important?

Biblical Foundations for Life

PART 1

THE IMPORTANCE OF THE LOCAL CHURCH

215 | We need each other

There is a story of a young man who had given his life to God; but after a time of disappointment and disillusionment, he began to withdraw from other Christians. The young man's pastor stopped in for a visit one cold, blustery winter evening and with the wind howling outside, they sat and talked.

After awhile, the wise pastor walked over to the fireplace, and with a pair of prongs picked up a hot coal from the fire, placing it on the bricks in front of the fireplace. He continued to converse with the young man. Then glancing at the ember on the bricks, he said, "Do you see that piece of coal? While it was in the fireplace it burned brightly, but now that it's alone, the ember has almost gone out."

The pastor took the prongs, picked up the ember and placed it inside the fireplace. Within minutes, the dying ember was again burning brightly.

It suddenly dawned on the young man what the pastor was trying to tell him. When we move away from the warmth and encouraging fires of fellow believers in the body of Christ, we will eventually cool down spiritually. Joining with others as a community of believers in a local church body helps keep our fires glowing. From that day on, the young man made a decision to join regularly with other believers in a local church in his community. He did not want to take the chance of his fire going out again.

The Bible says in Hebrews 3:13, *"But encourage one another daily, as long as it is called Today, so that none of you may be hardened by sin's deceitfulness."* It is extremely difficult to live the Christian life alone. Believers need to fellowship together and encourage one another daily because it is easy to become increasingly tolerant of sin in our lives otherwise.

A friend of mine once said, "Lone Rangers often get shot out of the saddle." He was referring to the popular U.S. television show in the 1950's called "The Lone Ranger." This lone lawman rode to rid the wild west of outlaws and was often vulnerable to attack. If we try to live our Christian lives alone, without the support of other believers, the devil can easily destroy us spiritually. We need each other. Hebrews 10:24-25 tells us, *"And let us consider how we may spur one another on toward love and good deeds. Let us not give up meeting together, as some are in the habit of doing, but let us encourage one another—and all the more as you see the Day approaching."*

Jesus Christ is coming back soon. We need to stir one another up to be on fire for our Lord Jesus Christ. Meeting together regularly encourages each of us to hold firmly to Christ. God has a plan for us to assemble together on a regular basis so that we can receive teaching, encouragement and be equipped for the work of ministry. He calls this group of believers the "church." In this book, we will learn about the importance of being solidly connected to a local church.

Why do we need to be connected to believers in the local church?

Why does Hebrews 10:24-25 say we should spend time with other believers?

216 | The church—"called out ones"

What is the *church*, exactly? The church is not a building or a meeting or a program. The church of Jesus Christ is simply *people*. As believers, we are the church. The word *church* literally means *called out ones*. The church then, is a group of people who have been called out of spiritual darkness into the light of God's kingdom.

When we come to Christ, we are immediately a part of the universal church of Christ which includes every believer who has ever named the name of Christ from every nation of the world. Jesus talks about His universal church in Matthew 16:18. *And I tell you that you are Peter, and on this rock I will build my church, and the gates of Hades will not overcome it.* I have had the privilege of traveling to six continents of the world. Everywhere I go, I find believers from completely different backgrounds, different skin colors and different cultures who have one thing in common. They all have the same heavenly Father, have received Jesus Christ as Lord, and are part of the same family.

One time, while flying in an airplane, the businessman sitting next to me began to tell me about the corporation he represents. Then he asked me, "What do you do?" I told him that I am a part of the largest corporation in the world. "In fact," I said, "we are now in every country of the world." Of course, I was talking about the kingdom of God—God's wonderful and universal family, the church of Jesus Christ.

The Bible is talking about the universal church when it says that all the saints of the whole church of God, and all His children in heaven and earth will acknowledge that Jesus Christ is alone worthy...*with your blood you purchased men for God from every tribe and language and people and nation* (Revelation 5:9).

Jesus has promised that He will build His church and the gates of hell will not prevail against it (Matthew 16:18). We can be assured that regardless of what happens in the world today, Jesus Christ is building His church, and we have the privilege of being a part of it.

But the word *church* also refers to the *local* church. Within God's universal church family are *local* churches in each community which provide the support and love each believer needs.

217 | A baby Christian needs a family

Every believer needs a "support system" to survive. When I have the privilege of leading someone to Christ, I often tell him that he is now a "baby Christian" and needs to understand four important truths of spiritual nourishment. First of all, every baby needs to eat and drink. That's why the Bible says in 1 Peter 2:2 that baby Christians need to first drink the milk of God's Word so they can begin to grow. *Like newborn babies, crave pure spiritual milk, so that by it you may grow up in your salvation.*

What is the church?

What is the universal church?

What is the local church?

What are the four things a spiritual baby needs in order to grow spiritually?

Biblical Foundations for Life

What does our heavenly Father call us (2 Corinthians 6:18)?

Second, to remain alive, every baby needs to breathe. Baby Christians (and mature ones!) breathe spiritually through prayer—through communicating with our Father in heaven. The Bible tells us to "pray continually" (1 Thessalonians 5:17).

Third, we need to exercise—to share our faith with others. The scriptures tell us, "Let the redeemed of the Lord say so..." (Psalms 107:2 NKJ).

And fourth, baby Christians need to stay spiritually warm. We stay warm through being committed to other believers in a local church and having regular fellowship with them. We are a part of a spiritual family—a family of the redeemed who are joined under one Father in Christ. *For this reason I kneel before the Father, from whom his whole family in heaven and on earth derives its name* (Ephesians 3:14-15).

In the local church, we are part of a spiritual family united under Christ. This spiritual family gives us a place to grow and learn from other believers how to live our Christian lives. We need this input from others.

You will find that there is no perfect local church. However, this is no excuse for not getting involved in a church. If we could find a church that was perfect, the moment we joined, the church would no longer be perfect, because we are not perfect!

Our salvation, of course, does not come through being joined to a local church; it comes by knowing God our Father through a personal relationship with Jesus Christ. When we join to Christ, we become sons and daughters of our Heavenly Father. *"I will be a Father to you, and you will be my sons and daughters," says the Lord Almighty* (2 Corinthians 6:18).

However, once we are children of God, we should want to join other Christians so we can receive their love and encouragement. As soon as we are saved, we should ask the Lord where He desires to place us in His family within a church in our community.

218 | The local church is God's army

We need one another. We are not supposed to live the Christian life alone. The Lord has called us to be a company of spiritual soldiers who serve in His spiritual army. *Endure hardship with us like a good soldier of Christ Jesus* (2 Timothy 2:3).

Why must we be like soldiers?

A former military officer once told me that what kept him going in the war more than anything else was the camaraderie that he developed with fellow soldiers. We are in a spiritual war. We need the support of our fellow Christian soldiers because we are fighting the devil who is out to kill, steal, and destroy the people of God (John 10:10).

Armies are made up of small groups called platoons. In the New Testament church, the believers met from house to house (in small groups) as well as in the temple (in large groups). Meeting in a local church fellowship is especially important because it allows us to be encouraged and trained as spiritual soldiers. It is so important to find the place where God can use us best in His kingdom.

The local church is not only for training to go into the world. Just as all armies have medical units, the church is also a place we can be cared for, healed and strengthened when we are weak. It is a place where we can be set free to live transformed, victorious lives so we can go out to the spiritual battlefield with power. By the power and authority of Jesus Christ, in local churches, people can be set free from besetting sins, life-controlling problems and bad habits.

Sometimes churches look more like social clubs than spiritual armies. People attend meetings for the social interaction and forget their true purpose. God has called His church to return to its original purpose to be a standard of righteousness in our generation. Isaiah 59:19 (NKJ) says that *when the enemy comes in like a flood, the Spirit of the Lord will lift up a standard against him.* The church of Jesus Christ is a standard that the Lord is raising up against the enemy who wants to destroy this generation. Each of us needs to find our place in God's army, the local church, and do our part.

219 | Fitting together

Like a building that is made up of blocks that have been placed on a wall with mortar, as the church, we are living stones built together through relationships with one another.

As you come to him, the living Stone—rejected by men but chosen by God and precious to him—you also, like living stones, are being built into a spiritual house to be a holy priesthood, offering spiritual sacrifices acceptable to God through Jesus Christ (1 Peter 2:4-5).

For we are God's fellow workers; you are God's field, God's building (1 Corinthians 3:9).

In these scriptures, notice that the Lord calls us a "building" and also a "field." Not only are we to be in relationship with other believers, we should know where we fit in our spiritual "field."

Many times when I fly over countries that have beautiful farm lands, I can see various crops growing in distinct fields. Each local church is a distinct field with believers planted there so they can grow and reproduce within that particular "field." The Lord's desire is for us to reproduce the life of Jesus in others. It all starts when we are committed to Jesus and to a local church where we can receive help to grow in Christ and help others to grow in the Lord.

That's why it is so important for the local church to be made up of small groups of believers who meet together. It is impossible for a believer to be relating to hundreds of people, but in smaller groups we can practically touch a few people. In some churches these may be called Sunday School classes or Bible study groups. Other churches may use the term home fellowships or cell groups or house churches.

Kelly, a young divorced mother of two, learned just how valuable the relationships she had with those in her small group were. She had let the insurance lapse on her car and then had an accident causing her driver's license to be suspended

Who are we fighting (John 10:10)?

How are you God's field and building (1 Corinthians 3:9)?

Do you know where you fit into God's kingdom?

Biblical Foundations for Life

for three months. She wondered how she would care for her children because she would lose her job as a school bus driver. Her small group rallied around her in prayer and practical help. During her three months without a job, she had a ride whenever she needed one. Bags of groceries appeared at her doorstep. Kelly learned that God provides through the people she was "built together with."

Jesus had a small group of twelve disciples. Moses was commanded by the Lord to break the Israelites down into groups of tens (Exodus 18). We all have a need for relationships and to get to know others who can provide mutual support as we learn to grow in God and fulfill His purposes in our lives. This best happens in smaller groups with everyone working toward a common goal.

220 | The local church provides leadership and protection

What are some things spiritual leaders provide in the local church (1 Thessalonians 5:14-15)?

Why, you may ask, is it so important to be involved in a local church? For one thing, the local church provides leaders to equip us in our Christian walk. The early church was encouraged to appoint elders in every city (local church). *The reason I left you in Crete was that you might straighten out what was left unfinished and appoint elders in every town, as I directed you* (Titus 1:5).

One of the Lord's purposes for the local church is to provide eldership or spiritual leadership who can equip us, encourage us and serve us as "undershepherds" under Jesus (who is the Chief Shepherd). These leaders have clear instructions what their role is. *And we urge you, brothers, warn those who are idle, encourage the timid, help the weak, be patient with everyone. Make sure that nobody pays back wrong for wrong, but always try to be kind to each other and to everyone else* (1 Thessalonians 5:14-15).

This verse tells us that the Lord provides protection and discipline for His people through leaders in the local church. Leaders are to be people of love and patience as they encourage those they serve. They are there to give guidance and correction in love.

In Matthew 18:15-17, Jesus tells how the local church can provide discipline and restoration to a wayward member. *If your brother sins against you, go and show him his fault, just between the two of you. If he listens to you, you have won your brother over. But if he will not listen, take one or two others along, so that "every matter may be established by the testimony of two or three witnesses." If he refuses to listen to them, tell it to the church; and if he refuses to listen even to the church, treat him as you would a pagan or a tax collector.*

If a Christian believer sins against us, Jesus instructs us to confront him one-on-one. If he does not listen, we should go with "two or more" believers and again appeal to him to repent. If he still does not hear us, we should "tell it to the church." This is referring to the local church, because it would be impossible to take it to the universal church! The local church leaders will help to restore such a person back into fellowship.

Local church leaders have the responsibility to keep watch over us by protecting, directing, correcting and encouraging us. *Keep watch over yourselves and all the flock of which the Holy Spirit has made you overseers* (Acts 20:28).

221 | Vulnerable without a local church

Sometimes, through disillusionment, disappointment or spiritual pride, believers find themselves uninvolved in a local church. This leaves them very vulnerable. The Bible tells us in 1 Corinthians 10:13, "*No temptation has seized you except what is common to man. And God is faithful; he will not let you be tempted beyond what you can bear. But when you are tempted, he will also provide a way out so that you can stand up under it.*"

The local church is often "the way out" the Lord has prepared for His people during an onslaught of the devil. When we fellowship with other believers, we realize that we are not alone in the temptations that we face. We receive spiritual protection, strength and oversight from the spiritual leaders the Lord has placed in our lives. The Lord's plan is to use the local church to protect us, help us grow, and equip us to be all that we can be in Jesus Christ.

D.L. Moody, an evangelist from the late 1800's, was used of the Lord to lead a million people to Christ. Many times when he preached, he had a choir that included singers from many churches in the community in which he was preaching. A lady came to him one day and said, "Mr. Moody, I would like to sing in your choir." When Moody asked her which local church she represented, she said, "I am involved in the universal church."

Moody said to her, "Then find the pastor of the universal church and sing in his choir." In other words, Moody was concerned about this lady's noninvolvement in a local church. He recognized the need to be committed to a local church for spiritual protection and accountability.

Spiritual leaders and other believers in the local church are there to exhort you, comfort you and uphold you in prayer!

Why are we vulnerable without a local fellowship of believers to support us?

PART 2 SPIRIUTAL FAMILY RELATIONSHIPS

222 | The church is made up of family relationships

Many young couples who get married are in for a big surprise. They thought they were only marrying one person, but they realize after the wedding they married into an entire family! They have to get to know grandparents, uncles and aunts, cousins, dad and mom and all the rest of the in-laws. In the family of God, when you and I make a decision to become a part of a local church, we become a part of an entire church family. Galatians 3:26 tells us that sonship with God involves brotherhood with Jesus. Christians are related as family. We are all brothers (and sisters) through Jesus. *You are all sons of God through faith in Christ Jesus.*

In the Old Testament, God's people were always described as part of a larger family. The children of Israel were involved in one of twelve tribes. Each tribe was made up of a group of clans, and each clan was made up of a group of families. Gideon mentions his family, clan and tribe in Judges 6:15. *My clan is the weakest in Manasseh [tribe], and I am the least in my family.* Even today, the Lord continues to see each of us as a part of various spiritual spheres or families.

First, I believe the Lord sees me as an individual believer bought by the blood of Jesus.

He also recognizes that I am a part of a spiritual church family. For me, that spiritual family starts with the small group of believers I meet with weekly. In small groups, we are nurtured, equipped to serve and given the opportunity to reach out. Most churches have small groups of believers who meet together—Sunday School classes, youth groups, Bible studies, or in fellowships of believers who meet in homes. This kind of small group fellowship is one aspect of a spiritual family.

Another aspect of spiritual family life happens when whole clusters of small groups relate closely together to form a *congregation* of believers. When I meet on a Sunday morning with my local church congregation, my small group and many others come together to worship and receive the Word of God together. This is an extended spiritual family. According to Romans 16, the believers in Rome met together in homes. It also is clear they were in relationship with one another throughout the city in extended spiritual family relationships or congregations.

A third sphere of spiritual family relationships often refers to a church denomination or *family of churches*. Whenever a group of churches work together as a "network of churches" or an "apostolic fellowship" they form a larger sphere of family relationships. Our church is a part of a family of churches which partner together from various parts of the world, representing a larger spiritual family.

The Israelites were made up of twelve tribes and a multitude of clans and families. They were corporately known as "the children of Israel." In the same way, the church of Jesus Christ is made up of believers in small groups, congregations and denominations who together represent the kingdom of God.

Describe the way your local group of believers relates to other groups.

Do you feel like a part of the church family?

223 | Family relationships bring unity

No matter what our church affiliation or denomination, we become one family through Christ. When we realize that the walls have been broken down and we need each other as fellow believers in Christ, we will know for sure that every church group in the body of Christ is important to Him. *There is neither Jew nor Greek, slave nor free, male nor female, for you are all one in Christ Jesus* (Galatians 3:28).

Every church in every community and every denomination or family of churches has certain strengths to contribute to help the greater body of Christ. God uses many different church families to accomplish His purposes here on earth. We are called by the Lord to link arms with other churches, denominations and groups of believers so we can with one voice glorify our God and work together to build His kingdom.

Throughout history, there have been many times when, by His Holy Spirit, God would raise up various "movements," new families of churches and denominations to bring reform or refreshment to the church. For example, many Methodist churches are traced back to the 18th and 19th centuries when John Wesley and the team of men who worked closely with him obeyed the call from the Lord to share the gospel of Jesus Christ and to "plant" new groups of believers in the nations of the world. Today you can find Methodist church buildings all over the world.

The town I live in has a Moravian church. The Moravians, who have their roots in Europe, were sent to many nations of the world to share the gospel. In fact, they prayed around the clock twenty-four hours a day for a hundred years, as they sent missionaries to the nations of the world to share the gospel of Jesus Christ and start new churches. They had a real sense of *family* as they labored together.

Throughout the 1960s and 1970s, the Charismatic movement literally exploded throughout the world. God was telling His church that every believer needs to be filled with the Holy Spirit and experience the gifts of the Holy Spirit. God continues to move among His people who are citizens of His kingdom. We are linked together in unity by our family relationships!

224 | New wineskins bring new life

I believe the Lord wants to pour out His Spirit in our generation. As He does, thousands of people will come into the kingdom of God. Jesus tells us to open our eyes and realize there are many lost in the world who need to be saved. *I tell you, open your eyes and look at the fields! They are ripe for harvest* (John 4:35).

But how can these new believers be "harvested?" Traditional, modern-day church structures and programs cannot accommodate a huge harvest. They already have their hands full. I believe we constantly need new churches starting up to provide new wineskins or structures for new believers in Jesus Christ.

Why is it important to recognize we need each other in the body of Christ?

_____

_____

_____

_____

Why do local churches need to be in relationship with other churches?

_____

_____

_____

_____

_____

_____

Biblical Foundations for Life

Who are those "ripe for harvest" (John 4:35)?

Why are new wineskins important to new Christians?

Neither do men pour new wine into old wineskins. If they do, the skins will burst, the wine will run out and the wineskins will be ruined. No, they pour new wine into new wineskins, and both are preserved (Matthew 9:17).

A new wineskin is like a balloon—flexible and pliable. Putting a new Christian (new wine) into an old church structure can cause the structure to break, and the new Christian may be lost. New Christians should be placed in new church structures that are flexible and able to encourage their spiritual growth. Such new "wineskins" may be a small group of believers meeting in a house church or cell group. In small groups, people can be easily nurtured, discipled, and trained as leaders.

I believe the Lord will be raising up many new wineskins to help bring in the harvest. God is preparing laborers to reach the masses with the gospel of Jesus Christ in our generation. He will require many of us to be involved with new groups of believers (new wineskins) in the future as the Lord calls us to the nations of the world. The newer house church networks (see Day 243) and cell groups will work with the more traditional churches already in our neighborhoods today.

We must work together. Sometimes people involved in newer churches have a tendency to look down on churches that have been around for awhile. Instead, they should honor their "fathers"—those who have gone before them. And those in older churches should be glad when new movements and churches are started because they help to bring the gospel of Christ to a dying world.

We need every church body to be involved in planting new churches throughout the nations of the world. Every local church should have a vision that is much larger than themselves. Jesus instructed His disciples before He ascended into heaven. *But you will receive power when the Holy Spirit comes on you; and you will be my witnesses in Jerusalem, and in all Judea and Samaria, and to the ends of the earth* (Acts 1:8).

In other words, the Lord is calling us as His church to share the gospel, make disciples and start new churches in our home town (Jerusalem), our region (Judea), our neighboring state or country (Samaria) and to the end of the earth (the nations of the world)!

225 | Meeting house to house as a family

The early church understood the need for new churches to meet the needs of all the souls coming to the Lord. They met from house to house in small groups and also together in the temple, to receive teaching from the Word of God and worship the Lord together. *Every day they continued to meet together in the temple courts. They broke bread in their homes and ate together with glad and sincere hearts, praising God and enjoying the favor of all the people. And the Lord added to their number daily those who were being saved* (Acts 2:46-47).

After I gave my life to Jesus Christ in 1968, I had a tremendous hunger for God and for His Word. I started meeting with other young believers who were a part of a local church in our community to study the Bible and pray. One day we realized that God had called us to reach the lost around us, yet we were just sitting around enjoying a Bible study. We needed to become fishers of men (Mark 1:17).

During the next few years, my fiance and I helped start a youth ministry with a small band of young people who began to reach out to the unchurched youth of our community in Lancaster County, Pennsylvania, USA. We played sports and conducted various activities throughout the week for spiritually needy youngsters and teenagers. This kind of "friendship evangelism" produced results, and during the next few years, dozens of young people came to faith in Christ.

Those of us who served in this youth ministry were from various churches, so we also attempted to help the new believers find their place in our local congregations. Although the Christians in the local churches were friendly and helpful, something still wasn't "clicking." These young believers from unchurched backgrounds were just not being incorporated into the life of the established churches in our communities. We began to realize there needed to be "new wineskins" for the "new wine."

The Lord clearly spoke to me about starting a new wineskin (new church structure of small groups) for the new wine (new Christians). After receiving the affirmation and blessing of the leadership of the church who had sent us out to start this new work, we stepped out in faith to start a new church in October 1980. Since that time we've had the privilege of seeing people come to Christ and being built together in local churches throughout various nations of the world.

The church is people who are built together in a relationship with God and with one another who have been called by God with a common purpose and vision. They serve one another, reach out to those who need Christ, and support the local leadership that God raises up among them.

Real church is much more than going to a meeting every Sunday morning. For example, although we may not think about it often, a healthy tree needs to have a strong root system. In the same way, we have found in the church that what happens "underground" in cell groups (small groups where relationships are built) is of vital importance. When relationships are healthy and strong in small groups meeting together from house to house, the other church meetings will also be filled with life.

226 | Families are connected

Can you imagine a builder taking a thousand bricks, throwing them on a big pile and calling that a building? Ridiculous! In order to build a building, a master planner needs to take hundreds and thousands of bricks and strategically place one upon another and then mortar them together. The mortar that God uses to build His kingdom is the mortar of relationships. God, the master planner, takes you and me and places us in His body in strategic places with others so we can fulfill the Lord's purposes.

Many times we call a building on the street corner the "church," but in reality

How did the early church come together (Acts 2:46-47)?

What happens when people are built together in relationship?

From what is the church called out?

How are we connected as a family?

Why does God want us in a particular place in His church (1 Corinthians 12:18)?

the true church is "people." Praise God for buildings that we can use to worship Him and to be taught the Word of God; however, let's never confuse the church building for the true church, the people of God.

The Bible calls us "living stones." Each believer has been made alive through faith in our Lord Jesus Christ. The Lord builds us together with other Christians into a type of spiritual house or community. *You also, like living stones, are being built into a spiritual house to be a holy priesthood, offering spiritual sacrifices acceptable to God through Jesus Christ* (1 Peter 2:5).

We said before that the term "church" simply means "called-out ones"—those who are called out from the world's system to be a part of God's kingdom. To be a believer in Jesus Christ is to live counterculture to the world's system of selfishness. We live a new life in a new way, obeying the Word of God.

Jesus Christ lives in His church, which means He lives in His people, His called-out ones. Jesus dwells inside us as His people, His body. *From him the whole body, joined and held together by every supporting ligament, grows and builds itself up in love, as each part does its work* (Ephesians 4:16).

Like a human body, our shoulders and arms are linked together by joints and ligaments. These joints and ligaments, spiritually speaking, are relationships in the body of Christ. Believers joining together in a relationship who realize that Jesus Christ lives in them can supply one another with spiritual strength and life. That's why we need to be connected with other brothers and sisters in the body of Christ. I need my brothers and sisters to supply what I need to grow spiritually.

227 | Where has God placed you?

The Lord who has created our bodies tells us that we are like a spiritual body. Aren't you grateful that your hand is attached to your arm? If your hand was attached to your ear, it would cause a lot of problems for your body! We need to be placed properly in the body of Christ so we can be effective.

1 Corinthians 12:18 tells us God arranges us just where He wants us to be. *But in fact God has arranged the parts in the body, every one of them, just as he wanted them to be.* It is important that we know where God has placed us in His church so that we can serve effectively. You see, it is not the church of *our* choice, but it is the church of *His* choice.

There are different sizes and shapes of churches in our communities in which we can get involved. What I call a "community church" is a traditional church, meeting in a building on a Sunday and reaching the local populace in the surrounding community. It is often about 50-500 in size. A "mega-church" also meets in a church building on a Sunday but it reaches a much broader geographical area. It is often well over 1,000 in size. Finally, what I call a "house church network" is a group of individual house churches, often meeting in homes, which are complete little churches led by their own elders. Each house church or "micro-church," meeting together at least once each week, works with other house churches and other types of churches in their area.

Where is God placing you in the body of Christ? There are many wonderful churches throughout the world today. The issue is not which church is best. Every church family has strengths and weaknesses. The issue is this: where has God called you to be placed in His church? Which group of believers has the Lord called you to labor with during this season of your life?

The Lord wants you to grow spiritually and use you to reach other people for Christ. Find a church family you can relate to and then get involved in reaching out to people. Perhaps the Lord wants to use your home as a place where a small group of believers can meet and grow spiritually. Open up your home! You can reproduce yourself spiritually by mentoring or discipling others to grow in their Christian lives. Find your niche in the body of Christ!

What other options, beside the more traditional community church or mega-church, are there for you to experience "church"?

228 | Families will multiply

We read in the book of Acts that the early church grew and multiplied. The Lord had given them His Holy Spirit and a clear strategy from His Word for the church to grow. These early believers remembered the words of our Lord Jesus before He went back to His Father in heaven. He told them to *"go and make disciples of all the nations..."* (Matthew 28:19). A few weeks later as they met from house to house throughout the city of Jerusalem, believers realized that they were responsible to help other new believers grow in their relationship with God.

This is called the principle of multiplication. Believers in small groups are taught and trained to grow in the Lord, and many will eventually be trained to lead their own small groups. This causes the church to rapidly multiply! The believers in each new group continue to supply what the other believers need in order to grow spiritually, according to Ephesians 4:16.

In order for the local church and the home cell groups to stay healthy, they need to get a vision from God to grow in numbers and then to multiply to start other groups. The early church rapidly increased.

In those days when the number of disciples was increasing...the word of God spread. The number of disciples in Jerusalem increased rapidly...(Acts 6:1, 7).

The church of Jesus Christ was multiplied. Every group of believers meeting in a small group needs to have a vision to multiply and start other cell groups or house churches. In this way the church will continue to be healthy and strong. People in a church or a cell group that do not reach out to bring people to Christ often stagnate and eventually die spiritually.

Our bodies are made up of cells. Cells in our body go through a process called mitosis. The process of mitosis is simply this: one cell divides and becomes two. Those two cells then in turn divide and become four. In our bodies, a cell that will not produce will eventually die. The same principle applies to the church of Jesus Christ. Believers in cell groups and house churches are called by God to have a vision to reach out to new people and see them saved and become a part of the body of Christ. As they grow, people are being multiplied through "spiritual mitosis."

God has called each of us and every local church to pray, to evangelize, and to make disciples. Let's expect the Lord to use us as He multiplies His life through us to others.

Explain the principle of multiplication. What had to be spread before the church could multiply in Acts 6:1,7?

Biblical Foundations for Life

PART 3

WHO IS WATCHING OUT FOR YOU?

229 | The importance of commitment to other believers

The early Christians had a very effective way of looking out for each other. They met from house to house in small groups so they could *"practice loving each other." Practice loving each other, for love comes from God and those who are loving and kind show that they are children of God, and they are getting to know him better* (1 John 4:7 TLB).

Love does not just happen. It must be practiced. It is not just a feeling of goodwill but a decision that motivates us to help people and meet their needs. We cannot practically be committed to love and care for hundreds or thousands of other people. Although we can worship and learn from the Word of God together in a large group, we can only be practically committed to a small group of people at a time. Paul ministered in large public meetings as well as small house groups, according to Acts 20:20. *I...have taught you publicly and from house to house.*

Practical Christianity happens when believers meet together to reach their neighbors and co-workers with the gospel of Jesus Christ and help each other grow spiritually mature in Christ. Believers in my church family regularly meet in small cell groups where we pray for those who are sick and hurting as we extend God's love and forgiveness to each other. Our commitment to each other is heartfelt and real. We really do look out for each other. Our home cell group is our spiritual family.

In some churches, believers show their commitment to other believers in their home cell group or house church by making a simple pledge to commit to them as their local church family. Making this commitment is not so much a doctrine or a philosophy but a commitment to Jesus and His people to look out for each other. I believe that a commitment to the local church is a commitment to God, His Word and other believers more than it is commitment to an institution or an organization. We really show our commitment to other believers in our small group by faithfully interacting and building relationships with them. They will know we care if we make them a priority in our lives.

Although the elders of our church are the ones who watch out for our spiritual welfare (as we will see in the next section), I am very grateful for the believers in my small group who practically serve me, pray for me and encourage me in my walk with Jesus Christ.

230 | Leaders give us spiritual protection

According to Hebrews 13:7, 17, God places spiritual leaders in our lives who are accountable to God to watch out for us. *Remember your leaders, who spoke the word of God to you. Consider the outcome of their way of life and imitate their faith.*

Obey your leaders and submit to their authority. They keep watch over you as men who must give an account. Obey them so that their work will be a joy, not a burden, for that would be of no advantage to you.

How is a small home group a great way to promote true fellowship?

How have you helped to meet the needs of others in your small group?

Spiritual leaders in our lives give us spiritual protection, and we need to follow their example as they place their faith in Jesus Christ. We should remember them, receive the Word of God from them, obey them, be submissive to them, and do all that we can so their responsibility is joyful and not grievous. The Bible tells us that the devil is like a roaring lion seeking to devour us (1 Peter 5:8). That's why we need church leaders—to protect us and encourage us.

According to 1 Thessalonians 5:12-13, the Lord has called us to recognize and honor those He has placed in our lives as spiritual leaders. *Now we ask you, brothers, to respect those who work hard among you, who are over you in the Lord and who admonish you. Hold them in the highest regard in love because of their work. Live in peace with each other.*

I have spent much of my time traveling to various nations of the world in the past years, and I have been blessed over and over again by the spiritual leaders that the Lord has placed in my life. Our small group leaders, local pastors and elders have provided a tremendous sense of encouragement and protection to me and my family. Many times these precious brothers and sisters in Christ have prayed, encouraged and exhorted us. These spiritual leaders have encouraged me and held me accountable to take enough time with my family even though my travel schedule can be hectic. I am grateful to God that my spiritual leaders have my best interests at heart.

231 | Leaders help keep us on track

The Bible tells us in Acts 2:42 that the early believers "continued steadfastly in the apostles' doctrine and fellowship, in the breaking of bread, and in prayers." The early believers continued to study the scriptures and learn from the preaching and teaching of the early church leaders. Paul, the apostle, told the Ephesian elders in Acts 20:28-31 that the enemy will try to bring heresy into the church of Jesus Christ. *Keep watch over yourselves and all the flock of which the Holy Spirit has made you overseers. Be shepherds of the church of God, which he bought with his own blood. I know that after I leave, savage wolves will come in among you and will not spare the flock. Even from your own number men will arise and distort the truth in order to draw away disciples after them. So be on your guard! Remember that for three years I never stopped warning each of you night and day with tears.*

The Lord has given us His Word and places spiritual leaders in our lives to keep us from heresy (wrong teaching that is spiritually destructive). There are many "voices" today vying for our attention. We can trust the Word of God and we can trust spiritual leaders who have good "fruit" (character and integrity) in their lives (Matthew 7:15-20).

I am grateful for the spiritual leaders God has raised up worldwide. There is no one church or family of churches (denomination) who has all of the truth. We need to study the Word of God and learn from spiritual leaders, not only in our local church, but in the greater body of Christ. Spiritual leaders help us to keep from becoming sidetracked by minor issues (Romans 14:5) and heresies that would try to come into the body of Christ.

Biblical Foundations for Life

List ways your spiritual leaders have watched out for you.

Why is heresy so devastating to a church?

How do we keep from heresy, according to Acts 2:42?

Name the five ministry gifts given to the body of Christ.

Have you been equipped and released in a particular gift so that you can minister to others?

232 | Leaders equip

God calls believers with spiritual leadership abilities to build up and strengthen the believers in the church so that all believers can fulfill their work of service. God releases specific leadership gifts in the body of Christ so the people with those gifts can equip us for service according to Ephesians 4:11-12. *It was he who gave some to be apostles, some to be prophets, some to be evangelists, and some to be pastors and teachers, to prepare God's people for works of service, so that the body of Christ may be built up.*

These five ministry gifts (apostle, prophet, evangelist, pastor, teacher) are given to various individuals in the body of Christ who are then responsible to train and equip others. The gifts are "deposited" in spiritual leaders who are called by the Lord to train us to minister to others effectively. Those who have these gifts are able to train each believer for a lifetime of ministry.

Apostles are given to the church to help us receive a vision from the Lord to reach the world. Prophets are given to train us to listen to the voice of God. Evangelists are called of God to train us and to "stir us up'" to reach the lost. Pastors are commissioned by the Lord to encourage us, protect us, and show us how to make disciples. Teachers have a divine anointing to assist us in understanding the Word of God. Some spiritual leaders may have more than one gift in operation in their lives.

God's plan is to use these five gifts in His local church as much as possible to equip us (the saints) for the work of ministry. When we are equipped, we will be able to minister, too! Every believer is a minister. A pastor or church leader is not the only one who can minister. Every believer is called to minister to others in Jesus' name. You can receive input from someone with a spiritual leadership ability (gift) and be equipped and strengthened as you come to maturity as a Christian.

233 | Leaders lead

What can we learn from the New Testament about how leadership works practically in a local church? Acts 15 tells about a dispute in the church and how they solved it. Paul, sent out as an apostle, met with the leadership of the church in Jerusalem to discuss a problem. James was the clear leader of the Jerusalem church along with a team of elders who worked with him. *The next day Paul and the rest of us went to see James, and all the elders were present* (Acts 21:18).

James and his team of elders were responsible to work out solutions to problems as they prayed and heard from the Father. At every local church, there should be a team of elders, along with one person who is called to give clear oversight to this team and the local church. In fact, this principle applies in every area of the church. God calls teams of people to work together for a common goal; however, someone always has been chosen by the Lord to be the leader of this team. *May the Lord, the God of the spirits of all mankind, appoint a man over this community* (Numbers 27:16).

Every local church, every family of churches and every cell group or house church needs to have a clear leadership team, along with someone who has been chosen of God to give leadership to the team. For example, in a husband-wife relationship, there is a real sense of teamwork. In a healthy marriage, the husband and wife make decisions together; however, the husband is called to be the head of the home and should love and care for his wife. When, in times of crisis, a decision has to be made, the husband is responsible for the final decision.

When an airplane is flying, everyone works together as a team. However, during times of crisis, take off, and landing, who is in charge? The pilot. This is based on a spiritual truth. For instance, in your local church, God has called someone to give clear leadership to the church, yet at the same time, there should be a real sense of teamwork among the leadership team.

Acts 14:21-23 tells us that Paul and Barnabas were concerned that every local church in every area had clear eldership (spiritual leadership) appointed among them. In the New Testament, we see various types of spiritual leadership mentioned. Acts 15:6 says, *"The apostles and elders met to consider this question."* The elders were those who gave oversight to the local congregations. The apostles were those who had a larger sphere of oversight because they were called to oversee church leaders from various parts of the world. As "apostolic overseers," they were responsible to care for, oversee, encourage and equip local elders who served the people in their local area or sphere of influence. *We, however, will not boast beyond measure, but within the limits of the sphere which God appointed us—a sphere which especially includes you* (2 Corinthians 10:13 NKJ).

Paul, the apostle, told the Corinthian believers that they were within his sphere of responsibility. Paul was not a local elder in the Corinthian church; however, he was responsible to give oversight to the eldership who oversaw the work of God in that area. Paul called himself an apostle. Various denominations use different terminology when referring to these apostolic overseers in today's church; however, they still fulfill a similar role of overseeing pastors and elders in the local church.

234 | Leaders chosen by God and confirmed by His people

Since it is the Lord's plan for His church to grow and multiply, He is constantly desiring to release new leaders in His church. The leadership at the church of Antioch came together to fast and pray, and then the Holy Spirit called Barnabas and Saul to a new work of planting churches. *In the church at Antioch there were prophets and teachers...While they were worshiping the Lord and fasting, the Holy Spirit said, "Set apart for me Barnabas and Saul for the work to which I have called them." So after they had fasted and prayed, they placed their hands on them and sent them off* (Acts 13:1-4).

Barnabas and Saul were sent out to do God's work by the Holy Spirit. The Holy Spirit is the One who calls church leaders and believers into areas of ministry. After they were called, the spiritual leaders at Antioch affirmed the new

Biblical Foundations for Life

According to Acts 15, how did the early church model the fact that team leadership is more effective than one single person leading alone?

Why is it important to have clear leadership for a team?

What does church government by theocracy mean?

leaders, laid their hands on them, and prayed for them to be sent away to fulfill the Lord's call on their lives.

In today's church, different church families have various ways of choosing leadership. Some churches are governed by a democracy. A democracy is basically a church ruled by the people. Either a committee is formed or there is a type of consensus or vote to make decisions about church leadership.

Others are governed by a theocracy. I am of the persuasion that God is restoring theocracy to His church. Church government by theocracy means the leadership of the church fast and pray, and the Holy Spirit speaks to them about whom He is calling to spiritual leadership. God's people then, through fasting and prayer, give their affirmation to the Holy Spirit calling this person to spiritual leadership. In the New Testament, spiritual leaders were called by God this way.

How was Jesus the model for servant-leadership?

It is my understanding that leadership in a local church (or in a cell group) should be appointed because *God* is the One who has called this spiritual leader into an area of oversight and spiritual service. When God calls a person to leadership, he will be confirmed by other leaders and the body of Christ around him. Remember David the shepherd boy who was called to be the king of Israel? The Lord called David as a young boy. He was anointed with oil through Samuel the prophet (1 Samuel 16:13); however, it was many years later before David was affirmed by others to be the new king of Israel. Between the time of his call and the time of the fulfillment of this prophecy, David experienced many dark hours hiding out from a demonized king who was trying to kill him. But the day came when David was confirmed to be the king of Israel by other leaders around him and then eventually by the people of God.

I believe it is advantageous to have spiritual leaders from outside the local congregation also involved in this process of discernment regarding leadership. In Titus 1:5, Paul tells Titus to be responsible for the process of choosing leadership in the churches in Crete. *The reason I left you in Crete was that you might straighten out what was left unfinished and appoint elders in every town, as I directed you.* Anyone who has been given authority by the Lord needs to also be under authority. Titus was serving under Paul's leadership as an apostle in the early church.

235 | Leaders are always servants

Leaders in the body of Christ are called to be servants. Jesus Christ was the greatest leader who ever lived, and He said, *whoever wants to become great among you must be your servant, and whoever wants to be first must be your slave—just as the Son of Man did not come to be served, but to serve, and to give his life as a ransom for many* (Matthew 20:26b-28).

If someone comes to me and says he feels called to be a leader, I am not impressed with how much charisma he has or with his knowledge of the Bible. The real key to his ability to lead depends on whether or not he loves Jesus, loves His people and is willing to serve.

Churches often acknowledge individuals within their congregation who have a special ministry in serving as "deacons." The Bible tells us that deacons were first to be tested before they were set apart as deacons (1 Timothy 3:10). When someone desires to be involved in any type of church leadership, there should first be a period of time for him to be tested. Does he really have the heart of a servant? This is not implying that there is something wrong with him; it simply means that he needs to have time to see how he fits in with the other believers in the local church.

People are like pieces to a puzzle. Some people fit together and others do not. That's the way it is in the kingdom of God. It takes time until we know whether or not God has placed people together so they can work smoothly and effectively with one another.

Sometimes there are problems in churches which have occurred because the pastor or leader was brought in with good intentions, but the pieces just didn't seem to fit. If my arm is broken, a doctor would set it with a cast. It would take some time for it to be bonded back together. People need time to be bonded together. As the Lord calls you to be involved in a local church, allow the Lord to take enough time for you to be knit together in relationships with those in the church. It takes time for these relationships to be built. Relationships are built on trust, and trust takes time. These relationships can be built effectively with a small group of believers.

Consequently, when someone comes into a local church and becomes a part of a small group, wise spiritual leaders will give God the time He needs to work in the life of this believer before placing him into spiritual leadership. As the grace of God is evident in this believer's life, it will not be long until people around him will begin to look to him for leadership. Spiritual leaders who are sensitive to the Holy Spirit will begin to release him into areas of leadership, perhaps as an assistant leader in the small group. This can be a training ground for future leadership.

Why must leaders be tested before leadership responsibility is given to them?

Biblical Foundations for Life

PART 4 — COMMITMENT TO THE LOCAL CHURCH

236 | Common vision in the church

Did you ever go to a church meeting and feel like it was a really nice group of believers, but somehow you just didn't fit in? Although there was nothing wrong with this church, God simply wasn't calling you there. Every believer needs to be placed within the body of Christ so that he will be working hand-in-hand with believers with whom he shares a common vision. At the same time, we need to confirm the rest of the body of Christ around us so that God's purposes can be fulfilled. Remember, God is a creative God. In the same way the Lord created you and me, He created various kinds of congregations in His church family. Together they fulfill the purposes of God.

The scripture says that we should not plow with a donkey and an ox together (Deuteronomy 22:10). Why? Because they move at different paces. We need to be sure that the people we are "walking with" in our local church are those with whom the Lord has placed us, so that we can walk in unity, and He can command a blessing.

How good and pleasant it is when brothers live together in unity! ...For there the Lord bestows his blessing, even life forevermore (Psalms 133:1, 3b).

You can make hamburgers at McDonald's, but if you go to work at another restaurant, they will make hamburgers a bit differently from the way you were trained to do it. Every church has a different way of doing things. They have different visions the Lord has given them to fulfill.

For example, some churches prefer singing hymns while others prefer choruses and worship with a band. Some churches may focus more on systematic Bible teaching, while others are more focused on evangelism. We need to be a part of a church where we can agree with the basic "values" the spiritual leaders are teaching us.

In a cell-based church or house church, everyone is a part of a small group where they can be accountable to their brothers and sisters in the way they live their Christian lives. These smaller groups have a vision to nurture believers and help them with "blind spots" in their lives.

A church's vision encourages us to support and submit to the leadership that God raises up among us. When a church body agrees to a common vision, it will be easier to "live together in unity!"

When you join a church family, it is important to understand its "roots." Find out why God "birthed" your church. Understanding the past will give you a clear sense of what makes your local church tick. You will see the faithfulness of God.

History about the early days of your church or denomination may appear online or check with your church leadership for more information. The history of our church family, DOVE International, is written in the book, *Our Journey with God: The DOVE International Story*.[1] We encourage everyone who is called

---

How does your personal vision compare with your church's (or small group's) vision?

to be a part of our church family to read this book to understand where we've come from and what the Lord has called us to do.

Someone once said, "We build on the shoulders of those who have gone on before us." Many times mistakes are made because we have not heeded the lessons learned by our spiritual forefathers.

Although each local church needs to have a clear vision, we must remember that nothing happens except by the grace of God. The responsibility to make something happen is God's. You and I simply need to be obedient. We "plant our seeds" in faith and expect them to grow, but it is not our responsibility to make them grow. We co-labor with God for His glory.

237 | Know where you are called

Maybe you are saying, "How do I really know where God has placed me in His church?" First of all, you need to pray. Ask God, "Who are the Christian believers with whom I have a relationship?" Remember, the Lord places His people in relationships so they can serve Him. The scripture also tells us we must *let the peace of Christ rule in our hearts* (Colossians 3:15). In other words, you will know as you pray and take steps of faith and obedience.

According to Colossians 3:15, what is the basic evidence that you are where God wants you to be?

We are living in the last days, and God tells us He is going to pour out His Spirit on all flesh. You can expect it to happen. The Bible says in Acts 2:17-18, *"In the last days," God says, "I will pour out my Spirit on all people. Your sons and daughters will prophesy, your young men will see visions, your old men will dream dreams. Even on my servants, both men and women, I will pour out my Spirit in those days, and they will prophesy."*

When the Lord poured out His Spirit in Acts, chapter 2, the church was birthed in Jerusalem. Believers met from house to house all over the city. As God pours out His Spirit in our generation, there will be a need for many new "wineskins." New churches will be raised up to take care of the coming harvest as new believers are birthed into the kingdom of God. Some may be community churches, others mega-churches and still others house churches or "micro-churches." God may call you to be part of a new fellowship of believers in the future.

Trust God to lead you to spiritual leaders who are open and transparent with their own lives. Spiritual leaders need to be transparent with their Christian lives, sharing their weaknesses as well as their strengths.

Ask the Lord to lead you to believers who will be willing to pray with you to help you discern where the Lord is placing you in His body. God wants you connected to a local church where you can be trained, protected and available to serve others.

238 | Agreement in the local church

All believers in a local church should know what their church believes. Every local church should also have a clear "statement of faith" and a written statement of the specific vision the Lord has given them to fulfill. Billy Graham and a group of spiritual leaders met in Lausanne, Switzerland, in 1974 and the

Biblical Foundations for Life

What is your responsibility in keeping unity in your small group, your church, your family?

_____
_____
_____
_____

Why is it so important for believers in a local church to agree (1 Corinthians 1:10)?

_____
_____
_____
_____

Describe how the body of Christ is like the human body.

_____
_____
_____
_____
_____
_____
_____

Lord gave them a statement of faith called the *Lausanne Covenant[1]*. This is the covenant that our church, along with thousands of other churches throughout the world, has used as a statement of faith. This statement of faith declares that there is one God and that the Bible is the inspired Word of God. It states all of the major doctrines that are so precious to us as true believers in Jesus Christ.[1] If you are considering joining a church family, ask for their statement of faith.

Besides knowing and agreeing with your church's statement of faith, it is God's will for church leadership and all of God's people to work together in unity. *Make every effort to keep the unity of the Spirit through the bond of peace* (Ephesians 4:3).

As we preserve the unity in our local church family, God will continue to pour out His blessing on us. If someone comes to you regarding a problem with leadership in your local church, tell him that he needs to talk to the person with whom he has the problem. There is no place for gossip or slander in the kingdom of God. The enemy will use it as a wedge of disunity. If believers in your small group do not agree with the leadership of the local church, they need to pray and then discuss their problem with the leadership, not with other believers in the church. Those in leadership should be open to listening to the concerns of those they lead. Godly leaders will want to hear your appeals.

The enemy knows that a breakdown of unity will hinder the work of God more than any other thing in the local church. That's why the scripture says in 1 Corinthians 1:10 that we should appeal to each other. *I appeal to you, brothers, in the name of our Lord Jesus Christ, that all of you agree with one another so that there may be no divisions among you and that you may be perfectly united in mind and thought.*

[1] A copy of the Lausanne Covenant appears at www.dcfi.org.

239 | Support your church's vision

If every person called to be a part of a local church is committed to a relationship with a small group of believers within the church, there will be healthy relationships throughout the church. In the New Testament, God's people met as small groups of believers in homes. Everyone was needed. *Now the body is not made up of one part but of many. If the foot should say, "Because I am not a hand, I do not belong to the body," it would not for that reason cease to be part of the body. And if the ear should say, "Because I am not an eye, I do not belong to the body," it would not for that reason cease to be part of the body. If the whole body were an eye, where would the sense of hearing be? If the whole body were an ear, where would the sense of smell be? But in fact God has arranged the parts in the body, every one of them, just as he wanted them to be* (1 Corinthians 12:14-18).

Just as every member of the human body is important, every member of the local church should know where and how he is connected to the body of our Lord Jesus Christ. If you have questions about the specific vision of your local church, it is important that you sit down with church leadership to gain a clear understanding of what the Lord has called your church to do. It is of utmost importance that believers support the vision and the leadership of the local church in which they serve. If you cannot support the leadership and the vision of your local church, then the Lord may be calling you into another local church.

What should you do if you feel you do not fit in?

Did you ever notice how a group of houses in a community may all look the same on the outside because they were built by a builder with one particular style? Most of these houses, however, are different inside. In the same way, although they may "look" similar, various churches have different callings from the Lord, and as a spiritual family, have their own uniqueness.

We need to be sure we are placed within a spiritual family where we can grow and support the leadership and the vision of our local church. God has called us to be committed to Him, His Word and His people in a practical way through the local church.

240 | Unified but not exclusive

It is important to have the same basic vision within a church family because if we do not dwell together in unity, God cannot command a blessing (Psalms 133:1-3). But we cannot be exclusive. In the book of 1 Corinthians, one of the believers said, "I am of Paul," and another said, "I am of Apollos," another said, "I am of Cephas (or Peter)," and another said, "I am of Christ" (1 Corinthians 1:12).

Why is division so detrimental to the body of Christ?

Paul wrote back and told them that this was wrong. "Is Christ divided?" he asked. There can be no division in the body of Christ, neither should it be exclusive. The Lord warns us of placing one church (or one cell group or house church) as better than another. The scripture says in 1 Corinthians 12:5-6, *There are different kinds of service, but the same Lord. There are different kinds of working, but the same God works all of them in all men.*

We are called to love and encourage people from many different churches. However, we also need to be committed to and in unity with those in our church family, whether in our small group, local congregation or house church.

Why is exclusiveness detrimental?

Sometimes believers want to change from one local church to another. If someone believes the Lord is asking him to become involved in another church, he should talk to his trusted spiritual leaders first. If there is a difficulty in his former church, he needs to go the "hundredth" mile to be sure he has a clear relationship with that church and their leadership. If he doesn't, his problem may follow him.

When our church began in 1980, we were commissioned out of our former church. Although our new church has a different "personality" than the church we were commissioned from, we still have a wonderful relationship with the precious people in our former church.

241 | A unified church will multiply

One kernel of corn planted in a field will produce approximately 1,200 kernels of corn. If these 1,200 kernels of corn are planted the following year, they will produce 1,440,000 kernels of corn. This is called the principle of multiplication. Every church should multiply. One person shares with another person the good

Biblical Foundations for Life

According to Matthew 28:19-20, what is our goal and responsibility on this planet?

_____

_____

_____

_____

What will happen if we fulfill that responsibility (Acts 2:47)?

_____

_____

_____

_____

news of Jesus. This person receives Christ into his life and shares with another. And the church grows. Growing churches start new churches!

The Lord's desire is for His church to go forth in power and authority as Christians go from house to house in every community, throughout every city, town and nation of the world. In a vision the Lord gave me many years ago, I saw missiles shooting out of our home area to the nations of the world. These missiles represented believers who were sent out to other nations to share the gospel of Jesus Christ and to plant new churches. God wants to use you in your local church to touch the world.

Every church needs a local, national, and international vision. Churches without a mission vision will eventually stagnate. Jesus says in Matthew 28:19-20 that we should go and make disciples of all nations. That's why He left us on this planet. Years ago, our local church had the privilege of encouraging a new church to start in Nairobi, Kenya. Today they have grown to more than 200 churches in Kenya and Uganda and have reached many nations of Africa with the Gospel.

God wants Christians to work together, stand together, and pray together as He builds His church through small groups of believers. In small groups, Christians can be trained and then sent out as a spiritual army to take localities and the nations of the world back from the devil. Jesus Christ will continue to add to His church. The Bible says that the early church was *"praising God and enjoying the favor of all the people. And the Lord added to their number daily those who were being saved"* (Acts 2:47).

Although God's purpose for us in our churches, cell groups and house churches is to reach people for Christ, we will experience fellowship with one another at the same time. Fellowship with others is an added blessing to those who are serving Jesus. However, may we never forget why the Lord has placed us on this earth—*to know Him and to make Him known.*

242 | Roots and the grace of God

Throughout the Bible, we see examples of the Lord asking His people to set up monuments and altars as a remembrance of the things the Lord had done. In 1 Samuel 7, the prophet set up a stone as a reminder to God's people that the Lord had helped them. The Bible tells us in Deuteronomy 4:9, *"Only be careful, and watch yourselves closely so that you do not forget the things your eyes have seen or let them slip from your heart as long as you live. Teach them to your children and to their children after them."*

God was concerned the children of Israel would forget the phenomenal things that He had done throughout their history. He commanded them to teach their children and grandchildren.

In the New Testament, we are exhorted in Scripture to participate in taking communion to remember all that Jesus has done for us through His life, death and resurrection. When we take a piece of bread and drink from the cup, we receive again by faith the resurrection power of Jesus Christ. He is our Savior, our Deliverer, our Healer and our returning King.

Jesus shared the first communion with his disciples in the upper room before he went to the cross and told them: "Take and eat; this is my body." Then he took the cup, gave thanks and offered it to them, saying, "Drink from it, all of you. This is my blood of the covenant, which is poured out for many for the forgiveness of sins" (Matthew 26:26-28).

Paul the apostle told the early church: And when he had given thanks, he broke it and said, "This is my body, which is for you; do this in remembrance of me." In the same way, after supper he took the cup, saying, "This cup is the new covenant in my blood; do this, whenever you drink it, in remembrance of me. For whenever you eat this bread and drink this cup, you proclaim the Lord's death until he comes" (1 Corinthians 11:24-26).

Communion can be observed in a large congregation, in a small group, or whenever two or three gather together in His name. When we share communion together, we show our participation in the body of Christ. We are to personally examine our walk with God so we do not eat and drink in an unworthy manner (1 Corinthians 11:27-32).

God bless you as you allow the Lord to place you in His body in a way that pleases Him. Remember, it is not the church of your choice, but the church of His choice. Expect the Lord to use you as He builds His church through you from house to house, city to city, and nation to nation.

Why is it important to participate in communion in remembrance of Christ?

243 | Three kinds of churches

The Lord is using different types of churches to build His church today. Let's examine three kinds: community churches, megachurches and micro churches.

Community churches appear in nearly every community around the world. They meet in a church facility each Sunday morning in addition to holding various meetings throughout the week. Their specific target area is the local community.

There are many styles and flavors of community churches. They usually average between fifty to two hundred members, sometimes more. Community churches are like community stores. Most people buy groceries in a store that is near where they live. Proximity and ease of access are a big part of the nature of the community church.

Megachurches Fifty years ago, nearly every church in America was a community church. However, with a new mentality of small groups (cell groups) meeting within a larger church body, rapid multiplication and growth occurred. Megachurches began to mushroom across America and the nations. These churches often have one thousand or more people in their services.

Megachurches, like the Walmart superstores, are large and they offer an abundance of services to the believer. However, unlike the community church where you may know nearly everyone, at a megachurch you probably know only a few people. Yet, church members thoroughly enjoy a megachurch since everything is easily accessible in one location.

What type of church have you been involved in?

Biblical Foundations for Life

Micro churches and micro church networks The concept of micro churches requires us to think about church in a new way. Micro churches are small and can therefore meet anywhere—in a house, in a college dorm room, in a coffee shop, or in a corporate boardroom. A micro church is meant to be a complete little church. Each church is led by a spiritual father or mother who functions as the elder along with a small eldership team. The church leaders are mostly bi-vocational. Believers in micro churches focus on growth by multiplying new micro churches.

A micro church network would be equivalent to the stores in a shopping mall. If the average store were taken out of the mall, it would likely not be able to stand on its own. Each specialized store flourishes together within the cluster of the others. The house churches function like these shopping mall stores. They are individual and specialized, yet they flourish when they network together with other house churches. Remember, the New Testament church met in homes (Acts 2, Acts 20:20).

Into which type of church has God called you during this season of your life?

244 | The holy building myth and the holy man myth

The holy building myth is the idea that the church is a building. The holy man myth is the idea that the pastor is the one who is supposed to do all the ministry in a church. Neither of these are true. What does the Bible say about these concepts?

Jesus said, *"I will build my church"* (Matthew 16:18a). Jesus did not mean that He was going to lay one stone upon another in order to construct a church building. The church is people—called out ones. Every person is important and chosen by the Lord. The company of people God has called out meets both from house to house and publicly (in the temple). (Matthew 16:18; Acts 20:20). We do not go to church; we are the church!

Ephesians 4:11; 4:15-16 tell us, *"So Christ himself gave the apostles, the prophets, the evangelists, the pastors and teachers, to equip his people for works of service…. Speaking the truth in love, we will grow to become in every respect the mature body of him who is the head, that is, Christ. From him the whole body, joined and held together by every supporting ligament, grows and builds itself up in love, as each part does its work."*

The believers are called to do the work of ministry, not just one "holy man." God has given each of His children gifts, talents, and ministries for building His church. Many of these can be most effectively nurtured in a small group setting.

When I was a senior pastor for fifteen years, more than 90% of the actual ministry was done by the believers in the church who served in small groups. When all members are functioning properly in their gifts and ministries, the church will grow and prosper. The pastors and elders will no longer be held up as holy men on pedestals doing all the ministry. Instead, they will be released to train each believer to be a minister.

What did Christ give the church?

FOUNDATION 9

Authority and Accountability

245 | Introduction to foundation 9

In this teaching on Authority and Accountability, we will learn that the Lord has chosen to give His authority to men and women in various areas of life including the government, our employment, the church, and our families. If we have a healthy understanding of the fear of the Lord, we will understand why God places authorities in our lives.

The Lord delegates responsibility to the authorities so He can use them to bring protection, adjustment, and structure into our lives. A proper understanding of authority will bring security into our lives. Romans 13:1-2 tells us we are to submit to the governing authorities. *Everyone must submit himself to the governing authorities, for there is no authority except that which God has established...Consequently, he who rebels against the authority is rebelling against what God has instituted....*

It all begins with an understanding of the fear of the Lord. When we have a healthy sense of the fear of the Lord, we will not want to sin against Him. *To fear the Lord is to hate evil...* (Proverbs 8:13). That leads us to practical accountability. The meaning of accountability is "to give an account to others for what God has called us to do." We are first accountable to the Lord regarding how we live out our commitment to Christ. Our lives need to line up with the Word of God. Then we are accountable to fellow believers. These persons are often the spiritual leaders God has placed in our lives. Hebrews 13:17 says these leaders are accountable to God concerning us because they...*keep watch over you as men who must give an account....*

Having a healthy biblical understanding of the fear of the Lord, godly authority, and practical accountability will prepare us for a healthy, fulfilled life of obedience to the Lord.

Why is it so important for us to have a healthy understanding of the fear of the Lord?

Biblical Foundations for Life

PART 1   UNDERSTANDING THE FEAR OF THE LORD AND AUTHORITY

246 | The fear of the Lord causes us to obey

Jonah was a prophet in the Old Testament who made a major mistake. The Lord called him to go to the wicked city of Nineveh and warn the people of God's impending judgment. But Jonah knew that his God was a compassionate God. He figured that the people in Ninevah would repent and be spared God's judgment, and he really did not want God to have mercy on any nation but Israel. So, instead of obeying, he boarded a ship that was going in the opposite direction to the farthest place possible.

In the midst of the voyage, the Lord sent a huge storm that nearly wiped out the ship. The sailors were frightened as they cried out to their heathen gods. In the turmoil, someone found Jonah asleep in the lower part of the ship. The captain implored Jonah, "What are you doing sleeping? Get up and call on your God; maybe He'll keep us from perishing!"

Even though the sailors did not believe in the true God, they were spiritual men and believed in the supernatural. They cast lots to see whether or not someone on board was the cause of the storm that was about to destroy them. The lot fell on Jonah. Jonah then confessed...*I fear the Lord, the God of heaven, who made the sea and the dry land* (Jonah 1:9 NKJ).

Jonah felt guilty for disobeying God and putting the sailors at risk. He instructed the sailors to pick him up and throw him into the sea and promised that the sea would then stop raging. After repeated attempts to bring the ship to land, but to no avail, they reluctantly threw Jonah overboard. Immediately the sea grew calm. *At this the men greatly feared the Lord, and they offered a sacrifice to the Lord and made vows to him* (Jonah 1:16).

These men understood the fear of the Lord. The fear of the Lord causes people to place their faith in the Lord for salvation. It also causes them to realize that God judges sin because He is a holy God. We need to have a healthy understanding of the fear of the Lord. If we understand the fear of the Lord, we will want to live a life of obedience to Him.

247 | The fear of the Lord causes us to reverence God

The Bible tells us in Proverbs 9:10a that if we have a deep reverence and love for God, we will gain wisdom. *The fear of the Lord is the beginning of wisdom....*

A healthy understanding of the fear of the Lord is simply to be awestruck by His power and presence. *To fear the Lord* means *to be in awe and to reverence the Lord*, understanding that we serve a mighty God. Our Father in heaven loves us perfectly. He wants the best for our lives. He is a God who has created the entire universe and has all power and authority in His hand. As Christians, we should possess a holy fear that trembles at God's Word. *"Has not my hand made all these*

In the story of Jonah, how did the sailor's fear of their heathen gods differ from the fear of the Lord they experienced in Jonah 1:16?

things, and so they came into being?" declares the Lord. "This is the one I esteem: he who is humble and contrite in spirit, and trembles at my word" (Isaiah 66:2).

This is not to say that God wants us to cower in a corner. That's not what the fear of the Lord is about. The Lord does not desire for His children to be afraid of Him, but to honor and respect Him. God's Word tells us that *"perfect love casts out fear"* (1 John 4:18). In other words, where there is God's perfect love, fear cannot dwell; or to say it another way— where there is the presence of fear, there is the absence of love.

However, if we love, honor and respect our God, we will want to obey Him because the fear of the Lord also involves a fear of sinning against Him and facing the consequences. I grew up with an earthly father who loved me. I was not afraid of him. However, whenever I was disobedient, I feared the consequences of the discipline I knew would follow. Yet, I knew that even the discipline was from a father who loved me. Our heavenly Father loves us so much, yet He hates sin.

Our God is a God of complete authority in this universe. Ask the Lord to give you the grace to experience the fear of the Lord in your life. Expect to be awestruck by His presence in your life!

If God does not want us to be afraid of Him, what kind of "fear" are we talking about?

248 | The fear of the Lord causes us to turn away from evil

When we have a healthy fear of the Lord, we will not want to sin against Him. *To fear the Lord is to hate evil...*(Proverbs 8:13). We know that sinning against a holy God means we will have to face the consequences. Although we realize that God is not a God with a big stick just waiting for us to make a mistake, God *will* punish sin.

The Bible tells us in Acts 9:31 that the New Testament church understood what it meant to walk in the fear of the Lord. When we have a proper understanding of the fear of the Lord, we will hate evil, knowing that evil displeases the Lord and destroys God's people. *Do you not know that the wicked will not inherit the kingdom of God? Do not be deceived: Neither the sexually immoral nor idolaters nor adulterers nor male prostitutes nor homosexual offenders nor thieves nor the greedy nor drunkards nor slanderers nor swindlers will inherit the kingdom of God. And that is what some of you were. But you were washed, you were sanctified, you were justified in the name of the Lord Jesus Christ and by the Spirit of our God* (1 Corinthians 6:9-11).

In other words, true Christians will not live a life of sin. The good news is this: when we repent and turn from our sin, Jesus washes us clean. And the "fear of the Lord" keeps us from going back to our old way of living.

There are many examples of the fear of the Lord in the New Testament. After Ananias and Sapphira lied to the Holy Spirit and were struck dead, God's judgment on their sin caused the believers to increase in their awe and fear of the Lord. *Great fear seized the whole church and all who heard about these events* (Acts 5:11).

What do we hate when we have a healthy fear of the Lord, according to Proverbs 8:13?

What does the fear of the Lord lead us to?

Biblical Foundations for Life

In Revelation 1:17, John had an encounter with God. *When I saw him, I fell at his feet as though dead. Then he placed his right hand on me and said: "Do not be afraid. I am the First and the Last."*

Our fear of the Lord is not a destructive fear but one that leads us to God's presence and purity. When we understand and experience the fear of the Lord, we will hate sin and turn away from it. We will trust Jesus to wash, cleanse and make us new.

249 | Why authorities are placed in our lives

Who are the governing authorities in your life?

List ways each one is used by the Lord to mold, adjust and structure your life.

The Lord has chosen to give His authority to men and women in various areas including the government, our employment, the church and our families. If we understand the fear of the Lord in a healthy way, we will understand why God places authorities in our lives. The Lord delegates responsibility to the authorities so that He can use them to mold us, adjust us, and structure our lives. If we resist these authorities, scripture indicates we are resisting God and bringing judgment upon ourselves. Romans 13:1-4a tells us, *"Everyone must submit himself to the governing authorities, for there is no authority except that which God has established. The authorities that exist have been established by God. Consequently, he who rebels against the authority is rebelling against what God has instituted, and those who do so will bring judgment on themselves. For rulers hold no terror for those who do right, but for those who do wrong. Do you want to be free from fear of the one in authority? Then do what is right and he will commend you. For he is God's servant to do you good...."*

The authorities that are in our lives have been placed there by God. For example, police officers and government officials are ministers of God. That does not mean they are being obedient to God all of the time. However, God has placed them in our lives and wants us to respond to them in a godly way. If we're driving through a town and a police officer stands at an intersection and puts up his hand, every driver will stop because of his authority. It is not his own authority, but the authority of the government he represents. If we disobey the police officer, we are disobeying the government, because the police officer is under authority.

A proper understanding of authority will bring security into our lives. The scriptures teach us that *"rulers hold no terror for those who do right, but for those who do wrong"* (Romans 13:3). When there is no authority, there is chaos. One of the darkest periods of history for the people of God occurred because no authority was set in place. *In those days Israel had no king; everyone did as he saw fit* (Judges 21:25). Society does not tolerate chaos. There is always a need for some form of government or type of authority structure. If we do not have a godly authority structure, the vacuum will cause an ungodly authority structure to develop.

God delegates His authority to men and women. Anyone who has authority needs to be under authority, or he becomes a tyrant. I once heard a story of a sergeant in the army who relished his authority, taking great pleasure in telling men to obey his orders. When he retired, he attempted to apply the same principles in his hometown. He would bark an order at a store clerk, or a mail carrier, or a waiter in a restaurant. Needless to say, he was not very well received! The ex-sergeant soon realized he no longer had authority over those people, because he was no longer under military authority.

If we are not under the authority of Jesus, we can attempt to resist the devil and the demons of hell, but they do not need to submit to us. However, when we are submitted to God's authority in our lives, the devil must flee.

250 | What does it mean to submit to authority?

What does authority mean?

The Lord has set up delegated authorities to protect us and to help mold, adjust and structure us to be conformed to the image of Christ. For many people, this is a hard lesson to learn. There was a young man who was not willing to submit to the authority of his parents so he decided to join the army. Guess what? Now, he *really* learned to understand what submitting to authority was all about!

What does it mean to "submit to authority?" The word *submit* means *to yield, stand under, defer to the opinion or authority of another*. Submission is an attitude of the heart that desires to obey God and the human authorities that He has placed in our lives.

The word *authority* means *a right to command or act*. In other words, it is *the right given by God to men and women to build, to mold, and to adjust and structure the lives of others*. An authority is a person who has been given responsibility for our lives. At our workplace, it's our employer; in our hometown, it is our local government official; in the body of Christ, our authorities are the elders and pastors of our church; and for young people who are living at home, it is their parents.

How is resisting authority in your life actually resisting God?

Paul reminds believers in Titus 3:1 that it is important to be obedient to the authorities in their lives. *Remind the people to be subject to rulers and authorities, to be obedient, to be ready to do whatever is good.*

Submission to authority is not a popular topic today. Employees rebel against their employers, school children against their teachers, children against their parents and churchgoers against their pastors. The Lord wants to restore a proper understanding of the fear of the Lord and submission to authority to our generation. If we do not learn to properly submit to the authorities the Lord has placed in our lives, we are disobedient to God who has placed these authorities there.

Submission to authority seems foolish to many people, *but God chose the foolish things of the world to shame the wise; God chose the weak things of the world to shame the strong* (1 Corinthians 1:27).

Whenever I resist any authority the Lord has placed in my life—parents, employer, police, church authority—I am actually resisting God. (Unless, of course, the authority is asking me to do something that violates God's Word and causes me to sin. See Day 256). I have told young people, "When your parents ask you to be in by midnight or an employer tells you to be at work on time, the Lord is

Biblical Foundations for Life

using these authorities to train and mold you into the character of Christ. If you don't obey, you will have to learn the same hard lessons over and over again."

251 | Obedience is better than "sacrifice"

What did Saul do that displeased God so much?

God always requires obedience to His Word. In 1 Samuel 15:22-23, Saul rebelled and disobeyed God's clear instructions because he placed his own perception of what was right above what God said. Saul had been commanded to wait until the prophet Samuel came to offer a sacrifice. However, Saul feared the people instead of fearing God, and went ahead and offered the sacrifice. Samuel's admonition was very direct and to the point...*does the Lord delight in burnt offerings and sacrifices as much as in obeying the voice of the Lord? To obey is better than sacrifice, and to heed is better than the fat of rams. For rebellion is like the sin of divination, and arrogance like the evil of idolatry....*

Obeying from the heart is better than "sacrifice" (any outward form of service for the Lord). Rebellion (disobedience) is equated with the sin of witchcraft. Later, the Bible tells us that an evil spirit tormented Saul (1 Samuel 16:14). Saul's rebellion allowed room for an evil spirit to come into his life, and he lived as a tormented man for the rest of his life. He had refused to walk in the fear of the Lord.

Explain the phrase "obedience is better than sacrifice."

Unless we learn to submit to the authorities the Lord has placed in our lives, we cannot respond appropriately as an authority to others. Children who do not obey their parents and do not repent for their disobedience grow up with an unwholesome understanding of authority. They are often domineering over their own children. If we have not properly responded to the authorities the Lord has placed in our lives, the Lord may require us to ask forgiveness of the person(s) we have dishonored. Our confession can break the bondage of rebellion and stubbornness that may be operating in our lives.

252 | Delegated authority molds us

The authorities the Lord has placed in our lives will not be perfect. We do not submit to them because they are perfect, but we submit to them because the Lord has placed them there. I remember one of the jobs I had as a young man. I did not like the attitude of my employer. But, regardless of his attitude, I submitted to him because he was my employer. I have learned that it is a tremendous blessing to obey the authorities the Lord has placed in my life.

Wherever we go, one of the first questions we should ask ourselves is, "Who has the Lord placed in authority here?" People who are truly under God's authority see authority everywhere they go. They realize these authorities have been delegated and appointed by the Lord. Luke 17:7-10 explains this delegated authority. *Suppose one of you had a servant plowing or looking after the sheep. Would he say to the servant when he comes in from the field, "Come along now and sit down to eat"? Would he not rather say, "Prepare my supper, get yourself ready and wait on me while I eat and drink; after that you may eat and drink"? Would he thank the servant because he did what he was told to do? So you also, when you have done everything you were told to do, should say, "We are unworthy servants; we have only done our duty."*

This slave, after working hard all day, came in from the field and prepared his master's meal first. Did his master thank him? No, because it was the *responsibility* of the servant to prepare the food for his master. The servant had a clear understanding of God's delegated authority. Secure people have no problem with submitting to the authorities the Lord has placed in their lives.

It is our responsibility to submit to the authorities the Lord has placed in our lives, in our homes, employment, community and in the church. The Lord works His character in us as we learn this important principle. I have seen it happen over and over again when someone cannot submit to his employer—in most cases, he goes from job to job with the same problem, because the problem lies with the employee. The Lord uses His delegated authorities to teach us, mold us, and build the character of Christ in our lives. We, then, can be His loving authorities to others whom He places in our lives.

Put yourself in the place of the servant in this story. What would your attitude be?

PART 2 DELEGATED AUTHORITY IN GOVERNMENT, WORKPLACE, FAMILY AND CHURCH

Obeying governmental authorities

Matthew 17:24-27; 22:15-22
Romans 13:1-7
1 Peter 2:13-17

Why should we be careful who we call a "whitewashed wall"?

_____

_____

_____

_____

Why should we honor governmental authorities?

_____

_____

_____

_____

253 | Honoring authority in government

Let's look at four basic areas where God has delegated His authority to men and women. These four areas include the government, the workplace, the family, and the church.

First of all, let's look at government. In the fallen world we live in, we need order and restraints to protect us from chaos. That's why God ordained government. According to Romans 13:1-2 we are to submit to the governing authorities. *Everyone must submit himself to the governing authorities, for there is no authority except that which God has established...Consequently, he who rebels against the authority is rebelling against what God has instituted....*

Christians should obey the governing authorities because they are instituted by God. Romans 13:5-7 says we should be subject to authorities not because we are afraid of punishment but because they have been ordained by God and we must keep a clear conscience by obeying them. *Therefore, it is necessary to submit to the authorities, not only because of possible punishment but also because of conscience. This is also why you pay taxes, for the authorities are God's servants, who give their full time to governing. Give everyone what you owe him: If you owe taxes, pay taxes; if revenue, then revenue; if respect, then respect; if honor, then honor.* This scripture says that if we complain about paying taxes, we are complaining about the authorities the Lord has placed in our lives. Sometimes we tend to speak negatively about authorities—police officers, for example. We especially do this when they give us a ticket for a traffic violation! We must remember that police officers are God's ministers. We need to relate to them with a submissive attitude of honor.

Daniel, in the Old Testament, was taken to Babylon as a slave when he was sixteen years old. Even so, he lived in the fear of the Lord and was a man of prayer. He learned to honor the leadership in Babylon and was appointed prime minister under three different administrations.

Whether or not authorities in our lives are godly or ungodly people, the Lord has placed them there. One time, Apostle Paul was taken before the religious council. The high priest, Ananias, commanded those who stood by Paul to strike him on the mouth. Paul didn't realize Ananias was the high priest and responded by calling him a *"whitewashed wall"* (Acts 23:3). Those standing by said, *"How can you insult God's high priest?"* Paul immediately apologized, *"...Brothers, I did not realize that he was the high priest; for it is written: 'Do not speak evil about the ruler of your people'"* (Acts 23:5).

Even though the authorities in our lives may be ungodly, the Lord has called us to have an attitude of submission to them. We honor them for their position, not for their conduct.

254 | Honoring authority in the workplace

The second group of authorities the Lord has placed in our lives are our employers. Paul urges Christians to regard their jobs as service to the Lord. *Slaves, [employees] obey your earthly masters [employers] in everything; and do it, not only when their eye is on you and to win their favor, but with sincerity of heart and reverence for the Lord. Whatever you do, work at it with all your heart, as working for the Lord, not for men, since you know that you will receive an inheritance from the Lord as a reward. It is the Lord Christ you are serving* (Colossians 3:22-24).

In other words, our real employer is Jesus Christ. We need to see our jobs as serving the Lord Jesus Christ. If we have a tendency to do our best only when the boss is around, then there's a problem.

I have a friend who worked in a steak restaurant. He submitted to his boss as the authority he knew the Lord had placed over him. The owners and managers were so impressed with his attitude, they continued to hire his Christian friends. Within a short period of time, the majority of the employees at the restaurant were Christians. Why? Because this young man had an attitude of submission to the authority of his managers and employers.

The Lord calls us to work at our jobs enthusiastically with all of our hearts, realizing we are doing it unto the Lord. And imagine, as we're doing it unto the Lord, we are getting paid to serve Him in our places of employment!

255 | How God uses employers in our lives

If your boss is a Christian, do not think he should give you extra favors because you are a believer. Some Christians think, "My boss should understand why I'm late to work or why I'm slow. He is a Christian." Even if he is a believer, your boss needs to take the authority given to him by God and discipline you so that you can be truly conformed into the image of Christ.

All who are under the yoke of slavery [employees] should consider their masters [employers] worthy of full respect, so that God's name and our teaching may not be slandered. Those who have believing masters are not to show less respect for them because they are brothers. Instead, they are to serve them even better, because those who benefit from their service are believers, and dear to them... (1 Timothy 6:1-2).

Slaves [employees], submit yourselves to your masters [employers] with all respect, not only to those who are good and considerate, but also to those who are harsh. For it is commendable if a man bears up under the pain of unjust suffering because he is conscious of God. But how is it to your credit if you receive a beating for doing wrong and endure it? But if you suffer for doing good and you endure it, this is commendable before God. To this you were called, because Christ suffered for you, leaving you an example, that you should follow in his steps (1 Peter 2:18-21).

How are we really working for "employer" Jesus Christ on our jobs?

What should our attitude be toward our employer(s)?

How should we act if we are disciplined on the job by a believing boss for doing something wrong?

Biblical Foundations for Life

How is Jesus our example in the matter of submission?

If we are late for work or lazy on the job, our employer needs to deal with us properly so we can learn to be disciplined men and women of God. However, if we are doing a good job and our employer is harsh or critical, then the Lord promises us that He will reward us.

Jesus and Moses both learned to submit to their employer's authority before the Lord used them effectively. Jesus worked in the carpenter's shop for many years before being thrust into His ministry (Mark 6:3). Moses was herding sheep for his father-in-law for 40 years as God prepared him for leadership to lead the Lord's people out of the bondage of Egypt (Exodus 3). Their heavenly Father used these authorities in their lives to teach them to have a submissive spirit toward Him and a spirit of patience toward the people whom they served.

256 | Honoring authority in the family

The Lord has instructed us to submit to the authorities that He has placed in our lives. Families are another area of submission. Ephesians 6:1-4 tells us, *"Children, obey your parents in the Lord, for this is right. 'Honor your father and mother'—which is the first commandment with a promise—that it may go well with you and that you may enjoy long life on the earth." Fathers, do not exasperate your children; instead, bring them up in the training and instruction of the Lord."*

What is the promise for those who honor their parents (Ephesians 6:1-4)?

God commands children to obey the authorities He's placed in their lives, namely their parents. To the obedient, He promises a long life! Children who honor their parents will be blessed by God here on earth.

Parents, too, must honor their children. They honor them by submitting to the needs of their children—bringing them up in the instruction of the Lord without discouraging them with unrealistic expectations (Colossians 3:21).

Many times young people have asked me if they should obey their parents when their parents are not Christians and ask them to do something that is not right in God's sight. Acts 5:29b tells us, *"...we must obey God rather than men!"*

According to Acts 5:29, what should we do if an authority in our lives asks us to do something that is sinful?

If any authority in our lives asks us to do something that is sin, we need to obey God first! For example, Kako was a young Christian believer whose Buddhist parents wanted her to continue to attend and participate in their religious rituals. She could not obey her parents by continuing to worship these false gods and refused. God was her higher authority. Our obedience to any authority must always be based on a higher loyalty to God. So then, if parents or any other authority in our lives asks us to do anything that is against the Word of God, we need to obey God first (See Day 264.)

257 | Submit to each other in the home

To be in "submission" is to be *under the authority of the one responsible for the mission of our lives*. At work, we are *under the mission* of our employer. In school, we are *under the mission* of our teacher. On a basketball team, we are *under the mission* of the coach. In the church, we are *under the mission* of the spiritual leadership the Lord has placed in our lives. And in our homes, we are *under the mission* of the head of our home. Let's see how mutual submission is a principle applied to Christian families. *Submit to one another out of reverence for Christ. Wives, submit to your husbands as to the Lord. For the husband is the head of the wife as Christ is the head of the church, his body, of which he is the Savior* (Ephesians 5:21-23).

In families, the Lord has called husbands and wives to submit to each other. God wants husbands and wives to be in unity as a team. However, in every team, there's always someone the Lord places as leadership in that team. In the case of the husband and wife, the Bible says the husband is the head of the wife. His leadership must be exercised in love and consideration for his family. A husband has the responsibility to love his wife the same way Jesus Christ loved His church and gave His life for it (Ephesians 6:25).

As the leader in the home, a husband is responsible, in times of crisis, to make final decisions. A few years ago, my wife and I needed to make a decision about whether or not to send our children to a Christian school. We prayed and talked and prayed and talked, but finally we had to make a decision. My wife's response was that as the head of the home, I needed to make the decision and she would submit to my leadership. She trusted the Lord to lead me in making the right decision.

In a single parent home, the Lord gives special grace to moms and dads who do not have spouses to help them raise their children. The Bible says that our God is a father to the fatherless (Psalm 68:5). The Lord also desires to use the body of Christ (the local church) to assist moms and dads who are single parents (James 1:27).

258 | Honoring authority in the church

The fourth area of authority the Lord delegates to men and women is in the church. Hebrews 13:17 says, *"Obey your leaders and submit to their authority. They keep watch over you as men who must give an account. Obey them so that their work will be a joy, not a burden, for that would be of no advantage to you."*

The Lord places spiritual authorities in our lives who watch over us and they must give an account to the Lord for our spiritual lives. The Lord has placed elders and pastors in our lives to direct, correct and protect us. That's why it's so important for every believer to be connected to the local church; it brings spiritual protection to us.

Paul was willing to be accountable to the spiritual leaders the Lord had placed in his life. When Paul and Barnabas were sent out of the church of Antioch to plant churches throughout the world, they returned to their local church a few years later and reported all that the Lord had done (Acts 14:27-28).

We should honor the spiritual leaders the Lord has placed in our lives according to 1 Thessalonians 5:12-13. *Now we ask you, brothers, to respect those who work hard among you, who are over you in the Lord and who admonish you. Hold them in the highest regard in love because of their work. Live in peace with each other.*

How do husbands and wives submit to each other?

How do we honor spiritual authorities in our lives?

I meet people who say, "I don't agree with my pastor or my church leadership." I first encourage them to pray for God's blessing and wisdom on their spiritual leaders. After that, the Lord may also want them to appeal to their leaders in love about those issues, keeping in mind that they cannot change their leaders—that is God's responsibility. If the differences persist, they may also need to consider two other possibilities—maybe they have rebellion in their lives they need to deal with, or perhaps the Lord has called them to another church.

Jesus, when teaching His disciples about leadership, instructed them to not be like the Gentiles who rule over others, but to be servants (Matthew 20:25-28). Jesus was not suggesting that spiritual leaders have no responsibility or authority to give direction to the church, but that their attitude should be that of a servant. Spiritual authority and servanthood go hand-in-hand. For example, Nehemiah in the Old Testament, was a man of authority, but he did not lord it over the people like former governors (Nehemiah 5:15). He was a servant who walked in the fear of the Lord.

What are the things our spiritual authorities do for us?

The Lord's call on spiritual leaders is to help each believer draw closer to Jesus and learn from Him. The Lord has called us to have an attitude of submission toward the leaders He has placed in our lives. Years ago I heard a story of a little boy who insisted on standing on his chair during a church meeting. When his father took his hand and pulled him down into a seated position, the little boy looked up at his father and said, "I may be sitting down on the outside, but I'm standing up on the inside!" The Lord is concerned about our heart attitudes.

To summarize, we are called to pray, support, submit and appeal to our spiritual authorities. (We will talk more about appealing to authority in the next section). Likewise, our spiritual authorities—pastors and elders—should pray for us, teach us, protect us, and correct us as we need it.

259 | Sin in a spiritual leader's life

What should happen if a leader has sin in his life (1 Timothy 5:19-20)?

What happens if a spiritual leader falls into sin? We should not blindly submit to a leader who has sin in his life but instead confront him according to 1 Timothy 5:19-20. *Do not entertain an accusation against an elder unless it is brought by two or three witnesses. Those who sin are to be rebuked publicly, so that the others may take warning.*

If someone with spiritual authority (elder, pastor, cell leader, house church leader, etc.) sins and it is confirmed, those whom are placed over him spiritually are responsible to discipline him. Most local churches are a part of a larger "family of churches" or a denomination. The leadership of this family of churches has the responsibility, along with the other elders, to administer proper discipline. In fact, the Bible says the guilty one should be rebuked in the presence of everyone in the church. This is why all leaders should also have spiritual authorities who will give them the direction, protection and correction they need as they serve the Lord in the local church.

If we have sin in our lives, the Lord instructs our church leaders to lovingly discipline us and restore us to walking in truth (1 Corinthians 5, Galatians 6:1, Matthew 18:17). Loving earthly fathers will discipline their children, in love, because they care for their children. God has chosen to use people as His rod to discipline us (2 Samuel 7:14), but the discipline is to reclaim us, not destroy us. Being disciplined shows God loves us. In fact, the Lord tells us in Hebrews 12:8, *"If you are not disciplined (and everyone undergoes discipline), then you are illegitimate children and not true sons."*

Wherever you're committed in the body of Christ—in a small group (cell group), a local congregation or a house church—the Lord has called you to actively support and submit to the leadership He has placed there. If someone makes an accusation against a leader, tell that person to go directly to the leader. Do not pass on gossip or accusations. Do not allow gossip or slander to hinder the work of God in your midst. And remember, the Lord has placed godly authorities in our lives to help mold us into the character of Jesus Christ.

What should happen if we have sin in our lives?

PART 3

THE BLESSINGS OF AUTHORITY

260 | Submission to authority brings protection

Next we will look at some of the blessings we receive when we submit to the authorities the Lord has placed in our lives. Some people grow up with a healthy understanding of honoring authority in their lives and realize it is there for their protection. Others rebel against authority because they have an improper understanding of it. The Lord desires to renew our minds by His Word so we can properly respect the delegated authorities He's placed in our lives.

First of all, submitting to authorities is a commandment of God. *Everyone must submit himself to the governing authorities, for there is no authority except that which God has established. The authorities that exist have been established by God. Consequently, he who rebels against the authority is rebelling against what God has instituted, and those who do so will bring judgment on themselves* (Romans 13:1-2). Here the scripture is talking about submitting to governing authorities, but it applies to all authorities in our lives. There is no authority except that which comes from God. In fact, God appoints the authorities that exist. In most cases, if we resist these authorities, we are resisting Him. We need to submit to the authorities that He's placed in our lives, because these authorities give us protection.

For example, if we disobey the speed limit, we could be killed or kill someone else. If a parent tells a child not to play with matches and he disobeys, there could be the loss of a home or the loss of life. It would not be the parents' fault or God's fault; the child simply disobeyed the authority that was placed in his life. He moved out from under the umbrella of God's protection.

Having an attitude of submission toward the authorities God has placed in our lives will protect us from many mistakes. It also is a protection against the influence of the devil. The nature of the devil is rebellion and deceit. Lucifer fell from heaven because he said, "I will be like the Most High." He refused to submit to God's authority.

In the universe there are two major forces—the one is submission to the authority of God, the other is rebellion. Whenever we allow an attitude of rebellion into our lives, we are beginning to be motivated by the enemy which leads us to sin against God.

261 | Submission to authority helps us learn principles of faith

In order to be people of faith who see miracles happen in our lives, we must understand the principles of authority. When we submit to the authorities in our lives, we learn the principles of faith. The faith of the centurion in Matthew 8:8-10 was tied into his understanding of authority. *The centurion replied, "Lord, I do not deserve to have you come under my roof. But just say the word, and my servant will be healed. For I myself am a man under authority, with soldiers under*

Discuss the way God's authority acts like an umbrella.

How are the two forces in the universe controlling your life?

How can submitting to authority teach us about faith?

me. I tell this one, 'Go,' and he goes; and that one, 'Come,' and he comes. I say to my servant, 'Do this,' and he does it." When Jesus heard this, he was astonished and said to those following him, "I tell you the truth, I have not found anyone in Israel with such great faith."*

This centurion received a miracle from Jesus because he understood authority. As an officer, he could issue orders to his subordinates, and they would obey. He completely understood that Christ, who possesses all authority, could give a command, and His will would be done.

When Jesus says a sickness must go, it must leave. His life on this earth was filled with examples of healing people of various sicknesses and diseases. The scriptures teach us that we can expect miracles when we call for the elders of the church to pray for us if we are sick...*he should call the elders of the church to pray... and the prayer offered in faith will make the sick person well...*(James 5:14-15). The act of submitting to our spiritual leaders can release faith for healing in our lives!

262 | Submission to authority trains us in character

Yet another blessing we receive from learning to submit to the authorities in our lives is that it trains us in character to be a loving authority to others.

The Lord uses authorities in our lives who speak the Word of God to us. His Word chips away from our lives anything that is not from Him. Just as a blacksmith takes a piece of iron, makes it hot so that it becomes pliable and chips the impurities away with his hammer, God's Word purifies. *"Is not my word like fire," declares the Lord...*(Jeremiah 23:29). It destroys all that is false in our lives and leaves only the genuine "metal." In the same way, our character is strengthened as we become conformed into the image of Christ.

God placed authorities in our lives to make us pliable. When we react to authority in anger and bitterness because we do not get our own way, it is probably a sign that there are still impurities the Lord is desiring to chip away from our lives. The Word of God is a purifying fire that changes us more into His likeness.

If we haven't learned to submit to the authority in our lives in one setting, God will again bring someone into our new situation to whom we will have to learn to submit. He loves us that much. He is committed to seeing our lives motivated by the fruit of the Spirit: love, joy, peace, longsuffering, gentleness, goodness, faith, meekness and self-control (Galatians 5:22).

263 | Submission to authority provides guidance

We will also find that submitting to the authority the Lord has placed in our lives often provides guidance for us to know His will. While growing up, my parents asked me to break off my relationship with certain ungodly friends. At the time, I did not appreciate what they were telling me. I felt controlled; but in retrospect, I am thankful to God for having submitted to their authority. I realize now, it saved me from having my life shipwrecked.

What does faith have to do with miracles?

How is God's Word shaping you?

What is the Lord chipping away from your life?

To whose authority is Jesus submitted?

Biblical Foundations for Life

How have you ever submitted to an authority in your life and discovered God's will for your life as a result?

A contemporary Christian musician wanted to record an album; however, her parents asked her to wait. She found it difficult, but made a decision to submit to her parents. She later produced an album that has been a blessing to hundreds of thousands of people. God blessed this musician and gave her the right timing for the release of her album.

Joseph, in the Old Testament, submitted to the authority of the jailer, even though he was falsely imprisoned. The Lord later raised him up as prime minister for the whole nation.

Jesus himself submitted to His heavenly Father every day. Jesus says in John 5:30b, "...*for I seek not to please myself but him who sent me.*" Jesus was committed to walking in submission to His heavenly Father's authority. Jesus did nothing of his own initiative, but only that which was initiated by His heavenly Father.

264 | What if the authority is wrong?

Has there ever been a time when an authority wanted you to do something you knew was sin? What did you do?

Many times people have asked me, "What should I do if the authority in my life is wrong?" As we mentioned before, we should obey God rather than man if the authority in our lives requires us to do something contrary to God's Word. But what if we believe the godly authority in our lives is making a mistake? Philippians 4:6 tells us to make an appeal. *Do not be anxious about anything, but in everything, by prayer and petition, with thanksgiving, present your requests to God.*

First of all, we need to appeal to God. We should pray, making known our requests and concerns, as we appeal to Him as our authority. In the same way, this sets a precedent for us to appeal to the delegated authorities in our lives. According to Webster's Dictionary, the word *appeal* means *an earnest entreaty or a plea*. The Lord wants us to appeal to the authorities He has placed in our lives with an attitude of submission.

What is often the result of appealing to authority?

Instead of having a submissive spirit and appealing to authority, Aaron and Miriam accused Moses regarding the leadership decisions that He was making. They did not fear God or respect God's prophet, and this allowed a spirit of rebellion to come into their lives. Moses, who had learned his lesson about authority in the desert while herding sheep, did not defend himself. Instead he went to God, and God defended him.

Daniel and his friends, in the Old Testament, appealed to the authority in their lives and asked only to eat certain foods (Daniel 1:8,12,13). The Lord honored their appealing to authority and blessed them with health, wisdom, literary skill and supernatural revelation.

What is the result of rebellion?

Nehemiah appealed to the king to take a trip to Jerusalem (Nehemiah 1). His appeal to the authority in his life in an attitude of submission caused the king to grant his request. Nehemiah's attitude and obedience made it possible for the wall to be built around Jerusalem.

In conclusion, if any person in authority in our lives requires us to sin, we must obey God and not man (Acts 5:29). The early church leaders were told by the religious leaders of their day to stop proclaiming Jesus as Lord. They could not obey these orders; but, they still maintained a spirit and attitude of honoring the religious leaders. If the authorities in our lives are asking us to cheat, steal, lie, or sin in any way, we must obey the living God first! However, this is rarely the case. Usually God uses the authorities in our lives to help mold and structure our lives for good.

265 | Maintain an attitude of love and submission

God's concern is that we have an attitude of love and submission to our God and to those He's placed in authority in our lives. This is often opposite of what we see today—people are more concerned about being right in their own eyes and insist on "doing their own thing."

Korah was a priest in the Old Testament who rose up in rebellion against Moses with 250 other leaders in Israel. Rather than appealing in love and submission to Moses' and Aaron's authority, they challenged their authority. *They came as a group to oppose Moses and Aaron and said to them, "You have gone too far! The whole community is holy, every one of them, and the Lord is with them. Why then do you set yourselves above the Lord's assembly?"* (Numbers 16:3).

Korah and the other leaders were rebellious. They thought they could choose for themselves who would lead God's people. But God made it certain; He was in charge. The next day, the ground opened up and swallowed all of them alive. God hates rebellion.

Abigail, in 1 Samuel 25, realized David and his army were coming to destroy her husband and their people. She went to David and appealed to him, and he honored her and spared her family from death.

A friend of mine was required to sign a job-related document but realized that the technical wording would make him sign an untruth. He prayed and decided that he needed to obey God. Before he went to his supervisors to appeal to them, he asked the Lord for wisdom to fulfill his employer's intentions without compromising the truth. The Lord showed him a plan, but he was prepared to give up his job if required.

He told his supervisors he appreciated working at the company and explained why he could not sign the document. He admitted that it might inconvenience them or that he could lose his job; still, he needed to be faithful to God and not tell a lie. On his own time, he volunteered to make the change on the format of the document so it legally fulfilled their company's purpose at the same time. They accepted his idea, and the Lord gave him tremendous favor in that company.

Why does God want you to appeal to Him when you have a problem submitting to an authority?

266 | Understanding delegated authority

Sometime back, a missionary in a South American nation was teaching a Sunday School class on the subject of authority from Romans 13. A doctor stood up and said, "Do you mean that I must pay the taxes that my government requires?" At that time, this nation had a very ineffective tax collection system. Less than 25% of the entire population paid taxes. The government realized this

Biblical Foundations for Life

Name some people who have delegated authority over you in your family, church and workplace.

so they raised the quota to four times more than what it should have been to cover the expenses for those who did not pay.

Convicted of this biblical principle, the doctor made a decision that day to pay his taxes, but he also prayed and asked the Lord for wisdom. The Lord gave the doctor an idea how to change the tax collection system. He shared his new idea with the city officials, and they adopted his suggestion. It worked so well that 80% of the people started paying their taxes. The state then adopted the plan which was later adopted by the whole nation. The entire nation was blessed through one man's obedience. Let us dare to obey the Word of God and see what He does through our obedience.

When we understand the principle of God's delegated authority, it changes the way we think. Paul, the apostle, clearly understood delegated authority. God had given Paul delegated authority, so Paul delegated some of the Lord's authority to Timothy and sent him to the Christians at Corinth. *For this reason I am sending to you Timothy, my son whom I love, who is faithful in the Lord. He will remind you of my way of life in Christ Jesus, which agrees with what I teach everywhere in every church* (1 Corinthians 4:17).

Years earlier, Paul, (then named Saul), was on the road to Damascus and blinded by a bright light. The Lord had instructed him to go into the city and have Ananias pray for him. Paul did not say, "But I want Peter, the apostle, to pray for me, or James." He was willing to receive prayer from the servant the Lord had chosen. Consequently, he was filled with the Holy Spirit and received his sight. Ananias probably was an "unknown" Christian in the church world at that time, but both Paul and Ananias understood the principle of God's delegated authority, and God honored them both.

THE BLESSING OF ACCOUNTABILITY

PART 4

267 | What is personal accountability?

The meaning of *accountability* is *to give an account to others for what God has called us to do*. We are first accountable to the Lord regarding how we live out our commitment to Christ. Our lives need to line up with the Word of God. Then we are accountable to fellow believers. These people are often the spiritual leaders God has placed in our lives. Hebrews 13:17 says these leaders are accountable to God concerning us because they...*keep watch over you as men who must give an account....*

Many times I've asked others to keep me accountable for a goal I believe the Lord has set for me. Several years ago I asked one of the men in a Bible study group in which I was involved to hold me accountable with my personal time in prayer and in meditating in God's Word each day. Every morning at 7:00 AM I received a phone call as my friend checked up on me. Accountability enabled me to be victorious. There is a tremendous release that happens in our lives when we are willing to ask others to hold us accountable for what the Lord has shown us for certain personal areas in our lives that need encouragement and support.

I want to emphasize that personal accountability is not having others tell us what to do. Personal accountability is finding out from God what He wants us to do and then asking others to hold us accountable to do those things. Spiritual abuse can occur when someone in a position of spiritual authority in our lives misuses that authority and attempts to control us. This is not biblical accountability! The purpose for someone in authority is to help build us up. If someone's seemingly "godly" accountability attempts to manipulate us rather than free us to do what God has called us to do, it is a misuse of power.

268 | Accountable to Jesus first

As we just mentioned, we are first accountable to the Lord as to how we live out our commitment to Him. Mark 6 shows how the twelve disciples were accountable to Jesus. He had trained them and now they were ready to be sent out on a task. In verse seven, Jesus sends them out two by two so they could comfort and support each other in their mission. *Calling the Twelve to him, he sent them out two by two and gave them authority over evil spirits.*

After they had ministered, verse 30 says that the disciples reported back to Jesus what they had experienced. This is an example of accountability in operation. *The apostles gathered around Jesus and reported to him all they had done and taught* (Mark 6:7, 30).

Another time, when seventy-two disciples were sent out, they also came back and were accountable to Jesus. Luke 10:1,17 tells us, "*After this the Lord appointed seventy-two others and sent them two by two ahead of him to every town and place where he was about to go. The seventy-two returned with joy and said, 'Lord, even the demons submit to us in your name.'*"

Who "keeps watch over you"?

Give an example of personal accountability from your own life.

How were the disciples accountable to Jesus in Mark 6?

How are you accountable to Jesus?

Biblical Foundations for Life

If the early disciples needed to be accountable to Jesus, the One who had sent them out, how much more we need to be accountable to our Lord Jesus Christ! We are accountable by living our lives in obedience to God's Word as we put our hope in His promises (Psalms 119:74) and hide it deep within our hearts (Psalms 119:11).

269 | Accountable to others

What does admonish mean?

We are often faced with serious spiritual battles that we must learn to overcome. Others can help us face those battles. Accountability consists of someone loving us enough to check up on us and seeing how we are doing in our personal lives so we can stay on track. Paul wrote to the Roman Christians to remind them of the truths they already knew. He wanted to encourage them to correct and hold each other accountable in a loving way. *Now I myself am confident concerning you, my brethren, that you also are full of goodness, filled with all knowledge, able also to admonish one another* (Romans 15:14 NKJ).

Have you ever humbled yourself to ask another person to hold you accountable?

According to Webster's Dictionary, *admonish* means *to counsel against wrong practices, to caution or advise and to teach with correction.* We all need people in our lives to admonish us and hold us accountable. It doesn't just happen. We need to ask. *God resists the proud, but gives grace to the humble* (1 Peter 5:5b). It takes humility to ask others to hold us accountable for the way we live our Christian lives, but God gives grace to those who are humble and willing to open their lives to others.

One time, after spending a few days praying with a group of Christian leaders, I asked one of the fellow leaders to hold me accountable for the way I conducted myself as a Christian leader. He consented and asked me to do the same for him. There is tremendous freedom and protection in being accountable to someone else. The devil dwells in darkness and will try to isolate us from other believers. Jesus desires for us to walk in the light of openness and accountability.

270 | Accountability helps us stand under temptation

How has God used other people to help you stand up under temptation?

Many times a Christian will begin to grow in his Christian life and then fall back into a mediocre Christian experience. Other times believers are overtaken by temptation and fall into sin. Accountability to another person helps us to stay on fire for God and stand up under temptation...*God is faithful; he will not let you be tempted beyond what you can bear. But when you are tempted, he will also provide a way out so that you can stand up under it* (1 Corinthians 10:13).

We should not be afraid to be honest about our struggles and shortfalls. One of the benefits of accountability is that often we find that we are not the only one who struggles in a particular area. Knowing we are not alone with our problems helps us to be more transparent to admit our weaknesses so we can be healed. *Therefore confess your sins to each other and pray for each other so that you may be healed* (James 5:16).

Who are the people the Lord has placed in your life? Ask them to hold you accountable to do what the Lord has called you to do. Perhaps you need accountability in handling your finances properly. Or perhaps you need to be accountable for how you relate to your spouse.

If you desire to lose weight, you'll find a tremendous blessing in being accountable to someone for your eating habits and daily exercise. I once heard a man say that he had lost over 20,000 pounds in his lifetime. He would lose a few pounds and then gain the weight back, lose it again, then gain it back again. The cycle went on and on. Although he was exaggerating and joking about his physical condition, the truth is, he desperately needed to be accountable to someone in his life. Accountability is freeing! It encourages us to move on to maturity and victory in our lives.

Accountability keeps us from becoming lazy in our relationship with the Lord and provides a "way out" for us when temptation hits. The Bible tells us to encourage one another daily, so we do not become hardened by sin's deceitfulness (Hebrews 3:13).

271 | Accountability helps us with "blind spots"

Many drivers experience what we call a "blind spot" while passing, turning or backing up their vehicle. In this potentially dangerous blind spot, it is impossible to see oncoming traffic.

In the same way, many of us have blind spots in our lives that we often miss but others can see. There are many people in our lives that can help us with the blind spots. These people can hold us accountable as to how we are living our lives. At work, we may be accountable to a foreman. In the home, husbands and wives are accountable to one another. Children are accountable to their parents. We are accountable to the leaders in our church. The scriptures tell us in Proverbs 11:14, *"...in the multitude of counselors there is safety"* (NKJ). A friend of mine once said, "Learn to listen to your critics. They may tell you things that your friends may never tell you." This is good advice.

Something to remember when we hold others accountable is that we should not judge their attitudes. Instead, we help them see certain actions in their lives that may be displeasing to the Lord. We should speak it in a way that will encourage them. We are accountable for the words we speak. *But I tell you that men will have to give account on the day of judgment for every careless word they have spoken. For by your words you will be acquitted, and by your words you will be condemned* (Matthew 12:36-37).

At one point in my Christian life, I was convicted by the Lord to develop a more intimate relationship with Him. I shared honestly about this need in my life with one of the men in my small group. There were certain things that I knew I needed to do to pursue my relationship with Jesus, and this Christian friend "checked up on me" or held me accountable by encouraging me to do them.

Matthew 18 describes a slightly different case scenario of accountability in the church. When a professing Christian brother or sister sins against us privately, what should we do to hold them accountable to that sin? This scripture says we should not go to someone else about the problem. We must love the offender

What does Hebrews 3:13 tell us to do daily?

What is a "blind spot"? Has anyone ever helped you with one?

What are the accountability steps listed in Matthew 18 to handle a problem between you and another Christian?

Biblical Foundations for Life

According to Hebrews 10:24-25, why is it important to fellowship with other believers?

enough to go directly to him. If he has sin in his life and does not receive you, the Bible says we should then take one or two Christian friends along and talk to him again (Matthew 18:15-17). The goal is to see him restored and healed.

The goal of accountability is always to reach out in love and humility to an individual so that he receives a reaffirmation of God's love in his life and is restored to Christlikeness.

272 | Accountability in a small group

God did not create us to live without fellowshipping with other believers. When it comes to the everyday experience of living for Jesus, we need people in our lives with whom we are in close relationship to encourage us.

And let us consider how we may spur one another on toward love and good deeds. Let us not give up meeting together, as some are in the habit of doing, but let us encourage one another—and all the more as you see the Day approaching (Hebrews 10:24-25).

If one falls down, his friend can help him up. But pity the man who falls and has no one to help him up! (Ecclesiastes 4:10).

Why is it easier to be accountable to others in a small group?

Fellow believers can help to keep us accountable to those things the Lord is saying to us. A small group of believers in a Sunday School class, a cell group, a youth group or in a house church is a great place to express the desire for accountability. We cannot be accountable to everyone in a large setting, but in a small group of people we can more easily share our struggles and receive the help we need to overcome a problem or temptation.

In a small group, we can be trained, equipped and encouraged in the things of God. No one should try to live his or her Christian life without the support of others. We can save ourselves many heartaches by learning the principle of accountability and applying it to our lives within a small group.

273 | Our ultimate authority is Jesus

The very authority of God is given to His people on the earth! Explain.

Our ultimate authority and accountability must come from Jesus, not from other people. Jesus gives us His authority to live victorious lives. *I have given you authority to trample on snakes and scorpions and to overcome all the power of the enemy; nothing will harm you* (Luke 10:19).

Jesus is the One from whom we receive authority. Even though God uses delegated authorities in our lives and requires us to have an attitude of submission to them, God is the one who gives us ultimate authority. We even have authority over the demons in Jesus' name because of the authority of Jesus Christ. When we receive that authority by knowing Him and living in an intimate relationship with Jesus, His Word gives us authority.

When Jesus spoke, people listened. As we draw close to Jesus, we also will speak with the authority of Jesus Christ. *When Jesus had finished saying these things, the crowds were amazed at his teaching, because he taught as one who had authority, and not as their teachers of the law* (Matthew 7:28-29).

God is restoring the fear of the Lord in our generation. He has called us to submit to the authorities He's placed in our lives. As we submit to these authorities, the Lord teaches us the principles of faith. The Lord gives authority to His delegated authorities to mold, shape, and form us into the image of Christ. These authorities are found in governments, places of work, in our families, in our communities, and in our church.

The Lord has called us to have an attitude of submission to the authorities He's placed in our lives, realizing that ultimate authority is His. We should never obey any authority that is causing us to sin (Acts 5:29). We must obey God rather than man. If we believe the authorities in our lives are causing us to sin, we need to pray and appeal to them.

Who are the authorities the Lord has placed in your life? Who is holding you accountable? A proper understanding of authority and accountability brings tremendous security and freedom to us. Knowing that the Lord loves us enough to place authorities in our lives to protect us and to mold us is wonderful! To know that the people the Lord has placed in our lives love us enough to hold us accountable with our actions is a tremendous blessing. We do not have to live our Christian lives alone! God bless you as you experience the loving authority of Jesus Christ and the blessing of accountability.

What does a proper understanding of authority and accountability bring into our lives?

274 | Blessings for those who submit to authority

The Scriptures teach us, *"Everyone must submit himself to the governing authorities, for there is no authority except that which God has established. The authorities that exist have been established by God. Consequently, he who rebels against the authority is rebelling against what God has instituted, and those who do so will bring judgment on themselves"* (Romans 13:1-2).

What are some of the blessings we receive when we submit to the authorities the Lord has placed in our lives? First, God has placed authorities in our lives for our protection. If we disobey the speed limit, we could be killed or kill someone else. If a parent tells a child not to play on the road and he disobeys, there could be loss of life. It would not be the parents' fault or God's fault; the child simply disobeyed the authority that was placed in his life and moved out from under the umbrella of God's protection.

Having an attitude of submission toward authority will also protect us from many mistakes. It also is a protection against the influence of the devil. The nature of the devil is rebellion and deceit. Lucifer fell from heaven because he refused to submit to God's authority (Isaiah 14:14).

There are two major forces in the universe—one is submission to the authority of God, the other is rebellion. Whenever we allow an attitude of rebellion into our lives, we are beginning to be motivated by the enemy. This leads us to sin against God.

The centurion in Matthew 8 received a miracle from Jesus because he understood authority.

What are some of the blessings we receive when we submit to the authorities the Lord has placed in our lives?

As an officer, the centurion could issue orders to his subordinates, and they would obey. He completely understood that Christ, who possesses all authority, could give a command, and His will would be done.

Learning to submit to the authorities in our lives also trains us in character to be a loving authority to others. May God bless you as you experience the blessings of honoring authority and biblical accountability.

FOUNDATION 10

God's Perspective on Finances

275 | Introduction to foundation 10

In this Biblical Foundation teaching, God's Perspective on Finances, we will learn that Scripture has a tremendous amount to say about money and material possessions. Money is such an important issue because a person's attitude toward it often is revealing of his relationship with God. God wants to restore a healthy, godly understanding of finances to the body of Christ today.

We will learn from Scripture that God wants to bless us financially! God desires to meet our needs and provide abundantly for us to minister to others.

We know that God introduced Himself in Genesis 17 as El Shaddai...the God of more than enough. He desires to meet our needs and provides over and above for us so we can bless many others. We are merely managers of the material goods we possess.

We will learn together that God also associates our ability to handle money with our ability to handle spiritual matters. One day Jesus made an amazing statement regarding this truth. "Whoever can be trusted with very little can also be trusted with much, and whoever is dishonest with very little will also be dishonest with much. So if you have not been trustworthy in handling worldly wealth, who will trust you with true riches?" (Luke 16:10, 11).

Our God desires to bless us in every way. *Beloved, I pray that you may prosper in all things and be in health, just as your soul prospers* (3 John 1:2 NKJV). He also wants to teach us to be good stewards and good managers of all He has given us to manage for Him.

God associates our ability to handle money with our ability to handle spiritual things.

Why is it so important for us to have a healthy biblical understanding of finances?

Biblical Foundations for Life

PART 1

MANAGERS OF GOD'S MONEY

276 | God loves a cheerful giver

God wants to bless us financially! John 3:16 says that "God so loved the world that He *gave*..." God introduced Himself to Abraham in Genesis 17 as *El Shaddai*...the God of *more than enough*. He met Abraham's needs and provided abundantly for Abraham to bless the nations. God desires to meet our needs and provide abundantly for us to minister to others.

Many Christians have an unhealthy understanding of finances. They may give out of a sense of duty or obligation. Giving should come out of a sense of faith in God's grace (2 Corinthians 8:1-4): it should never be done grudgingly or out of a sense of compulsion. *Each man should give what he has decided in his heart to give, not reluctantly or under compulsion, for God loves a cheerful giver* (2 Corinthians 9:7). A Christian friend of mine visited a non-believing friend one weekend and asked his friend to attend church with him. My friend recalls how embarrassed he was when he realized the purpose of the service that Sunday morning was to collect money to purchase a new organ. They began to ask for pledges—thousand dollar pledges, five hundred dollar pledges, and one hundred dollar pledges. In fact, it took the entire meeting to prod and beg the people to make pledges. The non-Christian friend was so disillusioned by what he experienced, he never wanted to return to church!

Scripture has a tremendous amount to say about money or material possessions. Sixteen of the thirty-eight parables of Jesus deal with money. One out of every ten verses in the New Testament address this subject. Scripture has 500 verses on prayer, less than 500 verses on faith, but over 2,000 verses on the subject of money and material possessions. Money is such an important issue because a person's attitude toward it often is revealing of his relationship with God.

God wants to restore a healthy, godly understanding of finances in the body of Christ today. Let's be open to what God's Word says about finances.

277 | We are managers only

First and foremost, we must realize that everything we have belongs to God. We are merely stewards (managers) of any material goods we possess. God owns everything we have, but He makes us managers of it. *Let a man so consider us, as servants of Christ and stewards of the mysteries of God. Moreover it is required in stewards that one be found faithful. And what do you have that you did not receive...?* (1 Corinthians 4:1-2, 7b NKJ).

When my wife, LaVerne, and I served as missionaries, we had the job of buying the food and supplies for the other missionaries at our base each week. The money we were using was not our own; we were simply managing it. It belonged to the mission board.

I shared this principle of being a manager of God's money in Nairobi, Kenya, one time, and it made complete sense to one of the ladies in the audience.

Why does God want to bless us financially?

What should be our attitude in giving?

What is your responsibility as a "steward" of God's money (1 Corinthians 4:2)?

She told me that, as a bank teller, she understood that even though she handles massive amounts of money daily, the money is not hers. It belongs to the bank. She is simply a manager.

I am a manager of the Lord's money. In reality, the money in my wallet is not mine; it is God's. Some Christians believe that ten percent of the money they receive is God's and the other ninety percent belongs exclusively to them. They are mistaken. It *all* belongs to God. We need to recognize His ownership in everything we have.

...for everything in heaven and earth is yours...wealth and honor come from you...(1 Chronicles 29:11b,12a).

"The silver is mine and the gold is mine," declares the Lord Almighty (Haggai 2:8).

For every animal of the forest is mine, and the cattle on a thousand hills (Psalms 50:10).

While LaVerne and I served as missionaries, I drove a van owned by the mission, and although I sensed responsibility for the van, I realized that it did not belong to me. Ultimately, it belonged to God. It was a good lesson in managing someone else's property that is similar to the responsibility God has given us to manage the wealth He has given us. God has given us a responsibility as managers of His wealth. It all belongs to Him. We have to stop thinking like owners, and start thinking like managers.

278 | We cannot serve God and money

Did you know God associates our ability to handle money with our ability to handle spiritual matters? One day Jesus made some amazing statements regarding this principle. *Whoever can be trusted with very little can also be trusted with much, and whoever is dishonest with very little will also be dishonest with much. So if you have not been trustworthy in handling worldly wealth, who will trust you with true riches? And if you have not been trustworthy with someone else's property, who will give you property of your own? No servant can serve two masters. Either he will hate the one and love the other, or he will be devoted to the one and despise the other. You cannot serve both God and Money* (Luke 16:10-13).

Money, in terms of true value, is a "little" thing. However, faithfulness in little things (money) indicates our faithfulness in big things (spiritual values). Jesus said that those who are not trustworthy in the use of their worldly wealth will be the same with spiritual things. Jesus said that we cannot serve two masters—God and materialism. It is impossible to hold allegiance to two masters at the same time.

Being surrounded with the world's riches may give us a false sense of security. Christians must not hold on too tightly to possessions because they have a way of deceiving us and demanding our hearts' loyalty. How we handle finances often is a reflection or indicator of our hearts. The Lord is very concerned with our use of finances because He knows that if He can trust us with finances, He can trust us with spiritual things.

Have you ever been entrusted with another person's money or possessions?

How did you feel about those things?

Why can't we serve both God and money?

How can money be like a "master" to us?

Biblical Foundations for Life

Why is God taking a risk by making us managers of His finances?

With financial blessing, what should we be careful of?

279 | We should expect financial blessings

It amazes me to see how God constantly takes risks on His creation. When God created the angels, He took a risk. The archangel, Lucifer (Satan), tried to exalt himself above the Lord, so God had to throw him out of heaven (Isaiah 14:12-17). When God created mankind, giving us free wills, He took a risk.

Did you know that every time God blesses us financially, He is taking a risk? He takes a risk with you and me when He asks us to be stewards (managers) of His finances and material possessions, because we may begin to serve money instead of serving the true God. God, at times, blessed Israel with wealth as a sign that He was fulfilling His covenant. *But remember the Lord your God, for it is he who gives you the ability to produce wealth…*(Deuteronomy 8:18). We should expect financial blessings from the Lord. God wants us to be fruitful.

However, with the blessing of wealth, the Lord instructed His people to be careful so that they did not forget the Lord their God. God knows that our tendency is to allow money to be our God. We must remember that our lives do not consist in the abundance of the things that we possess…*Watch out! Be on your guard against all kinds of greed; a man's life does not consist in the abundance of his possessions* (Luke 12:15).

In the first of the Ten Commandments, the Lord commands us to "have no other gods before Him." The last commandment says we should not "covet what belongs to our neighbors." To *covet* means *to desire enviously that which belongs to another*. If we covet others' financial blessings, we are putting money ahead of God. Material possessions do not give life to us. Only a relationship with Jesus produces life! We must not allow material wealth to distract us from our heavenly calling.

280 | Is it better to be rich or poor?

Christians may fall into one of two camps when it comes to what they believe is God's perspective regarding a Christian's financial life-style—some may take the viewpoint that all Christians should be poor and others may take the viewpoint that all Christians should be rich.

Those who believe all Christians should be rich often believe financial wealth is a clear sign of God's blessing. However, God's "blessing" cannot *always* be equated with personal material gain. It involves so much more! God certainly wants to bless us financially. He wants to bless us in every way. *Dear friend, I pray that you may enjoy good health and that all may go well with you, even as your soul is getting along well* (3 John 1:2).

However, if we believe, like the Pharisees did, that great wealth is a *sign* of God's favor, we will look down on people who are poor. The Pharisees looked down on Jesus for being financially poor (Luke 16:14). But Jesus did not do the same. In fact, we see that the people of the church at Smyrna were destitute, yet Jesus said they were spiritually rich (Revelation 2:8-10). Although God wants to prosper us in every way, including financially, financial wealth does not necessarily mean we are blessed by God. The Laodicean Christians were a case in point. Scripture tells us they were wealthy, yet they were considered spiritually "wretched" (Revelation 3:17).

On the other hand, many wealthy people *are* blessed by God because they use their finances unselfishly. Job was a rich and godly man who did not allow his money to become his god (Job 1). Abraham also had great wealth and was very godly (Genesis 13:2). Before he had an encounter with Jesus, Zacchaeus, a wealthy tax collector, trusted his riches instead of trusting in the living God. But after he met Jesus, he gave back four times what he had taken from others (Luke 19:8).

In the other camp, and often in reaction to the very seductive power of money in our lives, some believers take the viewpoint that all Christians should be poor. They often have a fear of what money can do to them. They fear its corrupting influence and believe money will cause them to backslide. Some may have been wounded by financial scandals in the church and now reject any kind of wealth as having an evil influence.

The truth is this: The Lord is not for or against money; it has no morality to Him. Money is amoral in and of itself. It is *what we do with it* and *our attitude toward it* that makes it moral or immoral. Money is not the root of evil like some people like to misquote in I Timothy 6:10. In this scripture, the Lord warns us to beware of the pitfall of *loving* money. It is the *love* of money that is a root of all kinds of evil. *For the love of money is a root of all kinds of evil. Some people, eager for money, have wandered from the faith and pierced themselves with many griefs* (1 Timothy 6:10).

We can be lovers of money, whether we have little or much. It depends on what we are placing our affections in. Rich or poor, if we begin to love money, it will lead us down the path of greed and cause much pain in our lives and in the lives of those around us.

281 | Giving keeps us from materialism

Although God wants to bless us materially, it should not be our focus. *People who want to get rich fall into temptation and a trap and into many foolish and harmful desires that plunge men into ruin and destruction* (1 Timothy 6:9).

The Lord does not want us to have money on our minds all the time. Materialism is a preoccupation with material rather than spiritual things. Our primary focus should be on the kingdom of God, not on money. However, it does take money to expand the kingdom of God. We should not be a slave to money because God's purpose for money is for it to be a servant to us. Money is for purchasing the necessities of life and giving to those in need and to finance the spread of the kingdom of God. This bears repeating: the real purpose for receiving God's prosperity is to expand the kingdom of God.

Giving keeps us from materialism. Giving breaks the power of money to become an idol in our lives. God wants to bless us so we can sow into His kingdom and help the poor.

Biblical Foundations for Life

Is money a sign of God's favor? Is money the root of all evil (1 Timothy 6:10)?

Then what is the root of all evil?

What can happen if our focus is on getting rich (1 Timothy 6:9)?

What is the real purpose for receiving God's prosperity?

To be blessed financially simply means we have all that we need to meet the needs in our lives, and an abundance left over to give to others. The purpose for having a job and working should be for...*doing something useful with [our] his own hands, that [we] he may have something to share with those in need* (Ephesians 4:28b).

When we diligently work and faithfully give of our finances, the Bible teaches that God "will meet all our needs according to His glorious riches" (Philippians 4:19). He wants to meet our needs and enable us to meet the needs of others. God promises to take care of us. He wants to bless and prosper us! If you are a businessman, an employee, a student or a housewife, the Lord desires to prosper you. Remember, God revealed Himself to Abraham as *El Shaddai*...the *God of more than enough*. He promised to bless Abraham abundantly, just as He desires to meet our needs and abundantly bless us in every way today. Giving really does keep us from getting materialistic.

282 | Give sacrificially and your own needs will be met

In Luke 21, Jesus gives a lesson on how God evaluates giving. Jesus and His disciples were watching people putting their gifts into the temple treasury. The rich put in large amounts of money because they could easily spare it, but then a poor widow dropped two small coins in the treasury. She gave all she possibly could, and it required great personal sacrifice. Jesus remarked that the poor widow put in more than all the others because of the amount of sacrifice it required of her.

Recall some instances where you gave sacrificially and God took care of your needs.

It is not the amount we give, but the sacrifice that is involved. When we give out of a heart of love and compassion for others, we will discover that God will take care of our own needs and more! As we give generously, God promises... *to make all grace abound to you, so that in all things at all times, having all that you need, you will abound in every good work...Now he who supplies seed to the sower and bread for food will also supply and increase your store of seed and will enlarge the harvest of your righteousness. You will be made rich in every way so that you can be generous on every occasion, and through us your generosity will result in thanksgiving to God* (2 Corinthians 9:8,10-11).

You can give either sparingly or generously. You are rewarded accordingly... *with the measure you use, it will be measured to you* (Matthew 7:2). When you give sacrificially, God resupplies what you have given and increases your giving capacity. The more you give, the more you are blessed, and the more you can give. God wants to bless you financially so you have enough for yourself and enough to share with others.

THE TITHE   PART 2

283 | Giving a portion of our income

The Lord gives us the responsibility to manage the resources He gives to us. He has set up a system to constantly remind us of His ownership in everything. This systematic way to give is a first step to allowing our resources to be used for God's kingdom. In the Old Testament, the Israelites were required to give one-tenth of all their income to the Lord. The Hebrew word for *tithe* means *a tenth part*. At the very heart of tithing is the idea that God owns everything. God was simply asking the Israelites to return what He first gave them. *Honor the Lord with your wealth, with the firstfruits of all your crops; then your barns will be filled to overflowing, and your vats will brim over with new wine* (Proverbs 3:9-10).

We honor God by giving Him the "firstfruits" or a portion of our income. It shows that we honor Him as the Lord of all our possessions. This tithe (10%) opens up a way for God to pour out His blessings on us. Every time we give our tithes, we are reminded that all of our money and earthly possessions belong to God. We are simply stewards responsible for what the Lord has given us. The word *tithe* is first mentioned in Genesis 14:18-20. *Then Melchizedek king of Salem brought out bread and wine. He was priest of God Most High, and he blessed Abram, saying, "Blessed be Abram by God Most High, Creator of heaven and earth. And blessed be God Most High, who delivered your enemies into your hand." Then Abram gave him a tenth of everything.*

Abraham gave Melchizedek a tithe before the Old Testament law had ever been written. Abraham was honoring the Lord and Melchizedek as the priest of the Most High God with ten percent of that which the Lord had given to him. He may have learned this principle from Abel who brought the firstborn of his flock to the Lord.

At the end of every month I face a stack of bills that I need to pay. One of these bills is my bill to God. It is called a *tithe*, my "firstfruit." This tithe reminds me that everything I have belongs to Him. I have learned to enjoy returning this 10% to the Lord. After all, Jesus has given to me 100% of Himself through His death on the cross. I am eternally grateful!

Why does God require a portion of our income?

What does the tithe symbolize?

284 | Don't try to steal from God

In the 1992 riots in Los Angeles, California, looting took place in many stores and businesses. A young man was asked by a reporter what he had stolen. He said, "I stole Christian tapes because I am a Christian." You might think that sounds ridiculous. Yet, in a similar way, there are many Christians who are stealing from God by keeping for themselves that which really belongs to the Lord—the tithe.

In Old Testament history, some of the Israelites were robbing God by selfishly holding onto money that belonged to God. They were required to give at least one-tenth of the livestock, the land's produce and their income to the Lord. In addition they were required to bring other offerings in the form of sacrifices

What does God promise in Malachi 3, if we bring our tithes into the "storehouse"?

or free-will offerings. But God says they were holding back. *"Will a man rob God? Yet you have robbed Me! But you say, 'In what way have we robbed You?' In tithes and offerings. You are cursed with a curse, for you have robbed Me, even this whole nation. Bring all the tithes into the storehouse, that there may be food in My house, and try Me now in this,"* says the Lord of hosts, *"If I will not open for you the windows of heaven and pour out for you such blessing that there will not be room enough to receive it. And I will rebuke the devourer for your sakes, so that he will not destroy the fruit of your ground, nor shall the vine fail to bear fruit for you in the field,"* says the Lord of hosts (Malachi 3:8-11 NKJ).

When the people asked God how they were robbing Him, He responded clearly, "In tithes and offerings." Notice, He not only tells us to bring "tithes," but also "offerings." We'll talk more about offerings in part 3.

Many of God's people today are robbing God in this same way. The Lord has promised us that if we obey Him and bring all of our tithes into the storehouse, He will open the windows of heaven, pour out a blessing on us, and "rebuke the devourer." Many people are struggling financially because the devil has been robbing and devouring them. The enemy has not been rebuked by the Lord, because they are not paying tithes into the storehouse.

We are blessed as God rebukes the devourer when we tithe. However, our primary motivation for tithing should not be to get something back from God. Our primary motivation for tithing is obedience—to God and His Word.

I've known some people who have said that when they initially began to tithe, the enemy attacked them, and they found themselves worse off financially than ever before. The enemy may test us when we obey the Word of God. When Jesus was baptized, the heavens opened, and the Lord said, "This is my beloved Son in whom I am well pleased." During the next forty days of His life, Jesus was tested by the enemy. Tests will always come; however, if we hold on, we will receive the blessing that comes from obedience. God's promises always prove to be true!

When I was a missionary, the enemy tested me in the area of tithing. "You gave your entire life to God," he told me, "how could the Lord expect you to give back a tithe from the small amount of money you are receiving?" By the grace of God, I refused the enemy's lies and began to tithe even the small amount the Lord had provided for us. The Lord blessed us over and over again in a supernatural way as we served in the mission field. God is faithful. He honors His Word.

285 | The tithe is a bill to God

The tithe is a numerical expression reminding us that all we have belongs to God. Some years ago, I was reading the book of Malachi and was convicted by the Lord in the area of tithing. I checked my bank ledger. I had a whole list of bills. In fact, one of the bills I was delinquent in paying was my bill to God. Every month, my bill to God grew. I was not paying my tithe because I thought I did not have enough money to pay it.

One day, I made a decision to obey God. When I received my next paycheck, I paid all of my tithes to God. Some time later, I realized something supernatural had happened after I had taken this step of obedience. Our money seemed to last longer! The Lord began to provide for us financially, often in supernatural ways. It didn't happen overnight, but God began to bless us in a new way, and the devourer was rebuked.

Some people say, "I can't afford to tithe." The truth is—they cannot afford to withhold the tithe. A tithe is money set apart for God. If we don't give it to God, the devourer will consume it. Let's read again what God says in His Word about rebuking the devourer when we give tithes and offerings into His storehouse. *And I will rebuke the devourer for your sakes, so that he will not destroy the fruit of your ground, nor shall the vine fail to bear fruit for you in the field...*(Malachi 3:11 NKJ).

The word *devour* in the original Hebrew text means *to eat, burn up or consume*. During the days of Malachi, God's people were experiencing famine, scarcity, unseasonable weather, and insects that ate up the fruits of the earth. According to the above scripture, the enemy will devour our blessings when we choose to not obey God's principles. When we walk out from under the umbrella of protection of obedience to the Word of God concerning tithing, it gives the enemy a legal right to devour our blessings.

According to Webster's dictionary, *a tithe is 10% of one's income paid as a tax to the church*. When you pay your taxes to the government, do you *feel* like paying it? Do we have to *feel* like paying our tithe back to God? Of course not. Whether or not we *feel* like tithing is not the issue. We need to tithe in *obedience* to Him.

Imagine going to the bank and paying off a loan or a mortgage. How does the bank teller respond when we pay? Does she pat us on the back and tell us how much she appreciates it that we came to pay our bill? No, and neither should we expect God to pat us on the back when we tithe. We are not doing God any great favor when we tithe. It belongs to Him anyway. It is our responsibility to tithe, and we do it out of obedience.

286 | Giving systematically

The Lord wants us to learn to give systematically just like the believers were encouraged to do in 1 Corinthians 16:2. *On the first day of every week, each one of you should set aside a sum of money in keeping with his income, saving it up, so that when I come no collections will have to be made.*

Some believers claim to "follow the Spirit" as to when they will tithe. That's like calling your electric company and saying, "I'm not sure if I will pay my bill this month. Maybe I'll pay it next month. I'm just going to follow the Spirit." If you did not pay, you would get your electric service disconnected. We should always follow the Holy Spirit within the framework of the Word of God. The Word of God teaches us to tithe systematically as an act of obedience, not just when we feel like it.

Imagine giving your employer a phone call and telling him, "I will come to work when I think the Spirit is prompting me to come." Guess what would

Who will devour our money if we do not tithe?

How have you experienced the blessings of God by tithing?

Why is it important to give systematically?

Biblical Foundations for Life

What does tithing teach us?

happen? You would probably lose your job! The same principle applies to giving to the Lord in a systematic way. Yes, we should follow the Spirit in our giving that is over and above our regular tithes. However, our God is a God of order and discipline. He instructs us to give tithes systematically so we do not have to "catch up on our giving" because we didn't give on a consistent basis.

Some believers say, "I think I'll pray about tithing." That's a bit like praying about whether or not we should read the Bible regularly or whether or not we should be part of a local church. These principles are clear in the Word of God, just like tithing.

I have been asked, "Should we tithe on the net (wages I receive after my taxes are paid) or the gross (wages I receive before the taxes are paid)?" When we pay our taxes to the government, do we pay taxes on the net or on the gross? We pay on whatever we have received (the gross amount). As Christians, we should desire to give everything we possibly can back to God because of what Jesus Christ has done for us. Remember, tithing is not an option. It is an act of obedience to God. It is a privilege to return to God what is already His.

287 | Attitudes toward tithing

What attitude do you have when you give to God?

Sometimes Christians believe that tithing is simply an Old Testament doctrine. Dr. Bill Hamon says, "One divine principle in biblical interpretation is that whatever was established in the Old Testament remains proper as a principle or practice unless the New Testament does away with it. For instance, tithing was established in the Old Testament, but since nothing is stated in the New Testament that abolishes it, then it is still a proper practice for Christians."[1]

Jesus confirms the Old Testament principle of tithing in the New Testament. However, He does not want us to tithe with the attitude of the scribes and Pharisees in Matthew 23:23. The Lord sharply rebuked their attitudes about tithing. *Woe to you, teachers of the law and Pharisees, you hypocrites! You give a tenth of your spices-mint, dill and cummin. But you have neglected the more important matters of the law—justice, mercy and faithfulness. You should have practiced the latter, without neglecting the former.*

The religious Pharisees appeared spiritual and godly, but they were not in right standing with God. They tithed right down to the last tiny mint leaf, but their hearts were selfish and hard.

What are you learning about the tithe?

The Lord affirms that we should tithe today, but He is concerned about our attitudes as we give to Him. In the Old Testament, God's people tithed because the law required it. Since the New Testament, we should tithe because the Lord has changed our hearts. It is a privilege to return the tithe back to Him. We tithe as an act of love for our God and also out of a heart of generosity and love for others.

Let's imagine you ask me to come to live in your house. The only stipulation is that, monthly, I need to pay 10% of all the things you provide for me. You fill the refrigerator, put gas in the car and provide all of my living expenses. It would be ridiculous for me to begin to think that everything is mine. Nothing is mine, because it belongs to you. Giving ten percent reminds me that it all belongs to you. That's what tithing is all about. The Lord's purpose for tithing is to remind us that everything we have belongs to Him.

[1] Dr. Bill Hamon, *Prophets And The Prophetic Movement*, (Shippensburg, PA: Destiny Image Publishers, 1990), p. 197.

288 | God will provide

When we recognize that everything we are and have belongs to the Lord, it will be easier for us to trust the Lord to provide for us when we tithe. Even if we do not have much, God will provide when we give to Him. Giving has a way of releasing our finances. Let's learn again from the widow who gave a mite (a fraction of a penny) into the temple treasury. She sacrificially gave more than the many others who threw in large amounts because she gave all she had. *Calling his disciples to him, Jesus said, "I tell you the truth, this poor widow has put more into the treasury than all the others. They all gave out of their wealth; but she, out of her poverty, put in everything—all she had to live on"* (Mark 12:43-44).

God knows our hearts and honors our obedience in tithing. It might seem like a sacrifice, but in the long run, it helps us to become masters over our money instead of becoming a master to it.

What about those who just cannot tithe? For example, if your spouse is unsaved, you may find yourself in a dilemma. He or she may not want you to tithe. If a spouse does not agree to tithe, you cannot give something that is not yours to give. If you are the co-owner of a restaurant, you don't tithe on all the money that you take in because half of it belongs to the other owner. In the same way, you should not give away your family's money against your spouse's wishes.

Here are a few recommendations: Appeal to your spouse in faith. For example, you could say, "Could I give some money to the church this week on a regular basis?" Pray and allow the Holy Spirit to work in his or her heart. Ask the Lord for personal money you could tithe. Perhaps you occasionally make some extra money at a side job—you could tithe on that personal money. Remember, God looks at our hearts and honors our obedience no matter how small our tithe may be.

289 | Where should the tithe go?

Where should we give our tithes? As we learned before, Malachi 3:10a says, *Bring the whole tithe into the storehouse, that there may be food in my house....*

According to this scripture, all the tithes should be placed into the storehouse. The storehouse is where spiritual food is kept to bless those who lead us, feed us and equip us for ministry. In the Old Testament, the Levites and the priests were responsible to spiritually lead and feed God's people. The tithe paid for the work of those who were set apart for the purpose of ministry to the Lord and to His people. The Levites were dependent upon the faithfulness of God's people in giving tithes to support them. *I give to the Levites all the tithes in Israel as their inheritance in return for the work they do while serving at the Tent of Meeting* (Numbers 18:21).

Explain how the poor widow put more in the temple treasury than the rich.

Do you believe God will meet your needs as you tithe?

Who should be financed from the "storehouse"?

_____

_____

_____

_____

Since the Old Testament is a "type and a shadow" of the New Testament, the principle of where to tithe applies in the New Testament. We should tithe to the storehouse of our spiritual leaders because they are called by the Lord to minister the Word and encourage us.

Church leaders are called to "equip the saints for the work of ministry" (Ephesians 4:11-12). They need to be financially supported so that they have enough time to devote to prayer and ministering the Word of God to the saints under their care. In Acts 6:4, the leadership of the early church knew their responsibility was to single-mindedly "give their attention to prayer and the ministry of the Word."

A man once told me, "I give my tithes whenever I see a need." This man did not know it, but he was not giving a tithe, he was giving an offering. An *offering* is anything we give over and above the 10%. Tithes are the first 10% of our income given into the storehouse to provide finances to help support those who are equipping and giving spiritual leadership to the saints in the local church. *The elders who direct the affairs of the church well are worthy of double honor, especially those whose work is preaching and teaching* (1 Timothy 5:17). The word *honor* refers to *giving financially* to those who labor among us in spiritual oversight, prayer, teaching and training in the Word of God.

Now that we know what a tithe is and where it should be given, let's examine the importance of giving both tithes *and* offerings next.

GIVE BOTH TITHES AND OFFERINGS — PART 3

290 | The difference between a tithe and an offering

As we just learned, we need to take care of the needs of those who give us spiritual oversight by giving them our tithes. As we give our tithes into the storehouse (the local church where we are fed spiritually), we are taking care of the needs of our spiritual leaders. Galatians 6:6 says that those who are taught God's Word should help provide material support for the instructors. *Anyone who receives instruction in the word must share all good things with his instructor.*

Verses 7-10 of the same chapter go on to say that if we refuse to give support to these faithful leaders, we are sowing selfishness and reaping destruction. But if we give to these leaders, it is part of "doing good to all people, especially to those who belong to the family of believers." These faithful leaders in our church are worthy of our support, and we are right in supporting them (1 Corinthians 9:14; 3 John 6-8; 1 Timothy 5:18).

Our tithe to our local church should be our first priority for giving. This kind of giving is only a place to start, however. We need to give over and beyond our tithes to many worthy causes. "Offerings" are monies given above ten percent. We should give offerings to many places and causes both within and outside our local church.

As Christians, we have a responsibility to give to the poor and needy, especially those within the church. We are encouraged to show a concern for the poor. Jesus expected that His people would give generously to the poor. Proverbs 28:27 says, *"He who gives to the poor will lack nothing...."*

In addition, we should also give to those who feed us spiritually from places other than our local church—perhaps through a book, a TV ministry, or another para-church ministry. These are some of the many, many places where we can give our offerings.

I have heard various radio Bible teachers say, "Do not send me your tithes; send me your offerings—that which is over and above ten percent. Your tithe belongs to your local church." I believe those Bible teachers are properly discerning the scriptures concerning the difference between tithes and offerings.

In conclusion, our tithe should go into the storehouse of the local church, and our offerings should go where we, cheerfully, voluntarily and generously, believe God is leading us to give.

291 | Heart and money matters

We usually place our finances in areas that are the most important in our lives. Matthew 6:21 says that wherever we place our money, that's where our hearts will be. *For where your treasure is, there your heart will be also.*

Riches can demand the total loyalty of one's heart. That's why God tells us we must decide in our hearts to serve God and not money in Matthew 6:19-24.

What is your responsibility to the one(s) who teaches you (Galatians 6:6)?

In your own words, explain the difference between a tithe and an offering.

Biblical Foundations for Life

What does Matthew 6:21 tell us about our hearts?

Why is tithing an issue of the heart and not the law?

How is trust a part of giving your tithe?

If we are robbing God, what should we do?

People who place their money in stocks, immediately check out the stock market page whenever they receive their daily newspaper or go online each day. Why? Because that is where their interests lie; they are concerned about where their finances are placed. Where we give both our tithes and our offerings shows what we place high value on.

Since the Lord has called us to faithfully support our local church, it is important that we are placing our tithes in the storehouse of the local church. We encourage God's people involved in our church to faithfully tithe in obedience to the Lord, because when we tithe to our local church, our hearts are with God's people and with those who serve among us. Consequently, tithing is an issue of the heart—not a law. If we have decided within our hearts to give to our local church and its leadership, we will joyfully give our tithes to the storehouse in our church.

Giving a tithe shows we trust our leadership. When we are not willing to give a tithe, we begin, even without knowing it, to sow seeds of distrust. Tithing is a test in trust; trust in our God and trust in those the Lord has placed in spiritual leadership over our lives.

292 | Tithing–a test in trust

Let's take a moment to review. A tithe, as we learned, is 10% of our income—a reminder that all we have belongs to the Lord. Offerings are gifts we give to the Lord, His people and His work that is over and above the 10% tithe. In the same way that unforgiveness opens the door for the tormenter to bring depression and confusion into people's lives (Matthew 18:34-35), robbing God of the tithe to the storehouse opens the door for the enemy to rob us. We must trust God and support His work with our tithes, according to Malachi 3:10b. *"Test me in this," says the Lord....*

God is speaking of faith and trust when He tells us to tithe to the storehouse, the place where provisions were kept for the local Levites who were serving God's people. God's people gave to the storehouse in faith because they trusted the Levites to distribute the money properly. Today the same principle of trust applies: the tithe goes into the storehouse of the local church to meet the needs of spiritual leadership who equip and encourage the church. God's plan is for those who spiritually feed and lead us to be supported by tithes. *If we have sown spiritual seed among you, is it too much if we reap a material harvest from you? If others have this right of support from you, shouldn't we have it all the more? But we did not use this right. On the contrary, we put up with anything rather than hinder the gospel of Christ. Don't you know that those who work in the temple get their food from the temple, and those who serve at the altar share in what is offered on the altar? In the same way, the Lord has commanded that those who preach the gospel should receive their living from the gospel* (1 Corinthians 9:11-14).

You may wonder, "Where should the pastor (lead elder) of a church tithe?" In some churches, the pastor tithes into the storehouse of those who give him oversight encouragement and accountability. This is often a team of spiritual leaders in the pastor's denomination or fellowship of churches.

293 | A question to ask: Are you tithing?

Malachi 3:8-12 asks the question, *"Have you robbed God?"* Our response usually is, "Who, me? How could I ever do that?" And then the Lord tells us how—"in tithes and offerings." Are you tithing? If not, according to the scriptures, you're robbing God. Today is the day to repent before the Lord and begin to tithe in obedience to the Word of God.

Perhaps you are disobeying the Lord by withholding tithes and offerings because you had a bad experience in the past. A young person, who is the product of a broken home, may not want to get married because of witnessing a bad marriage between his parents while growing up. However, marriage is still a wonderful plan of God. Even though you may have had bad experiences in churches where money was misused, it is still the Lord's plan for us to give our tithes and offerings into the local church. We need to press on...*forgetting what is behind and straining toward what is ahead, I press on...*(Philippians 3:13-14a).

The Lord will honor you by rebuking the devourer and opening the windows of heaven. You will also find a new sense of trust in your God and trust in those He has placed in your life who serve you in areas of spiritual leadership.

If we have had bad past experiences, what does Philippians 3:13-14 encourage us to do?

294 | Are you tithing to the storehouse?

After God tells His people in Malachi 3 where to tithe—to the storehouse, He promises to pour out a huge blessing if they are obedient...*and see if I will not throw open the floodgates of heaven and pour out so much blessing that you will not have room enough for it* (Malachi 3:10b).

God wants to bless us, but we should tithe where He recommends—the storehouse. Are we tithing, but not to our church family? That would be like buying a hamburger at McDonalds and paying for it at Burger King! In the Old Testament, when the tithe was withheld from the storehouse, the Levites could not fulfill their role. The same is true today. In some parts of the body of Christ, pastors and other spiritual leaders are struggling financially because the tithes are being withheld in the congregations in which they serve. Consequently, they do not have enough time to effectively serve the people of God because of needing to support themselves through "tent-making" (business). The enemy can devour God's people through disobedience. Of course, some leaders, like Paul the apostle, do choose to make "tents," and this is acceptable and encouraged if the Lord has led them to do so.

What are some examples of giving our tithes to other places besides the storehouse (our church)? Giving our tithes to para-church ministries, missionaries, evangelists or other ministries are a few examples. Although there are many missionaries, evangelists, and other Christian workers who are reputable men and women of God and need our financial support, according to my understanding of the scriptures, they should be supported through *offerings*, not through *tithes*. If we give our tithes to them, it can open the door for unbelief and lack of trust to come into our local church family. The tithe should be placed into the

What does God promise if we tithe to the storehouse (Malachi 3:10)?

What is wrong with designating where we want our tithe to go within the local church?

Biblical Foundations for Life

storehouse of our local church to be distributed to support those who give us spiritual protection and equip us to minister.

To clarify a common "tithing misunderstanding," David Wilkerson, founder of Teen Challenge and former pastor of the Times Square Church in New York City, wrote in his newsletter some time back, "Concerning my statement recently about sending your tithe to our ministry, I received about 35 letters, many from pastors, lovingly reminding me that tithes belong in the local church. I totally agree. I should have clarified my statement. We have quite a number of people on our readers' list who do not attend church, sometimes because their church is shut down or they do not have a suitable church home...Believers really need to find a church home and support it. Until then, however, often my messages are the only spiritual food some people have. Overwhelmingly, those who support this ministry are faithful to support their local church, and they give us over and above their tithes."

Another question to ask is this: are you tithing to the storehouse, but designating your tithe instead of freely giving it like the people in Malachi 3? Some believers are very willing to tithe to the storehouse, but try to control the church by withholding the tithe or a portion of the tithe, or by designating it to be used for certain things only. When we pay our taxes, we do not tell our government to spend some of the taxes on the army and another portion of our taxes to remodel a room or buy new furniture for our president or prime minister. Likewise, in our local church, when we give our tithes to the storehouse, we must trust our spiritual leadership to distribute it in a way that honors the Lord.

295 | Excuses to rob God

Have you ever used any of the excuses listed here for not tithing? Explain.

There are many reasons why Christians rob God of the tithes and offerings. One reason is simply **ignorance**. *Truly, these times of ignorance God overlooked, but now commands all men everywhere to repent* (Acts 17:30 NKJ). If you have been ignorant about this truth, you can repent (turn around) and begin to obey this spiritual truth. We serve a merciful God. He desires to bless us as we obey Him.

Some of God's people do not tithe and give offerings in direct **disobedience to the Word of God**. If we claim to know the Lord, but are not willing to obey His Word, the scriptures tell us that we are liars. We need to repent and obey the living God. *The man who says, "I know him," but does not do what he commands is a liar, and the truth is not in him* (1 John 2:4).

Another reason that some believers do not give tithes and offerings is because of **personal debt**. The Bible says in Galatians 6:7 that...*a man reaps what he sows*. The lack of giving could be part of the reason for being in debt. I read about a Christian businessman who was in debt ten times greater than his yearly income. Yet he obeyed the Lord and began to tithe and give sacrificial offerings. Within the next few years, he saw his entire financial situation turn around. God prospered him and he became a pastor of a church. The Lord began to use him to teach the truths of the Word of God regarding tithing and giving offerings and giving to hundreds of people in his community.

If you find yourself in debt, seek counsel from a trusted Christian who has wisdom in these matters. You may need to develop new habits in sound financial management. Many years ago, a Christian friend showed me how to set up a budget. Managing finances with a budget has been a real blessing to me. A budget will not control our finances, but it will give us a picture of where they are going and what the needs are.

Some people do not give tithes and offerings because they think they are **too poor**. The Lord is not concerned about the amount of money we give; He is more concerned about our attitude toward giving. Even if we have little, we can give in proportion to what God has given us. If we give nothing, we are like a farmer who eats his seed and does not have a crop for the following year. If we eat our seed (using our tithe for something other than what it was intended for), we are hindering the blessing of God in our lives.

This brings us to still another reason why many of God's people withhold their tithes and offerings. They simply **do not trust their leadership**. If we do not trust our leadership in our local church to handle the tithes we give, then we need to ask the Lord for grace to trust our spiritual leaders. If we still cannot trust them, we may be in the wrong church. 1 Corinthians 12:18 tells us that God places us in the body as He wills. It is not the church of *our* choice; it is the church of *His* choice. We need to be among a group of believers where there is a sense of faith and trust in the leadership that God has placed there.

296 | Receive new freedom

If you are not tithing and giving offerings, I exhort you to start today by tithing to your church. You will receive a new freedom in your life and relationship with others in the local church family in which you serve. Secondly, ask God to bless you in a way that you can give generous offerings to ministries of integrity. There are many ministries that are worthy of our gifts and offerings; however, be sure to check out where you give. The Lord holds us responsible to give offerings to reputable ministries. Do not be afraid to do your homework before giving.

Remember, tithing is a test in trust—a trust in our God who has promised to rebuke the devourer and open the windows of heaven. And it is also a trust in the spiritual leaders in our local church, as we tithe into the storehouse. The Lord desires to set us free to joyfully give our tithes and offerings to Him. And He desires to bless us as His children who obey His voice. John 8:36 tells us, "*so if the Son sets you free, you will be free indeed.*"

May the Lord bless you and open the windows of heaven for you as you walk in obedience to these spiritual truths. Next we will look at how to manage the money and material wealth with which the Lord has blessed us.

Describe ways you have been set free to give–in both your tithes and offerings.

Who should we trust more than money?

Biblical Foundations for Life

PART 4

MANAGING FINANCES GOD HAS GIVEN

297 | Faithful with what we have

The finances and possessions the Lord has given to us belong to Him. We are simply managers of that which He has given. 1 Corinthians 4:2 says, "*...Now it is required that those who have been given a trust must prove faithful.*"

We are entrusted with God's money. So then, the finances and possessions that we have should be used to honor God and build His kingdom. We must faithfully use what God has given us.

The Lord also wants us to be content with the finances that He's given to us. Paul said, "*...I have learned to be content whatever the circumstances*" (Philippians 4:11).

To be content means *to be free from complaining*. There are times that our family has lived with very little and other times we have been abundantly blessed. Either way, God has called us to be content and triumphantly live above our changing circumstances.

People today often want their needs gratified immediately, so they go deeply into debt to buy the things they think they cannot do without. This is a financial mistake and breeds discontent.

It is also a mistake to want to get rich quick instead of paying the price faithfully, obeying God, day by day. This kind of "lottery thinking" or "waiting until I get a big break" is really "poverty thinking." If we focus on a distant chance that may come, we will be hindered from moving forward financially today. Financial advancement comes to those who apply God's principles on a consistent, long-term basis (Hebrews 6:12).

Remember the parable of the talents (Matthew 25:14-30)? One man had five talents and was faithful with the five. Another man had two. The Lord knew he was responsible enough to handle two talents. The third man only received one. Why did God give him just one talent? That was all he could handle at that point. God knows what we can handle. When we are faithful with what He has given, He blesses us with more.

298 | Provide for our families

The Lord wants to bless us financially in order to meet the needs of our family. *If anyone does not provide for his relatives, and especially for his immediate family, he has denied the faith and is worse than an unbeliever* (1 Timothy 5:8).

For even when we were with you, we gave you this rule: If a man will not work, he shall not eat (2 Thessalonians 3:10).

A man gave his life to the Lord and was convinced he should spend all of his time witnessing. He spent his time out on the beach, witnessing every day, while his family was nearly starving. He believed that somehow God would be

---

What is the first requirement of a good manager according to 1 Corinthians 4:2?

Why are "get-rich-quick" schemes detrimental?

obligated to provide for his family, since he was so busy doing "God's work." When his Christian friends challenged him to take care of his family, he became defensive. "Wasn't he telling others about Jesus? What could be more important than that?" The truth was that he was disobeying the Word of God. God was not telling him to be out witnessing when his family was not being properly taken care of. If the Lord calls you as a missionary who "lives by faith," it is important not to do it at the expense of your family. I have been privileged to proclaim the gospel and train Christian leaders in various parts of the world. However, my first responsibility is for my own family. Any Christian who refuses to provide for his own family has denied the faith and is worse than an unbeliever.

Some people say to me, "I want to be involved in a full-time ministry, supported by the church." This can be a noble desire, however, the truth is that everyone is involved in a full-time ministry. If you are working at a secular job, you are in full-time ministry. You're called to minister at your job.

So why do we work? Is it to have money to buy expensive material possessions? Not at all. The Bible tells us we work to give to him who is in need (Ephesians 4:28). It starts with providing for our own families and helping those whom the Lord has placed around us.

It is a blessing to be able to work. Don't wait for the perfect job. Start somewhere and God will give you the perfect job in the future as you are faithful in the opportunity He has given you today.

299 | Investing our Master's wealth

How do we invest our Master's wealth to see His kingdom built in a way that will honor Him the most? First of all, we invest the Lord's money to evangelize the world. Remember the story of the prodigal son? His father gave half of his wealth to the son who promptly wasted it. That young man eventually came back to his father, but it cost his father half of his fortune. In other words, the father used all of that money to see one soul saved. The Bible tells us in Mark 8:36 that we cannot put a price-tag on a soul. *What good is it for a man to gain the whole world, yet forfeit his soul? Or what can a man give in exchange for his soul?*

In our church, we encourage every Christian to support a missionary somewhere in the world. Why? According to the Bible, wherever we place our money, that is where our heart will be (Matthew 6:21). And since God loves the world so much, our missionary support keeps our hearts at the same place as our God's—reaching the world. The money we give to support a missionary of our choice is not taken from our tithe. It is taken from the 90%—an offering. Anything that is given above the 10% is an offering to the Lord. By investing our offerings into someone like a missionary, we are helping to invest the Lord's money to evangelize the world.

A practical way to invest our wealth is to invest in stocks or bonds or mutual funds that give a financial increase. Like the man in the Parable of the Talents who invested wisely, we will receive an increase with wise investments. This increase can help expand the kingdom of God.

Biblical Foundations for Life

What does 1 Timothy 5:8 teach us about taking care of our families?

Examine your life; are you motivated to work for the right reasons?

How can you gain the whole world at the expense of your soul (Mark 8:36)?

In what ways are you investing your wealth for the kingdom of God?

Describe some times you have used your money to build a relationship.

_____

_____

_____

_____

Repeat Matthew 5:16 aloud while changing the word "your" to "my." Make it your prayer.

_____

_____

_____

_____

300 | Money and relationships

We can also use the Lord's money to honor Him and build His kingdom by using it to build relationships. Jesus told the story of a manager who was being fired. His boss said, "Clean up your accounts; you're going to be fired." So the manager quickly found a man who owed the boss eight hundred gallons of oil. He said to the man, "Pay me for four hundred gallons." He found someone else who owed a thousand bushels of wheat and said, "Just rip up the original bill and pay for eight hundred bushels." The boss of the corporation came back and saw what the manager had done. Instead of being angry, the Bible says in Luke 16:8-9, *"The master commended the dishonest manager because he had acted shrewdly. For the people of this world are more shrewd in dealing with their own kind than are the people of the light. I tell you, use worldly wealth to gain friends for yourselves, so that when it is gone, you will be welcomed into eternal dwellings."*

The manager was commended by his master because he was acting very shrewdly. He used his master's finances to build relationships. He knew he was going to be without a job and needed relationships with other people. Although this manager was dishonest, and Jesus never condones dishonesty, there is a truth we can learn from this story. Jesus says that the people in the world are shrewder than God's children. In other words, many non-Christians have learned to use finances to build relationships, while in the church, we have often not understood this important principle.

We need to use our finances to build relationships. Take someone out for a meal, and you will be building a relationship that will last for eternity. A young man once told me that as a little boy he met an older Christian man who bought him an ice cream cone. That thirty-five cent ice cream cone opened him up to God through his relationship with this Christian man. Do you know why? The man was using his money to build relationships.

Baking a cake for your neighbor will help to build a relationship. Inviting someone into your home for hospitality or for a meal is using the money the Lord has entrusted to you to build relationships with people that will last for eternity. The Bible says in Matthew 5:16, *"...let your light shine before men, that they may see your good deeds and praise your Father in heaven."*

Our actions speak louder than our words. The way we use our money can cause people in the world around us to fall in love with Jesus Christ and live eternally with Him. Remember, Jesus Christ lives in us (Galatians 2:20). People often learn to trust Jesus as they learn to trust us.

301 | Helping the poor is like investing in God's bank

In both the New and the Old Testament, the Lord requires us to give to help those who are poor. James 1:27 says, *"Religion that God our Father accepts as pure and faultless is this: to look after orphans and widows in their distress and to keep oneself from being polluted by the world."*

Deuteronomy 15:7-8 tells us, "*If there is a poor man among your brothers...do not be hardhearted or tightfisted toward your poor brother. Rather be openhanded and freely lend him whatever he needs.*"

Jesus said, "*For I was hungry and you gave me something to eat, I was thirsty and you gave me something to drink, I was a stranger and you invited me in, I needed clothes and you clothed me, I was sick and you looked after me, I was in prison and you came to visit me.*" (Matthew 25:35-36).

And then He said, "*...whatever you did for one of the least of these brothers of mine, you did for me*" (Matthew 25:40). In other words, when we help someone who is hurting because we love Jesus Christ, we are doing it unto Jesus.

I believe we will stand before God and He will say, "Remember the time you invited Me into your home?" or "Remember the time you helped Me when I was struggling financially?" Every time we invite someone into our home or help someone because of Jesus, we are doing it to Him.

If the Lord has blessed us financially, it is for the purpose of blessing those around us. *He who has pity on the poor lends to the Lord, and He will pay back what he has given* (Proverbs 19:17 NKJ).

According to the Bible, when we give to someone who is poor, we are placing the money in God's bank—the greatest bank in the whole world. If God tells you to give someone a certain amount of money, you are literally investing that money in the Lord's bank. The Lord will pay you back with His blessing when you invest money in His bank by giving to those who are poor.

302 | Give freely to meet needs in the kingdom

The Lord also wants to bless us so we can meet needs in the body of Christ. 2 Corinthians 8:14 tells us, "*At the present time your plenty will supply what they need, so that in turn their plenty will supply what you need. Then there will be equality.*"

In other words, when one person has an abundance, he will supply the lack that someone else has. It reminds me of a balance scale. If my side of the scale is too heavy, I take some of the weight off my side and place it on your side of the scale. If you have extra, you give to someone else so they can be blessed by your abundance. If they have extra finances and you are going through a financial struggle, they can give to you so that you also may have what you need.

There are enough resources in the body of Christ to meet every need. I am not talking about a type of communism. Communism coerces people and forces "equality" on people under its influence. People should never be forced to give. In the kingdom of God, the Holy Spirit gives the Lord's people a desire to give to serve those who have a need in the body of Christ both in our communities, and in the mission field.

As we give, the Lord wants us to have proper attitudes and motives. 2 Corinthians 9:7 gives us a few biblical attitudes to consider as we give. *Each man should*

List some of our responsibilities to the poor.

What is the difference between God's equality and communism's way?

How has it been a joy for you to give?

Biblical Foundations for Life

give what he has decided in his heart to give, not reluctantly or under compulsion, for God loves a cheerful giver.

First of all, let's give cheerfully. I know of one church in the state of Texas, USA where the people are so excited about giving that they cheer and clap every time there is an offering given.

God has called us to give freely and willingly. Matthew 10:8b says, "...*freely you have received, freely give.*" We also should not give grudgingly or because we have to. We need to give because we want to.

You may ask, "How much should I give"? When we go to a meeting of believers at our local church and they take a special offering, the Lord will give us a sense of peace so we can know how much we should give. The more we grow in the Lord and give, the more we grow in faith. Again, we don't give grudgingly or because we have to, but we give because it is a joy to give back to God that which is His already.

303 | Give and it will be given

A friend of mine, a new Christian, was serving in the military. One day his friend borrowed money from him and did not pay him back. My friend struggled with unforgiveness, until he read this scripture in Luke 6:33-35. *And if you do good to those who are good to you, what credit is that to you? Even "sinners" do that. And if you lend to those from whom you expect repayment, what credit is that to you? Even "sinners" lend to "sinners," expecting to be repaid in full. But love your enemies, do good to them, and lend to them without expecting to get anything back. Then your reward will be great, and you will be sons of the Most High, because he is kind to the ungrateful and wicked.* When we give or lend money to others, it must be in faith. Whether or not it is returned to us, we must strive to keep our attitudes pure and continue to love, even our "enemies."

God has called us to give in faith. Luke 6:38 says, "*Give, and it will be given to you. A good measure, pressed down, shaken together and running over, will be poured into your lap. For with the measure you use, it will be measured to you.*"

As we give, God says He wants to bless us by giving back to us the same measure we give to others. He is the One who is responsible to bless us. Although our motivation for giving must always be out of our love for God, the Lord desires to bless us when we give in obedience to Him. Many do not receive God's financial blessings because they have not experienced their faith and do not expect to receive God's abundance.

God also calls us to give liberally. 2 Corinthians 9:6 says, "*Remember this: Whoever sows sparingly will also reap sparingly, and whoever sows generously will also reap generously.*"

Let's give to others just as Jesus has been so faithful to give to us. It is, however, important to check out where we give. A pastor friend confided in me that his church had given thousands of dollars to a man in another nation, only to find out that this man was embezzling money from the church for his own personal

According to 2 Corinthians 9:6, how should we give?

use. Of course they stopped giving to the man. We need to be sure that we are giving to reputable Christian ministries. It is often good to give to those with whom we have a close personal relationship. We can trust them because we know them and see genuine spiritual fruit in their lives.

And finally, the Lord's desire is that we prosper. 2 Corinthians 8:9 says, *"For you know the grace of our Lord Jesus Christ, that though he was rich, yet for your sakes he became poor, so that you through his poverty might become rich."*

Jesus Christ took the curse of poverty for us. He wants us to be blessed spiritually, relationally, physically, mentally, and financially. But remember, when He blesses us, He takes a risk. We may choose to trust in our financial riches instead of trusting in the living God. He desires to bless us so that we can bless those around us. May the Lord bless you as you fulfill your responsibility as a good manager (steward) of the finances He has entrusted to you.

304 | Financial principles from God's Word

1. **God is the source of everything.** Philippians 4:19 says, *"My God shall supply all your need according to his riches in glory by Christ Jesus."* 2 Corinthians 9:8 adds, *"And God is able to bless you abundantly, so that in all things at all times, having all that you need, you will abound in every good work."* Whenever we need money or possessions, prayer is the answer. Look to the Lord, because He will provide it as we pray according to His will.
2. **Giving.** Luke 6:38, says, *"Give, and it shall be given unto you; good measure, pressed down, and shaken together…"* According to Deuteronomy 14:23, one purpose of tithing was to teach the people of Israel to put God first in their lives. Tithing is committing a tenth of our income-right off the top to the Lord's work. Proverbs 3:9-10 reads, *"Honor the Lord with your wealth, with the firstfruits of all your crops; then your barns will be filled to overflowing, and your vats will brim over with new wine."*
3. **Living with a margin.** Everyone ought to live on a margin…a physical margin, a spiritual margin, a time margin and a financial margin. Living on a margin simply means allowing room for things to happen. Having a savings to prepare for extra bills that can come up is a margin.
4. **Saving.** Proverbs 21:20 says, *"The wise store up choice food and olive oil, but fools gulp theirs down."*
5. **Stay out of unnecessary debt.** Borrowing for a house or car is one thing, but buying or borrowing beyond our ability to pay is not wise. Psalm 37:21 says, *"The wicked borrows, and pays not again."* The minute a person goes into debt, he loses a portion of his freedom. Too many people think we can buy now and pay later.
These financial principles have been a great blessing to my life.

Which of these principles do you need to work on?

Biblical Foundations for Life

305 | More financial principles from God's Word

1. **Contentment.** Being content with what we have is so important. Hebrews 13:5 says: *"Let your conversation be without covetousness; and be content with such things as you have."* And I Timothy 6:6 says, *"But godliness with contentment is great gain."*
2. **Budgeting and record-keeping.** God's Word says, *"Through wisdom is a house built; and by understanding it is established: and by knowledge shall the chambers be filled with all precious and pleasant riches"* (Proverbs 24:3,4). By keeping good records, having a plan and being honest with yourself, you will not get into financial trouble. I seldom see financially successful people who don't keep good records.
3. **Don't cosign.** Proverbs 27:13 advises that we should exercise caution in cosigning. The advice infers that the world's poorest credit risk is the man who agrees to pay a stranger's debt. The reason a person needs a cosigner is because the lender is unwilling to lend that money to the person requesting the loan.
4. **Hard work.** The Scriptures spell it out: *"In all labor there is profit: but the talk of the lips tends only to poverty"* (Proverbs 14:23). *"He that tills his land shall have plenty of bread: but he that follows after vain persons shall have poverty enough"* (Proverbs 28:19). It is important to work.
5. **Seek godly counsel.** Proverbs 15:22 declares, *"Without counsel purposes are disappointed: but in the multitude of counsellors they are established"* (Proverbs 15:22). Before buying a house, purchasing a car, or borrowing money, pray about it and seek the counsel of godly people. They can keep you from making a lot of mistakes. Don't be hurried or coerced into any deal.

In review, we have looked at ten biblical financial principles: God is the source, give first, live on a margin, save money, stay out of debt, be content with what you have, budget and keep records, don't cosign, work hard, and seek godly counsel. As we learn to follow these biblical principles in our personal finances, we will know the joy that comes from trusting and obeying God.

Which of these principles do you need to work on?

FOUNDATION 11

Called to Minister

306 | Introduction to foundation 11

In this basic Biblical Foundation teaching, Called to Minister, we discover that every Christian is called by God to minister to people. The Lord has called pastors and other spiritual leaders to train the saints (believers) so that every Christian can be involved in ministry and become mature in Christ. As each believer fulfills what the Lord has called him to do, God builds His church through His people. Ministry does not just happen in our church meetings; it happens at our schools, our places of work, and in our homes as we reach out to others.

Pastors and other church leaders are in place to train and equip every believer in Christ to be a minister. The Bible tells us in Ephesians 4:11-12 that the Lord releases spiritual leaders with specific gifts for two basic purposes: *"And He Himself gave some to be apostles, some prophets, some evangelists, and some pastors and teachers, for the equipping of the saints for the work of ministry, for the edifying of the body of Christ"* (NKJ).

To minister means "to serve, to wait, or to attend." If you go to a restaurant, the waiter or waitress is ministering to you. That is a type of ministry. If you go to a hospital, you will see hospital attendants who are serving or ministering to the patients. The terms serve and minister can be used interchangeably.

People often think that to minister means "to teach or preach." But that is only one of many ways we can minister in the name of Jesus. For example, cleaning someone's house or giving them a ride to work is a type of ministry. Encouraging others, praying for the sick, and serving children in a children's ministry are all types of ministry. The list is endless! God has called you to be a minister for Him.

Who are the true ministers in the church?

Biblical Foundations for Life

PART 1 EVERYONE CAN MINISTER

307 | We are equipped to minister

Recently a soccer enthusiast told me of his experience at one of the World Cup soccer games. He paid $150 for a seat and joined thousands of fans who watched twenty-two talented players kick a ball around on a soccer field. Although he loved soccer, he was not allowed to play—he was a spectator only. His story reminded me of the church today. Think about it. A group of "spectator" Christians gathers together each Sunday morning to watch as the pastor performs his duties. Is this what the Lord desires for His church? I do not believe so. Every believer can be a minister.

Pastors and church leaders are in place to help or equip every believer to minister. The Bible tells us in Ephesians 4:11-12 that the Lord releases spiritual leaders with specific gifts for two basic purposes. *"And He Himself gave some to be apostles, some prophets, some evangelists, and some pastors and teachers, for the equipping of the saints for the work of ministry, for the edifying of the body of Christ"* (NKJ).

According to this scripture, these spiritual leaders with particular gifts are given to "equip the saints to do the work of ministry" and to "build up (edify) the body of Christ." Christ gives these leaders specific leadership gifts so that they can prepare God's people for works of service and so the body of Christ can grow as God intended. When these leaders train and equip every believer to minister, the church grows. If every believer does not learn how to serve others, God's church becomes paralyzed: only part of the body is being used.

If most of your body parts would shut down, you would be suffering from a partial paralysis. Much of the church of Jesus Christ today has become paralyzed because the important truth of all the saints doing the work of ministry is overlooked. God is restoring a basic truth to His church which involves the dynamic of every believer being called as a minister.

The leadership of the early church, including apostles, prophets, evangelists, pastors and teachers, realized that their focus needed to be on prayer and ministering the Word of God. *We will…give our attention to prayer and the ministry of the word* (Acts 6:3b-4).

Before they could "give themselves continually to prayer and the ministry of the Word," the leaders had to train believers to minister, thus easing the burden of doing everything themselves. As they obeyed this principle, thousands came into the kingdom and the church grew rapidly during the first century.

308 | Everyone can serve

Since the scriptures tell us that the saints are called to do the work of ministry, let's look again at who the saints really are. The truth is this: If you are a Christian, born again by the Spirit of God, you are a saint. We do not become saints when we get to heaven. We are saints right now. When you look in the

---

What is the role of spiritual leaders in the church, according to Ephesians 4:11-12?

How do these leaders train us to minister?

mirror in the morning, I encourage you to say, "I am a saint." The Bible says the saints are the ones who are called to do the work of ministry (Ephesians 4:12). Thousands of believers today are unfulfilled because they are not fulfilling the purpose that God intended for them—to minister to others.

What does the word *ministry* or *minister* really mean? Webster's 1828 dictionary says, "to minister means to serve, to wait, or to attend." If you go to a restaurant, the waiter or waitress is ministering to you. They serve you or wait on you at your table. That is a type of ministry. If you go to a hospital, you will see hospital attendants who are waiting, serving or ministering to the patients. The term *serve* and *minister* can be used interchangeably.

Every Christian is called by God to minister to other people. It is a privilege to minister and to serve others in Jesus' name. There are many different ways to minister and many different types of ministry; however, each person is called to serve others in the name of Jesus. The Bible says in Mark 16:17-18 that some signs will accompany true disciples and confirm that the gospel message is genuine. *And these signs will accompany those who believe: In my name they will drive out demons; they will speak in new tongues; they will pick up snakes with their hands; and when they drink deadly poison, it will not hurt them at all; they will place their hands on sick people, and they will get well.*

This scripture speaks of various kinds of ministry to which the Lord calls His people today. It does not say that these signs shall follow pastors or apostles or evangelists. It says "these signs will accompany those who believe." Every Christian who truly believes in Jesus is called of God to be a minister to others and bring in the kingdom of God with power and authority.

309 | Are we exercising spiritually?

In today's church, we often have a warped understanding of what it means to minister. But God is beginning to train and teach us to have a proper understanding of ministry from His perspective.

In the past, we have often thought that the pastor of the local church is responsible for all of the ministry—that the ministry is accomplished only by the clergy, the trained or the supported. Because of this attitude, many believers in the church today are very weak, understandably so. If you and I were to never exercise, we would become physically weak. In the same way, if we do not exercise spiritually, we become weak spiritually. *But solid food is for the mature, who by constant use have trained themselves to distinguish good from evil* (Hebrews 5:14).

We become spiritually mature by practicing and experiencing what God has told us to do. God has called every saint to be a minister for Him. We can be only a few days old in the Lord and already begin to minister to others by telling them what Jesus Christ has done for us.

When the pastor does all of the spiritual exercise, he burns himself out. The saints in the church are not exercising spiritually and remain weak, causing the entire church to be weak. Imagine a pastor doing four thousand push-ups every day! In a spiritual sense, that is what has happened in the church today.

Biblical Foundations for Life

How do you minister to others?

Are any of the signs of Mark 16:17-18 happening in your life?

How do we exercise our senses to discern good from evil (Hebrews 5:14)?

What is lacking in a church where the pastor does all the ministry?

I firmly believe that the Lord has called pastors and other spiritual leaders to train the saints so that every believer can be involved in ministry and maturing in Christ. When God's people are not exercising, they are no longer growing. Since God has given each of us different gifts and abilities, we all need to use these gifts to minister.

As each believer is fulfilling what the Lord has called him to do, a wonderful thing happens. God begins to build His church through His people from house to house and in each community. Ministry does not just happen in our church services; it happens at our schools, our places of work, and in our homes as we reach out to others. All, then, are fulfilled because they are using the gifts God has given them. This is the Lord's plan for building His church.

310 | How to minister

List several things you are able to do for others.

There are various ways to minister. For example, washing someone's car or giving them a ride to work is a type of ministry. Others may be gifted to bake a cake, giving it to someone as a "labor of love." Encouraging others, praying for the sick, and serving children in a children's ministry or Sunday school are all types of ministry. Many times, people think that *to minister* means *to teach or preach*. But that is only one of hundreds of ways we can minister in the name of Jesus.

When Jesus walked on the earth, He could be at only one place at one time. God the Father's strategy was for Jesus to go to the cross, then be raised from the dead, ascend into heaven and later send the Holy Spirit to His people. The Holy Spirit then would indwell the Lord's people. Now, rather than only Jesus walking the earth offering hope to people, there would be thousands of believers filled with the same Holy Spirit, ministering in Jesus' name throughout the world.

Where does your strength and ability come from according to 2 Corinthians 3:5-6?

We have received the Holy Spirit and are called by the Lord to be ministers. Everywhere Jesus went, He ministered to people. Everywhere we go, God has called us to minister to others—in our homes, communities, schools and jobs, and we can do it only by His strength. *Not that we are competent in ourselves to claim anything for ourselves, but our competence comes from God. He has made us competent as ministers of a new covenant—not of the letter but of the Spirit; for the letter kills, but the Spirit gives life* (2 Corinthians 3:5-6).

I will never forget the first time I ever taught at a Bible study as a young man. I was scared, because this was something new for me. I also realized that God's strength in me would pull me through. My competence was from God.

Many years ago, I served as a worship leader. The first time I ever led God's people in worship was in a church meeting where there were no musical instruments. I was given a small, round pitch pipe to get the proper key for the song. The first time, I blew the pitch pipe exceptionally loud and was extremely embarrassed! I looked for a hole in the floor to fall through, especially when I noticed that some of the people were giggling at my expense. It was a humbling experience, but by the grace of God I got through that first song. As I continued to practice, realizing I was called by God to minister in this way, I began to enjoy leading others in worshiping our Lord.

311 | Let's move out of our comfort zone

Each of us has an area in our lives that is comfortable, that we sometimes call our "comfort zone." We often find it hard to move out of our comfort zone into new things, but God has called us to take steps of faith. When Peter walked on the water, he moved far beyond his comfort zone!

God has called us to be people of faith and depend on the ability of God within us to help us accomplish His work. The Bible says, "...*without faith it is impossible to please God*" (Hebrews 11:6). Ministry to others will often require us to move beyond our comfort zone.

Our homes are excellent places of ministry. Jesus spent much of His time in the homes of people. The book of Acts is filled with examples of people meeting in homes: fellowshipping together, learning together and ministering to one another. Invite people into your home—for a meal or to spend time in fellowship. Exciting things can happen when people sit down together to eat a meal, play a game or just talk and laugh together. People can relax when we meet them on their own level and let them know we, too, are real people with real problems. We can ask the Lord for an opportunity to pray with them, and it can be a life-changing experience. Keep in mind that you are a saint who is called to minister.

The Lord may want to use you to give someone godly counsel. You may feel that since you're not a professional counselor, God can't use you, but the Bible says in Isaiah 9:6, "...*He will be called...Wonderful Counselor.*" Jesus is the "Counselor" and He lives within us. When people need solutions to problems in their lives, and I don't know the answers, I know that Jesus, the Counselor, lives in me. He has the answers. I pray and ask the Lord to speak to them and tell them what to do. Sometimes I can steer them toward other Christians who may be able to answer their questions.

Remember, the Lord has given you a powerful testimony! As you share your testimony with others, you'll find that the Holy Spirit will use you to speak the truth and others will be built up in faith. Perhaps you are afraid someone will ask you a question that you don't have the answer to. If you are unsure of the correct answers, it is appropriate to say, "I don't know, but perhaps I can ask someone who does know." None of us have all of the answers. That's why the Lord placed different gifts in different people in His church. We need one another.

Describe some situations when you moved out of your "comfort zone."

312 | It is not our ability, but His

The Lord wants us to be available for Him to use us to minister to others in many different ways. When our new cell-based church first started, one Sunday morning I was responsible to preach and the next Sunday morning I was responsible to minister to the children. Ministering to the children helped prepare me for other types of ministry the Lord would call me to in future years.

Regardless of the ministry the Lord has called you to, you do not minister by your own ability but by His ability that is within you. If you serve in a nursery, you can pray, laying your hands on these special children, ministering to them in Jesus' name. God has called each of us as Christians to minister wherever we go,

What happened when you were "crucified with Christ"?

Biblical Foundations for Life

255

What things died and what things became new?

What does perfect love do (1 John 4:18)?

How does the grace of God operate in your life?

asking the Lord to open our eyes so we can see people as He sees them. John 3:16 tells us, *"God so loved the world that He gave His only begotten Son, that whoever believes in Him should not perish but have everlasting life."* God loves people, and He lives in us! He has called us to encourage and serve the people around us.

Service is often done in practical ways. The Lord may call you to minister by helping a neighbor change a flat tire in the rain. God repairs a car through you! Sometimes serving requires us to do what the Lord has called us to do rather than what we *feel* like doing. If we have been truly crucified with Christ, the Bible tells us we are dead to doing what we want to do. *I have been crucified with Christ and I no longer live, but Christ lives in me. The life I live in the body, I live by faith in the Son of God, who loved me and gave himself for me* (Galatians 2:20).

The old "you" is dead and Jesus Christ now lives inside of you. He has called you to be a minister for Him.

313 | Love conquers all

I was speaking to a professional counselor who had years of psychological training. "You know," he said, "some people think that in order to help others they need to have all kinds of training." Then he went on to say, "I find that what people really need is just to have someone to love them." This counselor was not minimizing the need for training; however, he was talking about meeting the deeper need that is in the hearts of men and women today—the need to be loved.

That is what ministry is really all about. Jesus has called us to love people. We love people by listening to them and genuinely caring about the needs they have. We should not feel fearful or inadequate to minister to others. The Bible says, *"...perfect love drives out fear..."* (1 John 4:18).

When I realize that God loves me and He loves the person to whom I am ministering, His perfect love will cast out the fear. The more we spend time with Jesus, the more Christ will be able to minister through us. As we spend time with Jesus, those around us will perceive that we have the ability to minister to them because His love and boldness will be evident in our lives just as it was with Peter and John. *When they saw the courage of Peter and John and realized that they were unschooled, ordinary men, they were astonished and they took note that these men had been with Jesus* (Acts 4:13).

When we feel weak, it is then that we can be truly strong, because we know God's grace is sufficient for us. Paul pleaded with the Lord to take away a "thorn in the flesh." But the Lord told him that His strength would be made perfect through Paul's weakness, according to 2 Corinthians 12:9-10. *But he said to me, "My grace is sufficient for you, for my power is made perfect in weakness." Therefore I will boast all the more gladly about my weaknesses, so that Christ's power may rest on me. That is why, for Christ's sake, I delight in weaknesses, in insults, in hardships, in persecutions, in difficulties. For when I am weak, then I am strong.*

God's grace is always sufficient to live our daily lives. When we draw near to Christ, He will help us in every situation, giving us strength and comfort. We can minister to others by faith, through the strength of Jesus Christ.

WE ARE CALLED TO SERVE

PART 2

314 | What to do, if you want to be great

One day the mother of James and John came to Jesus with a special request. *Then the mother of Zebedee's sons came to Jesus with her sons and, kneeling down, asked a favor of him..."Grant that one of these two sons of mine may sit at your right and the other at your left in your kingdom"* (Matthew 20:20-21).

The Bible tells us that the other disciples were indignant. They couldn't believe that James and John had the audacity to expect to sit on the right and left hand of Jesus in His kingdom. They, of course, were still thinking that Jesus was going to set up an earthly kingdom here on earth. The twelve disciples had a wrong understanding of ministry and leadership entirely. Jesus tried to correct this wrong thinking when He told His disciples...*You know that the rulers of the Gentiles lord it over them, and their high officials exercise authority over them. Not so with you. Instead, whoever wants to become great among you must be your servant, and whoever wants to be first must be your slave—just as the Son of Man did not come to be served, but to serve, and to give his life as a ransom for many* (Matthew 20:25-28).

Jesus told His disciples that those who are under the world's system do not understand the principle of ministry and servanthood. Someone who is a leader in the world is often a person who exercises his power and control over people. But Jesus advocated a new way. He said that true leadership exemplifies servanthood. Servanthood is characterized through serving. Jesus Christ, the king of the universe, came to this earth to be a servant. Every chance He got, He served people and set an example for us. We also are called to be ministers (servants) to others in His name. We must minister to and help others—this is a true measure of greatness.

What should you do if you want to be great, according to Matthew 20:26?

What did Jesus say that He came to do on the earth in Matthew 20:28?

315 | Serving and ministry—one and the same

What, then, does it really mean to serve? As was mentioned earlier, the word *serving* and *ministry* are really synonymous. James and John wanted to be great in the kingdom. They thought greatness came from having the right position, but Jesus said greatness came through serving. Greatness does not depend on our talents or our abilities, but on our willingness to serve.

A servant is simply a person who is devoted to another. I love to watch people. And as I travel throughout the world, I've found an amazing truth. Wherever I find a truly "great man or woman of God," I notice that he or she has the heart of a servant.

Years ago, as a young pastor, I was at a leadership meeting in Dayton, Ohio. I found myself watching an elderly man, a leader in the body of Christ, who has now gone on to be with the Lord. Everywhere he went, he served others. I watched him as he reached out to a bell boy in the hotel, telling him about Jesus Christ. I watched him as he responded in gentleness and compassion to those who came and asked him questions about spiritual things. He was truly a servant.

In what ways are servant-leaders exalted by the Lord?

Biblical Foundations for Life

257

Describe ways you have served in the background.

_____
_____
_____
_____

What builds people up in the Lord, according to 1 Corinthians 8:1?

_____
_____
_____

How have you developed a servant's heart?

_____
_____
_____
_____

The mark of greatness in the kingdom of God is our willingness and obedience to serve others. One day, Jesus told a parable to a group of guests who were invited into the house of a ruler of the Pharisees. *When someone invites you to a wedding feast, do not take the place of honor, for a person more distinguished than you may have been invited. If so, the host who invited both of you will come and say to you, "Give this man your seat." Then, humiliated, you will have to take the least important place. But when you are invited, take the lowest place, so that when your host comes, he will say to you, "Friend, move up to a better place." Then you will be honored in the presence of all your fellow guests. For everyone who exalts himself will be humbled, and he who humbles himself will be exalted* (Luke 14:8-11).

The Lord warns us that we should never exalt ourselves or try to take the best places. Instead, we need to be willing to serve in the background. D. L. Moody, the great evangelist of the last century who was used of God to see more than one million souls come into God's kingdom, always liked to sit in the background. He was truly a servant. If we honor the Lord with humility and servanthood, in due time we will be exalted.

316 | Serving in love

A friend of mine serves as a Christian leader in our nation. Years ago, when he was a young Christian, he moved to a major city. He has a charismatic personality and had studied the Bible. He was enthusiastic and excited to teach others. One evening he went to a Bible study and offered to teach the Word at future meetings. The group leader told him he appreciated my friend's willingness; however, he really needed someone to set up the chairs. So week after week, my friend could be found setting up the chairs for the meeting. He was willing to be a servant, and today he is a noted leader in the body of Christ, teaching the Bible throughout the world.

The scriptures tell us in 1 Corinthians 8:1, *"…knowledge puffs up, but love builds up."* Too much knowledge can make us arrogant, but love will always build others up. I have met people who thought that to be involved in ministry meant they were called to preach or teach rather than serve the people of God. Preaching and teaching are valid ministries that are needed in the church today. However, all ministry, including the ministry of preaching and teaching, must come from a heart of love and compassion. Preachers and teachers who are called by God have a desire to serve those whom they teach. Only love will build people up. Too much knowledge, including knowledge of the Bible, without a heart of love and compassion, can cause us to be puffed up with pride.

Many times God's people need to minister in menial and practical ways before the Lord will release them into a ministry of preaching and teaching. Those who are willing to serve in these humble beginnings often are being prepared by the Lord to minister in greater ways because they have developed a servant's heart. Regardless of how much training or knowledge a person may have, the Lord is looking for those who are willing to serve. If we are willing to serve, He can truly make us great. If we are not willing to serve, regardless of our training or background, we cannot be great in the kingdom.

317 | How can I serve you?

Why didn't Jesus take you and me to heaven as soon as we were born again? I believe the answer is so we can serve here on the earth and help many people come into His kingdom through a relationship with Jesus Christ. Consequently, the bottom line is this: Every believer is called to serve. We are called to serve our families, people at our place of employment, the people to whom we are committed in our small groups, and other believers in our local church. The question we should ask ourselves wherever we go is, "How can I serve today?"

Maybe in your church you could serve by participating in a drama ministry, or serve through clowning as you minister to children. You may be called to minister to prisoners. Some may serve by picking up litter in a neighborhood. Perhaps you could visit the elderly and pray for them or serve meals to those going through a stressful time in their lives. Providing transportation for someone in a time of need can be a tremendous act of service.

You are a true minister when you serve others. Jesus never said, "I am the king, come worship me." He simply served. James 4:10 says, *"Humble yourselves before the Lord, and he will lift you up."*

Some time back, a pastor who had served the Lord faithfully for many years became a member of our church. One of the first questions that he asked when he came was, "How can I serve?" He was not thinking, "When can I preach a sermon?" He understood the importance of true ministry, serving in the body of Christ. It is people with the attitude of a servant whom the Lord will use to build His church in a powerful way.

I have found I am drawn to others who are willing to serve. As Jesus went about serving others, people were attracted to Him. When we have the heart of a servant, the Lord will cause people to be drawn to us so we can pray for them and minister to them. As we reach out beyond ourselves to serve others, people will be drawn into the kingdom of God. People usually do not come to Jesus because we have a lot of Bible knowledge, even though it is important to understand the scriptures. People are attracted to Christ when they see the heart of a servant exemplified through our lives.

List some specific ways you have served others.

How can you remain humble if you are recognized as an expert or authority on a subject?

318 | Touching others by serving

According to the Bible, people around us will glorify our God in heaven because of the way they see us serve. Jesus said, *"…let your light shine before men, that they may see your good deeds and praise your Father in heaven"* (Matthew 5:16).

A family I know made a commitment one winter to keep two elderly neighbors' sidewalks clean after it snowed. They shoveled cheerfully, even though they got an extraordinary amount of snow that winter!

I served as a pastor for many years. Because of the many people who came to our church, I was not able to meet everyone who came to our Sunday services. There were simply too many people. But do you know who they met? They met the people who parked the cars, those who greeted them at the door, those who

How do you let your light shine so people see Jesus?

Biblical Foundations for Life

ushered them to their seats, those who invited them to a meeting in their small group and those who served their children in the children's ministry. They experienced Jesus in these precious saints who were ministering to them and their children. By this, they were drawn into the kingdom of God.

You see, it is Jesus working through each of us that makes all the difference in the world. As the people in our church touched those around them with the love of Jesus Christ, hundreds of precious people became part of God's kingdom and became committed to our local church. Jesus used hundreds of ministers, through practical service, to minister to those whom God drew into His kingdom.

Everywhere I go, I find people in the church who have servants' hearts. One time in Africa, I was blessed by a businessman who was constantly finding opportunities to serve. He was not looking for a position in the church, but his desire was to be supported by his business so he could better serve Jesus and the people of God in his local church. He was truly a minister.

Although the Lord does call specific people to be supported by the local church so they can equip others to minister, let us never forget that *every* saint is called to be a minister.

319 | The ministry of "helps"

What is the ministry of helps?

Have you ever served in this kind of ministry? How?

Jesus spent His time training, encouraging and modeling for His twelve disciples what the kingdom of God was all about. These disciples also served Jesus in a ministry of *helps* similar to what we see in 1 Corinthians 12:28...*God has appointed these in the church: first apostles, second prophets, third teachers, after that miracles, then gifts of healing, **helps**, administrations, varieties of tongues* (NKJ).

The ministry of *helps* is a ministry of giving aid, assistance, support or relief to another person involved in ministry. It is giving practical assistance to someone so he can fulfill his responsibilities to God. Jesus' disciples helped Him fulfill the ministry that His Father had given to Him. A group of women also aided Jesus in His ministry (Luke 8:1-3) who served in many ways so that Jesus had time to pray, preach and minister healing to the people around Him.

One day, Jesus sent His disciples into Jerusalem to find a colt, untie it and bring it back to Him so He could ride it to Jerusalem (Matthew 21:1-11). Another time, the disciples prepared the upper room for the Last Supper (Matthew 26:17-30). They were serving in the ministry of helps.

Yet another time, thousands of people were gathered together to hear Jesus teach. It was getting late and the people were hungry. When Jesus asked what was available to eat, they discovered they had only five loaves of bread and two fish. Jesus prayed over the loaves and fish, it supernaturally multiplied—in fact, twelve basketfuls were left over after all the people were fed (Matthew 14:13-21). The disciples were involved in the ministry of helps as they distributed the food to the hungry people. I personally believe there was one leftover basketful of food for each disciple who had served.

Another time, Jesus realized He needed to pay the temple tax, so He sent Peter to catch a fish. When the fish was caught, a coin was found to pay the taxes! (Matthew 17:27). Peter was serving in the ministry of helps when he caught the fish and paid the taxes.

I am constantly looking for future spiritual leaders. The leaders God is looking for are those who are willing to serve in the ministry of helps as God prepares them for future leadership.

320 | Training for future ministry

Jesus' disciples learned faithfulness by serving practically. If we are faithful in small things, God knows He can trust us with greater responsibilities. *He who is faithful in what is least is faithful also in much; and he who is unjust in what is least is unjust also in much* (Luke 16:10 NKJ).

Moses was trained to be a leader by serving. Before he delivered the children of Israel out of Egypt, God placed him in the ministry of helps—serving his father-in-law by tending sheep in the desert for forty years.

Later on, Joshua served Moses in a ministry of helps capacity while he was being trained to take over Moses' responsibility of leadership for the children of Israel. Many men and women of God today have been trained through practically serving another Christian leader for years before the Lord opens up a door of public ministry or leadership for them.

In fact, Jesus Himself spent thirty years in His father's carpentry shop—in the ministry of helps. Stephen and Philip were powerful evangelists; however, they both were also involved in serving tables (Acts 6:1-7). I encourage you to ask yourself, "How can I serve a leader whom the Lord has placed in my life?" Tell him or her you are willing to serve in the ministry of helps as the Lord trains you for future ministry.

For years, I served in the ministry of helps in a youth outreach. We played basketball and other sports with young people so we could share Christ with them. My responsibility in the basketball club was to bring the basketball and to be the chauffeur who brought the young people to the basketball court week after week. Sometime later, I was asked to take a small group of new believers and start a believers' Bible study. The Lord used these acts of serving in my life to train me for future ministry.

If you want to find your ministry, a place to start is by serving in the ministry of helps as prescribed in the Word of God. Often, those people who try to push themselves into the limelight are the very ones who need to serve behind the scenes where the Lord can work His heart of a servant in them. I believe God desires to exalt us, but He asks us to humble ourselves first, so He can exalt us in due time (1 Peter 5:6).

If we serve in small things, what happens, according to Luke 16:10?

Biblical Foundations for Life

PART 3

MINISTERING WITH COMPASION

321 | Loving regardless of the response

Whenever Jesus ministered to others, His ministry came from a heart of love and compassion. *When he saw the crowds, he had compassion on them, because they were harassed and helpless, like sheep without a shepherd* (Matthew 9:36).

Jesus loved the people He served and has called us to do the same. 1 Corinthians 13 is often known as the "love chapter" in the Bible. The scriptures in this chapter teach us that we can do all kinds of good deeds and "ministry," but unless it is done from a heart of love, it will be of no profit for us or others.

Love is not just a feeling but a decision you make. *Love is giving with no expectancy of return.* Jesus Christ loved us. He went to the cross and made a decision to love us regardless of our response to Him. In the same way Jesus gave His life for us, He has called us to love others and give our lives for them. We can love others because Jesus Christ loved us first. Since Christ lives in us, His love is in us. Every day we need to allow the love of God to be released in our lives. Either we live by what the Word of God says and by the truth of Christ living in us, or we live by our emotions and by the way we feel. Here is an excellent checklist to use as you minister to others: *But the wisdom that comes from heaven is first of all pure; then peace-loving, considerate, submissive, full of mercy and good fruit, impartial and sincere* (James 3:17). If you want to give someone counsel, you can readily decide whether or not you have Christ's compassion by asking: "Am I willing to yield?" "Is the counsel I'm giving pure?" "Is it bringing peace, or is it bringing confusion?" God is not the author of confusion but of peace (1 Corinthians 14:33 NKJ).

Many times we may say the right thing but in a wrong attitude. This will not produce the spiritual results that God desires. We can respond like a lamb or a snake to those around us. A lamb is willing to yield and even be taken to the slaughter (Isaiah 53:7). The devil will always rise up in resistance like a snake: "Who are *you* telling *me* what to do?" God has called us to respond to others and minister to them like a lamb—with love and compassion.

322 | Start small

As we minister to others out of a heart of love and compassion, we need to recognize that there are many different kinds of ministries the Lord has given to His people. 1 Corinthians 12:4-7, 11 says, "*Now there are diversities of gifts, but the same Spirit. There are differences of ministries, but the same Lord. And there are diversities of activities, but it is the same God who works all in all. But the manifestation of the Spirit is given to each one for the profit of all: But one and the same Spirit works all these things, distributing to each one individually as He wills*" (NKJ).

I have met people who feel they are called to minister to others by singing or leading in worship when, in actuality, they cannot carry a tune. The Lord

---

What is the difference between serving with compassion and serving without it?

Name the things on the checklist of James 3:17 that will be evident as you minister to others.

simply has not given them the ability to sing. We need more than an inward motivation for a spiritual gifting, we also need to be enabled to perform it. God is the One who gives us the power to perform ministry of any kind. We will know when we are functioning in the ministry God has given us because it will produce certain results.

A great place to begin to minister to others is in a small group setting such as a cell group or house church. Maybe God has called you to prophesy. Start in your small group. Perhaps the Lord has given you a song to sing that would be a blessing to other believers. The place to start is in a small group of believers. When you are faithful in this smaller setting, the Lord can then release you in larger settings in the future.

Sometimes people have what may be called a "preacher's itch." They constantly think they are responsible to preach and teach at every meeting they go to. Desiring to preach the Word is a very noble desire. However, ministry is serving. As was mentioned previously, Stephen and Philip served tables, and then God released them as mighty evangelists. They started by practical service. We should follow their example.

323 | What counts for eternity

Many years ago we spent much of our time ministering to a group of young people who grew up in homes without Christ. One day, some of these youngsters sat on our Volkswagen's sunroof, damaging it. From that time on, whenever it rained, water would leak from the roof and drip on my knee as I drove. For awhile, I had to watch my attitude. Was it really worth it to minister to these young rowdy people who caused my car's sunroof to leak and showed no appreciation for what we did for them? Soon I realized, "What does it matter anyway?" All that matters is where these youngsters spend eternity. Today, some of those young people are dynamic Christians.

As we see life from God's perspective, we realize that all that really counts is our relationship with God and our relationship with others as we serve those around us. God's call on our lives is first to love Him, and then to love people. Paul, the apostle, said in 1 Corinthians 9:22, *"To the weak I became weak, to win the weak. I have become all things to all men so that by all possible means I might save some."*

If we really love people with the love of Jesus Christ and see them from God's perspective, we will be willing to do whatever it takes to relate to help them come to know Jesus and fulfill the call of God that is on their lives. Many issues that we consider of major importance are really minor in God's eyes. Let's just love Jesus and one another and realize we are ministers. Then let's reach out to those around us in His name. God is calling many kinds of people to become part of His church, according to Galatians 3:28. *There is neither Jew nor Greek, slave nor free, male nor female, for you are all one in Christ Jesus. If you belong to Christ, then you are Abraham's seed, and heirs according to the promise.*

Biblical Foundations for Life

How can you begin to allow the Lord to use you in your spiritual gift(s)?

How can you "become all things to all men" (1 Corinthians 9:22)?

Why is it important to love all people, regardless of race, culture, gender, social position, wealth or age?

I get excited when I go to a meeting of believers and see them loving and accepting one another. One person wearing a suit sits next to someone wearing an old pair of jeans. There are no social, national, racial or gender distinctions with regard to our relationship with the Lord. It is not what is on the outside that is so important, but what is on the inside—a heart that is being changed by Jesus Christ.

324 | God uses imperfect people

Let's take a moment and look at the kind of people that God calls into leadership to minister effectively to others. This may surprise you. Let's start with Moses. *But Moses said to God, "Who am I, that I should go to Pharaoh and bring the Israelites out of Egypt?" And God said, "I will be with you..."* (Exodus 3:11-12).

Moses didn't feel like he was capable to do the job the Lord was asking him to do. Most Christians called to ministry feel the same way. They know they will have to rely on God's strength and not their own. The first small group Bible study I ever led seemed like a monumental task, but I took a step of faith because I knew God would give me the strength. Joshua was fearful when he responded to the Lord's call on his life. God told Joshua, *Have I not commanded you? Be strong and courageous. Do not be terrified; do not be discouraged, for the Lord your God will be with you wherever you go* (Joshua 1:9).

The Lord had to continually encourage Joshua in his new role as a leader. We do not depend on our ability but upon God's ability in us. If you feel you do not have all the natural gifts you need to be able to minister to others effectively, be encouraged. You have a lot of company. Moses and Joshua and others throughout the scriptures felt the same way. But God used them anyway. The Bible tells us God has chosen to use imperfect people to fulfill His purposes to confound the wisdom of those who seem to be wise in this world (1 Corinthians 1:27).

325 | Do not be afraid

Gideon was another individual who struggled when the Lord called him to areas of ministry and leadership. *"But sir," Gideon replied, "if the Lord is with us, why has all this happened to us? Where are all his wonders that our fathers told us about...But now the Lord has abandoned us and put us into the hand of Midian."*

The Lord turned to him and said, "Go in the strength you have and save Israel out of Midian's hand. Am I not sending you?"

"But Lord," Gideon asked, *"how can I save Israel? My clan is the weakest in Manasseh, and I am the least in my family."*

The Lord answered, "I will be with you, and you will strike down all the Midianites together" (Judges 6:13-16).

Have you ever felt like Gideon? You may know the Lord has called you to minister, and yet when you look at your own "track record," you can hardly believe it is possible that the Lord could use you. Yet if you seek to serve the Lord, He promises to be with you (Matthew 28:19-20).

Describe any times you felt inadequate to minister but the Lord gave you the grace to do it.

What does the Lord promise in Joshua 1:9?

Have you ever refused God?

Jeremiah was another individual who felt the same way that many young people feel when they realize God has called them to minister to others. Jeremiah, a young man, told the Lord in Jeremiah 1:6-8.

"Ah, Sovereign Lord," I said, "I do not know how to speak; I am only a child."

But the Lord said to me, "Do not say, 'I am only a child.' You must go to everyone I send you to and say whatever I command you. Do not be afraid of them, for I am with you and will rescue you," declares the Lord.

A feeling of "I can't do it" is a common thread that runs through each of these individuals' responses when the Lord called them to ministry and leadership. This is the type of person the Lord will use—those who are completely dependent on Him. No matter what your task, the Lord promises to be with you and help you.

Maybe you feel you've made too many mistakes and the Lord can never use you again. Look at Jonah. After running from God and being swallowed by a great fish, the Bible states, *Then the word of the Lord came to Jonah a second time* (Jonah 3:1).

God is always the God of a second chance. We need to put all of our trust in Him. We must be convinced that if God doesn't show up, it's all over. God has a "track record" of using those who feel like they cannot do the job. Man looks at the outward appearance, but God looks at the heart (1 Samuel 16:7). When our heart is at the right place—in complete submission to Him—it is amazing what the Lord can do to prepare and equip us for the responsibilities that lie ahead.

Has He given you a second chance?

326 | Connected and protected

God's purpose in the earth today is to build His church (Matthew 16:18). His universal church is made up of multitudes of local churches in every part of the world. Their goal is to preach the gospel, bringing men and women into a saving relationship with Christ. Each local church should desire to motivate their members to reach out. The early church leaders in Antioch got together to fast and pray, and then sent out a dynamic missionary team. *In the church at Antioch there were prophets and teachers...While they were worshiping the Lord and fasting, the Holy Spirit said, "Set apart for me Barnabas and Saul for the work to which I have called them." So after they had fasted and prayed, they placed their hands on them and sent them off* (Acts 13:1-3).

Paul and Barnabas were not sent out on a lone mission, the church supported and encouraged this missionary team, and they reported back to the church telling all that had happened. *From Attalia they sailed back to Antioch, where they had been committed to the grace of God for the work they had now completed. On arriving there, they gathered the church together and reported all that God had done through them...*(Acts 14:26-27).

This shows the importance of being sent out to minister from our local church and reporting back to them what the Lord is doing through us. God's desire is to continue to build His church—the congregations of believers in your local community. Jesus told His disciples that the gates of hell will not prevail against the church of Jesus Christ (Matthew 16:18).

How are you connected to and protected by the church?

What can happen if you are not connected?

Biblical Foundations for Life

Sometimes, because of zeal or a lack of understanding of the scriptures, Christians get excited about ministering to others without being properly connected to the local church. I have met various people through the years who have not been properly connected to the body of Christ and have gone through many kinds of struggles that were unnecessary. As we minister to others, it is important to be properly connected and protected through the local church.

327 | We are all kings and priests

Although we may find it hard to admit, at times we base our understanding of God on our preconceived ideas and our past experiences. Baptists grow up with a Baptist understanding of the scriptures, and the same can be said of Methodists, Lutherans, Charismatics and so forth. Depending on our church's denomination, we are convinced that our brand of theology is correct.

The truth is, we should be sure what we believe is based on the Word of God and not on a distorted traditional understanding. The Berean Christians refused to take everything that Paul preached at face value. They went home and studied the scriptures to be sure that the things Paul said were really true...*for they received the message with great eagerness and examined the Scriptures every day to see if what Paul said was true* (Acts 17:11).

Is it possible that certain traditions we consider to be completely scriptural are not based on the Bible at all? Could it be that the real reason we do certain things is because our spiritual parents and grandparents did them? I've heard the story of a young mother who always cut off the ends of a whole ham before baking it in the oven. When she was asked why she always followed this procedure, she said, "Because Grandma did it that way." Little did she know that grandma's roast pan was too small for the entire ham—that was the only motivation grandma had to cut off the ends!

Some traditions are good; however, we need to be sure that our ways of thinking are the same as God's. I believe a poor tradition (unbiblical, unscriptural) in the church has been the understanding that the pastor should do all the ministry, while the other saints simply come week after week to be fed. As we've learned from the scriptures in this book, every saint is called to be a minister, otherwise the church will never be built as the Lord intended.

Many Christians today have elevated pastors of a local church as holy men who stand between them and the Lord. The scriptures tell us He has made all of us kings and priests. *And has made us to be a kingdom and priests to serve his God and Father...*(Revelation 1:6).

We all have direct access to the Lord through the shed blood of Jesus Christ. Praise God for pastors, elders, and spiritual leaders the Lord has placed in our lives, but we should not expect them to do all of the ministry. We are called by God to minister to others. Our spiritual leaders should encourage us, equip us, and train us to be servants who minister to others. Let's expect to be a minister today. Ask the Lord to open your eyes to see needs around you. Then expect the Lord to give you the grace and the strength to minister to others.

How are you responsible for what you believe?

How does Revelation 1:6 relate to this responsibility?

WE ARE ON JESUS TEAM! — PART 4

328 | Live each day to the fullest

How would you feel if the President or Prime Minister of your nation personally asked you to serve on his team? I have even more awesome news for you—the King of the entire universe has handpicked you as one of His personal ministers! When we get up in the morning, rather than dreading the day ahead of us, we can be assured that God wants to use us as one of His ministers. As we go to work, to school, or serve in our homes or communities, God has called us to be ministers. God is orchestrating His plans in our lives so we will meet people who need Jesus Christ and His ministry. As we trust Him in faith, He will unfold His plans before us.

One of the tricks of the enemy, aimed at trying to keep us from being fulfilled in God and in ministry, is to try to tempt us to live in the past. If that doesn't work, the enemy will tempt us to be overly concerned about our future. God wants us to live to the fullest in the present and allow Him to reign in the midst of our problems. Matthew 6:33-34 tells us, *"But seek first his kingdom and his righteousness, and all these things will be given to you as well. Therefore do not worry about tomorrow, for tomorrow will worry about itself. Each day has enough trouble of its own."*

Every problem that you have is an opportunity for a miracle. As you read through the Bible, you'll find that every miracle was preceded by a problem. The Red Sea parted because the children of Israel had a problem—they had to flee the pursuing Egyptians. Jesus fed the five thousand because there was a problem—the people were hungry. The blind man was healed because he had a problem—he could not see. God desires to use you as an instrument of His miraculous power.

Sometime back, I was talking to a small group of people and I felt an impression from the Lord that one of the ladies was living with a fear that had been tormenting her for many years. As I shared this with her and the others in the room, she began to cry. We prayed for her, and Jesus ministered His peace and healing. Keep your eyes open, there are needs all around you. You can speak words that bring life to others.

329 | Expect Jesus to use us

Some Christians believe they need to have their whole life planned out for them. But really, the way to live for Jesus is one day at a time. Life is much like a football game. The football coach could not possibly plan out every play, because every play is dependent on the plays the opposing team has just made. In the "game of life," the enemy has plans and God has plans. We stand in the middle of the playing field. Let's trust Jesus day by day and minute by minute and expect Him to use us to minister to others.

When we learn to fellowship with the Lord and listen to His voice, we will realize that He is always at work around us. Jesus said, *"...My Father is always*

What are the things that will be given to you when you seek God's kingdom first (Matthew 6:33-34)?

_____
_____
_____
_____
_____

When you speak words of encouragement to others, what happens?

_____
_____
_____
_____
_____

How do we discover God's plan for our lives?

What have you learned about God's love from these verses in the book of John?

How can we love others like Jesus?

at his work to this very day, and I, too, am working...I tell you the truth, the Son can do nothing by himself; he can do only what he sees his Father doing, because whatever the Father does the Son also does. For the Father loves the Son and shows him all he does. Yes, to your amazement he will show him even greater things than these" (John 5:17, 19-20).

What is God the Father doing around you right now? Let's find out what the Father is doing and then partner with Him as one of His vital ministers. Remember—God is the initiator; we are the responders. *No one can come to me unless the Father who sent me draws him...*(John 6:44).

God is drawing people to Jesus Christ. Let's watch and pray and then respond as the Holy Spirit leads us to minister to others.

330 | Minister out of His love

Never forget—even though it is important to minister to others, God desires a personal love relationship with each of us. He really loves us. How can we know that Jesus loves us? Because He laid down His life for us at the cross 2,000 years ago. Jesus loves us as much as the Father loves Him!

As the Father has loved me, so have I loved you. Now remain in my love. If you obey my commands, you will remain in my love, just as I have obeyed my Father's commands and remain in his love. Greater love has no one than this, that he lay down his life for his friends (John 15:9-10, 13).

My daughter once prayed with a young lady in another nation. "Do you love Jesus?" she asked her. "Oh yes," the young lady responded, "but I do not love God the Father." She went on to explain that her father had molested her and, because of this devastating experience, she could not trust the Father in heaven. My daughter explained to her that God, our heavenly Father, loves her perfectly.

How do we know God loves us perfectly? Because of the cross. Jesus went to a cross and died for us. The cross of Jesus Christ is the proof of His love. As we minister to others, we need to minister out of an understanding that God loves us. We never should minister to *be* accepted by God or others. We minister because we *are* accepted by God, and we are able ministers of His love. In Isaiah 43:4, God expresses His love for Israel. *Since you are precious and honored in my sight, and because I love you....*

That same love applies to you and me today. God really loves you! He has redeemed us and we belong to Him. As we experience this love, we then can effectively minister that love to those around us. Lovers tell one another every day that they love each other. We need to tell our God how much we love Him. Jesus has told us in His Word over and over again how much He loves us. We can be effective in ministering to others as we experience our God's acceptance and love in our own lives.

331 | Partner with Jesus

We are privileged to partner together with God and be involved in what He is doing on the earth today. The Bible tells us in John 15:16, *"You did not choose me, but I chose you and appointed you...."*

God chose to use us. When I was a young boy, I played baseball with my school mates. However, since I was not a very good baseball player, sometimes I was not chosen for the team. I can remember standing in a row of young boys, waiting to be picked to play on the team. It felt so good when I was chosen. God wants you to know that He has chosen you to serve on His team. He has appointed you to bear fruit for Him.

Everywhere you go this week, ask Jesus, "Lord, what are You doing around me? Open my spiritual eyes to see as You see. I know that You love me, so how do You want me to be involved in Your work this week?" Maybe He wants you to give an encouraging word to someone or write them a note. Perhaps the Lord will lead you to pray for someone who needs to be encouraged and strengthened. The Lord may call you to minister to some children or listen to someone who has been going through a stressful time in their lives.

I don't know why God chose to use people, but He did. If I was God, I probably would not have chosen to use people. We make so many mistakes as human beings. But God chose to use us for His purposes on this planet. Let's remain secure in His love for us, so we can minister effectively to others in His name.

How does it feel to be a partner with Jesus?

How are you bearing fruit for Jesus?

332 | Decide to obey

In order to be effective as a believer in Jesus Christ, we need to make a decision every day to obey Him as His minister. Paul wrote to the Corinthian church encouraging them to obey the Lord in everything, no matter what came their way. *The reason I wrote you was to see if you would stand the test and be obedient in everything* (2 Corinthians 2:9).

Life is a series of decisions. Today you will make decisions that may affect the rest of your life. Let's be sure to constantly acknowledge the Lord in all of our decision-making, so we can truly partner together with Jesus to be His minister.

Naaman, in the Old Testament, desiring to be healed, came to the prophet Elisha (2 Kings 5). Elisha told him to wash in the Jordan River seven times. At first he reacted negatively, but then he made a decision, at the prompting of his servants, to obey the voice of the prophet. As he washed in the Jordan River, he was made whole. Obedience paid off for Naaman.

It always pays to be obedient. Every day you and I have the opportunity and privilege to be a minister to others. The enemy will try to cause us to be self-centered and think only of ourselves and our own needs and problems. However, when we make a decision in Jesus' name each day to be a partner with Jesus, life takes on a whole new meaning.

I'm very grateful to those who have ministered to me. I'm grateful for the young lady who told me about Jesus Christ many years ago. I'm grateful for a

How do you obey Jesus in your decision-making?

Biblical Foundations for Life

pastor who was patient with me and ministered to me when I was baptized with the Holy Spirit. I'm grateful for my parents and others who provided for me when I was a young boy as they ministered to me in practical ways. I'm grateful for other believers who have encouraged me. The Bible tells us that much will be required of those who receive much (Luke 12:48). God has been very good to us. He now requires us to minister to others. Let's make a decision today to do it!

333 | Please God rather than man

As you reach out in faith and minister to others, you will find there will be times you will be misunderstood. For example, when Jesus ministered healing to the blind man, both Jesus and the man who was healed were misunderstood. When the religious leaders asked the blind man if he thought Jesus was a sinner or not, he replied, *"...Whether he is a sinner or not, I don't know. One thing I do know. I was blind but now I see!"* (John 9:25).

This man refused to defend himself. He simply spoke the truth. When you and I choose to obey the living God and minister to others in Jesus' name, we should not be surprised if there are times we are misunderstood. Remember—it is God whom we serve first, not man. We will find that everyone will not always understand. Jesus and His apostles were misunderstood many times. In fact, Paul, the apostle, writes, *"Am I now trying to win the approval of men, or of God? Or am I trying to please men? If I were still trying to please men, I would not be a servant of Christ"* (Galatians 1:10).

Pleasing God must be our top priority. If we desire to please people rather than please God, we are no longer effective as ministers of Jesus Christ. When I was baptized with the Holy Spirit, many people misunderstood—even well-meaning people. Sometimes, when I have the privilege of leading people to faith in Jesus Christ, their friends and family members have been upset at me. But this is the price we may have to pay as believers in Jesus Christ who are called to minister to others.

When we minister to others in Jesus' name, we are called to love them and speak in a way that brings God's peace and blessing on them. *If it is possible, as far as it depends on you, live at peace with everyone* (Romans 12:18). However, we cannot focus on pleasing others more than pleasing Jesus. The early apostles declared boldly, *"We ought to obey God rather than men"* (Acts 5:29).

334 | God has chosen you

One of the greatest ways for us to experience and continue to build a love relationship with the Lord is to partner with Him. He desires to do His greater works through us. *I tell you the truth, anyone who has faith in me will do what I have been doing. He will do even greater things than these, because I am going to the Father. And I will do whatever you ask in my name, so that the Son may bring glory to the Father. You may ask me for anything in my name, and I will do it* (John 14:12-14).

During the year that I was engaged to be married, we spent much of our

Did you ever endeavor to live at peace with someone, but had to obey God first?

time in ministry to young people. As we partnered together in ministry, the Lord allowed us to get to know one another better. This same concept is true in our relationship with our Lord Jesus. As we partner with Jesus and minister to others, we will continue to get to know Him more intimately.

Keep your "spiritual eyes" open. What is Jesus doing in your life, in the lives of your loved ones or in the lives of those He has placed around you? How has He called you to partner with Him to minister and serve others? Expect the Lord to use you today, and remember ...*we have this treasure in jars of clay to show that this all-surpassing power is from God and not from us* (2 Corinthians 4:7).

We have the treasure, our Lord Jesus Christ, within us. The power we have to minister to others is not of us—it is from Him. We are weak "jars of clay," but Jesus lives powerfully within our human weakness.

When you lay hands on sick people and pray, expect them to recover. Christ lives in you! As you speak words of encouragement to others, expect the Lord to use you to boost their faith. And never forget—God, the King of the whole universe, has chosen *you* as one of His choice ministers!

What are the results of being a partner with the Lord (John 14:12-14)?

335 | Teaching with Confidence

One of the ways we minister to others is by teaching God's Word. Most people who are good at teaching do not come by their ability naturally. They have learned certain skills and put them into practice.

Let me share with you five simple keys I have learned to help make teaching less stressful so you can be more effective as a teacher.

Key 1: An effective teacher loves people

To be an effective teacher, you must have a genuine love for the people you teach. Loving and serving people overflows out of your love for Jesus. Teaching others one-on-one or in a small group is simply imparting truth to others that you love. Ask God to give you a genuine love for the people you teach.

Key 2: Pray, pray, pray!

In order for a teaching to become a part of our lives so we can impart it to others, it must be bathed in prayer. Luke 6:12 tells us how Jesus prayed: "Now it came to pass in those days that He went out to the mountain to pray, and continued all night in prayer to God." Prayer will prepare people's hearts and cause the teaching we give to be received, so they can be changed and become more like Jesus.

Key 3: Teach the Word, not your opinions

Someone once said that opinions are like the nose on your face; everyone has one! A teacher needs to teach the Word, not ideas and opinions. Our opinions will never change anyone's life; only the Word of God changes lives. Teachers need to "Preach the word! Be ready in season and out of season" (II Timothy 4:2). God's Word stands up by itself. It is powerful.

Biblical Foundations for Life

List the five keys to teaching with confidance

Key 4: Use visuals and stories and illustrations

Most people are visual learners. Mental pictures always help to focus a message and make it easier to remember. Be practical in your teaching and use illustrations people can readily understand. Jesus constantly used parables or story illustrations that conveyed a spiritual meaning.

Key 5: Teach with enthusiasm. . . it's a sin to be boring!

Did you ever sit in a meeting in which the speaker droned on endlessly and practically put you to sleep? God has called us to minister His life when we teach. It is not the only the words themselves that are going to cause people to listen, but how we say them. Revelation 3:19 tells us to "repent and become enthusiastic about the things of God." Enthusiasm is a choice. We need to realize that we are preparing people for eternity—it is important to capture people's attention by being enthusiastic.

Apply these five keys to your life and enjoy ministering the truth of the Word of God to others!

FOUNDATION 12

The Great Commission

336 | Introduction to foundation 12

As disciples of Jesus Christ, our marching orders are to go and make disciples. God has called us as His church to touch every nation of the world, but we must ask the Lord where He has called us to specifically. Although some believers will go to another country to make disciples, many believers will reach out to others right where they live.

One effective way of making disciples is by mentoring others as a spiritual father or mother. This task is for every one of us.

Spiritual fathers and mothers are those who gently help develop and encourage those whom they mentor to walk the path of becoming spiritual fathers and mothers themselves. This kind of mentoring challenges all believers to both have spiritual fathers and mothers, and to become spiritual parents, thus producing lasting and far-reaching results. In fact, this entire series of Biblical Foundation teachings were written to serve as a tool for any believer who is willing and obedient to make disciples according to the plan of our Lord Jesus Christ.

God wants to use you to change the world! He meets us right where we are. I was a young chicken farmer when God called me to start discipling others. I am so grateful for the privilege the Lord has given me over many years to become a spiritual father to many others who have gone much farther ahead of me in influence than I have ever gone. This is the call from God for all of us, to become a disciple and to make disciples to bring glory to God.

As believers in Christ, we are all commanded by the Lord to reach people from all nations (Matthew 28:19). It happens one person at a time as we obey the Lord each day.

What are our "marching orders" from the Lord?

Biblical Foundations for Life

PART 1 — WHAT IS THE GREAT COMMISSION?

What is a commission?

Where are you called to make disciples?

337 | Go and make disciples

After Jesus had risen from the dead and was ready to go back to His Father in heaven, He called His twelve disciples together and gave them some last minute instructions. We often refer to this as the "Great Commission." We read about it in Matthew 28:18-20. *Then Jesus came to them and said, "All authority in heaven and on earth has been given to me. Therefore go and make disciples of all nations, baptizing them in the name of the Father and of the Son and of the Holy Spirit, and teaching them to obey everything I have commanded you. And surely I am with you always, to the very end of the age."*

Wouldn't you like to have been there when Jesus gave these last minute "marching orders" to His disciples? Even though He would leave them to go to be with His heavenly Father, He promised to be with the disciples to the end.

Their mission on earth would be to make disciples in all nations. Jesus is still giving this commission to us today. As disciples of Jesus Christ, our marching orders are to go and make disciples.

A *commission* is *a set of orders or instructions*. "Going" is not an option with Jesus' instructions to make disciples of all the nations. Some Bible scholars tell us that the word "go" when translated from the original Greek language implies "having gone." In others words, as we live our lives for Jesus Christ, God has already called us to make disciples wherever we are. We may fulfill this call on the job, in our families, in our communities, in the church or on the mission field. Everywhere we go, we are called to make disciples.

In this Biblical Foundation book, *The Great Commission*, we will learn what it means to go as a spiritual force (army) to evangelize, make disciples and mentor others and see the kingdom of God advance! We will discover an effective way of making disciples is by mentoring others in a spiritual father or mother capacity. Spiritual fathers and mothers are those who gently help develop and encourage those they mentor to walk the path of becoming spiritual fathers and mothers themselves. This kind of training by mentoring challenges all believers to both have and become spiritual parents, thus producing lasting and far-reaching results. In fact, this book of Biblical Foundations was written to serve as a tool for any believer who is willing and obedient to make disciples according to the plan of our Lord Jesus Christ.

338 | Reach the nations

An important part of the Great Commission is sending missionaries to areas of the world that have never heard the good news of Jesus Christ. There are many groups of people in areas of the world who have never heard the gospel. Christians are commanded by the Lord to reach people from all nations...*therefore go and make disciples of all nations*...(Matthew 28:19).

God has called us as believers in Jesus Christ to carry the gospel to the very ends of the earth. Missionaries are those who have heard the call of God to live out their witness for Jesus within another culture in a region of the world unfamiliar with the gospel. They hear God's heart to carry the news of eternal salvation to those dying without truth. Missionaries want to express their faith in the language of the common person in the country in which they live. They go into a nation, learn to speak the language and live among the people to explain the gospel and love people as they are drawn into the kingdom of God.

A person called to be a missionary wants to see the gospel penetrate the hearts of people and the societies in which they live. As they live in their "adopted" nation, they reach out to those the Lord places in their lives. God is looking for men and women who will go as missionaries to live out their faith in Christ in their new surroundings. Perhaps God will use your life to bring the message of salvation to needy people in another country.

All of us are called to be involved in missions in some way. Some are called to go while others are called to both pray for missionaries and to support them financially. Ask the Lord to reveal His plan to you regarding world missions.

339 | The strategy

The Great Commission of our Lord Jesus Christ is really very simple. It is a call to make disciples. You may ask, "How do we go to all the world to make disciples?" We start right where we are! God has called us as His church to touch every nation of the world, but we must ask the Lord where He has called us specifically. Although some believers will go to another country to make disciples, many believers will reach out to others right where they live. God places people all around us we can disciple and train.

Disciples are made one at a time. Jesus ministered to multitudes of people, but He spent most of His time with just twelve disciples. Jesus had different levels of relationships among those He ministered to. John was probably Jesus' closest friend, according to John 13:23. John was joined by Peter and James, another circle of intimate friends Jesus had. The rest of the twelve disciples comprised another level of friendships for Jesus. Jesus also spent time with seventy of His disciples as well as with the 120 who witnessed Him ascending to His Father in heaven (Acts 1:15).

So then, in the same way Jesus had levels of friendships, you will also have various spheres of friendships. The Lord desires for you to walk closely with a few people at a time so that you can "pour your life" into them. The church of Jesus Christ is built through relationships according to 1 Peter 2:5. *You also, like living stones, are being built into a spiritual house....* Each of us is a building stone for God to use in building His kingdom. We are built together and are held together by these God-ordained relationships.

God's intention is to raise up spiritual parents who are willing to nurture spiritual children and help them grow up in their Christian lives. Billy Graham was once asked what he would do if he wanted to impact a city. His plan was

Where are we commissioned to carry the gospel, according to Matthew 28:19?

How can we practically obey the Lord to reach the world?

How are disciples made?

Think of your spheres of friendships; how can you make disciples within those spheres?

simplistic and strategic. He would find a few key men in the city, spend time with them, and literally pour his life into them, training them in the things the Lord had shown him. As their spiritual father, he then would encourage each of these men to do the same—to find other men and to pour their lives into them. This is the essence of discipleship and spiritual parenting. The renowned evangelist believed he could see an entire city affected for Christ through this strategy. I heartily agree. The Lord is bringing back the truth of discipleship and spiritual parenting to the church of Jesus Christ.

340 | Relationships last forever

Why is a small group a more effective setting for discipling than a larger group?

The Lord has called us to build relationships with one another. Relationships, although they may change, last forever. When you and I get to heaven, all that is really going to count is the relationship we have with God and with one another. Church buildings and church programs will crumble, but relationships last throughout eternity. The early church met "house to house" so they could experience family-type relationships to the fullest. Relationships were the key to the kingdom of God as they met in each other's homes to nurture, equip and serve each other. *So continuing daily with one accord in the temple, and breaking bread from house to house, they ate their food with gladness and simplicity of heart, praising God and having favor with all the people. And the Lord added to the church daily those who were being saved* (Acts 2:46-47 NKJ).

New people were continually added to the church family because these early Christians practiced loving one another. They met in small groups so that disciples could be made more easily. More and more churches today utilize small groups because they are a place where everyone's gifts and talents can be exercised and experienced. In small groups, fellow Christians can pray for one another and experience God personally as they obey God's mandate to make disciples.

You see, making disciples does not just happen. Pray and ask God to show you those relationships He desires for you to build so you can "pour your life" into others and help them become mature believers in Jesus Christ. The Word of God has power to transform lives.

I am not ashamed of the gospel, because it is the power of God for the salvation of everyone who believes: first for the Jew, then for the Gentile (Romans 1:16).

For the message of the cross is foolishness to those who are perishing, but to us who are being saved it is the power of God (1 Corinthians 1:18).

The gospel is powerful! Some people have a career of handling dynamite, knowing just how to blow holes in sides of mountains in order to construct roads. The explosive properties of dynamite, when used properly, are quite effective. We can be effective, too, when we realize we can spread the gospel which will be explosive in a positive way in our communities to change lives! During the Welsh Revival of the early 1900's, many police officers had nothing to do; crime had diminished due to the impact of the gospel. The police force instead formed quartets and sang for community functions!

341 | Your life is read like a book

Paul, the apostle, instructed the early believers to follow his life-style as he followed Christ. *Imitate me, just as I also imitate Christ* (1 Corinthians 11:1 NKJ).

People will imitate us when our lives imitate a love for God and others. They will be attracted to Jesus because of seeing His character in our lives. Do you know that the only spiritual book that some people ever read is the book of your life? In fact, the Bible says in 2 Corinthians 3:2-3, "*You yourselves are our letter, written on our hearts, known and read by everybody. You show that you are a letter from Christ, the result of our ministry, written not with ink but with the Spirit of the living God, not on tablets of stone but on tablets of human hearts.*"

In the Old Testament, the laws of God were written on the tablets of stone at Mount Sinai. But now, under the new covenant of Christ, the Holy Spirit writes God's law in people's hearts. This internal law consists of our love for God and others. People "read" our lives like a book. This is a tremendous privilege, because we are modeling the kingdom of God to those around us as people watch our lives.

If you are a parent, people watch how you relate to your children. If non-believers play sports with you, you have the privilege of showing them godly attitudes as you play. In your home, workplace, community, or school, people are watching to see if your life really exemplifies the principles of God. If they see you fail or make a mistake, they will hopefully also see you repent and make it right. People are looking for real Christians, not religious people who live by a legalistic set of man-made laws. They are looking for people with the love of God written on their hearts.

My life has been most profoundly changed through watching the example of others who have lived their Christian lives in front of me. Although I have enjoyed reading good books and listening to great preachers, the most powerful impact that Christ has had in my life comes from seeing Him modeled through other believers. Sometimes those that I've been patterning my life after have made mistakes. But I've also seen their sincere repentance. Their example has spurred me on to "love and good deeds" (Hebrews 10:24). I'm eternally grateful for those the Lord has placed around me to help me grow in my Christian life and be conformed to the image of Jesus Christ.

342 | Major on Jesus; minor on differences

One of the reasons many of God's people have lost sight of making disciples is because the enemy has deceived them, causing them to focus on problems and differences in the church. We need to focus on Jesus and on making disciples. Matthew 6:33 tells us, "*But seek first his kingdom and his righteousness....*"

God's kingdom is simply the King, Jesus Christ, and His domain. God is the ruler and the King of the whole universe. We are His servants and a part of His domain. His kingdom includes every believer who names the name of Jesus Christ. It includes every congregation and family of churches who honor Him as Lord and believe in His Word.

Who should we imitate (1 Corinthians 11:1)?

Describe a time you saw Christ in someone and it influenced your life.

What do you think the spotless bride of Christ will look like?

His kingdom has variety. When I have the opportunity to attend a family reunion, I am amazed at how different each of us looks, even with some common characteristics. Just as each family has its own distinctive characteristics, every congregation, denomination, or family of churches in God's kingdom has its own distinguishing characteristics. Instead of majoring on the differences, the Lord's desire is for us to major on Jesus and the things we can agree on.

For example, some Christians may have a personal conviction as to whether or not they should celebrate certain holidays. We need to be careful that we do not allow these issues to divide us. The Bible tells us, *"One man considers one day more sacred than another; another man considers every day alike. Each one should be fully convinced in his own mind"* (Romans 14:5).

We need to know what we believe about these minor issues and not be pressured by others into seeing these issues in exactly the same way. We should also be careful not to try to force everyone else to believe as we do on these minor issues.

We are called to join together in unity to build His kingdom. Let's focus on Jesus and on fulfilling His Great Commission. When we get to heaven, we will probably all find out that we were wrong about certain things. It's reassuring to know that Jesus is committed to us, regardless! In Jesus' prayer for believers in John 17:20-21, He prays for their spiritual unity. *My prayer is not for them alone. I pray also for those who will believe in me through their message, that all of them may be one, Father just as you are in me and I am in you. May they also be in us so that the world may believe that you have sent me.*

Our oneness is based on our common relationship to Jesus. We do not have to think exactly alike, but God wants His children to have the same basic attitudes toward God's truth as revealed in His Word. The devil has tried to divide the church of Jesus Christ for generations. Do not allow the devil to use you to criticize His church. Jesus Christ is coming back for a church who is in love with Him and with one another. Our God is coming back for a spotless bride… *to present her to himself as a radiant church, without stain or wrinkle or any other blemish, but holy and blameless* (Ephesians 5:27).

Although the church is far from perfect, we are being conformed into the image of Christ and becoming the spotless bride our Lord Jesus has called us to be.

343 | Prayer, evangelism and discipleship

Jesus' life was characterized by the basic values of prayer, evangelism and discipleship. These basic values characterizing the life of Jesus remind me of a three-legged stool. I live in a farming community. Many of those who have grown up on a farm can remember their parents using a three-legged milking stool to sit on while milking the cows each morning and evening. Why were there only three legs on the stool? Because no matter where you would set the stool on the barn floor, it would always be stable.

In the same way, we believe God has given His church a three-legged stool of truth as He uses prayer, evangelism and discipleship to build His church. When we give our lives to help others by praying for them, reaching out to them and discipling them, the Lord will make sure we are blessed in return. In fact, the greatest way to be blessed is to do what the scripture says in Luke 6:38. *Give, and it will be given to you. A good measure, pressed down, shaken together and running over, will be poured into your lap. For with the measure you use, it will be measured to you.*

Ecclesiastes 11:1 tells us, "*Cast your bread upon the waters, for after many days you will find it again.*" Taking the time and effort to reach out to disciple and mentor another person may look like you are throwing away your chance for having your own needs met, but by sowing into others' lives, we are promised to reap a return. Proverbs 11:25 says, "*...he who refreshes others will himself be refreshed.*"

A friend once told us about a time she was sick and needed to be healed. Instead of focusing on her own problem, she started to pray for someone else who needed healing. During the prayer, the Lord miraculously touched our friend's body and brought healing into her life. As she refreshed someone else, she was refreshed.

When we pour our lives out for others, what are we promised in Luke 6:38?

In Proverbs 11:25?

Biblical Foundations for Life

PART 2

How often should we encourage each other, according to Hebrews 3:13?

_____

_____

_____

_____

_____

How do you encourage others?

_____

_____

_____

_____

_____

READY FOR ACTION! SPIRITUAL WARFARE

344 | We are a spiritual army

Throughout the scriptures, Christians are exhorted to be spiritual soldiers, fighting in spiritual battles. Imagine how absurd it would be if all you did in the army was go to meetings to learn how to be in the army. True soldiers do more than go to meetings! They have to endure hardship and suffering in the world. *Endure hardship with us like a good soldier of Christ Jesus* (2 Timothy 2:3). They engaged in warfare.

Likewise, in God's kingdom, we are called to be a spiritual army, willing to endure suffering and difficulties as we help other people come out of spiritual darkness into the kingdom of light. The reason Christians get together in small groups or in larger church meetings is to be trained from the Word of God so they can go out into the world as victorious spiritual soldiers. God has called us to help people come to know Jesus Christ.

The church is like an army with a medical unit. If God's soldiers get wounded, they can receive healing and get back on the battlefield. As the church, we can help people come to know Jesus Christ and grow in Him. God is building His kingdom. His kingdom is made up of many different churches, families of churches, and denominations who are called to work together throughout the world.

We must encourage other Christians to continue in the faith...*encourage one another daily...*(Hebrews 3:13a). Let's encourage and strengthen one another so we can stand together as a strong army, preparing for the return of our Lord Jesus. We are called to encourage people every day throughout the body of Christ through cards, texts, phone calls and acts of kindness. The devil lies to God's people by telling them they are no good, that they will never fulfill the Lord's purpose for their lives. God wants us to build His people up and strengthen and encourage them. We counteract the lies of the devil by speaking the truth of God's Word to others and encouraging them.

In this part, we will look at the weapons of spiritual warfare the Lord has given us as we accomplish the Great Commission.

345 | Prayer—A spiritual weapon to wage war

Spiritual warfare is real. The spirit world is real. Two major tactics of the enemy are to first make us believe he is not real, and secondly to produce an overemphasis on him. Some people choose to believe the devil is just a fairy tale—a guy in a red costume with pointed ears and a tail. Just because we cannot see the devil does not mean he is not real. We cannot see radar, radio waves or nuclear radioactivity, but they are still very real.

Other people blame everything on demons and the devil. They overemphasize his power instead of the Lord's. We must keep our focus on Jesus, not on the enemy. Sometimes, instead of blaming everything on demons and the devil, there may be an area in our lives the Lord wants to discipline. We must continually war against those things that limit God's work in our lives.

How does a Christian wage war? We must be strong in the Lord and put on the whole armor of God to engage in our spiritual conflict with evil. We wage this spiritual warfare by the power of the Holy Spirit (Romans 8:13). Paul tells us in Ephesians 6:10-12 to put on spiritual armor like a soldier does so we can stand against Satan's schemes. *Finally, be strong in the Lord and in his mighty power. Put on the full armor of God so that you can take your stand against the devil's schemes. For our struggle is not against flesh and blood, but against the rulers, against the authorities, against the powers of this dark world and against the spiritual forces of evil in the heavenly realms.*

Our fight is not with people; the real war is with the demons of hell, the angels of darkness. The only weapons to which they respond are spiritual weapons. Prayer is a powerful spiritual weapon against the powers of darkness. 2 Corinthians 4:3-4a tells us, "*And even if our gospel is veiled, it is veiled to those who are perishing. The god of this age has blinded the minds of unbelievers, so that they cannot see the light of the gospel....*"

Satan blinds the minds of people who do not believe. Those who do not submit themselves to Jesus are under Satan's rule. He "veils" their eyes to the truth of the gospel to keep them from believing in Jesus Christ. Imagine driving down a road and seeing a sign alerting you that a bridge is washed out. You immediately know you should follow the detour. Now imagine a drunk driver seeing the same sign. With his impaired judgment, he may read the sign without truly comprehending the dangers. It is possible he may drive off the edge of the bridge to his destruction, because he was blinded to the truth. People all around us today are going to hell. The Bible makes it clear that we can pray and bind the powers of darkness in Jesus' name, so that people will see the truth. Matthew 18:18 says, "*I tell you the truth, whatever you bind on earth will be bound in heaven, and whatever you loose on earth will be loosed in heaven.*"

Jesus says we can bind (tie up spiritually) the demonic strongholds that are in people's lives. There is power in prayer. As we bind these strongholds in Jesus' name, people will be set free to hear the gospel and respond to Jesus Christ.

A young man once told me, "The only reason I am a Christian today is because my mother prayed for me." This mother understood the principles of the kingdom of God. Let's get serious about praying for those whom the Lord has placed in our lives and who need to draw closer to Jesus. We can bind the blinding spirits deceiving them so that they can understand and respond to the good news of Jesus Christ.

346 | Truth keeps you grounded

We saw in Ephesians 6:10-12 that before we wrestle with demonic strongholds (principalities and powers), we need to put on the whole armor of God. The next two verses mention the first piece of armor to put on. *Therefore put on the full*

How do we stand against Satan's schemes (Ephesians 6:10-12)?

Biblical Foundations for Life

What ways does the devil try to knock you off your feet and make you ineffective in battle?

How does God's Word, His truth, keep you stable?

How do we obtain righteousness?

How can you be a peace-maker? Explain.

armor of God, so that when the day of evil comes, you may be able to stand your ground, and after you have done everything, to stand. Stand firm then, with the belt of truth buckled around your waist...(Ephesians 6:13-14a).

When Paul, the apostle, was writing this, he was sitting in a prison cell looking at soldiers who surrounded him. He was able to write from a spiritual perspective about what he saw in the natural realm. He was able to stand his ground in his day of trial. Some days may be very easy for you and other days you may find yourself under intense attack from the devil. These attacks may come in the form of depression, oppression, fear or confusion. When the "evil day" comes, we need to learn how to stand as good soldiers of Jesus Christ. If we do not stand firmly, we will get knocked off our feet. We must stand, having "truth buckled around our waist."

The Bible tells us that Jesus Christ is the way, the truth and the life (John 14:6). The armor and each of the weapons strapped fast to the soldiers guarding Paul in his prison cell were stabilized by a belt. This is why we need to have the spiritual belt of truth in place in our lives. We build everything in our Christian lives on the truth of the Word of God and on the truth of Jesus Christ.

Speak the truth of God's Word every chance you get. Quote the scripture to yourself and to others. Remember, God's truth will set you free.

347 | What covers your heart and feet?

As Christian soldiers, our spiritual armor includes a full suit. Ephesians 6:14b-15 continues on to name more spiritual pieces of armor to put on...*with the breastplate of righteousness in place, and with your feet fitted with the readiness that comes from the gospel of peace.*

Righteousness refers to our *right standing with God,* which comes only by faith in Jesus Christ (Romans 4:3-5). Sometimes, we may see ourselves through the eyes of our own mistakes. However, as we repent and come to the cross, God always sees us as righteous. He sees His Son, the Lord Jesus, the perfect lamb that was slain. Whenever we have a problem, the enemy will tell us that God is probably punishing us or something is wrong with us. We must stand against the enemy in Jesus' name. We need to know we are righteous through faith in Jesus Christ.

We also need to make sure our feet are fitted with the "readiness that comes from the gospel of peace." The Lord has called us to walk in peace with our God and with all men. The Bible tells us in James 3:18, *"Now the fruit of righteousness is sown in peace by those who make peace."* We can negotiate life's obstructions more easily if we attempt to live peaceably with others. If peace is broken, it doesn't matter whose fault it is; we are called to be peacemakers and be reconciled to our brothers and sisters in Christ. If we need help, the Lord has provided the elders of the local church as mediators to help with these kinds of difficulties. We need to be ready and prepared to declare that the gospel of Jesus Christ brings peace with God and peace with our fellow man.

Therefore, if you are offering your gift at the altar and there remember that your brother has something against you, leave your gift there in front of the altar. First go and be reconciled to your brother; then come and offer your gift (Matthew 5:23-24).

If it is possible, as far as it depends on you, live at peace with everyone (Romans 12:18).

The Lord asks us to do all we can to pursue peace with others, and then trust Him to do the rest. Only God can change people's hearts and cause them to be reconciled.

348 | Hold your shield of faith in place

The piece of armor that a soldier really relied upon was the shield. The soldier's shield was a two foot by four foot shield behind which he stood in battle. It was an overall defense against attack because he could turn it in every direction to stop the arrows aimed at him. *In addition to all this, take up the shield of faith, with which you can extinguish all the flaming arrows of the evil one* (Ephesians 6:16).

How do we defend ourselves from Satan's "flaming arrows"?

When you and I look at our circumstances, at times we can get discouraged. However, when we protect ourselves with our shield of faith and believe that God's Word is true regardless of our circumstances, we can come through victoriously.

The fiery arrows of the enemy may include arrows of doubt, depression, condemnation, fear or confusion. The list goes on and on. We need to keep up our spiritual shields, so that when the enemy shoots arrows our way, we can respond with faith. Remember, "Faith comes by hearing, and hearing by the word of God" (Romans 10:17). Let's speak forth the promises of the Word of God and not allow the fiery arrows of the evil one to begin to burn a hole in our spiritual armor. We need to quickly extinguish them by speaking and believing the Word of God.

Even though we live in an instant society, we need to learn to live by faith. We may not always get results immediately, but we should continue to believe God's Word as truth, even in the midst of seemingly insurmountable circumstances. God is faithful. We can trust Him as we keep our shield of faith held high.

A few years ago, I met a lady whose son had strayed from the faith. While he was in rebellion, she continued to believe God would speak to him. She knew the Lord had given her a promise in Isaiah 59:21b...*My words that I have put in your mouth will not depart from your mouth, or from the mouths of your children....* This mother chose to believe God's Word. As she kept her shield of faith high, her son was convicted by the Lord at an unlikely place—a rock and roll concert! Today he is a pastor. Remember, we live by faith and not by sight!

349 | Your helmet and sword

Much of the Christian's battle is in the mind. Neither a Christian nor a soldier fighting a battle would fight very well if he did not have the hope of victory. We need to protect our heads with the helmet of salvation because the hope of salva-

Biblical Foundations for Life

How does the helmet of salvation help us fight the battle?

tion will defend our soul and keep it from the blows of the enemy. The helmet of salvation gives us the hope of continual safety and protection, built on the promises of God. *Take the helmet of salvation...*(Ephesians 6:17a).

Remember, to be *saved* does not only mean *to be set free from sin and live eternally with God*. Salvation also includes *healing, deliverance* and *to be set free from the powers of darkness*. I often travel to nations that do not have the same quality of medical expertise that we have in our western culture. I am amazed at the ability of God's people to truly believe Him for everyday miracles in these settings. It is impossible to figure out how miracles work. We simply accept by faith that God is a God of miracles. Our helmet of salvation keeps us from being confused by the powers of darkness and helps us to rely on God's great salvation and healing.

Why is the sword of the Spirit so important?

The Lord tells us to take up the final piece of armor—the sword of the Spirit. The sword was the only piece of armor a soldier carried that was offensive as well as defensive. For a Christian, the sword of the Spirit is the powerful Word of God...*and the sword of the Spirit, which is the word of God. And pray in the Spirit on all occasions with all kinds of prayers and requests. With this in mind, be alert and always keep on praying for all the saints* (Ephesians 6:17b-18).

When we are armed with the truth of God's Word, the Holy Spirit living within us helps us deal with temptations that come our way. We do not rely on our own wisdom, but on the Lord's. When we know His Word, we can withstand Satan's lies. As we hide the Word of God in our hearts (Psalms 119:11), we can resist sin.

The Bible tells us that the gates of hell will not prevail against the church of Jesus Christ. As Christians, we are called to take over enemy territory. Do not settle for less. Take the Word of God seriously and confess it, believe it, live it, and expect to experience it in your life.

In order to be alert and stand our ground, the Bible says (Ephesians 6:13) that we must take up the whole armor of God. We must put on the belt of truth and the breastplate of righteousness. We prepare ourselves with the gospel of peace and take up the shield of faith. In addition, we use the helmet of salvation and the sword of the Spirit. All this armor is a protection and helps us to pray effectively. Paul, the apostle, says we should pray always and be watchful as we pray for all the saints. We are called to pray for one another. Spiritual warfare calls for intensity of prayer. It is not an option, it is a life and death matter.

350 | Ready for action!

We really do need to pray for one another. Prayer allows us to enter the conflict of spiritual warfare and win the victory by working with God in this way. Paul, the apostle, asks for prayer in Ephesians 6:19-20 so he could be bold in his witness for Christ. *Pray also for me, that whenever I open my mouth, words may be given me so that I will fearlessly make known the mystery of the gospel, for which*

I am an ambassador in chains. Pray that I may declare it fearlessly, as I should.

The Lord wants us to be bold witnesses for Jesus Christ, but boldness comes from our prayer closet. As we pray for those in our small groups, churches, youth groups, communities, homes and workplaces, we will experience the boldness of the Lord to proclaim His Word to our generation. One time, while I was in the nation of Scotland, I found myself compelled to speak to a young man that I met on the street about Jesus. I knew that my boldness to speak out came because of prayer warriors who were praying for me.

If Paul, the apostle, needed others to pray for him to be bold, how much more do we need to be praying for one another to be bold today? In order for us to fulfill the Great Commission, we must be people of prayer. Remember to pray for missionaries the Lord has placed in your life to be bold for the Lord. And as we put on the full armor of God and pray each day, we will listen to our heavenly Father for orders from heaven. Then we will experience Jesus using us to make disciples in our generation.

It has been my experience that most spiritual failure happens when Christians fail to keep their spiritual armor in place. When you get up in the morning, declare that your armor is in place. Declare that you have placed the belt of truth around your waist. You are righteous through faith in Jesus Christ; the breastplate is in place. You have peace with God through your Lord Jesus Christ (Romans 5:1) because you are justified through faith. You walk in complete forgiveness toward anyone who's hurt you and you have pursued peace with them as much as possible (Romans 12:18). You have taken up the shield of faith and will not allow the fiery darts of the enemy to hurt you. You will quench them in Jesus' name through faith in the Word of God. The helmet of salvation is secure. You know you are born again and that Jesus Christ has changed your life. You take the Word of God and boldly, aggressively confront the powers of darkness in Jesus' name. You pray as a soldier who has properly placed on the armor that the Lord Jesus has given. You are ready for action! The world around us is waiting for us to declare the truth that will set them free.

When we pour our lives out for others, what are we promised in Luke 6:38?

In Proverbs 11:25?

Biblical Foundations for Life

PART 3

REACHING THE LOST AND MAKING DISCIPLES

351 | True evangelism

God places a much higher priority on evangelism than we usually do. Why? Because God truly loves people. *"God so loved the world..."* (John 3:16). As Christians, we often become ingrown and look within instead of trying to find ways to help people around us. God has called us to look outward. God's heart is for the world—for people. Evangelism is sharing the good news of Jesus Christ with others.

Many times Christians have a warped understanding of what evangelism really is. Some think that evangelism means they must knock on doors and pass out gospel tracts. Although this can be an effective way to share your faith, the Lord may not call you to evangelize in that way. To others, evangelism means going to crusades. Praise God for crusades, but for most Christians, crusade evangelism is not the type of evangelism they are called to.

I believe evangelism for most people is being so filled with Jesus that wherever they go, they discover people who need a relationship with God. Our responsibility is to share with people what God has done in our lives and help to encourage them to receive the good news of Jesus Christ into their lives.

In the story of the Good Samaritan (Luke 10:33-37), the Samaritan found a man lying in the gutter and helped him even though some of the religious folks of his day passed on by without lending a hand. The Samaritan practiced the principles of the kingdom of God by loving the person whom God brought into his path. Jesus made it very clear that we should *love the Lord...and love your neighbor as yourself* (Luke 10:27).

Loving God is a call to love others. Compassion for the lost and those in need is a sign that we really love God. After Jesus told the story of the Good Samaritan, he quizzed a nearby religious leader, asking, *"'Who was a neighbor to the man who fell into the hands of robbers?' The expert in the law replied, 'The one who had mercy on him.' Jesus told him, 'Go and do likewise'"* (Luke 10:37).

We must operate in mercy and love. In Luke 15, Jesus gave three more stories about loving those around us. The first story was the parable of the lost sheep. Out of 100 sheep, one got lost, and the shepherd searched until he found it. The second parable involved a lost coin. The owner of the coin looked all day for it, putting all his effort into finding it. The third story is that of a prodigal son who took half of his father's fortune and left home to do his own thing. The Bible tells us his father waited for him and then reached out lovingly when his son returned.

You see, God places a high priority on people who are hurting or lost. God has called us to reach out to those around us, even the "unlovely," so He can fulfill His purposes through us. Jesus has called us to be fishers of men. *"Come, follow me,"* Jesus said, *"and I will make you fishers of men"* (Mark 1:17).

Let's learn how we can "catch men" and lead them to faith in Jesus Christ.

What does evangelism mean to you?

How did Jesus evangelize?

352 | The *oikos* principle

How did Jesus and the early church lead people to faith? We sometimes call this the "*oikos* principle." The Greek word *oikos* means *household* or *family*. Our *oikos* includes those with whom we relate on a regular basis. *Oikos* refers to one's personal community or those with whom we are in relationship.

The scriptures tell us in Acts 10 that there was a man named Cornelius—a devout man who feared God with all his household, gave generously to the poor, and prayed to God regularly. One day Cornelius received a supernatural visitation from God through a vision. God told him to send messengers and call for Peter who would give him a message from God. Peter came to meet Cornelius who was...*expecting them and had called together his relatives and close friends* (Acts 10:24). Cornelius invited his *oikos* (relatives and friends) to this meeting with Peter and many of those people came to know Jesus Christ.

Another story showing how God used someone's *oikos* to bring people to Jesus occurs in Acts 16. Paul and Silas were in prison when an earthquake opened all the doors. The jailer was going to kill himself because he thought the prisoners would escape and he would be held responsible. Paul told him to refrain from harming himself because all the prisoners were safe. When Paul shared the Word of God with the jailer, his entire *oikos* (household) came to know Jesus Christ. All of us have people in our lives who are placed there by the Lord. They are the people with whom we can share the gospel most effectively and easily. No matter where we live in the world, the *oikos* strategy or building by relationship is the most natural way of fulfilling the Great Commission. People want the truth. They are waiting for Christians whom they can trust to give them the truth.

You may want to list your *oikos* members on a sheet of paper. Pray and ask God to show you two or three of the people whom you're most concerned about and begin to pray for these people and reach out to them. If they are unsaved, you will be involved in evangelism. If they are struggling in their Christian lives, God may call you to be involved in discipleship by becoming a spiritual father or mother to them.

The scriptures tell us in the book of Acts that new believers were *added* to the church daily as they were being saved (Acts 2:47). However, as we continue to read the book of Acts, we see the Lord taking the church another step. God's people began to grow in numbers. *Then the churches throughout all Judea, Galilee, and Samaria had peace and were edified. And walking in the fear of the Lord and in the comfort of the Holy Spirit, they were multiplied* (Acts 9:31 NKJ).

God's will is for us to be *multiplying* ourselves. In order for us to multiply, we need to get our eyes off ourselves and reach out to those who need to experience the life and power of Jesus Christ. We will see God's kingdom expand and our own spiritual growth accelerate. Jesus spent His time here on this earth doing two things—talking to God about people and talking to people about God. He has called us to do the same.

What does "oikos" mean?

List people in your oikos.

Biblical Foundations for Life

353 | Kinds of people in your *oikos*

Explain how you have released your faith in the past week.

There are several groups of people in our *oikos* or personal community. First of all, there are family members and relatives. Your uncle Jack and aunt Sally are all part of your *oikos*, even if they live far away. If you maintain regular contact with them, they are part of your *oikos*. Second, those who share common interests with you are part of your *oikos*. They may play sports with you or share an interest in computers, or sewing...the list goes on. Third, those who live in your geographical location are part of your *oikos*—this, of course, includes your neighbors.

Those with whom you share a common vocation—your fellow employees—would fit into a fourth category. The fifth area of persons that are part of your *oikos* would be others with whom you have regular contact, including your dentist, family doctor, auto mechanic, sales people, school officials, classmates, and so on. People in your *oikos* group will be much more receptive to the gospel because they trust you—you have built a relationship with them.

When Levi invited Jesus for dinner, he invited his *oikos* members or business associates. Luke 5:29 tells us of this occasion. *Then Levi held a great banquet for Jesus at his house, and a large crowd of tax collectors and others were eating with them.*

Because Levi already had a relationship with them, these tax collectors gladly came to listen to what Jesus had to say. Jesus had the opportunity to share with members of Levi's *oikos,* and they were presented with the hope Jesus offered. When we invite our *oikos* to meet Jesus, they have the opportunity to be presented with the truth that will set them free.

Nathanael was Philip's *oikos* member; they lived in the same town. Through their friendship, Philip led Nathanael to faith in Jesus Christ. The Bible tells us in John 1:45 that, "...*Philip found Nathanael and told him, 'We have found the one Moses wrote about in the Law, and about whom the prophets also wrote—Jesus of Nazareth...'*"

The scriptures are filled with examples of people who came to know Jesus through someone with whom they had a relationship. Sometime back, a small group leader in our church received a phone call from a woman in his small group. "Do you have any holy water?" he was asked. The group leader did not grow up in a Roman Catholic tradition and was not expecting this type of request. When he asked her for further details, she shared her concern for her daughter and her daughter's boyfriend. Strange things were happening in their home. An object had jumped off the stove and other unexplainable supernatural things were happening in their house. "May I come over to your daughter and her boyfriend's home to pray?" he asked.

"Oh yes," she explained, "and I want to be there when you come." The small group leader and his wife went over to the young couple's home to pray. After a time of sharing the Word of God, the young man received Jesus Christ as Lord. His girlfriend also expressed a desire to follow the Lord, and they were married a short time later. The demonic occurrences in their home stopped when the couple was set free spiritually. It all happened through a small group *oikos* relationship that expanded to include family *oikos* relationships. *Oikos* evangelism has a way of multiplying outward!

354 | Spend time mentoring others

Jesus Christ called us to make disciples. The key to making disciples can be found in Mark 3:14-15a. *He appointed twelve...that they might be with him and that he might send them out to preach and to have authority....*

Jesus was looking for twelve men with whom He could spend time so that He could show them the principles of the kingdom of God. He wanted His disciples to experience God's principles as He modeled these truths for them through His own life. Discipleship often involves this kind of training through mentoring or modeling.

Jesus reached out to the disciples for companionship and training, so that they might, in turn, go out to minister themselves. Dicipling others is caring for them as friends and training them to grow in their Christian lives. Making disciples is not telling other people what to do. Making disciples is literally laying down our lives for others and taking the time needed to see them grow spiritually. We can pray, encourage and help others focus on the Word of God which gives clear instructions how we should live our lives in Christ.

Biblical discipleship reminds me of serving as a coach for a sports team. The coach's responsibility is to help his players to be the best they can possibly be. Unless we are reaching out and helping others, we become stagnant and ingrown. Like an ingrown toenail, pain will eventually occur. God has called us to reach out to others and train them at the same time.

The Dead Sea is world-renowned "stagnant" sea. Waters run into it, but nothing runs out. There is life in a river, but a sense of death remains in a stagnant pool. When we give out to others, the power and life of God will flow freely through our lives.

List some practical ways we can make ourselves available to train disciples.

355 | Learn and teach by example

I love to play the guitar. I have had the privilege of teaching many others to play the guitar during the past 50 years. In fact, many of my students now play the guitar much better than I. If I taught you how to play the guitar, I would sit down with you and a guitar. I'd show you how to play by teaching you exactly where to hold your fingers on the frets and how to hold the pick as you began to strum.

The same principle applies to the kingdom of God. We are called to train, love and show others how to become disciples of Jesus Christ. You may say, "Larry, I have only been a Christian for less than a year." Great! You can begin to show others what you have learned in the past year. God wants us to immediately reach out to those around us and help them come into the kingdom. The good news is that we don't have to know all the answers. God is the One who has the

What are we responsible for, according to Deuteronomy 29:29?

Biblical Foundations for Life

How can we pass on what we have learned to others?

answers. We can freely share with others that we don't have all the answers, but our God does. In fact, the Bible tells us in Deuteronomy 29:29, *"The secret things belong to the Lord our God, but the things revealed belong to us and to our children forever, that we may follow all the words of this law."*

The Bible makes it clear that we are responsible to act on those things that have been revealed to us by the Lord. Even when we don't have the answers to some of life's problems, the Lord will bring into our lives spiritual fathers or mothers who will be used by the Holy Spirit to help and guide us. Then the Lord will help us to do the same—to serve others and be a spiritual father or mother to them. As we work together, we can see God's kingdom built as dozens and hundreds of lives in our communities are changed through the power of Jesus Christ.

Imagine, for a moment, every Christian you know, training two or three others in the basic truths and experiences of walking with Jesus. These "disciples" would be encouraged to do the same. The results would be astounding. In fact, if you and I each discipled another believer every six months and encouraged each person we disciple to do the same, and the pattern was repeated every six months, in less than thirty years the entire population of the world could be won to Christ!

356 | Hospitality in homes

What does hospitality mean to you?

Do you know that one of the most powerful ways we can be involved in discipleship and evangelism is through hospitality? Hospitality is a biblical principle that simply means *cheerfully sharing food and shelter and spiritual refreshment with those that God brings into our lives.* 1 Peter 4:9 tells us, *"Offer hospitality to one another without grumbling."*

I believe the Lord wants to use our homes to build His church. Our homes are to be used as places where people can be encouraged, filled with the Holy Spirit and come to know Jesus Christ. The presence of God is in your home because Jesus Christ lives in you.

How should we offer hospitality, according to 1 Peter 4:9?

Because Christ lives in you, you can be assured that every place you go, the presence of God will be there—in your home, at school, at the local restaurant, or at the store. God's kingdom can be built as we eat breakfast with another person, laugh together, cry together, or just have fun sharing life together. The principle of hospitality can be a tremendous blessing as we make disciples and fulfill the Great Commission.

The book of Acts opens and closes in a home. Homes are so important to the work of the kingdom of God. Dr. Cho, the pastor of the largest church in the world located in Seoul, Korea, was asked the question, "Where is God's address?" His answer was that God's address is *our* address. In other words, God lives inside you and me. Wherever you live, wherever you are, that is where God is. There are many people who would not feel free to go to a church meeting, but they would talk to you while sitting in your house eating a meal or playing a game in your living room.

Romans 12:13 tells us that we should *"practice hospitality."* You may think,

Biblical Foundations for Life

"My home is not nice enough to invite people in." Be assured, when people come into your home, they will sense the presence of God because He lives in you—they won't care about your house. When my wife, LaVerne, and I were first married, much of our hospitality was in a tiny mobile home. We had people coming in and staying overnight, eating with us and praying with us, and they did not care that it was small. Expect the Lord to use your home, no matter what size, to build His kingdom.

357 | Sowing spiritual seeds in others' lives

Praying, reaching the lost and making disciples is a bit like sowing seeds in a garden. When we sow spiritual seeds into people's lives through prayer, encouragement and discipleship, we expect to get a crop eventually. We sow that seed in faith.

If I go out to my garden and dig up the seed every day and say, "I don't think it's growing," I will never get a crop. In the same way, we sow the truth of God's Word into people's lives in faith, knowing that regardless of what we see today, we will get a crop in due time. We know, because we sowed our seeds in faith.

The scriptures tell us in Mark 4, that when we sow the seed of the Word of God into people's lives, several things can happen. For one, individuals may hear God's Word but fail to respond to it because Satan immediately steals it away (v. 15). It is at these times that we should bind demonic bondages in seekers' lives, so they can be free to hear and accept God's Word.

The scriptures also tell us that some people will hear the Word of God and immediately receive it with gladness. However, their roots are shallow, and they only endure for a time. When they go through hard times, they immediately stumble (v. 16).

Others may hear the Word but allow the things of this world to get in the way of their commitment to Christ. *Still others, like seed sown among thorns, hear the word; but the worries of this life, the deceitfulness of wealth and the desires for other things come in and choke the word, making it unfruitful* (Mark 4:18-19). Because of the worries of this life, these people may find the Word of God being choked from their lives. If we sow seeds of encouragement into their lives and pray for them, we can keep the spiritual thorns from choking the Word of God out of their lives. They need some extra assistance during this time. Do you know that some varieties of trees, when first planted, need to have a stake driven into the ground next to the tree? A rope then is tied around the tree and stake until the tree can grow tall and strong enough to hold itself. God has called you and me to be "stakes" for people, helping to stabilize their lives until they can make it on their own.

Finally there are those who hear God's Word and believe and persevere. They will bear fruit according to Mark 4:20. *Others, like seed sown on good soil, hear the word, accept it, and produce a crop—thirty, sixty or even a hundred times what was sown.*

How do you sow spiritual seeds?

What does faith have to do with planting seeds in others' lives?

As the Spirit of God, through us, pours His Word into people's lives, we are going to see a mighty harvest of people coming to know Jesus Christ. Someday we are going to stand before the Lord accompanied by multitudes of others—they are the result of the seeds that were sown—multiplying in numbers by the grace of God.

Have you ever heard of Mordecai Ham? Very few people have heard of him, and yet he has had a profound effect on the nations of the world. While Mordecai was preaching at a revival meeting in a tent, a young man came one evening and gave his life to Jesus. That man's name was Billy Graham. Every person who has come to know Jesus Christ through Billy Graham's ministry is a product of the obedience of a man named Mordecai Ham.

D. L. Moody, a hundred years ago, was responsible for leading more than a million people to Jesus Christ. Yet the man who shared the gospel with Mr. Moody was a common, ordinary man who made a decision to share Christ with the young boys in his Sunday School class. The Bible says the mustard seed is the smallest of all seeds, but grows to be a majestic tree (Matthew 13:31-32). As we are obedient to God in the "little areas," the Lord promises there will be a great spiritual harvest.

The Great Commission is simply sowing seed. Good spiritual seed is sown through prayer, encouragement, and by sharing the Word of God with others. As we continue to sow in obedience, the seed will grow. The multiplication process will continue on and on. Healthy Christians are those who pray and reach out to those whom God brings into their lives. Let's rise up in faith together and labor with Jesus to fulfill the Great Commission.

BE A SPIRITUAL FATHER OR MOTHER

PART 4

358 | The need for spiritual fathers and mothers

Jesus invested three years of His earthly ministry in the lives of twelve men. It was valuable time spent fathering His spiritual children. This time of mentoring prepared and equipped the disciples to "go into all the world" and fulfill the Great Commission.

We briefly mentioned the concept of "spiritual fathering and mothering" earlier in this book. While "discipleship" is similar in that it involves a few people getting together and helping the younger Christian, spiritual parenting has a much wider scope. Spiritual parenting has the intention of developing and encouraging others to walk the path of becoming spiritual fathers and mothers themselves. The spiritual father or mother mentors and trains another, and in doing so, imparts his or her inheritance to the younger Christian.

New Christians desperately need spiritual fathers or mothers to nurture and encourage them in their spiritual walk. The man who served as a pastor in my church for many years told me that when he received Christ, he was in his mid-twenties. A 77-year-old "spiritual father" from his church took him under his wing and discipled him. It made all the difference for this future pastor's spiritual maturity.

Paul, the apostle, told the Corinthian church that they should not overlook the need to make lasting spiritual investments in others' lives. He said they had many guardians or teachers in the church, but not many spiritual fathers and mothers who were willing to spend time nurturing new believers, according to 1 Corinthians 4:14-15. *I am not writing this to shame you, but to warn you, as my dear children. Even though you have ten thousand guardians in Christ, you do not have many fathers....* These Christians were immature as believers because they lacked true fathers to give them an identity and proper training and nurturing. They needed spiritual fathers and mothers who were willing to spend time with them.

Many times, new believers never really grow to their full potential in God because they never had a spiritual parent to care for them. True spiritual parents are sincerely concerned about the welfare of their spiritual children.

359 | God wants to "turn the hearts of the fathers to the children"

Why is raising up spiritual parents who are willing to nurture spiritual children and help them grow up in their Christian lives so important? For one, it is a fulfillment of the Lord's promise in the last days to...*turn the hearts of the fathers to the children, and the hearts of the children to their fathers...*(Malachi 4:6).

The Lord wants to restore harmony among fathers and their children, both naturally and spiritually, so fathers can freely impart their inheritance to the next generation. He wants spiritual fathers and mothers to take up the mantle to train

Why were the Christians immature in 1 Corinthians 4:14-15?

Are you willing to become a spiritual father or mother?

Biblical Foundations for Life

What happens when spiritual sons and daughters are mentored and equipped by spiritual parents?

their children so they no longer flounder in the sea of life. Children need to have the kind of parents in their lives providing the character they need, telling them they are valuable, that they are gifts from God. Parents need to put expectation into children's hearts so that they believe in themselves.

Paul says in verse 17 of 1 Corinthians 4 that he is going to send Timothy to the Corinthian church because he would *remind you of my way of life in Christ Jesus.* As a spiritual father, Paul faithfully trained Timothy. Now Timothy was ready to impart *his* spiritual fatherhood to the Corinthian church. Christian believers need to see spiritual fathering and mothering modeled so they can be equipped to pass on a legacy to the next generation of believers.

Paul trained Timothy, his beloved and trustworthy spiritual son, and now Timothy was coming to train them. Paul trusted Timothy to help the Corinthian church because Paul had trained him like a son. With this example, they would soon be producing their own spiritual sons and daughters. This kind of mentoring relationship of training and equipping sons and daughters was a spiritual investment that could continue to multiply as equipped and mature believers went out into the world to spread the gospel.

360 | Spiritual children go through growth stages

What are the growth stages for a new Christian to become a spiritual parent himself?

According to the Bible, we go through life in stages—as little children, young men, and fathers. At each point in our journey, we function in a particular way and have distinct tasks to perform. John addresses all three spiritual stages in 1 John 2:12-14. *I write to you, little children, because your sins are forgiven you for His name's sake. I write to you, fathers, because you have known Him who is from the beginning. I write to you, young men, because you have overcome the wicked one. I write to you, little children, because you have known the Father. I have written to you, fathers, because you have known Him who is from the beginning. I have written to you, young men, because you are strong, and the word of God abides in you, and you have overcome the wicked one.*

Coming to a place of fatherhood is the cry of God's heart. Since fatherhood is so crucial to God's divine order, He established a natural training ground consisting of "growth stages." Baby Christians grow to fatherhood as they progress through each of these stages. Only then can they receive the heart and revelation of a father or mother.

Our stages as babies in Christ, young men and women, and spiritual fathers and mothers have nothing to do with our chronological age but everything to do with how we eventually progress on to spiritual maturity. Children are expected to grow up. Only then can they become fathers and mothers.

If we fail to take the next steps to become spiritual parents, we remain spiritual babies—spiritually immature and lacking parenting skills. It is sad, but it is this scenario which is often the very case in the church. Many times there is no provision for believers to develop within our church systems.

Nevertheless, with the restoration of New Testament Christianity, as people meet together in small groups, God is providing an ideal setting to develop spiritual parents. Each person is given the opportunity to "do the work of ministry" and connect in vital relationships with each other. Through modeling and impartation, spiritual reproduction happens naturally.

God's intention is to bring new believers to the place of spiritual fatherhood and motherhood after going through spiritual childhood and young adulthood. Paul, the apostle made it his concern to properly instruct everyone so they could be grounded in the faith...*teaching every man in all wisdom, that we may present every man perfect in Christ Jesus* (Colossians 1:28).

The Lord's call has not changed. Every believer, after being equipped, can become a spiritual parent. Meanwhile, we have to progress through the stages of growth.

361 | Growing from spiritual children to young men and women

Spiritual babies in the body of Christ are wonderful! According to 1 John 2:12, they are *children whose sins are forgiven.* This forgiveness of sin puts them in fellowship with God and other believers. Spiritual children or new believers are alive to what they can receive from their Savior. They freely ask the Father when they have a need. Did you ever notice how new believers can pray prayers that seem to be theologically unsound, yet God answers almost every prayer a new believer prays? The Father is quick to take care of these little ones.

A new believer's focus is forgiveness of sins, getting to heaven and getting to know the Father. Like natural babies, they know their Father, although it is not necessarily a thorough knowledge of God. A new believer will often act like a natural child with the marks of immaturity, including instability and gullibility. They will need constant assurance and care. They often do the unexpected because they are still learning what it means to follow Jesus. Spiritual parents are happy to spend extra time with spiritual children in order to guide them in the right direction.

But what happens when spiritual babies do not grow up? Not only new believers are spiritual babies in the church today. Older Christians who lack spiritual maturity are "adults in age" but "babies in spiritual growth." They may be 20, 30, 40 or 50 years of age, Christian believers for years, and have never spiritually matured. They live self-centered life-styles, complaining and fussing and throwing temper-tantrums when things do not go their way. Some do not accept the fact that God loves them for who they are. Others may wallow in self-pity when they fail. Many spiritual children in our churches today desperately need to grow up and move on to the next stage as spiritual young men and women.

Spiritual young men and women no longer have to be spoon-fed. According to 1 John 2:14, "*the Word of God abides in them and they have learned to feed on the Word to overcome the wicked one.*" They don't need to run to others in the church to care for them like babies because they have learned how to apply the

Biblical Foundations for Life

What happens if we fail to go through these stages?

What are some characteristics of spiritual children?

Of spiritual young men and women?

Word to their own lives. When the devil tempts them, they know what to do to overcome him. They use God's Word effectively and powerfully!

Spiritual young men and women must be encouraged (1 Timothy 4:12). They are strong in the Word and Spirit. They have learned to use the strength of spiritual discipline, of prayer and the study of the Word. They are alive to what they can do for Jesus.

On the other hand, the temptations of spiritual youth may be a trap for those who have not yet developed a strong sense of right and wrong. Youth are cautioned to run from their youthful passions that might lead to scandal (2 Timothy 2:22).

Spiritual young men or women may have attained a certain level of spiritual maturity, but they are not yet spiritual parents. They sometimes can become arrogant and dogmatic. After returning from the latest seminar or after reading a recent book, they may think they have all of the answers. They need to be tempered by parenthood. They must become fathers and mothers to experience its joys and disciplines. Again, it bears repeating: becoming a spiritual parent has nothing to do with chronological age; it is a spiritual age!

362 | Spiritual fathers and mothers defined

How do spiritual young men and women become parents?

Just how do spiritual young men and women grow up to become spiritual fathers and mothers? There is only one way—to have children! You can become a spiritual parent either by natural birth (fathering someone you have personally led to Christ) or by adoption (fathering someone who is already a believer but needs to be mentored). Paul led Onesimus to Christ personally, so Onesimus was his natural spiritual son (Philemon 10). Timothy was also Paul's spiritual son, but by spiritual "adoption" because Timothy came to Christ earlier through the influence of his mother and grandmother (Acts 16).

Spiritual fathers and mothers are mature believers who have grown and matured in their Christian walk; they are called *fathers* according to 1 John 2:13. *I write to you, fathers, because you have known Him who is from the beginning....* This implies a profound and thorough knowledge of Jesus through knowing His Word. It also implies a deep sense of acquaintance with Him, by having a passion for Jesus.

Give a definition of a spiritual father or mother.

Mature Christians are awake to their calling to be like Jesus—to be a father like God's Son. They understand what it takes to be a spiritual parent and are willing to become one.

One of the greatest catalysts to maturity as a Christian is to become a spiritual parent. Even if prospective spiritual parents do not feel ready to become parents, as they take a step of faith, and draw on the help and advice of their own spiritual mom and dad, they will find great success and fulfillment.

Spiritual fathers and mothers could be called *mentors* or *coaches* because they are in a place to help sons and daughters negotiate the obstacles of their spiritual journeys. A coach is someone who wants to see you win. A coach tells you that you can make it.

Simply stated, my favorite definition of a spiritual father or mother is: ***A spiritual father or mother helps a spiritual son or daughter reach his or her God-given potential.***

With a mature spiritual parent at their side, sons and daughters will grow strong and learn quickly and naturally by example. The parent teaches, trains, sets a good example, and provides a role model. Spiritual parents raise children's awareness of attitudes or behaviors in their lives that need to be changed. They help new believers take an honest look at their lives and make adjustments so that their actions and behaviors can change.

363 | Our inheritance of spiritual children

Regardless of our own experience—whether or not we have had a spiritual father or mother—we can become a spiritual father or mother to someone the Lord has placed in our lives. Every believer can make a decision to co-labor with Jesus and make disciples by becoming a spiritual father or mother to someone who needs our assistance to grow in the Lord.

So how do we begin? The early Christians did not haphazardly "share their faith." Instead, people were built together, each doing a job, working as a team to accomplish the Great Commission. God will place people in our lives He wants us to reach out to. As we commit ourselves to train them, they will become conformed to Jesus' likeness. As new believers grow in Christ, they also will begin to make disciples, following the parent's example. Abraham was ninety-nine years old when God gave him the promise that he would be the *father of many nations* (Genesis 17:4). Galatians 3:29 says that those who belong to Christ are *Abraham's seed, and heirs according to the promise.* Therefore, as believers, God wants to birth in us "nations," too. These "nations" or groups of people, who come to know God because of our influence, will be our spiritual lineage—they are our posterity in God's kingdom. We have been promised it because we are children of promise. Our God desires to give us a spiritual posterity.

Years ago, I was a spiritual father to Bill, now a missionary in the Caribbean. On a visit to Barbados, Bill told me an interesting history of this island nation. Many of the people who now live in Barbados originally came as slaves from West Africa, specifically the nation of Gambia. Today, native Barbadians are being sent out from Barbados as missionaries to Gambia. Then he said something that moved me deeply, "Larry, do you realize the people being reached in Gambia are part of your spiritual heritage? You were one of my spiritual fathers." At the time I was a spiritual father to Bill, I was a young man myself, a chicken farmer, who led a Bible study of young people. Bill had gone into the world and trained others to go, and the results mushroomed! I was deeply moved! It was as if I was the recipient of a large inheritance!

How can we birth a spiritual lineage according to Galatians 3:29?

Biblical Foundations for Life

What is our spiritual legacy?

How does having and becoming a spiritual parent help you obey the Great Commission?

364 | Go into all the world and leave a legacy!

The promise of spiritual children is for every Christian! God has placed us here on earth because He has called us to become spiritual fathers and mothers in our generation. With this comes the expectation that our spiritual children will have more spiritual children and continue into infinity.

Our inheritance will be all the spiritual children that we can some day present to Jesus Christ. *For what is our hope, our joy, or the crown in which we will glory in the presence of our Lord Jesus when he comes? Is it not you? Indeed, you are our glory and joy* (1 Thessalonians 2:19-20). No matter what you do—whether you are a housewife, a student, a worker in a factory, a pastor of a church, or the head a large corporation—you have the divine blessing and responsibility to birth spiritual children, grandchildren and great grandchildren. You are called to impart to others the rich inheritance that God has promised.

If we would get serious about making disciples one at a time and training them so they could go and make more disciples, it would not take long for every person on the face of the earth to be confronted with the truth of Jesus Christ. This scriptural principle is so simple, yet many times God's people have failed to obey this Great Commission from our Lord Jesus. God has called us and given us His priority to make disciples.

God uses the principle of multiplication through spiritual fathering and mothering. When you and I are obedient to Him, reaching out to one, two, three, four or more people whom the Lord places in our lives, we will literally see God's kingdom being established over the whole world. God wants to establish His kingdom in our generation through the principle of multiplication through spiritual parenting. God's kingdom is built as we love people and spend time with them.

If you desire more training to become a spiritual father or mother, you may want to read my book, *The Cry for Spiritual Fathers and Mothers*. There is also a video training available. Now that you have learned the basic foundations of the Christian life through this *Biblical Foundation Series*, pray about helping someone else grow in the Lord and teach them what you have learned!

I believe an end-time sweeping revival is just around the corner. God's people need to be alert and ready to accommodate the great harvest this will bring into the kingdom of God. Spiritual parents must be ready to obey His call and take young Christians under their wings.

We are containers of the Holy Spirit, and God is going to pour His Spirit out on us that flows to others. Acts 2:17 tells us, *"In the last days,"* God says, *"I will pour out my Spirit on all people. Your sons and daughters will prophesy, your young men will see visions, your old men will dream dreams."*

Someday, you and I will stand before the Living God. I do not want to stand there by myself. How about you? Let's stand there with a multitude of our spiritual children, grandchildren and their future descendants! The Lord wants to give you a spiritual legacy. God has called you to be a spiritual parent!

365 | My Personal Challenge for You

God wants to establish His kingdom in our generation through spiritual fathering and mothering and making disciples, one person at a time. God's kingdom is built as we love people and spend time with them.

The promise of spiritual children is for every Christian! God has placed us here on earth to become spiritual fathers and mothers in our generation. With this comes the expectation that our spiritual children will also have spiritual children themselves as they pour their lives into the next generation…our eternal legacy that will bring glory to God.

Jesus discipled twelve men. Paul followed Jesus' example when he discipled Timothy, Titus, and Silas. The concept of making disciples has been all but lost in much of the body of Christ and has largely been replaced with a focus on meetings and programs. Now is the time for each of us to pick up the responsibility of spiritual fathering and mothering, make disciples, and continue the revolution started by Jesus.

Jesus spent most of His time with His twelve disciples—His spiritual sons. Peter, James and John were a part of Jesus' inner circle. Through this simple concept of disciple-making, Jesus reproduced Himself in His followers to start a revolution that changed the world. Call it what you want—mentoring, discipling, coaching, or spiritual fathering or mothering—it all basically boils down to the same thing: caring about the spiritual growth of another person.

Paul grasped this truth of disciple-making when he told Timothy, *"You then, my son, be strong in the grace that is in Christ Jesus. And the things you have heard me say in the presence of many witnesses entrust to reliable men who will also be qualified to teach others"* (2 Timothy 2:1-2). Paul exhorted Timothy, who was his spiritual son, to find other disciples who would disciple others.

I have personal challenge for you. Ask God for one person to personally disciple this year. Just one! It might be a coworker, a family member, someone from your church, or a friend. Ask the potential spiritual daughter or son to meet with you every few weeks or each month (maybe for coffee or tea) and talk about your walk with Jesus. Pray daily for your disciple. Encourage your spiritual daughter or son to disciple someone else next year.

As you find another person to disciple each year, in ten years you will have discipled directly or indirectly more than 1,000 people! After twenty years it escalates to one million disciples! And after thirty years it escalates to one billion disciples! No wonder the enemy has been hiding this truth from God's people.

I have been blessed to be making disciples for the past fifty years. It is not always easy, but it is so worthwhile. This is my one-person challenge for you: Ask God to help you find your Timothy. Model your life after Jesus and Paul. God has called you. What are you waiting for?

Ask God for one person to personally disciple this year.

Biblical Foundations for Life

366 | Ever-increasing multiplication

Who is a person the Lord may be calling you to disciple?

After ministering at a church in Dallas, Texas, a young man holding a Bible came up to me and narrated this story:

"My folks are not Christians, but recently I opened this Bible I found lying on the coffee table. After reading in it, I realized I needed Jesus. I gave my life to Christ and then drove around looking for a church family. I found a church building near where I live and walked in. The first person to greet me was a young lady. After telling her my story, she called her father over and said, 'Tell my dad what you told me.'"

The dad listened to my testimony and examined the Bible in my hands. "Fifteen years ago," he said, "I witnessed to a man I served with in the military. He declined to receive the Lord but agreed to take the Bible you are holding. The man I witnessed to was your father!"

The young Texan continued to explain that he was now engaged to the young lady he had met at the church, and they were both excited about serving as small group leaders.

When we obey the Lord and speak truth with love into the life of another, we may be amazed at what God will do.

God has called all of us to become spiritual fathers and mothers in our generation. With this comes the expectation that our spiritual children will have their own spiritual children who will have even more spiritual children, thus providing ever-increasing multiplication. No matter what you do—whether you are a housewife, a student, a factory worker, a pastor, or the head of a large corporation—you have the divine blessing and responsibility to birth spiritual children, grandchildren and great-grandchildren. You are called to impart to others the rich inheritance God has promised.

Jesus told us in Matthew 28:19 to *"Go and make disciples."* Yet many times we have failed to obey this Great Commission from our Lord Jesus. This scriptural principle is so simple. God uses the principle of multiplication through disciple-making as we become a spiritual father or mother to another person. You are called to impart to others the rich inheritance that God has given to you.

HELPFUL RESOURCES

Building Your Personal House of Prayer

Christians often struggle with their prayer lives. With the unique "house plan" developed in this book, each room corresponding to a part of the Lord's Prayer, your prayer life is destined to go from duty to joy! Includes a helpful Daily Prayer Guide to use each day. *By Larry Kreider, 254 pages:* **$15.99**

The Cry for Spiritual Mothers and Fathers

Returning to the biblical truth of spiritual parenting so believers are not left fatherless and disconnected. Learn how loving, seasoned spiritual fathers and mothers help spiritual children reach their full potential in Christ. Proven biblical keys you ned to become a godly mentor. *By Larry Kreider, 224 pages.* **$14.99**

A Practical Path to a Prosperous Life

A clear biblical, step-by-step approach to attaining abundant personal finances, building wealth and financing of the Great Commission in our day. Age-old biblical truths with practical, present-day applications to help your thinking line up with the God's Word. By Brian Sauder, *282 pages:* **$12.99**

Called Together
Pre and postmarital workbook

Designed for couple-to-couple mentoring use, *Called Together* prepares couples for a successful and God-honoring marriage. It supplies down-to-earth Biblical wisdom to help couples get off to a positive start. Includes postmarital checkups at three and nine months. Special sections for remarriage and intercultural marriages. *By Steve and Mary Prokopchak, 250 pages*: **$19.99**

House to House

The church is waking up to the simple, successful house to house strategy practiced by the New Testament church. *House to House* documents how God called a fellowship of believers to become a house to house movement., DOVE International has grown into a family of small group based churches and micro churches networking throughout the world. *By Larry Kreider, 264 pages.* **$15.99**

When God Seems Silent

Discovering His purposes in times of confusion and darkness Why does it sometimes feel like God is silent? Is He hiding from us? Larry and LaVerne Kreider help us examine these questions and many of the barriers that can block the voice of God in our lives. They also reveal their own struggle with God's silences and the breakthroughs that can be discovered. *By Larry and LaVerne Kreider, 208 pages:* **$12.99**

Finding Freedom

Becoming whole and living free The struggle is real. We desire to follow Christ, but too often we find ourselves entangled and tripped up, falling back into the old patterns of our former selves. Authors examine God's Word for the answers and share from their own lives and others who have experienced God's true freedom. *By Larry Kreider, Craig and Tracie Nanna 198 pages:* **$12.99**

Encountering the Supernatural

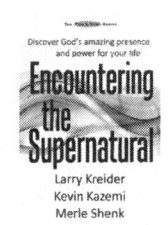

Discover God's amazing power and prescene in your life Wherever you are in your spiritual journey, this book will place you on a path to greater revelation of God's supernatural power in everyday life. By Larry Kreider, Kevin Kazemi and Merle Shenk, *220 pages:* **$12.09**

Battle Cry for Your Marriage

Discovering breakthroughs for today's challenges With raw honesty four couples tackle issues of spiritual, emotional and sexual intimacy along with other marital stresses. Biblically-based insights will inspire spouses to face issues, communicate honestly, find life-changing strategies and—most of all—love the One who gave them the gift of each other.
By Larry and LaVerne Kreider, Steve and Mary Prokopchak Duane and Reyna Britton, Wallace and Linda Mitchell, 204 pages: **$12.99**

MANY DISCOUNTS!

DOVE Store   1.800.848.5892

BIBLICAL FOUNDATIONS FOR LIFE

Presented by Larry Kreider

Sign up to receive our *FREE* 365 Day Devotional Video Series

Scan the QR Code with your mobile device's camera, or go to **dcfi.org/devos**

BFFL — BIBLICAL FOUNDATIONS FOR LIFE | BROUGHT TO YOU BY DOVE INTERNATIONAL

Made in the USA
Middletown, DE
08 August 2021